The Cambridge Companion to Vaughan Williams

An icon of British national identity and one of the most widely performed twentieth-century composers, Ralph Vaughan Williams has been as much misunderstood as revered; his international impact, and enduring influence on areas as diverse as church music, film scores and popular music, have been insufficiently appreciated. This volume brings together a team of leading scholars, examining all areas of the composer's output from new perspectives, and re-evaluating the cultural politics of his lifelong advocacy for the music-making of ordinary people. Surveys of major genres are complemented by chapters exploring such topics as the composer's relationship with the BBC, and his studies with Ravel; uniquely, the book also includes specially commissioned interviews with major living composers Peter Maxwell Davies, Piers Hellawell, Nicola LeFanu and Anthony Payne. The *Companion* is a vital resource for all those interested in this pivotal figure of modern music.

ALAIN FROGLEY has taught at Oxford and Lancaster universities, and since 1994 at the University of Connecticut; in 2008 he was Visiting Professor at Yale. In 2005–6 he was a Fellow of the American Council of Learned Societies. He is the editor of *Vaughan Williams Studies* (1996) and the author of *Vaughan Williams's Ninth Symphony* (2001); he has also contributed to the *New Grove Dictionary of Music and Musicians* and the *Oxford Dictionary of National Biography*.

AIDAN J. THOMSON taught at the universities of Oxford and Leeds before being appointed Lecturer in Music at Queen's University Belfast in 2003. His publications include articles and book chapters on Elgar (in *19th-Century Music*, *The Cambridge Companion to Elgar*, *Edward Elgar and His World*, *Elgar Studies* and *The Musical Quarterly*), Ethel Smyth and Arnold Bax.

The Cambridge Companion to

VAUGHAN WILLIAMS

EDITED BY

Alain Frogley
University of Connecticut

and

Aidan J. Thomson
Queen's University Belfast

CAMBRIDGE
UNIVERSITY PRESS

CAMBRIDGE
UNIVERSITY PRESS

University Printing House, Cambridge CB2 8BS, United Kingdom

Cambridge University Press is part of the University of Cambridge.

It furthers the University's mission by disseminating knowledge in the pursuit of education, learning, and research at the highest international levels of excellence.

www.cambridge.org
Information on this title: www.cambridge.org/9780521162906

© Cambridge University Press 2013

First published 2013
Reprinted 2014

Printed in the United Kingdom by Clays, St Ives plc.

A catalogue record for this publication is available from the British Library

Library of Congress Cataloguing in Publication data
The Cambridge companion to Vaughan Williams / edited by Alain Frogley and Aidan J. Thomson.
    pages   cm
Includes bibliographical references and index.
ISBN 978-0-521-16290-6
1. Vaughan Williams, Ralph, 1872–1958.   2. Composers – England – Biogaphy.   3. Vaughan Williams, Ralph, 1872–1958 – Criticism and interpretation.   4. Music – England – 20th century – History and criticism.
I. Frogley, Alain.   II. Thomson, Aidan J., 1975–
ML410.V3C36   2013
780.92–dc23
[B]
                                                        2013016199

ISBN 978-0-521-19768-7 Hardback
ISBN 978-0-521-16290-6 Paperback

In memory of
Ursula Vaughan Williams (1911–2007)
and
Richard Hickox (1948–2008)

Contents

Tables

Contributors

Byron Adams is Professor of Musicology at the University of California, Riverside. An accomplished composer, his music has been performed throughout North America and Europe. He has published widely on the subject of English music of the nineteenth and twentieth centuries; he is co-editor of *Vaughan Williams Essays* (2003), and a contributor to the revised edition of the *New Grove Dictionary of Music and Musicians*. In 2000, the American Musicological Society bestowed upon him the Philip Brett Award for his scholarly work on the intersections of gender and nationalism in British music. In 2007, Adams was scholar-in-residence for the Bard Music Festival, 'Elgar and His World', and was editor of the book connected to the festival, *Edward Elgar and His World*.

Jenny Doctor was awarded a Fulbright Grant to the UK in 1989 and remained there for over twenty-two years. Whenever time permitted, she rummaged around the BBC archives, leading to *The BBC and Ultra-Modern Music, 1922–1936* (Cambridge, 1999). With Nicholas Kenyon and David Wright, she co-edited *The Proms: A Social History* (2007), and with Sophie Fuller she is editing letters exchanged by composers Elizabeth Maconchy and Grace Williams. As Director of the Belfer Audio Archive and Associate Professor at Syracuse University, Jenny's current research focuses on British music history, sound recording archives and music on American radio.

Alain Frogley has taught at Oxford and Lancaster universities, and since 1994 at the University of Connecticut; in 2008 he was Visiting Professor at Yale. In 2005–6 he was a Fellow of the American Council of Learned Societies. A specialist in the music of the late nineteenth and twentieth centuries, particularly that of Britain and America, he has also worked extensively on Beethoven. His research has centred on sketch studies, reception history and musical nationalism; his most recent work explores music and the modern city. Frogley is the editor of *Vaughan Williams Studies* (Cambridge, 1996) and the author of *Vaughan Williams's Ninth Symphony* (2001); he has also contributed to the *New Grove Dictionary of Music and Musicians* and the *Oxford Dictionary of National Biography*.

Sophie Fuller is Acting Head of Postgraduate Studies at Trinity Laban Conservatoire of Music and Dance, London. Her research centres on aspects of music, gender and sexuality, in particular investigating music and musicians in late nineteenth- and early twentieth-century Britain. She is the author of *The Pandora Guide to Women Composers* (1994), and co-editor of *Queer Episodes in Music and Modern Identity* (2002) and *The Idea of Music in Victorian Fiction* (2004); her more recent publications explore Edward Elgar and the private musical world, and the career of singer Clara Butt. Projects in progress include a monograph on the late Victorian and Edwardian musical salon.

Julian Horton is Associate Professor and Head of the School of Music at University College Dublin. He is author of *Bruckner's Symphonies: Analysis, Reception and*

Cultural Politics (Cambridge, 2004), a contributor to *The Cambridge Companion to Bruckner* and editor of *The Cambridge Companion to the Symphony* (Cambridge, 2013). He has published articles on issues in the analysis of nineteenth-century music in *Music Analysis, The Musical Quarterly, Music & Letters* and the *Dutch Journal of Music Theory*, and is currently completing a monograph on Brahms's Piano Concerto No. 2.

Michael Kennedy was born in Manchester and started his career as a journalist in 1941. His first book, a history of Manchester's Hallé Orchestra, was published in 1960. Since then he has written studies of Elgar, Vaughan Williams, Britten, Walton, Mahler and Strauss, as well as biographies of the conductors Sir John Barbirolli and Sir Adrian Boult. He has also written the histories of the Royal Manchester College of Music and its successor, the Royal Northern College of Music (he served on its Board of Governors for over forty years). He also compiled the Oxford Dictionary of Music. He was appointed OBE in 1981 and CBE in 1997.

David Manning is a researcher with interests in early twentieth-century British music. His work has focused on the music and writings of Ralph Vaughan Williams. He edited an anthology of prose writings by this composer published in 2008 under the title *Vaughan Williams on Music*. He studied at the universities of Bristol and Oxford, before completing a PhD at Cardiff University. His doctoral thesis is an analytical study of Vaughan Williams's musical language informed by relevant theoretical perspectives. He has also written book reviews for journals including *Twentieth-Century Music* and *Notes*.

Christopher Mark is Senior Lecturer in musicology at the University of Surrey. He was founding Editor-in-Chief of the Cambridge journal *Twentieth-Century Music* and founder of the Biennial International Conference on Music since 1900, which held its first meeting in 1999 at the University of Surrey. He has published *Early Benjamin Britten* (1995), *Roger Smalley: A Case Study of Late Twentieth-Century Composition* (2012) and *Britten: An Extraordinary Life* (2013) as well as numerous articles, conference papers and book chapters on Britten, Smalley, Elgar, Vaughan Williams, Warlock and Tippett. He is currently working on a monograph on melancholy in twentieth-century English music.

Charles Edward McGuire, Professor of Musicology at the Oberlin College Conservatory of Music, studies British music of the nineteenth and twentieth centuries. His areas of interest include Elgar, Vaughan Williams, music festivals, sight-singing, and the intersection of choral singing and moral reform movements. McGuire has published articles in *19th-Century Music* and *The Musical Quarterly*, and the monographs *Music and Victorian Philanthropy: The Tonic Sol-fa Movement* (Cambridge, 2009) and *Elgar's Oratorios: The Creation of an Epic Narrative* (2002). He also co-wrote *The Historical Dictionary of English Music* (2011), with Oberlin colleague Professor Steven Plank.

Julian Onderdonk is a music historian specializing in nineteenth- and twentieth-century British music and society. Early experience as a boy chorister at St Thomas's, Fifth Avenue, inspired a lifelong enthusiasm for Vaughan Williams's music, and a Fulbright scholarship in London (1992–3) led to work on the composer's folksong collecting and hymn-tune arrangements. His essays have appeared in *Folk Music Journal, English Dance and Song, Current Musicology*, the Music Library

Association's *Notes, The RVW Society Journal, Vaughan Williams Studies* (Cambridge, 1996), *Vaughan Williams Essays* (2003), *Strengthen for Service: 100 Years of the English Hymnal* (2006) and *The Canterbury Dictionary of Hymnology* (2013). He has taught at New York University, St Francis University (PA), the Pennsylvania State University system and Williams College, and is now Professor of Music History at West Chester University of Pennsylvania.

Heather de Savage is currently completing a Ph.D. in Music History and Theory at the University of Connecticut; her dissertation examines the American reception of Gabriel Fauré, with a particular focus on the Boston area. She has co-authored articles on performance practices in fifteenth-century chanson and on the analysis of Liszt's songs, and has presented papers on the music of Heinrich Schütz. She currently teaches music history courses at the University of Connecticut and is the Editorial Assistant for the College Music Symposium.

Eric Saylor is Associate Professor of Musicology at Drake University. The co-editor of *Blackness in Opera* (2012), he has contributed articles and reviews to the *Journal of the Royal Musical Association, The Musical Quarterly, The New Grove Dictionary of American Music, Music & Letters, The Musical Times, Musik-Konzepte* and *Nineteenth-Century Music Review*, and compiled the Vaughan Williams entry for *Oxford Bibliographies Online*. In addition to the works of Vaughan Williams and his contemporaries, his research interests include English pastoral music, music and politics, historiography and shape-note hymnody.

Aidan J. Thomson taught at the universities of Oxford and Leeds before being appointed Lecturer in Music at Queen's University Belfast in 2003. His main research interests are the music and culture of early twentieth-century Britain and Ireland, particularly the relationship between reception, criticism and analysis. His publications include articles and book chapters on Elgar (in *19th-Century Music, The Cambridge Companion to Elgar, Edward Elgar and His World, Elgar Studies* and *The Musical Quarterly*), Ethel Smyth and Arnold Bax. He has served on the councils of the Royal Musical Association, the North American British Music Studies Association and the Society for Musicology in Ireland, and is currently the reviews editor of the *Journal of the Society for Musicology in Ireland*.

Acknowledgements

Acknowledgement for kind permission to reproduce illustrations and music examples is due to the following:

Illustrations

The photograph on the front cover (the identity of the photographer, probably professional, is unknown) is presumed to date from *c.* 1910, and is reproduced by kind permission of the British Library and the Vaughan Williams Charitable Trust.

Music examples

The author and publishers acknowledge the following sources of copyright material and are grateful for the permissions granted. While every effort has been made, it has not always been possible to identify the sources of all material used, or to trace copyright holders. If any omissions are brought to our notice, we will be happy to include the appropriate acknowledgements on reprinting.

Boosey & Hawkes
Ex. 2.1b: (c) Copyright 1911 by Boosey & Co. Ltd. Reproduced by permission of Boosey & Hawkes Music Publishers Ltd.

British Library and the Vaughan Williams Charitable Trust
Ex. 2.3 by permission.

Oxford University Press
Ex. 2.5b *Flos Campi* by Ralph Vaughan Williams © Oxford University Press 1928. Reproduced by Permission of CopyCat Music Licensing, LLC, obo Oxford University Press. All Rights Reserved.

Ex. 2.6 *Magnificat* by Ralph Vaughan Williams © Oxford University Press 1932. Reproduced by Permission of CopyCat Music Licensing, LLC, obo Oxford University Press. All Rights Reserved.

Ex. 2.7 *Job: A Masque for Dancing* by Ralph Vaughan Williams © Oxford University Press 1934. Reproduced by Permission of CopyCat Music Licensing, LLC, obo Oxford University Press. All Rights Reserved.

Ex. 2.8 *Riders to the Sea* by Ralph Vaughan Williams to text adapted from J. M. Synge.

© Oxford University Press 1936, 1972. Reproduced by Permission of CopyCat Music Licensing, LLC, obo Oxford University Press. All Rights Reserved.

Ex. 9.2 *The Lark Ascending* by Ralph Vaughan Williams © Oxford University Press 1925. Reproduced by Permission of CopyCat Music Licensing, LLC, obo Oxford University Press. All Rights Reserved.

Exx. 9.3 & 9.4 Concerto for Violin: *Concerto Accademico* by Ralph Vaughan Williams © Oxford University Press 1925. Reproduced by Permission of CopyCat Music Licensing, LLC, obo Oxford University Press. All Rights Reserved.

Exx. 9.5 & 9.6 Concerto for One or Two Pianos and Orchestra by Ralph Vaughan Williams © Oxford University Press 1973. Reproduced by Permission of CopyCat Music Licensing, LLC, obo Oxford University Press. All Rights Reserved.

Ex. 9.7 Concerto for Oboe and Strings by Ralph Vaughan Williams © Oxford University Press 1947. Reproduced by Permission of CopyCat Music Licensing, LLC, obo Oxford University Press. All Rights Reserved.

Exx. 10.1, 10.2a, 10.2b, 10.2c, 10.2d, 10.5 & 10.6 Symphony No. 4 by Ralph Vaughan Williams © Oxford University Press 1935. Reproduced by Permission of CopyCat Music Licensing, LLC, obo Oxford University Press. All Rights Reserved.

Exx. 10.3 & 10.7 Symphony No. 5 by Ralph Vaughan Williams © Oxford University Press 1946. Reproduced by Permission of CopyCat Music Licensing, LLC, obo Oxford University Press. All Rights Reserved.

Exx. 10.4, 10.8, 10.9 & 10.10 Symphony No. 6 by Ralph Vaughan Williams © Oxford University Press 1948. Reproduced by Permission of CopyCat Music Licensing, LLC, obo Oxford University Press. All Rights Reserved.

Exx. 10.11, 10.12 & 10.13 *Sinfonia Antartica* by Ralph Vaughan Williams © Oxford University Press 1953. Corrected 1968. Reproduced by Permission of CopyCat Music Licensing, LLC, obo Oxford University Press. All Rights Reserved.

Ex. 10.14 Symphony No. 8 by Ralph Vaughan Williams © Oxford University Press 1956. Reproduced by Permission of CopyCat Music Licensing, LLC, obo Oxford University Press. All Rights Reserved.

Exx. 10.15, 10.16 & 10.17 Symphony No. 9 by Ralph Vaughan Williams © Oxford University Press 1958. Reproduced by Permission of CopyCat Music Licensing, LLC, obo Oxford University Press. All Rights Reserved.

Stainer & Bell

Ex. 4.3 *A Sea Symphony* by Ralph Vaughan Williams © 1918 by Stainer & Bell Ltd, Victoria House, 23 Gruneisen Road, London N3 1DZ, www.stainer.co.uk.

Ex. 4.4 *A London Symphony* by Ralph Vaughan Williams © 1922 by Stainer & Bell Ltd, Victoria House, 23 Gruneisen Road, London N3 1DZ, www.stainer.co.uk.

Ex. 9.1 Phantasy Quintet by Ralph Vaughan Williams © 1921 by Stainer & Bell Ltd, Victoria House, 23 Gruneisen Road, London N3 1DZ, www.stainer.co.uk.

List of abbreviations

Unless otherwise stated, dates of works given throughout are those of primary compositional activity (e.g. 1911–13) as they appear in *KC*, or of publication in the case of short works, e.g. folksong arrangements.

Books

KC	Michael Kennedy, *A Catalogue of the Works of Ralph Vaughan Williams* (2nd edn, Oxford University Press, 1996).
KW	Michael Kennedy, *The Works of Ralph Vaughan Williams* (2nd edn, Oxford University Press, 1980).
LRVW	Hugh Cobbe (ed.), *Letters of Ralph Vaughan Williams 1895–1958* (Oxford University Press, 2008).
NM	Ralph Vaughan Williams, *National Music and Other Essays* (2nd edn, Oxford University Press, 1987).
UVWB	Ursula Vaughan Williams, *R. V. W.: A Biography of Ralph Vaughan Williams* (Oxford University Press, 1964).
VWE	Byron Adams and Robin Wells (eds.), *Vaughan Williams Essays* (Aldershot: Ashgate Publishing, 2003).
VWIP	Lewis Foreman (ed.), *Ralph Vaughan Williams in Perspective: Studies of an English Composer* (London: Albion Music, 1998).
VWOM	David Manning (ed.), *Vaughan Williams on Music* (Oxford University Press, 2008).
VWS	Alain Frogley (ed.), *Vaughan Williams Studies* (Cambridge University Press, 1996).

Periodicals

ML	*Music & Letters*
MMR	*Monthly Musical Record*
MN	*Musical News*
MO	*Musical Opinion and Music Trade Review*
MQ	*The Musical Quarterly*
MSt	*The Musical Standard*
MT	*The Musical Times*

Chronology

COMPILED BY HEATHER DE SAVAGE

Information for this chronology has been drawn from a variety of sources. Works are listed by the year of their first performance except where otherwise indicated; given the extent of the composer's *oeuvre*, only major works or those that represent an important phase of broader compositional activity are included. For a complete listing, see *KC* or the entry on Vaughan Williams in *The New Grove Dictionary of Music and Musicians*. Additional information on Vaughan Williams's family background may be found in Chapter 1.

Year	Life	Works
1872	Born in Down Ampney, Gloucestershire, 12 October.	
1875	Death of father; family moves from Down Ampney to Leith Hill Place, Surrey.	
1878	Begins music lessons with his aunt Sophy Wedgwood; first composition (four bars), *The Robin's Nest*.	
1879	Begins violin lessons.	
1880	Passes a correspondence course in music theory.	
1883–6	Attends Field House School, Rottingdean, Sussex.	
1887–90	Attends Charterhouse School, Godalming, Surrey.	
	In August 1888 plays violin in performance of his Piano Trio in G major in school concert.	Piano Trio in G major (lost).
1890–2	Attends Royal College of Music, London (RCM); studies theory with F. E. Gladstone, composition with Hubert Parry and organ with Walter Parratt.	Composes *Three Elizabethan Songs* ?1891–6.
1892–5	Attends Trinity College, Cambridge (Mus. Bac. 1894, BA in History, 2nd-class honours, 1895); continues lessons with Parry; also studies with Charles Wood (composition) and Alan Gray (organ).	'The Virgin's Cradle Song' 1894. Completes Piano Trio in C major 1895.
1895–6	Returns to RCM, studies composition with Stanford. Becomes friends with Gustav Holst. Appointed organist at St Barnabas Church, South Lambeth.	Begins Fantasia for Pianoforte and Orchestra (completed 1904).
1897	Marries Adeline Fisher, 9 October; honeymoon spent mostly in Berlin, where RVW studies composition for several months with Max Bruch.	Composes String Quartet in C minor 1897–8.
1898	Returns to London; lives at several addresses in Westminster, finally settling at 10 Barton Street early in 1899. Passes exams to become Fellow of the Royal College of Organists (FRCO).	Composes Serenade in A minor.

Year	Life	Works
1899		Completes *The Garden of Proserpine* and Mass submitted for Cambridge Mus. Doc. Degree.
1900		Completes *Bucolic Suite*.
1901	Awarded Mus. Doc., Cambridge; first performances of orchestral music, *Heroic Elegy* in London, Serenade in A minor in Bournemouth.	*Heroic Elegy and Triumphant Epilogue*.
1902	First work published, 'Linden Lea'; first University Extension Lectures; first articles for *The Vocalist* magazine.	'Rest'; 'Whither Must I Wander'.
1903	Receives enthusiastic critical notices from Edwin Evans and several other writers; begins work on *A Sea Symphony*; in December begins collecting folksongs.	*Willow-Wood*; *The Solent*; completes Piano Quintet in C minor.
1904	Begins work as editor of *The English Hymnal*, which will continue until 1906; publishes articles on fugue and conducting in *Grove's Dictionary of Music and Musicians* (2nd edn).	*The House of Life*; *Songs of Travel*; completes first version of *In the Fen Country*.
1905	Assists in founding of Leith Hill Festival and is appointed Principal Conductor; continues in this position until 1953. Edits first volume of Purcell's *Welcome Songs* for the Purcell Society. On November 1 Vaughan Williamses move to 13 Cheyne Walk, Chelsea, where they live until 1929.	*Pan's Anniversary*.
1906	Publication of *The English Hymnal*, which includes original contributions from RVW.	*Norfolk Rhapsody* No. 1; incidental music for *The Pilgrim's Progress*.
1907	In mid-December travels to Paris to begin study with Maurice Ravel.	*Toward the Unknown Region*; *Boldre Wood*; *Harnham Down*; *Norfolk Rhapsodies* Nos. 2 & 3.
1908	Returns from Paris in late February.	Completes *Three Nocturnes* based on poems of Whitman. Publishes *Folksongs from Eastern Counties*, arrangements of songs collected by the composer between 1903 and 1906.
1909	Ravel stays with Vaughan Williamses on first visit to London.	Incidental music for *The Wasps*; String Quartet in G minor; *On Wenlock Edge*.
1910	Edits second volume of Purcell's *Welcome Songs*; conducts premieres of *Fantasia on a Theme by Thomas Tallis* (September) and *A Sea Symphony* (October).	*Fantasia on English Folk Song*; *Fantasia on a Theme by Thomas Tallis*; *A Sea Symphony*. Begins work on first opera, *Hugh the Drover*, completed in vocal score 1914.
1911		*Five Mystical Songs*; incidental music to *Iphigenia in Tauris*, *The Bacchae* and *Electra*; begins work on *A London Symphony*, completed 1913.
1912		*Fantasia on Christmas Carols*; composes Phantasy Quintet.
1913	Works with F. R. Benson on Shakespeare productions at Stratford-upon-Avon.	Incidental music for a number of Stratford Shakespeare productions and plays by Maeterlinck; *Five English Folk Songs*.
1914–19	War declared 4 August 1914; enlists as Private in the Royal Army Medical Corps; serves as wagon orderly in 2/4 London Field Ambulance, sees action in France and Greece in 1916; given commission as Lieutenant in Royal Garrison Artillery in 1917, sees action in France in 1918; after Armistice is made Director of Music, First	1914: *A London Symphony*; composes *Four Hymns* and *The Lark Ascending* (version for violin and piano).

Year	Life	Works
	Army of the British Expeditionary Force, France. Demobilized February 1919.	
1919	Awarded honorary D.Mus degree by Oxford University; begins teaching composition at the RCM.	
1920	Revised version of *A London Symphony* published'; performed in London (May) and New York (December).	*Three Preludes on Welsh Hymn Tunes*; 'O Clap Your Hands'; *Twelve Traditional Carols from Herefordshire*.
1921	Appointed conductor of the Bach Choir; resigns position in 1928.	*The Lark Ascending* (version for violin and orchestra); *Merciless Beauty*.
1922	In late May embarks on first visit to the USA, to conduct American premiere of *A Pastoral Symphony* in Norfolk, CT; sees New York, Boston and Niagara Falls.	*A Pastoral Symphony*; Mass in G minor; *The Shepherds of the Delectable Mountains*.
1923		*English Folk Songs* (Suite for Military Band); *Old King Cole*.
1924	*On Wenlock Edge* performed at International Society for Contemporary Music festival in Salzburg.	First performances of *Hugh the Drover* (RCM). Begins work on *Sir John in Love*, completed 1928.
1925	Begins relationship with Oxford University Press. *A Pastoral Symphony* performed at ISCM festival in Prague; *Merciless Beauty* performed at ISCM festival in Venice. Conducts recordings of Overture to *The Wasps* and *Old King Cole*.	Concerto in D minor (*Concerto Accademico*), violin and orchestra; *Flos Campi*; *Four poems by Fredegond Shove*; *Three Poems by Walt Whitman*; begins work on *Riders to the Sea*, completed 1932.
1926		*Six Studies in English Folksong*; *On Christmas Night*; *Sancta Civitas*. Composes first two movements of Concerto in C major for Pianoforte and Orchestra, completed 1931.
1927		*Along the Field*.
1928	Publication of *The Oxford Book of Carols*, the music edited by RVW and Martin Shaw, and including original contributions from the composer.	Te Deum in G.
1929	In October Vaughan Williamses move out of London to The White Gates, Dorking. *Flos Campi* performed at the ISCM festival in Geneva.	*Sir John in Love*.
1930	Awarded Cobbett Medal; receives Gold Medal of the Royal Philharmonic Society.	*Job* (orchestral version); *Benedicite*; *Fantasia on Sussex Folk Tunes*.
1931	*Benedicite* at ISCM Festival, London; *Job* staged at Cambridge Theatre, London.	*Job* (staged ballet).
1932	Elected President of the English Folk Dance and Song Society. In September begins second trip to USA, to lecture at Bryn Mawr College, Pennsylvania; returns December.	*Magnificat*.
1933		Concerto in C major for Pianoforte and Orchestra.
1934	Death of Gustav Holst. Awarded Collard Life Fellowship; *National Music* published.	*The Running Set*; Suite for Viola; *Fantasia on 'Greensleeves'*.
1935	Accepts the Order of Merit.	Symphony No. 4.
1936		*Dona Nobis Pacem*; *The Poisoned Kiss*; *Five Tudor Portraits*.
1937	Conducts recording of the Fourth Symphony; awarded first Shakespeare Prize by University of Hamburg; Festival Te Deum performed at King George VI's coronation.	*Riders to the Sea*; *Flourish for a Coronation*; Festival Te Deum.

Year	Life	Works
1938	Meets Ursula Wood, whom he will later marry.	*Double Trio*; *Serenade to Music*; begins work on Symphony No. 5, completed in 1943.
1939	RVW's music banned by the Nazis. Active member of Dorking Committee for Refugees from Nazi Oppression; assists Myra Hess with organization of National Gallery Concerts instituted at outbreak of war.	*Five Variants of 'Dives and Lazarus'.*
1940	Composes first film score, for *49th Parallel*. Appointed Chair of Home Office Committee for the Release of Interned Alien Musicians.	*Six Choral Songs to be Sung in the Time of War.*
1941	Appointed to Council for the Encouragement of Music and the Arts (CEMA).	*Household Music*; *England, My England*.
1942		'Valiant for Truth'; *Coastal Command*.
1943	Conducts premiere of Symphony No. 5 at the Proms.	Symphony No. 5; *The People's Land*; *The Flemish Farm*.
1944		Concerto in A minor for Oboe and Strings; String Quartet in A minor.
1945		*Thanksgiving for Victory*; *Stricken Peninsula*.
1946		Introduction and Fugue for Two Pianos.
1947		*The Loves of Joanna Godden*; *The Souls of the Righteous*; 'The Voice out of the Whirlwind'.
1948		Symphony No. 6; *Scott of the Antarctic*; 'Prayer to the Father of Heaven'.
1949	Sits for Epstein bust.	*Dim Little Island*; *Fantasia (quasi variazione) on the 'Old 104th' Psalm Tune*; *An Oxford Elegy.*
1950	First full-length book on RVW published, *Ralph Vaughan Williams: A Study* by Hubert Foss.	*Folksongs of the Four Seasons*; *Bitter Springs*; *The Sons of Light*; Concerto Grosso.
1951	Death of Adeline Vaughan Williams; *The Pilgrim's Progress* staged as part of Festival of Britain.	*The Pilgrim's Progress*; *Three Shakespeare Songs.*
1952		*O Taste and See.*
1953	Marries Ursula Wood, 7 February; leaves Dorking and moves back to London, living at 10 Hanover Square, Regent's Park. Arrangement of *Old Hundredth Psalm Tune* performed at coronation of Queen Elizabeth II.	*Sinfonia Antartica*; 'Silence and Music'; *The Old Hundredth Psalm Tune.*
1954	In September embarks on third visit to the USA, at invitation of Cornell University; lectures there and at other institutions across the country; receives Howland Memorial Prize from Yale University. Vaughan Williams Trust established.	*Hodie*; Sonata in A minor for Violin and Pianoforte; Concerto in F minor for Bass Tuba and Orchestra.
1955	*The Making of Music* published.	
1956		Symphony No. 8; 'A Vision of Aeroplanes'; *The England of Elizabeth.*
1957		*Ten Blake Songs*; *Epithalamion*; Variations for Brass Band.
1958	Dies suddenly at London home, 26 August.	Symphony No. 9; *The First Nowell* (completed by Roy Douglas).

Introduction

ALAIN FROGLEY & AIDAN J. THOMSON

There can be few composers who have ridden such a reputational roller-coaster as Ralph Vaughan Williams. Lionized as a revered national figure, and across the English-speaking world in the latter part of his life, within a decade of his death in 1958 he seemed in danger of being consigned to little more than a historical footnote: a Spohr or Telemann, perhaps. His hymn tunes, songs, shorter orchestral pieces and some choral and band works did continue to be staples of the repertoire – Vaughan Williams has, in fact, always been one of those rare beasts, a popular twentieth-century composer. Yet such popularity soon became confined largely to the amateur realm, and while this would surely have offered some comfort to Vaughan Williams, a passionate advocate of the music-making of ordinary people, it was inevitably overshadowed by the precipitous decline of his standing in the world of elite performance and critical opinion. As for new research into his life or music, by the early 1980s musicological neglect was almost total. In 1996 one of the editors of the present volume introduced another book of scholarly essays on Vaughan Williams, the first of its kind, with the reflection that even a decade earlier such a project would have seemed 'to belong strictly to the realms of futuristic fantasy'.[1] Though there may been a touch of rhetorical hyperbole in that judgement, it was only a touch.

But by the mid-1990s the tide was finally turning. As the introduction to that book went on to argue, a variety of forces helped propel this revival in Vaughan Williams's fortunes. Perhaps most significant – and reaching well beyond this one composer – were the breakdown of a monolithic narrative of twentieth-century musical modernism, and a historical reassessment of the cultural politics of British nationalism and imperialism (the latter crucial for a figure who had become so associated with a particular version of national identity); in both cases, these concerns arose at least in part from the application of poststructuralist and postmodern approaches to a discipline, musicology, that had hitherto rejected them.[2] A new wave of interest in Vaughan Williams quickly gathered pace, and in the first decade of the new millennium continued to grow, spurred in part by the approach of the fiftieth anniversary of the composer's death in 2008. A wealth of ground-breaking research has now

[1]

appeared, including two further volumes of scholarly essays, several monographs, a number of important doctoral dissertations, and numerous periodical articles; this work has explored a wide variety of topics, including compositional processes, cultural contexts and reception history.[3]

In the perhaps more immediately influential realms of performance and recording, the Vaughan Williams revival has also borne very rich fruit, especially with performances of neglected or in some cases previously unknown works that have deepened and significantly changed our perceptions and understanding of the composer's development. The Ralph Vaughan Williams Society, founded in 1994, has been a vital agent of activism and fund-raising for a number of these projects, some of which have appeared on disc under its Albion Records imprint (the Society also publishes a lively journal). Vaughan Williams's music for the stage, the most neglected part of his output, has fared particularly well, with the opera *The Poisoned Kiss* and the complete incidental music for Aristophanes' *The Wasps* recorded for the first time ever, and even traditionally ephemeral genres such as film scores and incidental music for radio finding a home on disc. At the time of writing the Coliseum stage is still warm, as it were, from a historic production of the composer's most ambitious stage work, *The Pilgrim's Progress*, not given a full professional production since its premiere run at Covent Garden in 1951. *Sir John in Love* and *Riders to the Sea*, similarly neglected by professional companies, have also been produced by English National Opera in the last few years, in 2006 and 2008 respectively.[4]

The 2008 anniversary was celebrated in a number of ways, but the most significant landmark was arguably the appearance of a major collection of Vaughan Williams correspondence, edited by Hugh Cobbe, which has yielded innumerable new perspectives on the composer and his work. Also important, in part because of the extent of the press coverage they received, was the release of two highly contrasting documentary films, Tony Palmer's *O Thou Transcendent: The Life of Ralph Vaughan Williams* and John Bridcut's *The Passions of Vaughan Williams*. Particularly notable in the Palmer film is the inclusion of interviews with contemporary composers, including John Adams and Mark-Anthony Turnage, both of whom pay warm homage to Vaughan Williams; this reflects a broader reassessment of Vaughan Williams's legacy as a living force in twenty-first-century music.

Palmer also interviewed pop musician Neil Tennant, reminding us that Vaughan Williams's impact has always been felt well outside the realm of classical music. Frank Sinatra, for instance, who had a wide knowledge of classical music, revered Vaughan Williams and the composer's *Job* in particular, and musicians as diverse as the progressive rock band

Genesis, jazz-rock fusion pioneer Wayne Shorter, and, most recently, alternative rock singer PJ Harvey have all acknowledged his influence.[5] And in the domain of film music, salient markers of Vaughan Williams's style remain as reliable a point of reference, particularly for evocations of landscape, as the music of Copland. His continuing potency as a symbol of British national identity in the cinema was underlined in 2003 by the use of the *Fantasia on a Theme by Thomas Tallis* in the Oscar-nominated film *Master and Commander*. In this context it should be noted that Vaughan Williams has in recent years attracted attention from historians and other writers outside musicology, e.g. Peter Ackroyd, Jeffrey Richards, Robert Stradling and Meirion Hughes, as part of an increasing recognition of the crucial role played by music in broader constructions of British national identity.[6]

Yet some old attitudes die hard, as two recent and vexing inscriptions of them in the broader literature make clear. Richard Taruskin's monumental *The Oxford History of Western Music* ignores most British twentieth-century music except Britten's, and in a survey of almost 4,000 pages grants Vaughan Williams barely 6, as part of a chapter on nationalism and the nineteenth-century symphony.[7] Alex Ross's bestseller *The Rest is Noise: Listening to the Twentieth Century* likewise focuses on Britten and passes quickly over the rest of British music (though to be fair to Ross his book is a much more obviously personal view, which frees him in part from the responsibilities imposed by Taruskin's title).[8]

Both because of, and to some extent despite, all these recent developments, a volume on Vaughan Williams in the Cambridge Companion series seemed extremely timely. No comprehensive study of the composer's output has appeared since the 1998 revised version of James Day's 'Master Musicians' volume, originally published in 1961; Michael Kennedy's seminal 1964 study has not been significantly revised since 1980[9] (we are on that account doubly pleased to include here his reflections on more recent developments in Chapter 13). This Companion thus represents the first opportunity to incorporate into a comprehensive assessment the major findings of the more specialized research of the last twenty years, along with consideration of recently rediscovered or revived works that have been published and recorded during the last decade or so.[10] And while there has been a great deal of progress in our understanding of Vaughan Williams and his music, given the exceptionally long and rich life that he lived, and the sheer size and diversity of his *oeuvre*, it should come as no surprise that much work remains to be done.[11] To take just one example from the present volume, Julian Onderdonk's chapter on Vaughan Williams's hymn tunes, folksong arrangements and 'functional' church music is the first thoroughgoing survey of this part of the composer's output – despite the fact that it includes some of his most widely performed pieces. We hope, therefore, that this book will both consolidate recent advances in our knowledge of Vaughan Williams and suggest new avenues of investigation. As with other volumes in the series, the intention has been to provide a comprehensive survey of the composer's achievement that will be accessible and appealing to a broad non-specialist readership, but also to include new information and fresh perspectives, particularly in areas such as music analysis, cultural politics and reception history, that will be of value to students and more advanced scholars.

The book is divided into three main parts. The first part establishes the foundations of Vaughan Williams's musical and broader cultural attitudes and his place in British music, by examining the emergence of his beliefs and values, musical style and critical reputation in the period up to *c.* 1925 (about the midpoint of his career as a composer). The second part addresses his musical output according to the major genres in which he worked. The third broadens the scope to explore Vaughan Williams's wide-ranging role in British musical life, as an active writer and public figure (e.g. working for the release of interned Jewish refugees during World War II), his relationship with the BBC, and the vagaries of his critical reputation, both during his life and since (this section includes discussion of Vaughan Williams's considerable and often overlooked impact outside Britain, especially in the United States). Finally, building on the kind of perspectives suggested only by sound-bites in the Palmer documentary, we conclude the volume by opening up the discussion to the world of contemporary music, engaging in sustained dialogue with four leading composers of our time.

A volume of this kind clearly requires the support of many individuals, and it is possible to mention here by name only a few. Vicki Cooper at Cambridge University Press encouraged and advised us in the initial stages of the project; Rebecca Taylor, Rachel Cox, Gill Cloke and Fleur Jones steered it through a rather protracted gestation, and we are extremely grateful for their patience and professionalism. The University of Connecticut Research Foundation provided travel funding and, most importantly, support for an editorial assistant: Heather de Savage transcribed audio recordings of the composer interviews, compiled the chronology and bibliography, copy-edited chapters, and assisted in numerous other ways with the preparation of the manuscript. We are enormously grateful to Sir Peter Maxwell Davies, Piers Hellawell, Nicola LeFanu and Anthony Payne for agreeing (and taking the time) to be interviewed for Chapter 14. Hugh Cobbe of the Vaughan Williams Charitable Trust and Nicolas Bell of the Department of Manuscripts at the British Library offered generous assistance in a number of matters. We are grateful to our colleagues and students at the University of Connecticut and Queen's

University Belfast, who supported and stimulated us in the preparation of the book, sometimes unwittingly.

Finally, all those who work on Ralph Vaughan Williams and cherish his music owe an incalculable debt of gratitude to Ursula Vaughan Williams, who died in October 2007 at the age of ninety-six. Ursula was the complete opposite of the kind of obstructive surviving relative who sometimes complicates – and on occasion outright blights – the legacy of a great artist in the years after their death. She was unfailingly generous, most obviously in the bequest of the composer's manuscripts that she made to the British Library just a few years after her husband's death, but also in countless other ways in the help, hospitality and friendship that she offered to so many who were interested in Vaughan Williams's music. Her death just a few months before the beginning of the 2008 celebrations, albeit after a long and full life, inevitably cast something of a shadow over those events. No one could have known that before 2008 came to an end, a more shocking and quite unexpected death would rob British music, and Vaughan Williams in particular, of another one of their greatest champions: in late November the conductor Richard Hickox died suddenly, barely twenty-four hours after speaking to a joint meeting of the Elgar and Vaughan Williams Societies, and a few days before he was due to conduct the opening night of English National Opera's production of *Riders to the Sea*. This volume is dedicated to the memory of Ursula Vaughan Williams and Richard Hickox.

Notes

1 *VWS*, xi.

2 Both these factors stimulated the study of British nineteenth-century and twentieth-century music more broadly, a development reflected by the institution in 1997 of the biennial Music in Nineteenth-Century Britain conference and the foundation in 2003 of the North American British Music Studies Association, to take just two examples of the burgeoning of this sub-field of musicology.

3 See Bibliography for further information.

4 2008 also saw the release of the first commercially available DVD of a Vaughan Williams opera, a production of *Riders to the Sea* by NVC Arts in association with RTÉ in Ireland (Kultur DVD D4390), originally recorded for VHS in 1988.

5 See Charles L. Granata and Phil Ramone, *Sessions with Sinatra: Frank Sinatra and the Art of Recording* (Chicago University Press, 1999), 93, and Will Friedwald, *A Biographical Guide to the Great Jazz and Pop Singers* (New York: Pantheon Books, 2010), 680; interview with ex-Genesis keyboard player Tony Banks

conducted by Christopher Thomas in 2004, www.musicwebinternational.com/classRev/2004/Apr04/banks_interview.htm, and Edward Macan, '"The Spirit of Albion" in Twentieth-Century English Popular Music: Vaughan Williams, Holst, and the Progressive Rock Movement', *The Music Review* 53/2 (1992), 100–25; interview with Wayne Shorter in the *New York Times*, 24 December 2004, at www.nytimes.com/2004/12/24/arts/music/24shor.html?_r=0; interview with PJ Harvey in *The Sunday Times*, 23 September 2007, at www.thesundaytimes.co.uk/sto/culture/music/article71954.ece (Harvey included the *Fantasia on a Theme by Thomas Tallis* in her playlist for Radio 3's 'Private Passions' programme, presented by Michael Berkeley, broadcast on 20 April 2008).

6 For instance, Peter Ackroyd, *Albion: The Origins of the English Imagination* (London: Chatto & Windus, 2002), Chapter 53; Christopher Norris (ed.), *Music and the Politics of Culture* (London: Lawrence and Wishart, 1989), specifically the essays by

Meirion Hughes, Robert Stradling and Paul Harrington; Jeffrey Richards, *Imperialism and Music: Britain 1876–1953* (Manchester University Press, 2001); Bernard Porter, 'Elgar and Empire: Music, Nationalism and the War', in Lewis Foreman (ed.), *Oh, My Horses! Elgar and the Great War* (Rickmansworth: Elgar Editions, 2001), 133–73; Meirion Hughes and Robert Stradling, *The English Musical Renaissance 1840–1940: Constructing a National Music*, 2nd edn (Manchester University Press, 2001); Meirion Hughes, *The English Musical Renaissance and the Press 1850–1914: Watchmen of Music* (Aldershot: Ashgate, 2002).

7 *The Oxford History of Western Music* (Oxford University Press, 2005), vol. iii, 811–16.

8 New York: Picador, 2007.

9 James Day, *Vaughan Williams* (London: Dent, 1961), 3rd edn published by Oxford University Press, 1998. An updated version of the catalogue portion of Kennedy's book was published in 1996.

10 That said, the pace of developments in the latter area has been such that even this volume was not able to take into account the so-called 'Cambridge Mass', premiered in 2011, or the recordings and published scores of the *Bucolic Suite* and other early orchestral works that have appeared within the last year, though the latter were at least examined in manuscript for Chapter 4.

11 The world of high-level international performance also seems to exhibit some residual resistance to British music. Despite the sterling work of Richard Hickox, Vernon Handley and other British conductors, it is unfortunate that Vaughan Williams performance tends to be so thoroughly dominated by specialists in British music. Colin Davis's advocacy has been encouraging, but it remains disappointing that Simon Rattle has not taken up Vaughan Williams in any significant way, especially in Berlin (though Roger Norrington has performed Vaughan Williams in Berlin with the Deutsches Sinfonie-Orchester and other ensembles on the continent). Most tellingly, there are no leading foreign-born conductors, even among the various Finnish, Baltic and Russian conductors working in Britain, ready to take up the mantle of Bernard Haitink or Leonard Slatkin (who himself may be said to have succeeded André Previn). One wonders why Vaughan Williams's symphonies, at the very least the Fourth, Fifth and Sixth, should not have a similar place in the international repertoire as that enjoyed by those of Sibelius and especially Shostakovich. Why should we not have, say, a Gergiev cycle of Vaughan Williams symphonies? Vaughan Williams is perhaps hampered by the fact that his symphonies and shorter orchestral works are not complemented by traditional virtuoso concertos, or a cycle of string quartets or piano sonatas – still the linchpin genres of classical music programming – which puts him at a disadvantage in relation to composers such as Prokofiev and Shostakovich.

'Who wants the English composer?': forging a path, 1890–1925

PART I ...

"Who wants the English composer?"
forging a path, 1890–1925

1 The composer and society: family, politics, nation

JULIAN ONDERDONK

Assessing the social, political and religious views of a composer like Vaughan Williams is no easy task. He was a philosophically complex artist whose outspoken dedication to society and to the needs of musical amateurs coexisted with an intense privacy about the sources of his musical inspiration and a metaphysical belief in music as a spiritual force often far removed from worldly issues or concerns. A political radical and acknowledged atheist from early years, he cooperated with the most powerful political and cultural institutions of the day, including the monarchy and the Established Church. Further complicating the picture is the fact that these apparent contradictions have been flattened out and simplified at the hands of a 'nationalist' reception and historiography whose one-sided image of the composer has promoted conflicting interpretations of his work and influence. On the one hand, he has been hailed as a kind of populist hero whose determination to establish a national school of music, founded on the firmly democratic principles of folksong and musical amateurism, led to the establishment of a genuinely English compositional style that liberated native composers from foreign domination. On the other, he has been attacked as a cosy 'establishment' figure whose parochial focus on folksong and early English music resulted in the enshrinement of a genteel and reactionary pastoral musical idiom that exercised a generally harmful influence on British musicians who followed him.[1] So wide is the gulf separating the two images, and so acrimonious the debate between the two 'camps' forwarding them, that it is scarcely surprising that a coherent picture of his political beliefs and social assumptions has yet to emerge.

It helps that recent scholarship has begun to straighten out the tangled strands of the reception history. This work has shown that the competing images of the composer outlined above hinge on ideological attitudes towards nationalism and Vaughan Williams's associations with it. In this analysis, the

My thanks to Alain Frogley, Oliver Neighbour, Abe McCarmy, Nathaniel Lew, Peter Mondelli and Jeffrey Osgood for their generous assistance with this essay. Special thanks to Hugh Cobbe, whose monumental *Letters* have greatly expanded our understanding of Vaughan Williams's political views; and to Stephen Banfield who many years ago unknowingly inspired the direction of the research presented here.

composer's iconic identification with 'Englishness' was less of his own creation than socially constructed – the product of an unprecedented cultural
chauvinism that promoted an intense focus on the 'national' features of his
style while generally ignoring his cosmopolitan grounding in continental
music, including his obvious links to twentieth-century modernism.[2] This
was a development of the 1920s and 1930s, when the cataclysm and aftermath
of World War I, abruptly awakening Britain to the reality of its decline on the
global stage, prompted the wistful embrace of the nation's pre-industrial past.
While the resulting focus on Vaughan Williams contributed to the enormous
acclaim he enjoyed from the 1920s to the 1950s, the backlash against nationalism after World War II, compounded by a newly triumphant avant-garde
musical aesthetics, ensured the lasting decline of his critical reputation among
musicologists and cultural taste-makers from the mid-1950s on. Such judgements made little headway among non-specialists and amateur enthusiasts,
however, whose admiration for the composer continues even today to rely on
the attitudes and arguments of his mid-century peak. The result is the dead-
lock between popular and critical opinion characteristic of the 'pro' and
'contra' groups described above – ample proof, if any were needed, of
nationalism's continuing ability to polarize public debate.

Recently, scholars have sought a way around the problem by shifting
attention away from Vaughan Williams's nationalist legacy to his cosmopolitan interests and eclectic influences. This corrective approach is richly
merited and has already uncovered important aspects of his work that
have been too long obscured.[3] Yet there is a danger that this redirection
can go too far to the opposite extreme. Clearly, Vaughan Williams was not
the narrow nationalist claimed by advocates and detractors alike, but
neither was he the rootless internationalist valorized by twentieth-century
theories of modernist art. This is a man who entitled his most important
book of essays *National Music* and who declared: 'I believe that all that is
of value in our spiritual and cultural life springs from our own soil'.[4] Even
allowing for the possibility that popular acclaim prompted him to exag-
gerate his English influences and downplay his continental ones, his lifelong devotion to England's musical heritage as composer, conductor and
teacher cannot be disputed. He may well have been co-opted by the
chauvinistic mood of the interwar years, with the consequences traced
above, but we must not lose sight of the fact that he himself helped
determine the framework by which that co-option took place.

For Vaughan Williams's embrace of 'Englishness' dates to the two
decades *before* World War I, when the intense focus on the national past
that later reached its climax in the culture of the interwar years actually
began. From the late 1870s, a focus on the 'eternal' values of the English
countryside and a vogue for the English past, notably the Tudor and

Elizabethan periods, became an increasingly dominant strain in the national culture. Rural preservation societies, designed to protect commons, footpaths and historical buildings, emerged around this time, while agrarian communes and farming cooperatives joined with the rise of the wild 'English' garden, 'alternative' rural schools and planned 'Garden City' suburbs in extending these ideas to the population at large. The Arts and Crafts movement, with its embrace of pre-industrial processes, flourished in this period, while the dominant theme among many writers and artists became that of the countryside.[5] Here were the true beginnings of the cultural shift in the national image described above, one which, in a few short decades, had replaced the mid-Victorian celebration of Britain as 'the workshop of the world' with its polar opposite. That Vaughan Williams was caught up in this cultural shift is suggested by his youthful enthusiasm for Elizabethan and Jacobean poets – his first settings of Herrick date from 1895, those of Shakespeare possibly from 1890 – as well as his early efforts at musical landscape painting – *Happy Day at Gunby* (1892), *Reminiscences of a Walk at Frankham* (1894) – and his interest in native folksong. He discovered Stainer and Bramley's *Christmas Carols New and Old* (1871) in the late 1880s, began arranging folksongs in the 1890s, and started the lecturing that would lead directly to his first efforts at collecting folksongs 'in the field' in December 1903. His engagement with early English music, likewise, quickened around this time with commissions to edit Purcell's *Welcome Songs* (1905/1910) and *The English Hymnal* (1906). The latter, in particular, was a labour of love that took up two years of creative work and brought him into contact with Tudor and Jacobean sources that remained a source of inspiration to the end of his life.

The pre-war origins of this nationalism, both in Vaughan Williams's case and in that of English culture generally, are significant, for failure to place it in its correct historical context explains some of the errors of interpretation that surround discussions of his politics and beliefs. These are obvious with respect to the egregiously ahistorical judgements of modernist writers who, following a left-wing tendency traceable to T. W. Adorno, tend to lump all manifestations of nineteenth- and twentieth-century nationalism together with that which led to Hitler.[6] They also colour the attitudes of those supporters of Vaughan Williams who view his democratic embrace of folksong and musical amateurism, somewhat sweepingly, as a latter-day manifestation of the political liberalism of eighteenth- and nineteenth-century nationalist movements, or as an extension of the 'traditional English freedoms' handed down from the Glorious Revolution of 1688 if not the Magna Carta of 1215.[7] (A qualified defence of individual rights remained central to his political philosophy, as we shall see, but its relationship to these historical developments is far more complex than simple causal assertions imply.) More recent work by revisionist historians, particularly those of the folk revival of the turn of the twentieth century, has offered an improved specificity in the study of the composer's nationalism, firstly, by placing it in its proper pre-war location, and secondly, by rooting it firmly in the ruralist movement described above.[8] But even as this scholarship has opened up new avenues of interpretation, its narrow reliance on Marxist models of class analysis has promoted oversimplification and distortion. Any understanding of the complexities and nuance surrounding Vaughan Williams's nationalist activities must therefore take this scholarship as its starting point while also seeking ways to temper and qualify it.

What this revisionist scholarship suggests is that pre-1914 'Englishness' was centrally promoted by a newly forming social and cultural elite that sought appeals to patriotism as a means to meet perceived threats to the national interest. The emergence from the 1870s of Germany and the United States as military and trade rivals, the administrative challenges of maintaining an increasingly far-flung empire, and the sharpening of class antagonisms at home initiated a series of social and cultural negotiations designed to improve inter-class cooperation and understanding and ultimately increase national 'efficiency.' The first sign of this was a growing *rapprochement* in this period between the industrial bourgeoisie, traditionally identified with cities and the factory system as well as with religious Nonconformity, and the landed aristocracy, long linked to agriculture and the Established Church. These two classes had been locked in a 'culture war' since the eighteenth century, if not earlier, but tensions now eased as both groups recognized the necessity of uniting in the face of a common threat. Middle-class radicals and liberals slowed their attack on the 'unearned' income of aristocratic privilege and softened their demands for social and economic reform, while the landed classes, for their part, relaxed their criteria for aristocratic membership and overcame their traditional hostility to business and 'trade'. The result was 'a revitalized leadership which would effectively combine the "mechanical" qualities of [middle-class] utilitarianism and political economy with those of the more "organic" traditions of the aristocracy'.[9] The shift in the national self-image – from the urban and industrialized representations of the 1840s and 1850s to the firmly rural and neo-Tudor projections of 1900 – was only the outward sign of these developments.

This project of social consolidation and national solidarity necessarily encompassed the lower orders as well, but here accommodation was harder to effect, as the working classes had entered into a period of renewed political activism. In this reading, the embrace of the pre-industrial past was an essentially psychological and defensive, if largely unconscious, reaction on the part of the new elite to the rise of trade unions and labour agitation – 'disruptive' developments unmistakably associated with contemporary urban life. 'Englishness', by contrast, was safely rural: its appealing depiction of a communal and essentially classless society in which self-interest and class difference are subsumed in the pursuit of the common good seemed to offer a means to foster a sense of shared identity and solidarity. But because this communitarian message was a myth, neither faithful to the realities of Tudor or contemporaneous rural life nor a truly realistic alternative in a highly industrialized and stratified society, it represented instead a form of covert cultural politics, one in which the egalitarian pretence of 'national unity' actually served to maintain the very class divide it claimed to bridge.

Vaughan Williams's susceptibility to this analysis can readily be imagined, for his family background resembles aspects of the class convergence described above. He was descended on his mother's side from Wedgwoods, celebrated potters and middle-class industrialists from the Midlands, and on his father's side from a long line of churchmen and lawyers (his grandfather was knighted for his service as Judge of Common Pleas).[10] Wedgwoods had long been involved in radical causes – they joined Wilberforce's anti-slavery movement and fought for electoral reform; some even supported the French Revolution – while Vaughan Williamses, though not themselves drawn from the aristocracy or gentry, had close connections to the elite through their Oxbridge educations and occupations in the church and the law. Eventually, even Wedgwoods felt the pull of the aristocratic lifestyle, as financial success prompted various family members to marry into the gentry, buy landed estates, reject Nonconformity for the Established Church, and in some cases join the Conservative Party.[11] By 1868, when Ralph Vaughan Williams's parents married, his immediate family had distanced itself completely from the pottery and relied on outside investments – their money was in railways – to generate wealth.[12] It was these investments, no doubt supplemented by rents from their Surrey estate, Leith Hill Place, that paid for the composer's education at Charterhouse, Cambridge and the Royal College of Music, and that provided the private income which relieved him of the necessity of regular salaried work.[13]

Further, Vaughan Williams was outspoken in his frequent calls for inter-class cooperation and national cohesion. 'Is not folk-song the bond of union where all our musical tastes can meet?' he wrote. 'One day, perhaps, we shall find an ideal music which will be neither popular nor classical, highbrow or lowbrow, but an art in which all can take part'.[14] Such appeals reflected the agenda of the nationalist composer seeking to win popular support for English music; but they also reflected assumptions about the formation and implementation of cultural policy that ultimately derived from a privileged family background. For what stands out about Vaughan Williams's many pronouncements is their insistently *public* tone, the assertion that causes he supported were of 'national importance' or of significant cultural concern. This public orientation, in turn, was a reflection of the access to the foremost political and cultural institutions of the day that he enjoyed as a consequence of his social standing. The fiery (and numerous) letters to the editor, the high-profile committee work, the frequent communications with government officials and civil servants – all bespeak a familiarity with the workings of the 'establishment' and a readiness to use its power for social and cultural causes he believed in. Doubtless, his musical eminence greatly aided him in this work: his long association with the prestigious Royal College of Music and his later compositional acclaim clearly opened many doors and naturally encouraged his involvement.[15] But the impulse to address social issues was there from the first, as his earliest essays demonstrate, and there is no getting around the fact that social and family connections were crucial in helping him impact the highest levels of policy-making. His work on behalf of the Home Office Committee for the Release of Interned Alien Musicians during World War II was plainly expedited by personal access to Sir Cyril Asquith, chair of the Advisory Committee on Aliens.[16] Similarly, his successful campaign to have Cecil Sharp appointed a Government Inspector of Schools in 1919 – an important step in their crusade to prioritize anonymous and thus 'communal' folksong in the school curriculum – was a consequence of the private appeal he made to H. A. L. Fisher, President of the Board of Education and, not coincidentally, his brother-in-law.[17]

Finally, involvement in public life prompted Vaughan Williams at times to idealize the nation's pre-industrial heritage in ways that distorted the historical and contemporary reality of English working-class life. He located the 'folk' among unlettered peoples whose 'primitive consciousness' was the product of their isolation from urban life and culture. 'True' folksongs, as noted above, were 'anonymous' and 'communal' and were vastly superior to music hall songs, parlour ballads and other 'composed' and 'commercial' popular musics that he dismissed as 'vulgar' and 'banal'.[18] Such views betrayed deep-seated prejudices and did not fully resemble the singers' own practices and preferences, which Vaughan Williams occasionally ignored in his collecting work. His notebooks, indeed, reveal a sometimes blatant disregard for what he found in the field – urban and commercial songs, a high incidence of tonal (as opposed to modal) tunes, idiosyncratic departures from standard versions of well-known tunes – in the effort to paint a picture of a tightly knit, essentially 'homogeneous' national community.[19] A similar idealization informed a tendency to sanitize Tudor life, a world (as he described it) in which composers, in the 'spirit of gay and careless adventure', ignored continental developments, and where class divisions between aristocrat and labourer seemed hardly to exist in the shared enjoyment of a common culture.[20]

Such distortions would seem to place Vaughan Williams squarely in the trajectory of 'Englishness' that the revisionists trace. Yet it is important to recognize that his actions and opinions, even his family history, do not quite fit the model, and that the picture is considerably more complicated than this narrative suggests. Close examination of his collecting work, for example, shows that his misrepresentations of traditional singing culture were less extensive than those of many colleagues, including Cecil Sharp, and were more than offset by a genuine appreciation of his singers' preferences and personal contributions, even where these contradicted folksong 'theory'. He may at times have idealized the culture in ways described above, but in most other instances he recognized the currency of urban popular musics in singers' repertories, openly acknowledged any verbal or musical literacy among them, and actually drew attention to their creative departures from well-known tunes.[21] By the same token, the questionable assertions of his writings on Tudor music find frequent contradiction in the Tudor-inspired works, whose historical re-creations of the era are surprisingly realistic, especially compared to the self-serving 'Merrie Englandism' of his contemporaries.[22] Indeed, by all accounts, Vaughan Williams was fully aware of the dangers inherent in rural idealization. His essay on the Tudor period warned of the tendency for folk culture to be 'perverted by the sentimental rich', whose glib talk about 'bringing Life and Joy to the working classes' obscured the 'real nature' of that culture. And in the famous essay 'Who Wants the English Composer?' he actually pointed to urban popular musics like Salvation Army hymns, barrel-organ tunes and music hall songs as no less worthy than folksong to inspire young composers to express 'the whole life of the community'.[23]

For all its idealizing tendencies, in other words, Vaughan Williams's nationalist vision included room for the recognition of historical and contemporary realities. The sincerity of his stance, the proof that it was no mere populist 'pose', resides in what Bernard Shore called the composer's 'passionate support of the underdog' – his embrace of the marginalized and dispossessed.[24] This is evident from the subject matter of many works (Synge's tragic seafolk, Bunyan's persecuted Pilgrim, the urban unemployed depicted in the last movement of *A London Symphony*)[25] but also, and more crucially, from his everyday actions and deeds: the support he habitually gave to individuals in need, and the ready sympathy and aid he extended to historically underprivileged groups like women, Gypsies and Jews.[26] Then there are his political views and voting record, which testify to his sympathy with progressive social activism. Vaughan Williams 'stood out' as a Radical at Charterhouse; at Cambridge, he read the Fabian tracts and admired the success of the trade union leaders John Burns and Ben Tillett, who led the landmark 1889 London dockworkers' strike, and, 'in opposition to the majority of undergraduates', he became a socialist. Thereafter, with one important exception, he voted 'either Radical or Labour' to the end of his life.[27] A vote for either was a vote for progressive taxation and for the increased role of the state in the redistribution of wealth. Following the landslide Liberal victory in the 1906 election, radical elements within that party helped push through an ambitious programme of social reform, including the introduction of old-age pensions (1908), the Trade Boards Act (1909) that enabled the creation of a minimum wage, and the National Insurance Act (1911), which provided insurance for both health and unemployment. After the war, the Liberal Party, compromised by its historical connections to free trade, faded, and was replaced by a Labour Party that was better equipped to represent working-class interests. While Labour's time in government during the interwar period was relatively brief, they were triumphantly voted into office after World War II, and in perhaps the most far-reaching peacetime parliament of the twentieth century ushered in the modern welfare state with the National Health Service Act (1946).[28]

This impressive record has not so much been ignored by Vaughan Williams's revisionist critics as rejected as insufficient. His socialism, in particular, has been accused of actually bolstering the power structure of which it was critical.[29] Insofar as the developments described above did not result in the dismantling of capitalism in Britain, the charge has some point. But such a conclusion is also misguided and one-sided, the product of a disappointed Marxism that fails to appreciate the signal advance in working and living conditions that early twentieth-century social democracy brought to society's poorest members. It also overlooks the fact that 'progressivism' – the term that probably best describes Vaughan Williams's political philosophy – was responsible for the vast increase in civil machinery and governmental oversight that was actively overturning the principles of laissez-faire economics during this period.[30] Throwing his support behind a more collectivist and centralizing state, Vaughan Williams expressed his belief in the power of direct government action to correct the worst abuses of industrial capitalism, redistribute income and extend civil rights and equality of opportunity to the poorest segments of society.

But then, protest against the factory system and its cruel treatment of the labouring classes had always been one of the main messages of the ruralist movement itself. Traceable to the radical utopianism of figures like John Ruskin and William Morris, the embrace of the rural constituted not so much a rejection of the urban and industrial present as a condemnation of its dehumanizing effects. The idealization of a 'classless' pre-industrial world, in particular, was a call to reform a society in which mass production and commercialism had come to dominate the forms of contemporary culture, foisting the ready-made products of the 'business interest' on society as a whole and ultimately dampening individual creativity and self-expression.[31] This, surely, is the real explanation for Vaughan Williams's preference for rural folksong (what he called 'music made *by* the people') over urban popular song ('music made *for* the people'), as well as for his admiration of the Elizabethans, who by producing 'their own art' did not have to 'pay others to make it for them'.[32] Not that such 'anti-modernism' reflected only a progressive outlook. For some, the attack on urban squalor and commercial taint expressed reactionary concerns about physical and moral 'degeneration', and fed eugenicist fears about racial decline and its effects on military preparedness.[33] But for those who believed that unemployment and destitution were the products, not of individual laziness or shiftlessness, but rather of the inevitable cyclical depressions of an unregulated free market economy, the ruralist movement reflected a deeply humanitarian impulse to stem the abuses of industrial capitalism through the mechanism of the state. In these terms, ruralism played a major role in effecting the transition from an outmoded Victorian liberalism to new, twentieth-century forms of governmental and economic centralization.

In this way, 'Englishness' could be culturally backward-looking and politically progressive at once. That this was so in Vaughan Williams's case is borne out by his family background, a closer examination of which reveals patterns of behaviour and thought – generally overlooked by the revisionists – that help to explain how the composer could have connections to the 'establishment' and still remain on the political left. For while it is true that Wedgwoods generally abandoned industry and converted to Anglicanism in the early nineteenth century, the great majority did not go over to the Tories but rather remained staunchly radical in their viewpoint. This was possible because, in moving away from industry, family members – including some of those who bought country estates – eschewed landed *values* and entered the professions instead. Wedgwood sons and daughters became civil servants, mid-level government officials, lawyers, writers, journalists and university professors – occupations that elevated their social status while also situating them *outside* the merger of land and industry and thus in a still-subordinate position from which to criticize the elite above them. And criticize they did, especially as the professional class, released by the industrial revolution from its traditional dependency on the upper classes, had struck out on an independent course defending the principles of meritocracy and equality of opportunity against all forms of inherited property and privilege. These principles – the inevitable outgrowth of the professional focus on trained expertise and selection by intellectual ability – naturally placed professionals in opposition to land. But they also placed them at odds with industry, which was rapidly abandoning its entrepreneurial (and meritocratic) ideals in favour of the values of aristocratic preferment and entitlement that it had once opposed. Indeed, the real danger of the alliance of land and industry, from the professional viewpoint, was that it had created a 'new plutocracy' of enormous power and scope whose unfair political and economic advantage threatened to undermine the very basis of civil society. Only government action could curb this power, and here professionals, with their statistical training and managerial expertise, found their natural place. It was they who carried out the research, produced the reports and effectively implemented the progressive tax, the new commerce laws (including the repeal of free trade in 1931), and the long expansion of social services that culminated in the National Health Service. The natural champions and instinctive administrators of an expanding civic apparatus, professionals were in fact the chief architects of the centralized state.[34]

Thus even as they changed occupations and improved their social standing, Wedgwoods did not abandon their old ideals. If anything, their embrace of professional values intensified their moral opposition to entrenched privilege and gave them the statistical and analytical tools to prosecute the 'culture wars' more effectively than ever. Even conversion to Anglicanism signalled no real loss of radicalism since Wedgwoods embraced Evangelicalism, a socially committed (if narrowly tolerated) branch of the Established Church whose focus on humanitarian issues owed something to the traditions and old resentments of Nonconformity.[35] It was precisely this combination of religious and professional zeal, in fact, that put Wedgwoods at the very centre of an influential 'pressure group' that the historian Noel Annan famously dubbed the 'intellectual aristocracy'.[36] This was an extensively intermarrying cousinhood of high-minded, Evangelical and professional middle-class families, including the Wilberforces, Darwins, Wedgwoods, Butlers, Keyneses, Stephens and Haldanes, who became over the course of the nineteenth century the principal theorists and apologists of an expanding centralized state. Through their accomplishments in economics, medicine and the natural and social sciences, as well as their influential work at the universities and in civil administration, this 'aristocracy of exceptional talent' brought the professional ideals of meritocracy and public service into the mainstream of public opinion and policy.[37] Focusing their formidable analytical skills on the problems of society and communicating their views to the public by means of a direct literary style, they made the case for the State as the engine of humanitarian and democratic reform and the best means to ensure the common good. They valued hard work and intellectual endeavour, not merely because they felt duty-bound to account for the talents granted them by Providence, but also because freedom of thought and of conscience were necessary preconditions for freedom of contract and equality of opportunity. Personal duty and duty to society were thus twin pillars of a common impulse, and they came to view themselves as the disinterested arbiters of civility and common decency, criticizing the assumptions of the 'irresponsible' ruling class above them and establishing the principle of community over selfish class interest as a means to improve society as a whole.

Here is the true source of Vaughan Williams's social confidence and public-mindedness. His calls for social cooperation and national solidarity reflected his family's connections, not to a newly merging industrial and landed elite, but rather to an influential group of professional families independent of that elite who, for a variety of religious and historical reasons, saw themselves as stewards of the national culture. That Vaughan Williams identified with this Wedgwood inheritance is suggested by brief comments and anecdotes in letters and essays,[38] but also, and more importantly, by fundamental aspects of his life and personality. Upholding family traditions of independence, he refused a knighthood and the Mastership of the King's Music, and accepted the Order of Merit only on the grounds that it involved no 'obligations to anyone in authority'.[39] He placed high value on scholarship and learning, following the great Wedgwood and Darwin accomplishments in philology, moral philosophy and the natural sciences with his more modest but still important editorial work with hymn tunes and folksongs. (Proud of the Doctor of Music degree he earned from Cambridge in 1901, he preferred the academic title of 'Dr' to all others.)[40] An indifference to outward 'appearances' and the mindless social conventions of Victorian respectability, typical of a group that sought the general reform of society, was also characteristic of a man whose carelessness about his clothes, his handwriting and the shabby state of his home is the stuff of legend. He further conformed to type by marrying Adeline Fisher, a product of Oxbridge academics and high-ranking civil servants who shared connections with many of the same intellectual families as her husband.[41] Endogamy, as Annan points out, was a natural result of shared backgrounds and values, and was also an effective strategy for a group that relied on concerted action to influence public affairs.

Not that every feature of Vaughan Williams's personality fitted this profile. His ebullient high spirits and mischievous wit contrasted with the earnest humourlessness of many in the group, and he roundly rejected the Evangelicalism that surrounded him as a youth at Leith Hill Place, turning from its grey austerity and philistinism to embrace the High Church aestheticism of his dead father instead.[42] Nor as a musician did his work fit the typical professional pattern of applying expertise in law or civil administration to the creation of statistical reports and policy papers. In his insistence on music as a *public* art form, however, capable of exerting a positive moral influence on society, he clearly exhibited the assumptions of his class. Chiefly, this took the form of cultivating what he called a 'sense of musical citizenship': working with amateur musicians as composer, conductor and competition adjudicator, lecturing and writing essays aimed at non-specialized audiences, teaching, and providing financial and administrative assistance to numerous local musical organizations.[43] It also found expression in his outspoken advocacy for public arts funding, a practical endorsement of governmental centralization that he supported as early as 1902 and that culminated in his high-profile committee work, in the 1930s and 1940s, on the British Council, the Council for the Encouragement of Music and the Arts (CEMA) and its successor, the Arts Council.[44] His engagement at nearly every level of the nation's cultural life is striking, as are the values he characteristically promoted in this work: the emphasis on art as a spiritual necessity, the frequent appeal to democratic precept and moral argument, and above all the commitment to uphold standards of excellence for the benefit of all. 'Has it ever occurred to [the BBC governors] that they have a moral responsibility to *make* the best music popular?' he wrote in response to proposed cuts to the high-toned Third Programme in 1957.[45] As often with public statements by members of his class, the rebuke formed part of a larger campaign of letter-writing and face-to-face meetings with BBC officials organized by a group of eminent intellectual figures seeking to influence matters affecting 'the interests of the . . . nation as a whole'.[46]

Paternalistic assumptions are inescapable here, and serve as a reminder that even progressivism contained the seeds of a paradoxical conservatism and authoritarianism. For a group whose principled defence of democracy and promotion of the common good had elevated it to a position of cultural authority, this was perhaps inevitable. Thus the populism animating Vaughan Williams's embrace of folksong, that long-abused expression of the lower classes of society, also prompted him to condemn as 'positively harmful' the mass-produced Victorian parlour songs and hymn tunes that an 'undiscriminating' populace had taken to its heart.[47] It also informed a patronizing defence of elite culture, as in the fight over the

Third Programme cited above, or on those occasions when he expressed particular concern that children be exposed to 'good music' as a means to safeguard their 'spiritual health'.[48] And yet, as we saw earlier, he did not wholly reject urban popular musics, granting a limited place to them as source material for composers, even drawing on them himself in specific compositions. When organizing concerts in his home town of Dorking during World War II, he deliberately programmed the classics to educate the troops while still allowing them their popular favourites.[49] Nor did he always support the claims of high art. When in 1942 John Maynard Keynes, as CEMA chairman, sought to nurture professional performing ensembles at the expense of amateur groups, Vaughan Williams shrewdly checked him in committee meetings and secured amateur funding for the near future.[50]

This flexible and ultimately non-dogmatic approach to questions of popular versus elite culture is significant and gives the lie to claims that Vaughan Williams's 'public' stature necessarily led him to impose his views on others. A sense of cultural stewardship may indeed have prompted strong views and a 'crusading' activism, but a counterbalancing defence of civil liberties and respect for independence of thought – values also inherited from his family – guaranteed an open mind towards alternative viewpoints and an allowance for 'exceptions'. How else are we to explain the curious denials of omniscience and authority that creep into his highly opinionated essays,[51] or his remarkable defence of Alan Bush's and Michael Tippett's pacifism during World War II even though he himself was a firm believer in the war effort? (He protested against the BBC's 'victimisation of private opinion' in banning Bush's music by returning a BBC commission for one of his own works, while his testimony at Tippett's tribunal declared that he thought the younger composer's 'pacifist views entirely wrong, but I respect him very much for holding them so firmly'.)[52] That he should insist on these during wartime, when crisis conditions encouraged a culture of obedience to the state, suggests that the principle of individual freedom was even more important to him than the claims of 'nation'. Indeed, for all his faith in government centralization as the vehicle of social cooperation, he was quick to condemn the waste and inefficiency often attending bureaucracy and warned of the dehumanizing potential of a wholly regulated world. When, in an effort to streamline CEMA's administration of amateur groups, Keynes replaced a proven system of itinerant supervisors or 'music travellers' with impersonal, one-size-fits-all regional offices and officers, Vaughan Williams delivered a policy paper criticizing this substitution of real human contact with telephones and typewriters.[53] Looking back on the headlong expansion of centralized planning during the 1945–51 Attlee government, he asserted that socialism had overreached itself and created an 'unholy mess'.[54]

The contradictions and inconsistencies are striking, and yet were the logical consequence of a political philosophy that drew on eighteenth-century radical (i.e. individualist) arguments even as it embraced nineteenth- and twentieth-century notions of state collectivism as the best means to protect and extend individual rights. As he put it in a 1952 letter to Rutland Boughton: 'The truth is, I think, that when I am with Conservatives I become socialistic and when I am with Socialists I become a true blue Tory'.[55] The resulting tension between the claims of the individual and the group – between the private and the public, the local and the national, even the national and the international – meant that he could easily tip one way or another depending on the specifics of the case. Thus he sided with Hungarian dissidents who fought against Stalinist oppression in 1956 but also dismissed the protests of Ulster Protestants who felt threatened by Irish Home Rule in 1914. He condemned the Nazi suppression of free speech but also denounced as 'ruffians' independent-minded Greeks who called for the removal of allied British troops during World War II. Sometimes he took opposing positions on a single issue, as when he censured the government for fomenting 'class war' by recruiting volunteers to break the 1926 General Strike even as he could not 'deny the right' of any citizen to join up for this work.[56] What was nevertheless consistent in these instances was the effort, wholly characteristic, to work towards the 'common good': to examine carefully and dispassionately the rights and needs of the players involved (as well as any relevant practical or long-range strategic factors) in order to arrive at a solution that was fair to all. Where a situation did not admit of a clear solution, mutual cooperation and compromise – the give and take between competing interests negotiating in good faith – was essential. His self-memorandum on the General Strike strongly criticized both the trade unions and the government for 'refusing to budge' during negotiations, and he had even harsher words for the 'selfish [and] dishonest' behaviour of the Soviets, who craftily obstructed the drafting of the new United Nations charter after World War II.[57] Compromise and negotiation 'in good faith', indeed, drove his passionate embrace of Federal Union in the 1940s, and sustained his lifelong faith in graduated parliamentary reform, rather than revolution, as the only viable means to social change.[58] It is also what prompted him, in the 1945 election cited earlier, to reverse his usual practice and cast his lone vote for the Tories.[59] The 'mean trick' of the Labour party in 'forcing an election' lay in its abandonment of Churchill's government coalition for narrowly partisan goals directly after the peace was won, a move that, in Vaughan Williams's eyes, signalled Labour's rejection of the spirit of national unity and inter-class cooperation that the war had called forth.

Does this make Vaughan Williams, in the final analysis, a conservative? In a recent book on British music and modernism, Matthew Riley discusses the limitations of political progressives like Vaughan Williams, suggesting that their 'liberal humanism' had become outmoded in a twentieth century characterized by 'mass democracy' and a 'factional and polarized politics conducted by megaphone'.[60] There is some truth to the assertion, insofar as Victorian notions of 'character', 'self-improvement' and 'altruism' remained central to the vocabulary and social outlook of British progressives long after they had been jettisoned by other left-leaning intellectuals, and that these values met with increasing indifference and hostility from many different quarters of society as the century wore on.[61] (The Third Programme campaign of 1957, to give but one example, failed utterly to achieve its aim.) It is further true that some progressives, offended by the new class politics and despairing of an 'uneducable' working class distracted by consumerism and media manipulation, moved politically towards the right.[62] But this was hardly the case with all progressives, many of whom, like Vaughan Williams, continued to seek ways to extend the professional ideals of meritocracy and equality of opportunity to society's poorest members. Their achievement was to construct a humane state apparatus that redistributed wealth and empowered the underprivileged while still managing to safeguard individual rights, protect private property and promote entrepreneurial activity. Indeed, it was probably the currency of those same 'outmoded' liberal humanist values that ensured that mass democracy in twentieth-century Britain, when it came, preserved the civil liberties that helped her resist the plunge into fascism and totalitarianism that consumed so much of continental Europe.

All of which brings us full circle to Vaughan Williams's music and its reception. Modernist commentators like Riley make an important point by linking the paternalism that undoubtedly did inform the progressive agenda with the 'conservative' and 'accessible' idiom of much twentieth-century British music. Clearly, a sense of social responsibility and cultural leadership prompted composers like Vaughan Williams to take a utilitarian and 'didactic' approach to music that led them, in turn, to reject the most extreme forms of modernist technique in their own creative work. By focusing only on the shortcomings of progressivism, however – its uneasy relations with mass culture rather than its long-range social and political achievements – these commentators slip all too easily into the familiar pattern of modernist criticism that equates artistic quality only with forms of political and stylistic disaffection. Such a viewpoint not only misses the irony surrounding modernism's own elitist aesthetic – one far more contemptuous of the masses than progressivism's cautious populism, in fact – but also skirts the duty of the cultural historian to push past orthodox 'theory' to consider the legitimacy of alternative responses to the modern world.[63] Doing so

ourselves, we can recognize in Vaughan Williams's music an independent voice poised between modernism and conservatism, innovation
and tradition, that has its roots in his personal history and his family's
heritage of commitment to society and nation.

Notes

1 For only two examples of the 'populist' tradition, see Sidney Finkelstein, *Composer and Nation: The Folk Heritage in Music*, 2nd edn (New York: International, 1989), 228–37; and Frank Howes, *The English Musical Renaissance* (New York: Stein and Day, 1966), 230–45. For detractors, see Donald Mitchell, 'Vaughan Williams', in Christopher Palmer and Mervyn Cooke (eds.), *Cradles of the New: Writings on Music* (London: Faber and Faber, 1995), 87–97; and Robert Stradling and Meirion Hughes, *The English Musical Renaissance 1860–1940: Construction and Deconstruction* (1st edn, London: Routledge, 1993), 60–7, 135–79.
2 Alain Frogley, 'Constructing Englishness in Music: National Character and the Reception of Ralph Vaughan Williams', in *VWS*, 1–22.
3 Alain Frogley, *Vaughan Williams's Ninth Symphony* (Oxford University Press, 2001); Walter Aaron Clark, 'Vaughan Williams and the "Night Side of Nature": Octatonicism in *Riders to the Sea*', in *VWE*, 55–71. See also the essays on Vaughan Williams in the 'British Modernism' issue of *MQ* 91/1–2 (Spring/Summer 2008).
4 *NM*, 155.
5 Martin J. Wiener, *English Culture and the Decline of the Industrial Spirit 1850–1980* (Cambridge University Press, 1981); and Jan Marsh, *Back to the Land: The Pastoral Impulse in England, from 1880 to 1914* (London: Quartet Books, 1982). Frank Trentmann, 'Civilization and Its Discontents: English Neo-Romanticism and the Transformation of Anti-Modernism in Twentieth-Century Western Culture', *Journal of Contemporary History* 29 (1994), 583–625, though focusing on the interwar years, traces the movement to the 1890s.
6 Otto Deri, *Exploring Twentieth-Century Music* (New York: Holt McDougal, 1968), 148–50, 166–8 and 440, is representative.
7 James Day, *Vaughan Williams* (1st edn, London: J. M. Dent and Sons, 1961), 83; Wilfrid Mellers, *Vaughan Williams and the Vision of Albion* (London: Pimlico, 1989), 118–41. Hubert Foss, *Ralph Vaughan Williams: A Study* (London: George G. Harrap & Co., 1950), 53, roots British (and

thus the composer's) 'instincts . . . toward liberality' even more indistinctly in the culture of 'Celt and Saxon, Norman and Dane and Roman, German, even Phoenician'.
8 Vic Gammon, 'Folk Song Collecting in Sussex and Surrey, 1843–1914', *History Workshop Journal* 10 (1980), 61–89; Dave Harker, *Fakesong: The Manufacture of British 'Folksong' 1700 to the Present Day* (Milton Keynes: Open University Press, 1985), 198–210; Alun Howkins, 'The Discovery of Rural England', in Robert Colls and Philip Dodd (eds.), *Englishness: Politics and Culture 1880–1920* (London: Croom Helm, 1986), 62–88; Alun Howkins, 'Greensleeves and the Idea of National Music', in Raphael Samuel (ed.), *Patriotism: The Making and Unmaking of British National Identity*, 3 vols. (London: Routledge, 1989), vol. III, 89–98; Georgina Boyes, *The Imagined Village: Culture, Ideology and the English Folk Revival* (Manchester University Press, 1993), 1–119.
9 Brian Doyle, 'The Invention of English', in Colls and Dodd (ed.), *Englishness*, 89–115 at 90.
10 *UVWB*, 1, is incorrect in stating that Edward Vaughan Williams was the *first* Judge of Common Pleas. See N. G. Jones, 'Williams, Sir Edward Vaughan', in *Oxford Dictionary of National Biography* (online, accessed 11 June 2012).
11 Barbara and Hansleigh Wedgwood, *The Wedgwood Circle: Four Generations of a Family and Their Friends* (London: Studio Vista, 1980), *passim*, but esp. 105–6, 114, 137 and 238.
12 *UVWB*, 6; Wedgwood and Wedgwood, *Wedgwood Circle*, 250.
13 The only weekly salaried position that Vaughan Williams ever held, that of organist and choirmaster at St Barnabas, South Lambeth, from 1895 to 1899, was not a full-time job. It is, however, important not to overstate the family's wealth. Vaughan Williams's own description – 'I was born with a very small silver spoon in my mouth' – seems generally accurate given that 'until I was about forty . . . I could not financially afford to devote my whole time to composition – from the age from about 20 to 30 I supplemented my income

by playing the organ (very badly) and teaching and lecturing' (*LRVW*, 318). In conversation with the author (October 1992), Ursula Vaughan Williams described her husband's private income as 'small'.

14 *NM*, 39.

15 On the RCM, see Stradling and Hughes, *English Musical Renaissance*. See also *LRVW*, 228–9, 369–70 and 457–8 for examples of Vaughan Williams pulling strings for favoured pupils, performers and colleagues.

16 *LRVW*, 303–4.

17 *UVWB*, 151. See also Gordon Cox, *A History of Music Education in England 1872–1928* (Aldershot: Ashgate, 1993), 146.

18 *NM*, 21, 38. See also *VWOM*, 191, 193.

19 Gammon, 'Folk Song Collecting', 61–89; Harker, *Fakesong*, 198–210; Boyes, *Imagined Village*, 41–62, while focusing on Sharp's collecting methods, implicates Vaughan Williams as well.

20 *VWOM*, 69. See also *ibid.*, 47–50 and *NM*, 166–9.

21 See Julian Onderdonk in: 'Vaughan Williams's Folksong Transcriptions: A Case of Idealization?' in *VWS*, 118–38; 'Vaughan Williams and the Modes', *Folk Music Journal* 7/5 (1999), 609–26; and 'The Revised (1904) Version of the Folk Song Society's Hints to Collectors', *English Dance and Song* 62/3 (Autumn 2000), 21–5. See also Georgina Boyes's recent retraction of her previous views in '"An Individual Flowering": Ralph Vaughan Williams's Work in Folklore', in *RVW Society Journal* 46 (October 2009), 7–8.

22 Roger Savage, 'Alice Shortcake, Jenny Pluckpears, and the Stratford-upon-Avon Connections of Vaughan Williams's "Sir John in Love"', *ML* 89/1 (2007), 18–55 at 33–4.

23 *VWOM*, 50, 41–2. Vaughan Williams clearly also enjoyed music hall songs and performed them himself in private settings. See *UVWB*, 118 and 129; *LRVW*, 60.

24 Vaughan Williams Memorial Issue, *The Royal College of Music Magazine* 60/1 (February 1959), 35.

25 Alain Frogley, 'H. G. Wells and Vaughan Williams's *A London Symphony*: Politics and Culture in Fin-de-Siècle England' in Chris Banks, Arthur Searle and Malcolm Turner (eds.), *Sundry Sorts of Music Books: Essays on the British Library Collection. Presented to O. W. Neighbour on His Seventieth Birthday* (London: The British Library, 1993), 299–308.

26 Jennifer Doctor, '"Working for Her Own Salvation": Vaughan Williams as Teacher of Elizabeth Maconchy, Grace Williams and Ina Boyle' in *VWIP*, 181–201, details the

composer's generous treatment of female students throughout their careers. For his public statements defending Gypsies, see *VWOM*, 227–8; and Lavender M. Jones, 'The Song Seekers – Hereford', *English Dance and Song* 27/1–2 (December 1964–February 1965), 4–6, 38–40. His work on behalf of Jews as a member of the Dorking Committee for Refugees from Nazi Oppression is documented in *UVWB*, 224 and 229 and especially in Celia Newbery (ed.), *Vaughan Williams in Dorking: A Collection of Personal Reminiscences of the Composer Dr. Ralph Vaughan Williams, O.M.* (Dorking: private publication by the Local History Group of the Dorking & Leith Hill District Preservation Society, 1979), 14–15. For his personal generosity to individuals, drawn from all social classes and walks of life, see *ibid.* as well as the Vaughan Williams Memorial Issue, *RCM Magazine*, *passim*, especially the testimonies of Henry Steggles and J. Ellis Cook.

27 Quotations are from the composer's 1952 letter to Rutland Boughton in *LRVW*, 502–3. The references to Tillett and Burns come from a letter to Vaughan Williams written by G. M. Trevelyan, quoted in *UVWB*, 39. Paul Harrington, 'Holst and Vaughan Williams: Radical Pastoral' in Christopher Norris (ed.), *Music and the Politics of Culture* (London: Lawrence and Wishart, 1989), 106–27, provides a useful overview of the composer's left-leaning politics. See also *KW*, 388, for his admiration for William Booth, founder of the Salvation Army and champion of the urban poor; and *LRVW*, 403 and 560, for his views on economic levelling and the progressive tax. The 'important exception', mentioned in the same letter to Boughton, came right after World War II when Vaughan Williams voted for the Tories in the 1945 national election because 'I was so disgusted by what I considered the mean tricks of the Labour party in forcing an election'. I will return to this episode below.

28 Derek Fraser, *The Evolution of the British Welfare State* (London: Macmillan Press, 1973), *passim*.

29 Harker, *Fakesong*, 199; Stradling and Hughes, *English Musical Renaissance*, 77; Howkins, 'Discovery of Rural England', 75.

30 The term 'progressivism' is more often encountered in discussions of turn-of-the-century American political developments, though a short-lived Progressive party, allied to the Liberals, dominated the London County Council from 1889 to 1907. See Pat Thane, 'Labour and Local Politics: Radicalism, Democracy and Social Reform, 1880–1914' in

Eugenio Biagini and Alastair Reid (eds.), *Currents of Radicalism: Popular Radicalism, Organized Labour and Party Politics in Britain, 1850–1914* (Cambridge University Press, 1991), 244–70.

31 Marsh, *Back to the Land*, 8–17. See also Peter C. Gould, *Early Green Politics: Back to Nature, Back to the Land, and Socialism in Britain 1880–1900* (Brighton: Harvester Press, 1988).

32 *VWOM*, 46–7 (emphases added).

33 Paul Rich, 'The Quest for Englishness', *History Today* 37 (June 1987), 24–30; Bernard Semmel, *Imperialism and Social Reform: English Social-Imperial Thought 1895–1914* (Garden City: Anchor Books, 1968), 18–42; G. C. Webber, *The Ideology of the British Right 1918–1939* (New York: St Martin's Press, 1986), 57–62.

34 For the complex social and economic developments summarized in this paragraph, see Harold Perkin, *The Rise of Professional Society: England Since 1880* (London: Routledge, 1989) and *The Origins of Modern English Society, 1780–1880* (London: Routledge and Kegan Paul, 1969), 252–70 and 428–37. Perkin asserts that the merger of land and industry commenced in the 1840s and 1850s and that it resulted principally from industry's growing acceptance of landed aristocratic values, including, crucially, this notion of entitlement and preferment. Both observations contradict the revisionists' arguments that the alliance originated in shared concerns about national defence and social control – specifically, the threat of an unruly working class – and that it arose only in the last third of the century. Other important accounts of the period, including Wiener's *English Culture* and F. M. L. Thompson's still-influential *English Landed Society in the Nineteenth Century* (London: Routledge, 1963), support Perkin's analysis. See also Stefan Collini, *Public Moralists: Political Thought and Intellectual Life in Britain, 1850–1930* (Oxford University Press, 1991) for a rich portrait of the moral and intellectual life of the educated and professional classes in this period.

35 Wedgwood and Wedgwood, *Wedgwood Circle*, 194, 198–200, 221–2. For the Evangelical Anglicans, see Horton Davies, *Worship and Theology in England*, 5 vols. (Princeton University Press, 1961), vol. III, 210–40.

36 Noel Annan, 'The Intellectual Aristocracy', in J. H. Plumb (ed.) *Studies in Social History: A Tribute to G. M. Trevelyan* (London: Longmans, Green and Co., 1955), 241–87.

37 David Cannadine, *G. M. Trevelyan: A Life in History* (New York: W. W. Norton and Co., 1992), 8.

38 See especially *LRVW*, 90 and *NM*, 180, where Vaughan Williams credits Steven Massingberd, a Wedgwood cousin, for introducing him to Hubert Parry's dictum that 'a composer must write music as his musical conscience demands'. I am suggesting here that the composer's social outlook was formed principally by the Wedgwood, not the Vaughan Williams, side of his family. While the facts of his life appear strongly to support this – his father's early death, his upbringing among Wedgwood grandparents and aunts at Leith Hill Place, his close friendship with cousin Ralph ('Randolph') Wedgwood – more research is needed on the Vaughan Williams line to confirm or qualify this claim. Especially valuable would be a detailed understanding of the social and cultural negotiations involved in the union of the Vaughan Williamses, an 'old guard' professional and mainstream Anglican family, with the Wedgwoods, an Evangelical family only recently converted to professional life after a long involvement in 'trade'.

39 *LRVW*, 502. Significantly, he appeared at the OM investiture ceremony at Buckingham Palace in the plainest court dress allowable. See *UVWB*, 207.

40 *UVWB*, 207.

41 Annan, 'Intellectual Aristocracy', 277. See also the family tree diagrams in Paul Levy, *Moore: G. E. Moore and the Cambridge Apostles* (Oxford University Press, 1981), 22–5.

42 See Byron Adams, 'To Be A Pilgrim: A Meditation on Vaughan Williams and Religion', *RVW Society Journal* 33 (June 2005), 4–6 at 5; and Eric Seddon, 'Turn Up My Metaphors and Do Not Fail: Religious Meaning and Musical Iconography in Ralph Vaughan Williams's The Pilgrim's Progress', *RVW Society Journal* 38 (March 2007), 4–13 at 4–6. The turn to aestheticism was almost certainly motivated by personal and artistic, not conventionally religious, considerations. See *KW*, 39; *LRVW*, 201 and 489; and, for his impatience with Evangelicalism, the Vaughan Williams Memorial Issue, *RCM Magazine*, 9–12.

43 Quotation from *VWOM*, 41. Vaughan Williams's work with amateur groups is too wide-ranging to list here, though his long association with the Leith Hill Musical Festival, as chief conductor and president, must take pride of place. See Brian Tucker (ed.), *And Choirs Singing: An Account of the Leith Hill Musical Festival 1905–85* (Leith Hill Musical

Festival, 1985). 'Citizenship' extended to non-musical life as well, as Vaughan Williams served on regional education committees and preservation societies, joined the Rotary Club, and lent his name and time to many local causes. His service in World War I, as an ambulance orderly and later a gunner, is likewise exemplary, as are his exertions as an ordinary citizen during World War II, when he contributed to the war effort by collecting junk, filling sandbags, raising vegetables, storing barley and serving as an air raid warden. See *UVWB*, 229–30 and 395; and Newbery (ed.), *Vaughan Williams in Dorking*, 8, 11–12, 15–16.

44 *UVWB*, 63, 264; *KW*, 153.

45 *VWOM*, 120, with original emphasis restored. His broadside goes on to express alarm that the Third Programme might start broadcasting 'the kind of standardised entertainment which is already being mass-produced in every country', and concludes that 'we should defend to the last this service which maintains the highest standards of art and scholarship in our midst'.

46 Letter to *The Times*, 26 April 1957, 11, signed jointly by Vaughan Williams and fourteen others, quoted in Stefan Collini, *Absent Minds: Intellectuals in Britain* (Oxford University Press, 2006), 437–46 at 437. J. B. Priestley's thinly veiled portrait of Vaughan Williams as 'Dr. Mountgarret Camden', the craggy octogenarian composer and outraged scourge of frivolous government arts officials, in his satirical 1964 novel *Sir Michael and Sir George*, humorously captures many of the attitudes and methods of the intellectual aristocracy that I am discussing here. See Michael Gainsford, 'So Who Was the Model for Mountgarret Camden?', *RVW Society Journal* 4 (November 1995), 17.

47 Quotations from *VWOM*, 32–3.

48 Vaughan Williams used these very terms in his 1952 letter to the *Bournemouth Daily Echo* concerning the proposed disbanding of that city's orchestra. The letter continues: 'When [children] grow up, this spiritual exaltation will die away and fade into the light of common day unless we see to it that this splendid vision of the ultimate realities is preserved for them.' *LRVW*, 500–1.

49 Newbery (ed.), *Vaughan Williams in Dorking*, 17. Works incorporating urban popular music include the *London* and Sixth symphonies, as well as *The Poisoned Kiss* and the Intermezzo from the Partita for Double String Orchestra of 1948, a homage to the popular bandleader Henry Hall. The discrepancy between Vaughan Williams's

stated opinions and his actual practice is characteristic. For further examples, see Frogley, 'Constructing Englishness', 18–19, and the details of his editorial work with Victorian hymn tunes discussed in Chapter 7 of this volume.

50 Richard Witts, *Artist Unknown: An Alternative History of the Arts Council* (London: Little, Brown and Co., 1998), 104–7. My thanks to Andrew Pinnock for bringing this study to my attention.

51 See, for example, *NM*, 17, 55, 62, 67, 83, 84, 91, 108, 162, 176, and 206.

52 *UVWB*, 239, 255. Characteristically, a copy of the letter defending Bush, addressed to the Director-General of the BBC, was also sent to *The Times*. See *LRVW*, 314.

53 F. M. Leventhal, '"The Best for the Most:" CEMA and State Sponsorship of the Arts in Wartime, 1939–1945', *Twentieth Century British History* 1/3 (1990), 289–317 at 303.

54 *LRVW*, 501–2.

55 *LRVW*, 502–3.

56 *UVWB*, 378–9; *LRVW*, 93–4, 151–2, 249, 332. Hugh Cobbe (*LRVW*, 94) is uncertain about Vaughan Williams's Irish opinions, but the composer's talk of enlisting 'on the side of law and order when the fight comes' is a clear reference to the unprecedented chaos of 1913–14, when Ireland was on the verge of civil war owing to Tory mischief in derailing the Liberals' Home Rule bill. See George Dangerfield's classic 1935 account in *The Strange Death of Liberal England: 1910–1914* (New York: Capricorn Books, reprint, 1961), 74–138.

57 *LRVW*, 151–2, 471.

58 *LRVW*, 282, 290, 300, 307 and 397 provide both a brief introduction to Federal Union, a political theory and movement that stressed the union of 'free nations' operating under a 'common government', and examples of Vaughan Williams's enthusiasm for it. The composer's embrace of gradualism is clear from his undergraduate interest (cited above) in the Fabians, who urged the establishment of socialism through existing institutional channels, and from a comment in his essay on Holst about 'the weak points in [William] Morris's teaching' (*NM*, 135). Morris believed in revolution as the only means to achieve social change, and in 1887 led an unsuccessful workers' uprising in Trafalgar Square. Vaughan Williams's essay speaks admiringly of Morris's 'poetic socialism' and 'ideal of . . . comradeship', but the criticism makes it clear that he disapproved of his insurrectionist methods. The self-memorandum on the

General Strike does admit the possibility of 'revolution by violence as a last resort' but dismisses it on the grounds that the insurgents' plan for the future would probably not result in a '*better* state of things'; that being so, the 'temporary anarchy' that would necessarily accompany the revolution's first stages could hardly be justified. See *LRVW*, 152.

59 See note 27 above.

60 Matthew Riley, 'Liberal Critics and Modern Music in the Post-Victorian Age', in Matthew Riley (ed.), *British Music and Modernism, 1895–1960* (Farnham: Ashgate Publishing Ltd, 2010), 13–30 at 15.

61 Collini, *Public Moralists, passim*, esp. 85–90, 369–70; Collini, *Absent Minds*, 116, 446.

62 See, for example, Cannadine, *G. M. Trevelyan*, 158–61.

63 For an eloquent plea to judge twentieth-century British musical modernism on its own terms, see Jenny Doctor, 'The Parataxis of "British Musical Modernism"', *MQ* 91/1–2 (Spring/Summer 2008), 89–115.

2 Vaughan Williams's musical apprenticeship

BYRON ADAMS

for Oliver Neighbour

In her tribute to Vaughan Williams published in the 1959 memorial issue of *The RCM Magazine*, Elizabeth Maconchy emphasized that her teacher 'somehow imparted to his pupils his own attitude to composition, a complete and uncalculating devotion to music … He had no use for ready made solutions: he had worked out his own salvation as a composer and he encouraged his pupils to do the same'.[1] While invoking Vaughan Williams's pedagogical philosophy, Maconchy also echoed her teacher's vocabulary, for Vaughan Williams frequently had recourse to the word 'salvation' in connection to musical education – his own as well as that of his students. During a holiday in the late 1940s, Vaughan Williams dictated 'A Musical Autobiography' to the poet Ursula Wood, whom he would marry in 1953. In this laconic document, originally destined for his biographer Hubert Foss, the composer remembered that as a child, 'I had been taught the pianoforte, which I never could play, and the violin, which was my musical salvation'.[2] The son of an Anglican vicar, Vaughan Williams often employed language redolent of Christian aspiration and frequently quoted – and misquoted – the Bible. Raised in the final decades of Victoria's reign, Vaughan Williams was not alone in being steeped in the language of the Authorized Version, even if such habits were given special encouragement in his family.

As is clear from his writings and letters, Vaughan Williams eschewed religious faith in preference to devotion to music. Though written by a self-declared agnostic, Vaughan Williams's prose is shot through with such declarations as 'A work of art is like a theophany which takes different forms to different beholders' and 'The object of art is to stretch out to the ultimate realities through the medium of beauty'.[3] In this loosely defined system of metaphysical aesthetics, he posits that only

For their assistance in the completion of this chapter, the author thanks Nicholas Bell and the music staff of the British Library, Jenny Doctor, Eric Saylor, Charles Edward McGuire, Steven Bauer, Leanne Langley, the late Felix Aprahamian, Alain Frogley, Carlo Caballero, Marcus Desmond Harmon, Hugh Cobbe, Diana McVeagh and Lauren Cowdery. He also wishes to thank Dr Shantan Reddy, Dr Allen Hu and Dr Atul Jain, retinal surgeons whose extraordinary skill restored his eyesight and thus enabled him to complete this essay.

through art – and for Vaughan Williams, the 'art' under discussion is 'music' – can the composer himself receive salvation from the hell of a career strewn with unrealized conceptions. The goal of this pilgrimage is better than entrance into any heavenly habitation, for it is a nirvana-like dissolution into the beloved. As the elderly composer remarked seriously to Sylvia Townsend Warner shortly before his death, 'in the next world, I shan't be doing music with all the striving and disappointments. I shall be being it.'[4] But the burning question persisted for Vaughan Williams: musical salvation was greatly desired but how did an individual make one's way? Maconchy provides an important clue to his personal solution: 'He fully recognized the importance of an adequate technique, but for him the purpose of technique was how best to enable each of us to express his own ideas in his own way.'[5] Vaughan Williams's term for this process was doing one's 'stodge'. As another former pupil (and later colleague at the Royal College of Music), Gordon Jacob, recalled, 'his later pupils were put through the mill, or, as he put it "made to do their stodge", methodically. After all his musical demi-god was Bach, who surely, of all the great composers, combined profound spirituality with complete mastery of musical mechanics.'[6]

Unfortunately, Vaughan Williams talked and wrote a great deal of sheer nonsense about his supposed amateurishness. As revealed by his sketches and revisions, he was a perfectionist who polished his music continually, and yet in his autobiography he states 'I have struggled all my life to conquer amateurish technique and now that perhaps I have mastered it, it seems too late to make any use of it.' (In fact, he lived for almost eight years after dictating this memoir, during which he completed three symphonies, a large Christmas cantata, *Hodie*, and a violin sonata, among other scores.) A few pages later, this most relentlessly studious of composers makes the absurd claim, contradicted by his own testimony elsewhere in the same document, 'I have always found it difficult to study. I have learnt almost entirely what I have learnt by trying it on the dog.'[7] Given that Vaughan Williams had internalized such a powerful sense of inadequacy, it is not surprising to hear him resentfully dismiss the technical resources upon which he drew daily to compose his music. Jacob recalled that his teacher, newly appointed to the Royal College just after demobilization from active service during the First World War, 'was an instinctive poet in music and at that time had a horror of professional skill and technical ability'.[8] Jacob might have been more accurate to write that Vaughan Williams *expressed* a distrust of technical ability during the early 1920s, a period when he often feared that he had dried up due to the war. The composer of the lapidary and original *A Pastoral Symphony* (1921) can hardly be said to have demonstrated a 'horror of professional skill' in practice.

Part of Vaughan Williams's habitual self-deprecation was based in his privileged status as a member of the British gentry. Unlike Elgar, a trades-man's son who aspired to be a 'gentleman', Vaughan Williams rebelled against the constraints imposed by both his class and his upbringing. Vaughan Williams's family not only opposed his pursuit of a musical career but were censorious to his face and ridiculed him behind his back. Gwen Raverat, a cousin who would later collaborate on the composer's 'masque for dancing', *Job*, remembered one of her relations commenting waspishly about "'that foolish young man, Ralph Vaughan Williams", who *would* go on working at music when "he was so hopelessly bad at it"'. Raverat's Aunt Etty, who was Charles Darwin's daughter, wrote that the young Vaughan Williams 'can't play the simplest thing decently . . . They say it will simply break his heart if he is told that he is too bad to hope to make anything of it'. Aunt Etty also dismissed an early novel by E. M. Forster as 'too unpleasant for the girls to read'. Of such critiques, Raverat observed that 'these two were not great men then; this is what you have to go through to become great'.[9]

One can only speculate what the young Vaughan Williams 'had to go through', when, in an act of class rebellion, he announced his intention to become a professional violist at a time when orchestral musicians were considered a cut above servants, if that. His relatives must have been beside themselves with dismay. A 'compromise' was reached, however, and Vaughan Williams was allowed to pursue a less congenial but more respect-able career as an organist. With characteristic doggedness, Vaughan Williams worked hard at transforming himself, studying with two great teachers of the organ, Alan Gray and Sir Walter Parratt. Although Vaughan Williams later made fun of his attempts to play the organ – 'I have the distinction of being the only pupil who entirely baffled Sir Walter Parratt' – he passed the gruelling examination to become a Fellow of the Royal College of Organists, a test that today would defeat all but the most extraordinarily accomplished organists.[10] Sir Walter evidently prevailed and taught his awkward pupil a great deal despite Vaughan Williams's lack of tempera-mental affinity for the organ or for the life of a church organist. (When he resigned from his sole post of this kind, at St Barnabas, South Lambeth, Vaughan Williams left behind a box of 'daring' French novels with which he would while away the ennui that set in during sermons.)[11] In a pattern that was repeated often over the course of his musical education and after, his family and his teachers underestimated Vaughan Williams's potent mixture of innate musical ability and sheer determination. The gibes did not stop even after the signal accomplishment of earning his FRCO, however, for, as Vaughan Williams remembered, 'Sir Hugh Allen always insisted I must have bribed the examiners'.[12]

Despite his large frame and direct, at times heavily ironic, manner, the sensitive composer who lurked beneath this redoubtable public persona was surely wounded, perhaps deeply, by such remarks. As a result, he was endearingly considerate to his own students, treating them with gentleness, kindness and respect; as Maconchy noted, 'He was always on the side of the young, and ready with advice and practical help for any young composer whose music he thought worthwhile, whether or not he was a pupil'. Reflexively using another of Vaughan Williams's favourite pedagogical watchwords, Maconchy testified, 'His pupils continued to go back to him for criticism and advice, and above all for encouragement, for the rest of their lives'.[13]

For along with the transcendent notion of 'salvation', Vaughan Williams had frequent recourse to the more terrestrial term 'encouragement'. In 'A Musical Autobiography', he writes, 'With my own pupils now I always try to remember the value of encouragement. Sometimes a callow youth appears who may be a fool or may be a genius and I would rather be guilty of encouraging a fool than of discouraging a genius.' Vaughan Williams then makes his reasons for this policy plain by showing how encouragement is related to salvation: 'A fool, after all, may find his own salvation in artistic self-expression even though it means nothing to anyone else, and as to the genius, perhaps one may by analogy quote Lord Chesterfield, "If it's fine take an umbrella; if it is raining, please yourself."'[14] Despite the flippant twist at the end of this sentence, Vaughan Williams momentarily conjures the poignant wraith of his own disheartening experience as an apprentice composer made to feel as if his music meant 'nothing to anybody else'. In later years, Vaughan Williams divided his former teachers into two groups: those who offered encouragement and constructive criticism – those on the side of the angels, so to speak – and those who offered censure, formulaic solutions and discouragement. Unsurprisingly, Vaughan Williams's own practice as a composer, as well as his method as a teacher, was moulded during his protracted musical apprenticeship; in some instances, he was the heir of the traditional wisdom into which he was inculcated, but in other instances, he rebelled tenaciously against both the substance of what he was taught, and the manner in which he was taught it. To investigate Vaughan Williams's years of pilgrimage towards salvation illumines his lifelong passion for learning as well as the uses to which he put that learning in the search for his own voice.

Too Teutonic

In 'A Musical Autobiography', Vaughan Williams recalled, with a touchingly vivid childhood memory, the start of his musical salvation through learning to play the violin:

> I remember as if it were yesterday, when I was about, I think, seven years old
> walking with my mother through the streets of Eastbourne and seeing in a
> music shop an advertisement of violin lessons. My mother said to me,
> 'Would you like to learn the violin?' and I, without thinking, said, 'Yes.'
> Accordingly, next day, a wizened old German called Cramer appeared on
> the scene and gave me my first violin lesson.

Herr Cramer was the first of Vaughan Williams's teachers who were
immersed in the Teutonic tradition, and he would scarcely be the last.
During most of the nineteenth century, British music was dominated by
Italians at the opera and Germans in the concert hall; one need only recall
the names of Handel and Mendelssohn among the celebrated visitors from
Germany, the admiration of Sir George Smart and other British musicians
for Beethoven, and, later in the century, the virtual adoption of J. S. Bach as
a British composer known as 'John Sebastian'. Perhaps nowhere was this
more the case than the Royal College of Music, which Vaughan Williams
entered in 1890, and where, as he put it, 'Bach, Beethoven (ex officio),
Brahms and Wagner were the only composers worth considering'.[15]

Vaughan Williams was not the only student at the Royal College to be
initiated into the Teutonic mysteries. During his matriculation, and for
decades afterwards, the curriculum there was almost exclusively predicated
upon German music, with a special emphasis on Beethoven, due in part to the
tastes of its founding Director, Sir George Grove. Vaughan Williams's first
composition teacher at the Royal College, Hubert Parry, told him to study
Beethoven, 'especially the posthumous quartets, "as a religious exercise"' – an
unfortunate turn of phrase to use to his agnostic pupil. During one lesson
Parry even slammed through the 'Appassionata' Sonata (Piano Sonata No. 23
in F minor, Op. 57).[16] Despite his admiration for Parry, Vaughan Williams
resisted joining his teacher's worship at the Beethovenian altar. Vaughan
Williams's essay on Beethoven's Ninth Symphony tempers admiration with
trenchant criticism – he castigates the 'trivial arabesques' of the third movement, for example. He admitted late in his career, 'To this day the Beethoven
idiom repels me, but I hope I have at last learnt to see the greatness that lies
behind the idiom that I dislike'.[17]

If Parry presented Beethoven as a shrine to which incense must be
offered through study, he held up Brahms as the very model of a modern
composer; indeed, he composed an orchestral *Elegy in Memory of Brahms*
(1897). Along with others of the British musical establishment, Parry
admired but distrusted Brahms's aesthetic antipode, Richard Wagner:
the plots of Wagner's music dramas were too decadent; his harmonic
language too luscious; his orchestration too alarmingly colourful; and
his philosophy – both political and musical – too radical. (Only an outsider like Elgar, the self-taught Roman Catholic son of a provincial

piano tuner, could adopt and assimilate Wagner's example with impunity.) Despite the equivocations of Parry, who dismissed the pre-lude to *Parsifal* as 'mere scene-painting', Vaughan Williams remained unswervingly loyal to Wagner, in later life brushing aside criticisms aimed at the Mage of Bayreuth: 'Oh, you young people who run down Wagner'.[18]

As a consequence of his own haphazard early studies, Parry was not equipped to provide the technical training his students needed; but his character exercised a lasting influence on Vaughan Williams. As he wrote shortly after Parry's death in 1918, 'Half-a-dozen of his enthusiastic, eloquent words were worth a hundred learned expositions ... The secret of Parry's greatness as a teacher was his broad-minded sympathy.'[19] Parry often reacted to his students' personalities immoderately, erupting in either hearty approbation or violent dismissal. Luckily, Parry clearly liked Vaughan Williams; perhaps the young Vaughan Williams's mascu-line reticence and musical earnestness endeared him to Parry, who, by contrast, despised what he perceived as the effete glibness of Donald Francis Tovey.[20] Unfortunately, Parry indulged in the ill-advised practice of rewriting his students' music rather than leading them to find their own solutions. Vaughan Williams admitted that while Parry's 'criticism was constructive', the 'last two bars of my early part song "The Willow Song" were almost certainly composed by Parry'.[21]

Sent by familial fiat to Trinity College, Cambridge, in 1892, Vaughan Williams read modern history, taking a second in that subject for his Bachelor of Arts degree in 1895. He also took the Bachelor of Music, preparing for that degree with Charles Wood, an expatriate from Armagh who had been a member of the first class admitted to the Royal College in 1883.[22] Remembered for a handful of anthems and canticles designed for the Anglican liturgy, Wood possessed a suave fluency in polyphony and choral music.[23] Herbert Howells, who studied counterpoint with Wood at the Royal College, rated him 'the most completely-equipped teacher in his experience ... As a teacher Charles Wood was as gentle as any man could be in the presence of his pupils – gentle alike to the bunglers and the brilliant.'[24] While Vaughan Williams agreed with Howells's assessment of Wood's skill, he found this teacher's diffidence exasperating:

> Charles Wood was the finest technical instructor I have ever known. I do not say the greatest teacher. I do not think he had the gift of inspiring enthusiasm or of leading to the higher planes of musical thought. Indeed, he was rather prone to laugh at artistic ideals and would lead one to suppose that composing music was a trick anyone might learn if he took the trouble.[25]

Vaughan Williams thus found that Wood's emphasis on professional polish came at the expense of aesthetic vision: no salvation here.

As Parry had been appointed Director of the Royal College in 1895, Vaughan Williams returned to the College that same year as the pupil of Sir Charles Villiers Stanford, quite a different sort of Irishman from the reticent Wood. Whereas one of Wood's students claimed that his teacher 'was the shyest man that I have ever known', Stanford was quite the opposite.[26] Born in Dublin into a genteel middle-class Anglo-Irish family, Stanford gradually turned himself into a caricature of the bluff Irishman: his brogue became thicker with age and he wore a tam-o'-shanter to celebrate Saint Patrick's Day. His student Arthur Benjamin remembered Stanford as quarrelsome, impolitic and bigoted, abusive on a scale that is unimaginable today.[27] 'All rot, m'bhoy!' was the cry with which he denigrated a student's effort when displeased by either its perceived incompetence or unacceptable modernity.

Hardened by his family's opposition to his musical career, Vaughan Williams was among the tougher students who resisted Stanford's truculence and had the temerity to challenge his brusque critiques:

> Stanford was a great teacher, but I believe that I was unteachable. I made the great mistake of trying to fight my teacher ... The details of my work annoyed Stanford so much that we seldom arrived at the broader issues and the lesson usually started with a conversation on these lines: 'Damnably ugly, my boy, why do you write such things?' 'Because I like them.' 'But you can't like them, they're not music.' 'I shouldn't write them if I didn't like them.' So the argument went on and there was no time left for any constructive criticism.[28]

Unlike Parry, whose criticism was always 'constructive' and whose love of music was infectious, Stanford's curt dismissals simultaneously deepened Vaughan Williams's feelings of inadequacy and stiffened his resistance. The most telling sentence in Vaughan Williams's reminiscences of his teacher is also the most quietly damning: 'Stanford never displayed great enthusiasm for my work'.[29] Compared to his warm eulogy for Parry, Vaughan Williams's comments on Stanford's death were cool indeed: 'A composer cannot always be master of his inspiration, but he can see to it that his tools are always of tempered steel. This was preeminently the case with Stanford, so that whenever a true inspiration came to him he was ready for it.'[30]

An inveterate idealist, Vaughan Williams was dispirited by Stanford's pragmatic approach to composition. As evinced throughout *Musical Composition*, a distillation of his teaching method published in 1911,

Stanford's advice to young composers raised the acquisition of a comparatively narrow set of practical skills, including motivic development, formal balance and, above all, contrapuntal mastery, to the level of an obsession.[31] Although a deft orchestrator, Stanford puzzlingly mentions orchestration only in passing. This reflected his teaching, for Stanford infrequently commented upon orchestration in lessons, preferring instead for his students to compose an orchestral score, have it read by the College orchestra, and, if it failed, inform the hapless pupil to 'find some other way'.[32] Like Parry, Stanford harboured an almost ethical preference for diatonicism over chromaticism; both composers deplored the voluptuously chromatic post-Wagnerian idiom of such composers as Elgar, Scriabin and Strauss. Stanford, in particular, considered the idioms of these progressive composers to be a dire threat to the future health of British music. Practical to a fault, he believed that if a young English composer could write an accomplished anthem, motet, song, sacred cantata, oratorio, or perfectly articulated sonata movement in a smoothly diatonic idiom they were fully and finally equipped to build a successful career. Stanford was not being venal, however, for he sought to train his students in such a way as to give them a fighting chance towards making a decent living in the bustling, deeply conservative, and overwhelmingly commercial musical world of the Victorian and Edwardian periods. Even his cruelty may have been an attempt to toughen up his students so that, after surviving lessons with him, they could face any future discouragements with equanimity.

Stanford's biographer Paul Rodmell is surely correct when he avers:

> For all his weaknesses, Stanford was regarded by most of his pupils as a good teacher. His success . . . was founded in an uncharacteristic degree of flexibility for, whilst he was in many ways prescriptive and brutal, his list of pupils contains an enviable number of good and even great composers, most of whom were of the opinion that they had moved towards their goals aided by Stanford's guidance and not in spite of it.[33]

But Rodmell's shrewd observations do not take fully into account that many of Stanford's students – including Vaughan Williams – seem to have succumbed to a kind of institutional 'Stockholm syndrome' peculiar to composition graduates of the Royal College. Having been Stanford's hostages during lessons, Vaughan Williams and many of Stanford's other students invariably paid a standard, indeed almost formulaic, tribute to their teacher's ability – 'Stanford was a great teacher' – after which they proceeded to criticize, even mock, Stanford with impunity, usually through the retelling of 'amusing' anecdotes illustrative of his eccentric and, at times, sadistic behaviour. As impossible as he was all too often,

Stanford's mercurial temperament also included a hefty dollop of Hibernian charm, generosity, wit, pride in his students' accomplishments, and an endearing boyish ingenuousness. These contradictions made him a stimulating but maddening teacher, unable to provide the moral and emotional support that Parry had provided and Vaughan Williams needed.

That 'Parry and Stanford' have been coupled in the narrative of British music history is unfortunate as well as misleading, for Stanford differed sharply from Parry in many important ways both in character and aesthetics. One signal musical difference between the two was Stanford's love of opera, a genre that Parry could not abide. Indeed, Stanford was a *rara avis* among British musicians of his day in his admiration of Verdi, and he advised Vaughan Williams, whom he considered 'too Teuton already', to go to Italy.

Vaughan Williams disregarded his teacher's advice, however, and went to Berlin. There he sought out Max Bruch, with whom he studied for six months beginning in October 1897.[34] Like Stanford, Bruch was reactionary and quarrelsome, but he was a far more genial teacher.[35] One aspect of Bruch's work that must have interested Vaughan Williams was the German's lively interest in folksong, as is clear from such works as *Kol Nidrei*, Op. 47 (1881) and the *Scottish Fantasy*, Op. 46 (1880). Bruch was disturbed by his British pupil's predilection for parallel fifths as well as his preference for the flattened seventh degree of the scale, but, in a glowing letter of recommendation, called Vaughan Williams a 'sehr guter Musiker und ein talentvoller Componist'.[36] Decades later, Vaughan Williams gave Bruch this accolade: 'I only know that I worked hard and enthusiastically and that Max Bruch encouraged me, and I had never had much encouragement before'.[37]

Bruch's encouragement came too late to affect his pupil's habit of self-deprecation. As a result, both supporters and detractors of Vaughan Williams have echoed his remarks concerning his early lack of technical prowess without looking carefully at the scores written during his years of apprenticeship. With the recent publication and recording of this chamber and orchestral music, a sharper picture has emerged of a composer who had mastered fully the vocabulary, formal structures, voice-leading and polyphony that were characteristic of Brahms, Bruch, Thuille and other conservative German composers of the late nineteenth century. Vaughan Williams's String Quartet in C minor (1898), for example, composed just after his studies in Berlin, is expert and assured; it could easily be attributed to Bruch himself. Had Vaughan Williams been content to compose suave works in this idiom, he could have profitably done so for decades – and ended up as a historical footnote. Vaughan Williams's challenge was not that he lacked technique, but rather that he gradually realized that the technique that he had so laboriously acquired under Parry, Wood and Stanford was fatally constricted, unable to accommodate his engagement with both folksong and Tudor music. It was as if he had mastered the art of building carriages when the expertise he really needed was aerodynamics, so that in his aeroplane he could soar above Stanford's earth-bound precepts.

Even with a growing reputation, Vaughan Williams was frustrated with his technique and sought continually to expand his range and resources. After being politely rebuffed by Lady Elgar when he wrote asking for lessons from her husband, he went to the British Library and assiduously studied Elgar's music. Vaughan Williams went so far as to play *A Sea Symphony* (1909) for the indifferent Frederick Delius. Furthermore, he sought the advice of his peers, especially the unsparing critiques of his friend, Gustav Holst. All this striving brought him to a certain point but no further and left him dissatisfied. The key of promise that would unlock the door to his compositional salvation would come from a most unexpected source: to reach the portal of this House Beautiful, he must make a midwinter pilgrimage across the English Channel, across the snowy French countryside, to Paris.

A little French polish

In December 1907, Vaughan Williams wrote to the critic and musicologist M.-D. Calvocoressi to thank him 'for introducing me to the man who is exactly what I am looking for . . . As far as I know my own faults he hit on them all exactly & is telling me to do exactly what I half feel in my mind I ought to do – but it just wanted *saying*.'[38] Vaughan Williams had every reason to feel grateful, as Calvocoressi had steered him away from his original plan, recommended by the critic Edwin Evans, of studying at the Schola Cantorum in Paris with Vincent d'Indy, an even more dogmatic, utterly humourless, French version of Stanford.[39] Instead, Calvocoressi put forward a most unlikely candidate: the tiny, rouged, Baudelairean dandy of a composer, Maurice Ravel.

In many ways, Ravel was an outlandish suggestion. Ravel was three years younger than the English composer; he was then considered to be on the furthest fringe of the avant-garde; his career at the Paris Conservatoire, where he had studied with Gabriel Fauré, was undistinguished; and he had failed repeatedly to win the Prix de Rome.[40] In 1907, after all, Vaughan Williams was a 'coming man' in the British musical establishment whose 'choral song' *Toward the Unknown Region* had just been successfully premiered at Stanford's Leeds Festival. In contrast, Ravel remained a controversial figure in the eyes of many British composers and critics.

Vaughan Williams's former teachers at the Royal College must have been flabbergasted that he chose to study with such a suspect figure as Ravel – or any Frenchman, for that matter. Parry had scant respect for French music, which fell short of his Brahmsian ideal:

> The French have never shown any talent for self-dependent instrumental music. From the first their musical utterance required to be put in motion by some definite idea external to music . . . [T]he kernel of the Gallic view of things is, moreover, persistently theatrical, and all the music in which they have been successful has had either direct or secondary connection to the stage.[41]

According to Benjamin, Stanford dismissed both Debussy and Ravel as composers of 'eunuch music'.[42] This strain of criticism persisted for decades in British musical circles. In *A Survey of Contemporary Music*, published in 1924, the year of Stanford's death, the Scottish composer and critic Cecil Gray wrote:

> What, in the first place, are the most notable characteristics of the music of Ravel; what are the qualities in it that one either admires or dislikes? They are refinement, delicacy, restraint, clarity, according to some; preciosity, effeminacy, bloodlessness, insipidity, according to others. He is actually an extremely sentimental little person who is only rather too ashamed to show it.[43]

How did Calvocoressi persuade Vaughan Williams to choose Ravel over d'Indy? Aside from the *Pavane pour une infante défunte* (1899), Ravel's music had not yet attained the great affection of British audiences that it would enjoy a few years later. The first work by Ravel to be featured at a Proms concert was his Introduction and Allegro for harp, flute, clarinet and strings (1905), which was performed on 9 September 1907.[44] If Vaughan Williams attended this concert – he was a voracious concert-goer – the technical mastery and expert orchestration of this score must have impressed him deeply. Did Calvocoressi show Vaughan Williams the scores by Ravel that he kept in his personal library? In particular, did Calvocoressi, who was born in Marseilles to Greek parents, introduce the British composer to Ravel's arrangements of Greek vernacular songs, *Cinq mélodies populaires grecques* for voice and piano (1904–5)? Calvocoressi knew this work intimately, for it was he who had translated the folksongs from Greek into French, and had suggested to Ravel that he might set some of them; furthermore, the soprano Marguerite Babaïan premiered the work in a lecture-recital that Calvocoressi gave during the 1904–5 season.[45] Ravel's coruscating accompaniments to these vivacious, modal melodies would certainly have intrigued the British composer. As a critic reporting on the London scene, Calvocoressi was surely apprised of Vaughan Williams's activities as a collector and proselytizer for English folksong. Thus it is very likely that Calvocoressi pointed out Ravel's music to Vaughan Williams.

Unfortunately, there is only sparse documentation concerning Vaughan Williams's months of study with Ravel. Aside from a few extant letters from Vaughan Williams to Calvocoressi, there remains only an extended passage in 'A Musical Autobiography'. By the time that he dictated these memories, some forty-three years later, Vaughan Williams was caught between a desire to pay homage to Ravel's teaching and an understandable anxiety not to seem unduly influenced by a composer of his own stature. Unlike his reminiscences of Parry, Stanford and Bruch, which have a straightforward ring of truth, Vaughan Williams's recollections of Ravel, despite their seemingly forthright tone, are a study in selective memory:

> In 1908 [*recte* 1907] I came to the conclusion that I was lumpy and stodgy; had come to a dead-end and that a little French polish would be of use to me. So I went to Paris armed with an introduction to Maurice Ravel. He was much puzzled at our first interview. When I had shown him some of my work he said that, for my first lesson, I had better 'écrire un petit menuet dans le style de Mozart'. I saw at once that it was time to act promptly, so I said in my best French: 'Look here, I have given up my time, my work, my friends, and my career to come here and learn from you, and I am *not* going to write a "petit menuet dans le style de Mozart"'. After that we became great friends and I learnt much from him. For example that the heavy contrapuntal Teutonic manner was not necessary; 'complexe, mais pas compliqué', was his motto . . . He showed me how to orchestrate in points of colour rather than in lines. It was an invigorating experience to find all artistic problems looked at from what was to me an entirely new angle. He was against development for its own sake – one should only develop for the sake of arriving at something better. He used to say there was an implied melodic outline in all vital music and instanced the opening of the C minor Symphony [of Beethoven] as an example of a tune which was not stated but was implicit. He was horrified that I had no pianoforte in the little hotel where I worked. 'Sans le piano on ne peut pas inventer des nouvelles harmonies.'
>
> I practiced chiefly orchestration with him. I used to score some of his own pianoforte music and bits of Rimsky and Borodin, to whom he introduced me for the first time. After three months I came home with a bad attack of French fever and wrote a string quartet which caused a friend to say that I must have been having tea with Debussy, and a song cycle with several atmospheric effects, but I did *not* succumb to the temptation of writing a piece about a cemetery, and Ravel paid me the compliment of telling me that I was the only pupil who 'n'écrit pas de ma musique'. The fact was that

I could not have written Ravel's music even if I had wanted to. I am quite incapable, even with the pianoforte, of inventing his 'nouvelles harmonies' . . . I hope that I am not like the fox without the tail, but I feel content to provide good plain cooking and hope that the proof of the pudding is in the eating.

My French fever soon subsided but left my musical metabolism, on the whole, healthier.[46]

This *petite histoire* is nothing if not amusing, for Vaughan Williams was at his most charming when he was deploying his bluff, faux-bourgeois manner to rewrite history. Simply put, however, several crucial aspects of this story are about as accurate as the misremembered year at the beginning.

Did Vaughan Williams, who spoke fluent French, declare to Ravel at their first lesson 'I will *not* write a "petit menuet dans le style de Mozart"'? If he did so, it was in front of an acutely embarrassed Calvocoressi, for Vaughan Williams wrote to him at the time, 'it was awfully kind of you to have been present at the lesson – it was such a help'.[47] In fact, Vaughan Williams did compose a 'petit menuet dans le style de Mozart', for the second movement of his String Quartet No. 1 in G minor (1908) is indeed a minuet modelled on Mozart's practice. Furthermore, in that 'song cycle' with 'atmospheric effects', *On Wenlock Edge* (1909), the fifth song, 'Bredon Hill', is unmistakably about a cemetery, complete with a snowy churchyard and a persistent death knell. Finally, despite Vaughan Williams's claim that 'I could not have written Ravel's music even if I had wanted to', the opening of this same song is an unmistakable allusion to the last movement of Ravel's piano suite *Miroirs* (1904–5), 'La vallée des cloches' (see Ex. 2.1). The resemblance between the two is striking at times; Ravel may well have set Vaughan Williams the task of orchestrating part of 'La vallée des cloches' as an assignment.[48] Tail or no, the composer who dictated this autobiographical fragment was a sly old fox indeed.

Vaughan Williams was accurate, however, when he recalled, 'it was an invigorating experience to find all artistic problems looked at from what was to me an entirely new angle'. Indeed, it must have been humbling as well as invigorating, for two of Ravel's French pupils have testified to their master's strictness. Manuel Rosenthal remembered that 'he was a very stern teacher – I cried on many occasions when I left him – and I could not understand at first why he was so hard with me'. Rosenthal then cited his teacher's explanation, 'It's for your own benefit . . . [w]hat you learn, you have to learn the hard way and you will thank me for it later'. Ravel's candour was always used in the service of assisting his students by focusing their attention on their métier. Another pupil, Alexis Roland-Manuel, recalled that his mentor used to tell young composers, 'The truth of it is, you don't know anything'.[49] Thus it is hard to imagine even Vaughan

Ex. 2.1(a). Ravel, 'La vallée des cloches' from *Miroirs*, bars 3–6.

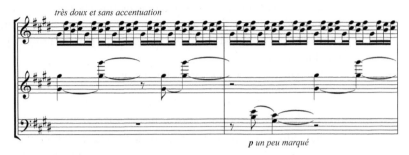

Ex. 2.1(b). Excerpt from the piano part, 'Bredon Hill', from *On Wenlock Edge*, bars 20–3.

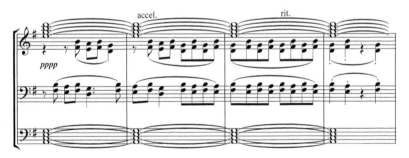

Williams refusing an assignment from such a teacher. Ravel may have been younger, shorter and conspicuously perfumed, but he was more than a match for the English composer – or anybody. Vaughan Williams was grateful for Ravel's honesty, however, for the Frenchman, like Max Bruch, paid him the signal compliment of taking his music seriously.

Despite a shared concern for their student's technical development, no two musical pedagogues could have been further apart than Ravel and Stanford. The French composer used honed surgical instruments to probe his students' deficiencies rather than hitting them over the head with a Celtic broadaxe. Ravel was at once more precise and open-minded than the Irish composer. Stanford, for example, warned against the use of the piano – 'The instrument should only be used as a test of work done, never ... as a suggestive medium for the materials of a work'.[50] Ravel, like Beethoven, Wagner and Stravinsky, composed at the piano and recommended that his pupils do so as well: 'Sans le piano on ne peut pas inventer des nouvelles harmonies.' (Vaughan Williams, who possessed an acute ear, mixed both methods depending on the work at hand.) Furthermore, the convictions held by Ravel and Stanford on the role of technique were diametrically opposed. For the Irishman, technique was a set of tools that composers acquired to provide themselves with a livelihood; for the Frenchman, however, composers had an ethical duty to care for and nourish their métier, which was a spiritual discipline that involved far more than the acquisition of mere practical skill.[51]

Ravel's strength of personality was reflected in the tenacity with which he espoused his aesthetics and devoted his life to his métier. The French composer adored Baudelaire and had absorbed his idea of the artist as an aloof dandy who retains an ironic detachment from the sordid business of life.[52] In contrast to Parry, Ravel distrusted the idea of 'sincerity' in art, for, as he once confided to Roland-Manuel:

> I am sometimes credited with opinions that appear very paradoxical concerning the falsity of art and the dangers of sincerity. The fact is I refuse simply and absolutely to confound the *conscience* of the artist, which is one thing, with his *sincerity*, which is another. Sincerity is of no value unless one's conscience helps to make it apparent. This conscience compels us to turn ourselves into good craftsmen. My objective, therefore, is technical perfection ... Art, no doubt, has other *effects*, but the artist, in my opinion, should have no other aim.[53]

As Roland-Manuel remembered, '[Ravel] was delighted by some words on the subject I discovered in a preface written by Remy de Gourmont: "Sincerity is barely an explanation: it is never an excuse"'.[54] To those who, disapproving of such aesthetics, accused Ravel of artificiality, he had a ready response: 'Mais est-ce qu'il ne vient jamais à l'idée de ces gens-là que je peux être "artificiel" par nature?' ('Doesn't it ever occur to those guys that I can be "artificial" by nature?')[55]

For Vaughan Williams, trained at the Royal College with a typically Victorian admixture of aspiration and pragmatism, Ravel's aesthetics must have come as a 'new angle' indeed. From the accounts of both Rosenthal and Roland-Manuel, it is clear that Ravel did not restrict himself in lessons to just technical instruction, and there is no reason to suppose that he treated Vaughan Williams – who, after all, took several lessons a week – any differently. By 1907 Vaughan Williams had worked out for himself that mere sincerity was not enough unless backed up by a fluent and progressive technique; Ravel's unsentimental teaching confirmed for him 'what I half feel in my mind I ought to do'.

Certain of Ravel's aesthetic precepts resonated throughout Vaughan Williams's career. In his own teaching at the Royal College, Vaughan Williams insisted that his students acquire an up-to-date technical mastery. Drawing on his own experience, he encouraged his most talented students to study on the continent to expand their techniques.[56] Moreover, Ravel's statement that a composer 'cannot do better . . . than say again what has already been well said' is echoed by Vaughan Williams when he declares, 'the duty of the composer is to find the *mot juste* . . . [i]t does not matter if this word has been said a thousand times before as long as it is the right thing to say at that moment'.[57]

The technical refinements that Ravel imparted to Vaughan Williams had just as lasting an effect as did his radical aesthetics. To quote the opening of Vaughan Williams's obituary tribute to Elgar: 'Of course, orchestration'. Compare, for instance, the elegantly judged and colourful orchestration of the Overture to *The Wasps*, written in 1909 after his study with Ravel, with the thick, undifferentiated textures of the withdrawn (and unrevised) second *Norfolk Rhapsody* of 1906. As for Vaughan Williams's statement that Ravel taught him to score in 'points of colour rather than in lines', Rosenthal inadvertently confirms this recollection when he quotes Ravel's conviction that 'orchestration is when you give a feeling of the two pedals at the piano; that means that you are building an atmosphere of sound around the written notes – that's orchestration'.[58]

Ravel's influence upon Vaughan Williams's technique went much deeper than just orchestration, however; his sophisticated methods of manipulating pitch materials had as lasting an impact upon his British pupil. The French composer was astonishingly inventive in his manipulations of modal and other resources. Ravel developed techniques of integrating various pitch collections that provided alternatives to traditional tonal practice. Ravel also developed a flexible manner of modulating rapidly through the use of modal inflection that was based on that of his master, Fauré; such rapid movement among modes created nonfunctional harmonic motion as well.[59]

While a full examination of the myriad ways in which Ravel's deployment of pitch materials influenced Vaughan Williams would indeed be revelatory, this investigation will examine just one such instance: the use of octatonic pitch collections. Ravel first encountered octatonicism in the music of the Russian Kutchka, which, on being imported to France by Saint-Saëns and Debussy, had proved a revelation to progressive Parisian musicians. Ravel closely analysed the music of composers like Borodin,

Rimsky-Korsakov and Mussorgsky, incorporating aspects of their work, including octatonic pitch collections, into his own idiom. Unlike the Russians, however, whose use of octatonic collections tends to be localized within certain dramatic situations in operas or in programmatic works, Ravel freely intersperses octatonic collections throughout his music, including non-referential, 'abstract' scores, so that they interact with modal, diatonic, and freely chromatic materials. (The American theorist Pieter van den Toorn refers to this technique as 'interpenetration'.)[60] In many of Ravel's works, especially those written before 1908, octatonic collections often appear at vertiginous climaxes, such as those of the first movement of his String Quartet in F major (1902–3) or of the Introduction and Allegro, the score that was performed at the Proms in 1907. In both these cases, sections of octatonic development succeed modal expositions; the climaxes occur at carefully plotted points near the end of the development at which the saturation of octatonic pitch materials disrupts any sense of a tonal centre (the climax of the quartet movement is shown in Ex. 2.2).

In his autobiography, Vaughan Williams recounted how Ravel exposed him to the music of the Kutchka and octatonicism: 'I used to score some of his own pianoforte music and bits of Rimsky-Korsakov and Borodin, to whom he introduced me for the first time.' Vaughan Williams mentions one score in particular to Calvocoressi: 'I have got Antar and have set to work on him'.[61] By assigning Rimsky-Korsakov's Second Symphony, *Antar*, to Vaughan

Ex. 2.2(a). Octatonic pitch collections.

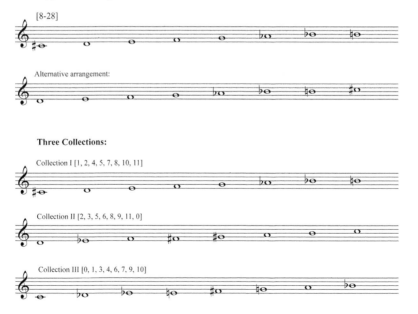

Ex. 2.2(b). Climax of the first movement, Ravel, String Quartet in F major, climax of the first movement, bars 115–20 (bars 115–19: Collection II; bar 120 juxtaposition of Collection III with whole-tone materials).

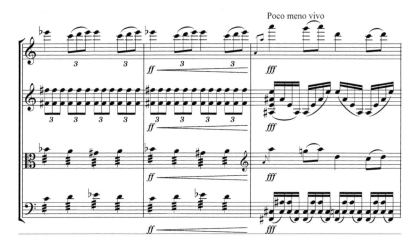

Williams, Ravel introduced his pupil to octatonic collections.[62] Aside from its stunning orchestral mastery, as lapidary as one of Fabergé's bejewelled Easter eggs, the melodic and harmonic materials of *Antar* are saturated with octatonicism, a characteristic of works by Rimsky-Korsakov that evoke the legendary and the fantastic.[63] Ravel himself used octatonicism to conjure an exotic and erotic atmosphere, as in his sensuous orchestral song-cycle, *Shéhérazade* (1903), or the darkly voluptuous 'Prélude à la nuit' that opens the *Rhapsodie espagnole* (1907–8).[64]

Vaughan Williams's initial experiments with octatonic pitch collections were tentative compared to Ravel's bold scores. An unpublished 1908 setting for baritone and orchestra of Walt Whitman's poem 'Whispers of Heavenly Death', which Vaughan Williams entitled *Nocturne*, is saturated with octatonic pitch-class sets: after a four-bar

Ex. 2.3. *Nocturne*, bars 1–8.

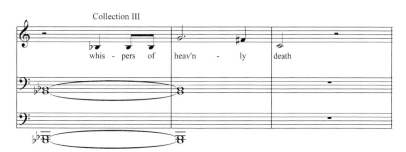

whole-tone introduction played by the low strings, the entry of the voice part pivots to an octatonic tetrad [0, 6, 7, 10] drawn from Collection III (see Ex. 2.3).

Ironically, an early appearance of an octatonic fragment in the English composer's published scores occurs almost furtively in the 'petit menuet dans le style de Mozart', the second movement of his String Quartet in G minor. Like the *Nocturne*, this quartet was completed in 1908 and may have been sketched in Paris; it is certainly among the first compositions that Vaughan Williams finished after his studies with Ravel. During the trio of the minuet, the first violin plays an octatonic pentad [4, 6, 7, 9, 10], drawn from Collection III (see Ex. 2.4a), that is immediately taken up by the viola. A further octatonic marker is a tritone (E–B♭) that is played *pizzicato* by the first violin five bars after rehearsal letter G (see Ex. 2.4b).

Sharing the same key as Debussy's string quartet, Vaughan Williams's work uses Parisian sophistication to approach British folk materials, and, as in Ravel's quartet, octatonicism appears in the context of an abstract work. Until his death in 1958, Vaughan Williams integrated octatonic pitch collections into ostensibly non-referential scores such as the Piano Concerto (1931), the Sixth Symphony (1947) and the Eighth Symphony (1955), to cite only three out of many.

Ex. 2.4(a). Octatonic pentad, Collection III, used in Trio of the second movement of String Quartet in G minor.

In other works, however, Vaughan Williams followed his teacher by using octatonicism to express both heightened emotional states, such as erotic desire, and powers beyond human agency, such as nature. For example, *Flos Campi* (1925), a suite for viola, wordless mixed chorus and small orchestra, is drenched in octatonic collections. Unsurprisingly, this is one of the most erotic of all Vaughan Williams's works, each movement being headed by a Latin epigram drawn from the Song of Solomon.[65] The suite is indebted to Ravel, and quite specifically to his ballet *Daphnis et Chloé*. (*Daphnis* influenced Vaughan Williams in other works, too: note, for example, the similarity between the undulating chords, announced in bar 6 and scored for stopped horns, that pervade the 'Introduction et Danse religieuse' of Part I of the ballet, and the swaying horn calls that open Vaughan Williams's Fifth Symphony.)[66] By the time that he composed *Flos Campi*, however, Vaughan Williams had so assimilated Ravel's techniques that the music of the suite contains only glancing reminiscences of the Frenchman's idiom. *Flos Campi* is therefore an example of sophisticated musical kleptomania; Herbert Howells recalled Vaughan Williams's humorous claim that he was just a 'simple kleptomaniac'.[67] But, despite Vaughan Williams's adaptations, there are still distinct reminiscences of Ravel's ballet in *Flos Campi*, such as the French composer's particular manner of using of the wordless chorus to depict frankly erotic yearning.[68] In *Flos Campi* Vaughan Williams integrates modal, chromatic, and diatonic music with passages that contain octatonicism. After the opening passage, which is drawn from a chromatic pitch-class set but is often described as 'bitonal', the viola and flute play a theme derived from two octatonic pitch collections (five bars before rehearsal number 1; see Exx. 2.5a and b).

Just as Vaughan Williams's use of Ravel's methods of modal inflection allowed him to pass rapidly from one mode to another, so he employs a similar procedure to move between octatonic collections. Vaughan Williams is never doctrinaire, however, for he does not hesitate to introduce a note (or notes) extraneous to either collection. These 'passing

Ex. 2.4(b). Trio of the second movement of String Quartet in G minor, bars 53–63.

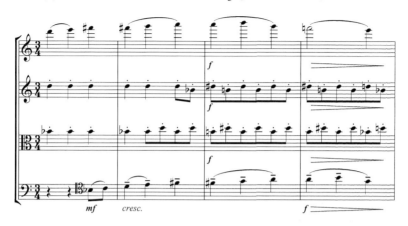

notes' are introduced to mould the pitch materials into expressive melodic contours.

Vaughan Williams differs from Ravel in that the Englishman employs octatonicism to evoke the numinous, something the Frenchman does

Ex. 2.5(a). Octatonic collections, *Flos Campi*, bars 5–10.

Ex. 2.5(b). Viola solo part, *Flos Campi*, bars 5–10.

exactly once in his orchestral music, at the appearance of the god Pan in *Daphnis et Chloé*. For example, in Vaughan Williams's seductive *Magnificat* for contralto, women's chorus, flute and small orchestra (1932), the erotic and the religious are intertwined through the use of the octatonic collections that the composer employs to create the uncannily sensuous and insinuating flute solos (see Ex. 2.6). Ursula Vaughan Williams quotes her husband as saying that 'he thought of the flute as the disembodied visiting spirit and the alto solo as the voice of the girl yielding to her lover for the first time'.[69]

In a far more disquieting context than the *Magnificat*, Vaughan Williams uses octatonic collections to create the minatory power of 'Satan's Dance of Triumph' in his 'masque for dancing', *Job* (1930) (see Ex. 2.7). In this dance, the obsidian brilliance and tonal instability of the music are a direct result of the structure of the octatonic collection itself, with its emphasis on the tritone and lack of a clear dominant – all techniques used to similar terrifying effect by Ravel in his evocation of the demonic 'Scarbo', the final movement of *Gaspard de la Nuit* (1908).

Similar in their unsettling effect are the octatonic fragments of a work begun much earlier than *Job*, in 1925, the one-act opera *Riders to the Sea*. As Walter Aaron Clark notes, 'in the 1920s a darker side of nature came to the fore in Vaughan Williams's music'.[70] What nature stands for in *Riders to the Sea*, however, includes what lies both without and within humankind, as the composer's psychological penetration has darkened as

Ex. 2.6. *Magnificat*, bars 15–17.

Ex. 2.7. 'Satan's Dance of Triumph' from *Job: A Masque for Dancing*, rehearsal letter P.

well. The protagonist, Maurya, and the pitiless sea are both characterized by music that has its origin in a single octatonic collection, Collection III (see Ex. 2.8). The first words in the opera, a reference to Maurya by her two daughters, are set to music derived from the same collection; furthermore, a motif derived from this collection occurs whenever Maurya has a premonition of approaching disaster. Most psychoanalytic schools treat the sea as a symbol of the submerged unconscious, so that Vaughan Williams's use of this particular octatonic pitch class uncannily links the sea with Maurya's deepest fears.[71]

By the time he composed *Riders to the Sea*, Vaughan Williams had absorbed Ravel's teaching into his own idiom. After 1925, Vaughan Williams deepened and intensified his use of octatonicism as a musical symbol of that 'which lies beyond sense and knowledge'. In a letter to Arthur Bliss, who had attended a private reading of Vaughan Williams's Fourth Symphony (1934), the composer wrote,

Ex. 2.8. *Riders to the Sea*, rehearsal figure 4: Collection III.

You mustn't think your advice has not been valuable because I have not followed it – when I give advice to my pupils I tell them that they can do one of 3 things

(a) accept it blindly – bad
(b) reject it kindly – bad but not so bad
(c) think out a 3rd course for themselves – sound.[72]

With these words, Vaughan Williams articulates the greatest lesson he took away from his French *maître*. Ravel, who admired his pupil's cultural nationalism, once remarked that Vaughan Williams had 'only realized his richness when he learned to be English'.[73] In a paradox that Ravel may have relished, Vaughan Williams learned to be fully English in France. As Vaughan Williams proudly recalled decades later in the memoir quoted earlier, Ravel had paid his student the supreme compliment of telling him 'that I was the only pupil who "n'écrit pas de ma musique"'.

Notes

1 Elizabeth Maconchy, 'Dr. Ralph Vaughan Williams, O.M.', *The RCM Magazine* 55/1 (Easter Term, 1959), 33–4. See *KW*, 372, where Kennedy virtually paraphrases Maconchy; and Hubert Foss, *Ralph Vaughan Williams: A Study* (London: Harrap, 1950).

2 Vaughan Williams habitually denigrated his skill as a keyboard player, but Donald Jay Grout recalled the alacrity with which the octogenarian composer spontaneously illustrated points during lectures he gave when visiting professor at Cornell University in 1954 by playing 'with a startlingly original, but none-the-less effective technique': see *The RCM Magazine* 55/1 (Easter Term, 1959), 54. For a pertinent comment on the origin of 'A Musical Autobiography', see Michael Kennedy, 'Preface to First Edition', in *NM*, xiii.

3 *NM*, 3, 189. For an exploration of Vaughan Williams's religious views, see Byron Adams, 'Scripture, Church, and Culture: Biblical Texts in the Works of Ralph Vaughan Williams', in *VWS*, 99–117.

4 Sylvia Townsend Warner, *Letters of Sylvia Townsend Warner*, ed. William Maxwell (London: Chatto & Windus, 1982), 168.

5 Maconchy, 'Vaughan Williams', 33–34.

6 Gordon Jacob, 'Dr. Ralph Vaughan Williams, O.M.', *The RCM Magazine* 55/1 (Easter Term, 1959), 31.

7 *NM*, 186, 190.

8 Jacob, 'Vaughan Williams', 31.

9 Gwen Raverat, *Period Piece: A Cambridge Childhood* (London: Faber and Faber, 1960), 273. Aunt Etty was christened Henrietta Darwin (1843–1927); she was Charles and Emma Darwin's second child.

10 *NM*, 178.

11 *NM*, 178, 186; *UVWB*, 58.

12 *NM*, 178.

13 Maconchy, 'Vaughan Williams', 34.

14 *NM*, 187. Vaughan Williams did not recall this quotation accurately; it runs, 'When *fine* take your umbrella; When *raining* please yourself.'

15 *Ibid.*, 183.

16 *Ibid.*, 181.

17 *Ibid.*, 110, 181.

18 *KW*, 14. According to Vaughan Williams, Parry's dismissal of the prelude to *Parsifal* was part of a broader pattern of musical inhibition, as his teacher evinced 'an almost moral abhorrence of mere luscious sound'. See *NM*, 183.

19 Ralph Vaughan Williams, 'Sir Hubert Parry', *The Music Student*, 11/3 (September 1918), in *VWOM*, 295–6.

20 Jeremy Dibble, *C. Hubert H. Parry: His Life and Music* (Oxford: Clarendon Press, 1992), 283–4.

21 *NM*, 182.

22 Ian Copley, *The Music of Charles Wood: A Critical Study* (London: Thames Publishing, 1978), 9.

23 Copley, *Wood*, 21.

24 Herbert Howells, 'Charles Wood', in Christopher Palmer, *Herbert Howells: A Celebration* (London: Thames Publishing, 1995), 305–6.

25 *NM*, 183.

26 Copley, *Wood*, 23.

27 Arthur Benjamin, 'A Student in Kensington', *ML* 31/3 (July 1950), 202–3. Arthur Benjamin (1893–1960) was a brilliant pianist, composer and conductor whose concert music was eclipsed by the enormous success of his *Jamaican Rumba* (1938). An ebullient and, for the time, quite remarkably open homosexual, Benjamin served in the Royal Air Force during the First World War; his gallant service won Stanford's admiration.

28 *NM*, 185.

29 *Ibid.* Notice that, unlike almost all of Stanford's other students who wrote about their dyspeptic teacher, Vaughan Williams does not attempt to transcribe the Irish composer's brogue into print phonetically, which suggests that for Vaughan Williams, at least, such tense confrontations were devoid of humour even in retrospect.

30 Ralph Vaughan Williams, 'Charles Villiers Stanford by Some of His Pupils', *ML* 5/3 (July 1924), 195, quoted in *VWOM*, 297.

31 See Charles Villiers Stanford, *Musical Composition: A Short Treatise for Students* (London: Macmillan and Co., Limited: 1911).

32 Paul Rodmell, *Charles Villiers Stanford* (Aldershot: Ashgate, 2002), 354.

33 *Ibid.*, 364. In his even-handed chapter on Stanford as pedagogue, Rodmell discusses with insight the economic and social context that informed the Irish composer's methods; see *ibid.*, 363–4.

34 *LRVW*, 75.

35 As Christopher Fifield notes, '[Bruch] was much loved by his students, who bore his intolerance with a forgiving nature and thought him a kind and considerate man'. Besides Vaughan Williams, Bruch's students included Oscar Straus and Ottorino Respighi. Stanford disparaged Bruch as a pedagogue, however, remarking to Dent, 'I wouldn't wish me worst enemy to go to Max Bruch'. See Christopher Fifield, *Max Bruch: His Life and Works* (Woodbridge: The Boydell Press, 2005), 251, 270, 285.

36 Rupert Erlebach recalled Vaughan Williams relaying an anecdote that could only have been about Bruch: 'Of one of these *Kapellmeisters* V.W. told me once that at a harmony lesson some consecutive fifths were pounced upon. "Ach, die Quints, Quints! Nein, Nein! You muss *not*! Quints, quints."' See Rupert Erlebach, 'Dr. Ralph Vaughan Williams, O.M.', *The RCM Magazine* 55/1 (Easter Term, 1959), 30; also *NM*, 187; *LRVW*, 23.

37 *NM*, 187.

38 *NM*, 62.

39 *KW*, 90. Interestingly, Stanford's own concise composition textbook has many points in common with d'Indy's massive *Cours de composition musicale* (1903–5).

40 For Ravel's career at the Conservatoire, see Arbie Orenstein, *Ravel: Man and Musician* (New York: Dover Publications, 1991), 33–44 *passim.*

41 C. Hubert Hastings Parry, *The Evolution of the Art of Music* (London: Kegan Paul Limited, 1905), 276.

42 Benjamin, 'A Student in Kensington', 201. However, Benjamin notes, 'Yet [Stanford] included [Debussy and Ravel's] works in College programmes'.

43 Cecil Gray, *A Survey of Contemporary Music* (Oxford University Press, 1924), 116, 120.

44 I am grateful to Leanne Langley for supplying me with this information.

45 Gerald Abraham, 'M.-D. Calvocoressi (1872–1944)', *MT* 85/1213 (March 1944), 83–5; Orenstein, *Ravel*, 41, 225.

46 *NM*, 191–2.

47 *LRVW*, 62.

48 In 1923 Vaughan Williams re-scored *On Wenlock Edge* – and thus 'Bredon Hill' – for full orchestra.

49 Roger Nichols, *Ravel Remembered* (New York: Norton, 1988), 67, 195.

50 Stanford, *Musical Composition*, 179.

51 For more on Ravel's attitude towards his métier, see Nichols, *Ravel Remembered*, 143.

52 Nichols, *Ravel Remembered*, 193.

53 Quoted in Orenstein, *Ravel*, 118. Amended translation.

54 Nichols, *Ravel Remembered*, 142.

55 Quoted in Nichols, *Ravel Remembered*, 180.

56 For example, Vaughan Williams sent Elizabeth Maconchy to study with K. B. Jirák in Prague, and Grace Williams to study with Schoenberg's pupil, Egon Wellesz, in Vienna. See Jennifer Doctor, 'Working for Her Own Salvation: Vaughan Williams as Teacher of Elizabeth Maconchy, Grace Williams and Ina Boyle', in *VWIP*, 181 *passim.*

57 Ravel's statement is quoted in Orenstein, *Ravel*, 119; Vaughan Williams's opinion is quoted in *NM*, 189–90.

58 Quoted in Nichols, *Ravel Remembered*, 68.

59 Fauré's innovations have been elucidated elegantly by Carlo Caballero in an unpublished paper 'Fauré and Multimodality' that was read at the American Musicological Society's National Annual Meeting in 2004.

60 Pieter C. van den Toorn, *The Music of Igor Stravinsky* (New Haven and London: Yale University Press, 1983), 67–8.

61 *LRVW*, 62.

62 As Rimsky-Korsakov completed the third and final revision of *Antar* in 1907, the score that Vaughan Williams obtained must have been the second version. Calvocoressi, whose primary area of expertise was nineteenth-century Russian music, and who made the French singing translation of Rimsky-Korsakov's last opera, *Le coq d'or*, may have helped Vaughan Williams find a copy of this comparatively rare item, or he may have lent the British composer his own copy.

63 Another such work, besides *Antar*, is *Sheherazade*; see V. V. Yastrebtsev, *Reminiscences of Rimsky-Korsakov*, ed. and trans. Florence Jonas (New York: Columbia University Press, 1985), 237 and Richard Taruskin, 'Catching Up with Rimsky-Korsakov', *Music Theory Spectrum* 33/2 (Fall 2011), 171–5.

64 See Steven Bauer, 'Ravel's "Russian" Period: Octatonicism in His Early Works, 1893–1908', *Journal of the American Musicological Society*, 52 (1999): 531–92. This passage is indebted to Bauer's original and subtle analysis.

65 Vaughan Williams's own copy of the Bible (BL Add. MS 63850) contains pencilled annotations in the Song of Solomon that do not always correspond with the epigrams in the manuscript score, which suggests that he may have initially contemplated using a text.

66 Another allusion to *Daphnis et Chloé* is found in the second trio of *A London*

Symphony in the original version of the work premiered in 1914. This extended passage is so obviously indebted to the 'Lever du Jour' music from Ravel's ballet that Vaughan Williams wisely excised it when revising the symphony in 1918.

67 *The Sunday Times*, 31 August 1958.

68 Vaughan Williams had used a wordless chorus as early as his song-cycle *Willow-Wood* (1908–9); the women's chorus in that work is marked *ad libitum*, and heightens the discreet Pre-Raphaelite sensuality of Dante Gabriel Rossetti's verse. The choral parts in *Flos Campi* are, as in Ravel's ballet, an integral part of the texture and are overtly erotic compared to *Willow-Wood*.

69 *UVWB*, 121–2.

70 Walter Aaron Clark, 'Vaughan Willliams and the "Night Side of Nature": Octatonicism in *Riders to the Sea*', in *VWE*, 55.

71 The pervasive octatonicism is washed away only after the dripping corpse of Maurya's last son has been placed on the kitchen table, when the mother sings of her transcendent resignation in music characterized by modally inflected diatonicism.

72 *LRVW*, 233.

73 Quoted in Orenstein, *Ravel*, 125, n.18.

3 Becoming a national composer: critical reception to *c*. 1925

AIDAN J. THOMSON

In an article written for the periodical *Musical Opinion and Music Trade Review* (hereafter '*Musical Opinion*') a few months before the outbreak of World War I, the eccentric British music critic Gerald Cumberland offered a prediction of how early twentieth-century British music might be viewed a hundred years later. Cumberland envisaged a 'rather long, but not altogether tedious' volume entitled 'History of European Music in the Twentieth Century', which included a chapter on the 'So-Called British School'. The author of this chapter, he believed, would observe that

> between the years 1900–1915 there was undoubtedly a great and gracious flowering of British genius in the field of musical composition, but no contemporary writer appears to have been conscious of the fact. On the contrary, everybody bewailed the general lack of musical genius, and the newspaper critics were continually deploring the dead level of merit of the music they were called upon to criticize.

The 'genius' on which Cumberland's imaginary twenty-first-century amanuensis focused in his article consisted of five composers: Edward Elgar, Joseph Holbrooke, Cyril Scott, Frederick Delius and Granville Bantock. Occasionally his comments about these figures are surprisingly close to what one might find written today, but more often they are wildly, even hilariously, inaccurate, none more so than his prediction that in 2014 Elgar would be 'little more than a name to-day', with *The Dream of Gerontius* having 'dropped out of public recognition . . . never likely to be revived', and that Bantock's work suffered from the 'revival of conventional religion [that] took place in the "[nineteen] forties" and "fifties"'.[1] Whatever Cumberland's strengths might have been as a critic, it is safe to say that they did not include crystal ball gazing.

Risible though his attempts at clairvoyance may seem in retrospect, Cumberland inadvertently makes an important counterfactual point: the history of twentieth-century British music is far from the seemingly inevitable, seamless narrative, running from Parry and Stanford, through Elgar, Vaughan Williams, Britten and Tippett, to the Manchester school, that it is sometimes made out to be. Much recent scholarship has been devoted to challenging this narrative, perhaps most controversially Robert Stradling's and Meirion Hughes's iconoclastic study of 1993, *The English Musical Renaissance, 1860–1940: Construction and Deconstruction.*[2] Stradling and Hughes attempt to deconstruct the political and aesthetic ideologies that underpinned early twentieth-century British musical culture – anti-Germanism (at least after 1914), aesthetic transcendentalism and English pastoralism (specifically the use of folksong as the essential foundation of a national musical style) – which, they argue, reflected the prevailing mindset of the Royal College of Music, the spiritual home of this renaissance in both composition and criticism. Thus composers estranged from the RCM, including the Royal Academy of Music-educated Bantock and Holbrooke, have found themselves marginalized from histories of British music, whereas those whose work exemplified the RCM's nostrums, by contrast, have taken centre stage.

Foremost among the latter was Vaughan Williams, who, Stradling and Hughes observe, had the support of influential music critics (such as J. A. Fuller Maitland and H. C. Colles of *The Times*, and Robin Legge of *The Daily Telegraph*), was closely connected to both the RCM (as a former student, and latterly as a professor) and the folksong movement, and who, in addition, came from the right social background:

> Vaughan Williams's personal qualifications were matchless. He was a member of the English aristocracy by birth and connection, yet was impeccably social-democratic in his convictions. He was an agnostic, yet treasured the heritage of English religion. His descent was from the finest scholarly lineage (he was a nephew of Charles Darwin), yet likewise was from the hardy 'stock' of English business enterprise (the Wedgwoods). He reached the solid age of 50 in 1922; he had helped to pioneer folksong research; he was a convincing exponent of the complementary revival of 'Tudor polyphony'. To such a man no door in the land was closed.[3]

And to such a man would come, almost as a birthright, the mantle of leadership of British music – or so one might infer from this portrayal. In fact, Stradling's and Hughes's depiction of Vaughan Williams here makes his leading position in interwar British music seem far more inevitable than was actually the case. They make much of Fuller Maitland's claim, in an early review of *Toward the Unknown Region*, that Vaughan Williams was 'foremost of the younger generation' of British composers, and of Colles's ecstatic eulogizing of *A Pastoral Symphony* in his review of that work's premiere in 1922.[4] But, influential though they were as critics and academics, Fuller Maitland's and Colles's were only two voices among many. Cumberland's article, written *after* the premieres of *A Sea*

Symphony, On Wenlock Edge and the *Fantasia on a Theme by Thomas Tallis*, indicates that Fuller Maitland's views were not shared by everyone, and that, even in 1914, there was no reason automatically to assume that Vaughan Williams would become the beating heart of British music within a decade.

My aim in this chapter is to trace how, when and why writing on Vaughan Williams, both critical and biographical, changed during the two decades that followed the publication of *The English Hymnal* in 1906. Rather than focus on the main British newspapers, where the writing is often ephemeral in nature, I concentrate on monthly and weekly musical journals, such as *Monthly Musical Record, Musical News, Musical Opinion* and *The Musical Standard*, which devote more space to assessments of new works, composers, repertories and topical musical issues.[5] The chapter is divided into four sections. Firstly, I consider the historiographical context of pre-war British music, in particular the composers who seemed to attract the most attention and praise from critics; the many different conceptions of, and approaches to, modernity adopted by active composers; and the attitudes to folksong. Secondly, I discuss critical reviews of Vaughan Williams's early works, focusing, for reasons of space, on five key pieces: *On Wenlock Edge, A Sea Symphony, Fantasia on a Theme by Thomas Tallis, Five Mystical Songs* and *A London Symphony*. Thirdly, I contextualize the increased interest in Vaughan Williams in the years immediately following World War I in terms of a realignment of the relationship between modernity, folksong and nationhood. Finally, I show how the idea of a 'national' composer is central to the reception of two early interwar works: *A Pastoral Symphony* and the Mass in G minor.

The context of Vaughan Williams's pre-war works

Vaughan Williams's early works were written in a period when British music was at a crossroads. The success in Germany of Elgar's *The Dream of Gerontius* meant that, for the first time in many decades, Britain could boast a composer of international standing who wrote in a more or less contemporary idiom. The Royal College of Music, founded in 1882 partly with the aim of improving British composition, had produced its first generation of composer graduates, Vaughan Williams among them, who were increasingly making their mark as professional musicians. Yet there was uncertainty about where the future of British music lay. Critics expressed doubts as to whether Elgar's music (notwithstanding patriotic potboilers like the *Pomp and Circumstance* Marches and the *Coronation*

Ode) was quite English enough to be considered the basis for a national music.[6] More crucially, there was no indication of how British composers might best engage with the compositional innovations of such composers as Strauss and Debussy, and latterly Stravinsky and Schoenberg. The multifaceted nature of early musical modernism posed a challenge to those who sought to develop a single national style, the more so because the half-generation of composers younger than Elgar was so diverse in its tastes. An article written in 1910 by one such composer, Edgar Bainton, illustrates this well. Bainton claimed that all British music of the period seemed to be reacting against the 'materialistic tendencies of the age', whether through Catholicism (Elgar, Walford Davies), orientalism (Bantock), Celticism, or, in Vaughan Williams's case, 'the broad humanity of Whitman', and that the leaders of the post-Elgar generation (in Bainton's view Bantock, Delius and William Wallace) sought their inspiration 'direct from Life and from Nature'.[7] But life, nature and a rejection of materialism were hardly unique to British composers as stimuli; far from identifying a unifying thread among the younger generation of British composers, Bainton inadvertently seems to have identified only their eclecticism.

Bainton was unusual in mentioning Vaughan Williams at all, for the most striking feature of Vaughan Williams reception before 1918 is how little he features in the major music journals compared with many of his contemporaries, whether in reviews or in more general assessments about the future of British music.[8] This reflects the relatively small number of performances that his works received, a consequence partly of the unusual scoring of some of his pieces, which made them difficult or expensive to perform. In London especially, most professional recitals tended to be given by a solo vocalist and piano accompanist, by a solo pianist, or by a chamber group; thus *On Wenlock Edge*, written for tenor, piano and string quartet, fell between several stools, and was performed infrequently. A similar problem affected larger-scale choral works. Pieces that were written for major choral festivals, such as the Three Choirs, Leeds, or Birmingham, did not lend themselves to regular performances in professional orchestral concert series, unless the composer had the status of Elgar or Bantock, particularly if they were technically demanding, or required soloists (or both); thus *A Sea Symphony*, premiered at the Leeds Festival in October 1910, was not heard in London until February 1913. Vaughan Williams's reputation as a composer (as distinct from his reputation as a folksong collector, or *English Hymnal* editor) was therefore based on a relatively small corpus of works that were not heard that often – and it suffered accordingly.

A survey of editorial reviews of the previous year's music in January numbers of music journals illustrates this point well. *Musical News*'s 'Music in 1909' survey makes no reference to the premiere of *On Wenlock Edge* or any other work by Vaughan Williams, but it does note the first performances of Granville Bantock's *Old English Suite*, Henry Walford Davies's *Noble Numbers* and Rutland Boughton's *Choral Variations on Two Folk Songs*. The equivalent column the following year highlights the premieres of Bantock's *Omar Khayyám* and *Sea Wanderers*, Samuel Coleridge-Taylor's *Hiawatha* and Bertram Shapleigh's *Lake of the Dismal Swamp* among others, but not those of *A Sea Symphony* or the Tallis Fantasia. *Monthly Musical Record*'s review of 1911 does not acknowledge the premiere of *Five Mystical Songs*, or Vaughan Williams's presence among the thirty-two British composers whose music was performed during the International Musical Congress in London that May. Three years later the premiere of *A London Symphony* is not considered worthy of mention, but those of Cyril Scott's Piano Concerto and Joseph Holbrooke's *Dylan* are.[9] While the absence of Vaughan Williams's name from lists of forthcoming concerts during the year may be attributed simply to the infrequency with which his works were performed, its absence in more general reviews would appear to suggest that his music was not considered worthy of the same attention as that of his more fecund peers.

Among those peers, three feature more prominently than most during the pre-war period: Bantock, Holbrooke and Scott (all of whom were among the five listed by Cumberland at the beginning of this chapter). In an article written in 1911, Ernest Newman, a champion of both Wagner and Elgar, described Bantock as, 'Next to Elgar, [the composer who] commands the largest following in England at present', and claimed that he had 'sharply wrested English music out of the sacred rut into which it had fallen'. Among the 'younger men', Newman identified Holbrooke as 'the next most important figure', and praised Scott as 'a delicate and sometimes subtle thinker and a fastidious workman', whose music he would like to hear more.[10] Newman was not alone. A few months later, George Lowe, in his review of Holbrooke's *Pierrot and Pierrette*, described its composer as forming 'a triumvirate from which the highest musical achievements are to be expected' with Elgar and Bantock.[11] The Birmingham-based critic Sydney Grew was so enraptured by the premiere of Bantock's *Atalanta in Calydon* that he predicted that 'January 25th, 1912 [the date of the premiere], may prove an historic date, – a date from which events in English choral music must be reckoned' alongside the premieres of Parry's *Scenes from Shelley's 'Prometheus Unbound'* and Elgar's *Dream of Gerontius*.[12] Scott, meanwhile, undoubtedly profited from Debussy's description of him as 'one of the rarest artists of the present generation', and in the 1910s his piano music and songs attracted considerable attention both in Britain and further afield.[13] Following a

Bechstein Hall recital that he gave in 1913, *Monthly Musical Record* noted approvingly that 'amongst all English composers of the younger school there is none who shows so strong an individuality as Cyril Scott; and the Continent is not slow in recognizing this fact, and his reputation abroad is steadily growing'.[14] M.-D. Calvocoressi – who, as Byron Adams notes in Chapter 2 of this volume, was influential in introducing Vaughan Williams to Ravel – wrote in 1914 that he had considered Scott's *Old Songs in New Guise* alongside works by Schoenberg, Berg, Bartók, Kodály, Stravinsky and Scriabin in terms of their significance to recent developments in music.[15] By 1920, Bantock, Holbrooke and Scott had all been the subjects of biographical monographs, something that was not the case at that time for Parry or Stanford, let alone Vaughan Williams.[16]

The popularity of Bantock, Holbrooke and Scott is indicative of the different strands and conceptions of modernity (and thus possible future stylistic paths) that existed in early twentieth-century British music. Bantock and Holbrooke appealed to those for whom 'modernism' meant lavishly scored symphonic poems after Strauss, and operas based on mythological themes after Wagner; that increasingly conservative strand persisted into the 1920s in the fleeting success of Boughton's Celtic opera, *The Immortal Hour*. Scott appealed more to those for whom modernism meant Debussy and Stravinsky, whose influence would also later be seen in the music of Lord Berners, Goossens and, at least initially, Bliss. But one strand of British musical life that was not readily associated with modernity was the folksong movement; and a particular difficulty for Vaughan Williams in this period was his close relationship with it.

Although many leading musical figures in Britain were sympathetic with the aims of the Folk-Song Society, which had been formed in 1898 – Parry, for instance, had given the inaugural address to the Society – many others were not, and were suspicious of Cecil Sharp's hope that the language of English folk music might form the basis of a national style of art music.[17] These suspicions were often outlined in the pages of the mainstream musical press. Grew, for instance, argued in 1909 that folksong

> cannot be made the base of English music; it is not comprehensive enough. The foundation of a national art must be as broad as humanity itself. . . It is a false and a specious plea that entreats the adoption of folk song as the main source of inspiration in national art. Its beautiful simplicity would be tortured beyond recognition in the strain of bearing an unwieldy superstructure; for insularity in art is impossible and what previous qualities it possesses would be lost without compensating gain elsewhere.[18]

Grew's fear – that folk music and art music were qualitatively different, and that composers risked using one in the other at their peril – was echoed by J. H. G. Baughan in an editorial in *The Musical Standard* in 1911, in which he argued that a composer's use of folksong was simply proof of a lack of melodic creativity.[19] For others, the folksong revival went against the notion of progress in art: Douglas Donaldson, writing in 1911, described folksong as a 'lapse . . . into the primitive', and although noting that the 'present craze for folk-song' was in some cases 'a craving for repose and relief from modern æsthetic complexities', such a 'purge' was 'a poor substitute for growth and vital extension'.[20] One of the most excoriating critiques of the movement came in 1912 from Gerald Cumberland, whose objections to it took four forms: the lack of discrimination in the material that was collected; the inauthentic nature of a movement led by educated urban sophisticates; a suspicion of the collectivist ideology that underpinned the folksong movement (which ran counter to the nineteenth-century values of artistic genius that he upheld); and the suspicion, echoing Baughan, that 'at least half of the younger school of British composers have borrowed old tunes to save themselves the trouble of inventing new ones' (and that the resultant works 'scarcely survive the year in which they are first produced').[21] While Cumberland's views were perhaps more trenchantly expressed than most, it is clear that the folksong movement was not quite as central to the identity of English or British music before the war as has sometimes been thought.

As one of the most prominent composers active in the folksong movement, Vaughan Williams was often singled out for special treatment by the sceptics (including Cumberland in the article quoted above). The critic of *The Musical Standard*, reviewing the premiere of the *Fantasia on English Folk Song* in 1910, expressed the wish that Vaughan Williams 'would leave our folk-songs alone, and give us, as the saying is, music out of his own head! It won't do at all to make a system of deriving his inspiration from other composers' inspirations.'[22] The correspondent of *Musical Opinion* took a similar position in his review of the *Fantasia on Christmas Carols*: 'Dr. Williams [*sic*] has on several occasions proved that he has ideas of his own to give to the world and many of us regret his devotion to a movement which appears to be curbing the growth of his own originality.'[23] In his opinion, the folk tunes were undistinguished and the orchestration too sophisticated for the melodies and harmonies that it supported. This complaint echoed a report in the same journal the previous year of the Midland Musical Competition Festival, at which Vaughan Williams's setting of 'Bushes and Briars' had been sung. 'One can have no reasonable objection to the innocent and mild pastime of collecting peasants' frequently feeble attempts at tune writing', the critic harrumphed, 'but when a scholar like Dr. Vaughan Williams offers a lugubrious little melody harmonised in the darkest of colours and set to words reminiscent of the

soil, it is high time to protest with all the earnestness at one's command'.[24]
In the eyes of such critics, Vaughan Williams's use of folksong did nothing
to further his credentials as a creative artist.

In the light of this, it is not surprising that a rare pre-war journal article
about Vaughan Williams played down the composer's folksong activities.
Grew's 1913 essay in *The Musical Herald* notes in passing that 'Dr. Williams
[*sic*] is one of our most consistent lovers of folk-songs ... in addition to
collecting and arranging examples of this class of music he frequently writes
in direct imitation of it', and acknowledges that he is 'always good when
mood and subject bring about ... folk-like melodies' such as 'I Got Me
Flowers' from *Five Mystical Songs*. But other than that he dwells little, if at
all, on that aspect of Vaughan Williams's career – a reflection, perhaps, of
his doubts about folksong in art music.[25] Instead, Grew focuses exclusively
on Vaughan Williams's early vocal works, specifically his settings of
Whitman, Housman, Stevenson, Herbert and the Rossettis. By far the
most impressive in Grew's opinion were the Housman settings of *On
Wenlock Edge*, which were 'as physically strong as the Herbert songs, and
as spiritually true as the Verlaine. They are probably the best that England,
as England, can or will ever produce... The fifth song, *On Bredon Hill* [*sic*],
is the composer's supreme achievement.' But this praise came with a caveat:
'since neither it ['Bredon Hill'], nor the group to which it belongs, is a
reflection of the widespread spirit we call "modernity," it cannot be said that
even *On Wenlock Edge* carries its author forward to the first line round the
great central chair of state'.[26] Rather than acknowledge that modernity
could come in different forms, including the Ravelian parallel triads of
'Bredon Hill', Grew was incapable of looking beyond his own narrow
definition of the term.

The reception of Vaughan Williams's pre-war music

In view of its unusual scoring, it is perhaps unsurprising that *On Wenlock
Edge* was premiered – by tenor Gervase Elwes, pianist Frederick Kiddle
and the Schwiller Quartet – in a concert at London's Aeolian Hall on
15 November 1909 that also included both chamber music (Vaughan
Williams's G minor String Quartet, which received its first public performance) and other songs. The song-cycle received little attention from the
critics; for instance, E. H. of *Musical News* wrote simply that *On Wenlock
Edge* was 'impressive and exacting', and instead devoted most of his review
to the quartet, which he damned as 'ultra-modern in style, and ... at times
discordantly chaotic' (neither piece was mentioned in the periodical's
review of notable new works in 1909).[27] Over the following decade,

however, the song-cycle made a greater impression, possibly because the subject matter of Housman's poetry – the premature death of young men, and resultant sense of loss – was felt particularly acutely during the First World War.[28] When Elwes and Kiddle again performed the work at Aeolian Hall on 27 December 1919, ten years after its premiere, one critic wrote that 'the cycle made its customary appeal'; it is not hard to imagine that a large part of this appeal was its poignancy.[29] While the composition of *On Wenlock Edge* obviously was not inspired by war in the way that, say, *A Pastoral Symphony* was, the events of 1914–18 undoubtedly enhanced its centrality within the Vaughan Williams canon.

A Sea Symphony made an immediate and generally very positive impression with the critics, a consequence, perhaps, of its having been written for the 1910 Leeds Festival, one of the biggest choral events in the country. Sydney Grew wrote a synopsis of the work for *Musical Opinion* prior to the premiere, in which he proclaimed that the symphony 'should stand out as the great work of the year. . . It is eminently sane and natural, yet often daring in its means of expression'. Grew was sufficiently impressed with the score that 'one would venture, on the authority of this work, to indicate [Vaughan Williams] as one of the five great composers of contemporary musical England'.[30] But the piece was not quite the finished article, in Grew's opinion; parts of the finale lacked the 'exquisite melodic thrill' of Bantock's *Sea Wanderers* (1906), or the 'irresistible charm' of his *Omar Khayyám* (1906–9).[31] Other critics, too, hinted at a lack of maturity. William Caunt, in *The Musical Standard*, while praising Vaughan Williams's technique, felt that the composer had 'over-estimated the power of appeal' of Whitman's poetry, 'and [its] sustainability for contrasted treatment under symphonic form . . . we get a bigness, but not a vestige of wonderment'. In *Musical News*, Arthur Eaglefield Hull noted the 'advanced and complicated methods [of] the young and gifted composer', and pronounced the work 'exceedingly difficult for chorus and orchestra'.[32] This last point was identified by Cyril Graham, in a review of a performance of the symphony in 1916 by the Bach Choir, as the main reason for the symphony's not getting performed more often; indeed, one wonders whether the Bach Choir would have performed the work at all on that occasion had the conductor not been Vaughan Williams's friend, Hugh Allen.[33]

Perhaps the biggest surprise in the reception of Vaughan Williams's early music is the divergence of opinion with regard to the Tallis Fantasia, which was premiered at the Gloucester Festival in 1910. The critics for the two main London newspapers were glowing in their praise. Legge described the work as 'pregnant with musical matter of real moment', while Fuller Maitland claimed:

> The work is wonderful because it seems to lift one into some unknown
> region of musical thought and feeling. Throughout its course one is never
> quite sure whether one is listening to something very old or very new ... it
> cannot be assigned to a time or a school but it is full of the visions which have
> haunted the seers of all times.[34]

But this view was far from universal. G. H., in *Musical News*, noted that
'the archaic nature of the theme has been well preserved, and treated with
considerable ingenuity, but the work as a whole is not of much musical
interest, and will probably survive only as a specimen of what a clever
composer can do with but slender material to work upon'; the critic for
Monthly Musical Record wrote that Vaughan Williams 'preserved the
serious, quaint character of the theme' but little else (and failed to mention
that this was a premiere); and Paul Seer, in *The Musical Standard*, does not
mention the piece at all in his review of the festival.[35] The critic of *Musical
Opinion*, who was 'disappointed' by the Fantasia, identified Bantock's
cantata, *Gethsemane*, as the highlight of the festival; so, too, did the
correspondent of *Monthly Musical Record* in its review of new works in
1910, in which the Fantasia was not even mentioned.[36] Although Graham,
in a review of the piece's London premiere at Queen's Hall on 11 February
1913, asserted that it was 'a thoroughly representative work' of its type
there is little evidence that it was widely played; indeed, the comment in
The Musical Times that it 'seemed over-long for concert use, but it has
many beautiful moments' smacks of damnation with faint praise.[37] For all
the work's popularity and esteem today, it clearly made little impact on
most critics when it was first performed.

A work that attracted more attention than the Fantasia was the *Five
Mystical Songs*, written for the 1911 Worcester Festival. The generally
positive reviews of the premiere in *Musical News* and *Monthly Musical
Record* indicate, like Fuller Maitland with the Fantasia, some uncertainty
as to whether the music was very old (the correspondent of *Musical News*
claimed that the songs 'all have rather a Gregorian character') or very new
(the writer in *Monthly Musical Record* noted the contemporary French
influence in Vaughan Williams's music, and stated that 'he keeps pace
with the times' without any 'attempt at sensational writing').[38] What
bridged the historical divide between Gregorianism and modern French
music was Vaughan Williams's use of modality, and it was this aspect
of the music that A. N. B. of *Musical News* explored in his review of
the work's London premiere at Aeolian Hall on 21 November 1911:
'Archaic alike in the modal character of the music and in the symbolism
of the words, it seems to reveal the soul of some fourteenth-century
contemplative to whom[,] by long weaning from the beauty of the senses,

new and strange doors have been opened.'[39] In these reviews, there is a growing awareness of a historicist paradox that would lie at the heart of Vaughan Williams's mature musical language: that modernity might be found as much in the past as in the present.

The possibility of a musical modernity that was not characterized by sensationalism features in reviews of the premiere of *A London Symphony*, the last major work that Vaughan Williams completed (at least in its original form) before the First World War. According to the critic of *Musical News*, S. H. C. W., the symphony was

> the most considerable contribution to contemporary British orchestral
> music since the First Symphony of Elgar. Thoroughly modern in feeling,
> though not in expression as contrasted with the advanced French and
> Russian schools, its chief merits are the strength of its thematic material and
> the clarity and directness of the treatment.[40]

The distancing of his symphony from the modern French and Russian schools (Debussy and Stravinsky respectively) is an indication that Vaughan Williams's particular type of modernity might become identified with the future direction of British music – the more so, perhaps, because of the setting of the work. As the reviewer from *The Musical Times* put it, '[t]here is a big impulse, a big rhythmic line underlying the whole design which makes it a real symphony and a real reflection of the London spirit, a spirit which we feel all the more strongly because it is disguised beneath a myriad attractions and distractions'.[41] This spiritual aspect of the work was remarked upon by both critics here: for S. H. C. W., the 'dreamy contemplation of Dr. Williams [*sic*] is his greatest asset'; for the *Musical Times* critic 'Dr. Vaughan Williams thinks about it all much as Walt Whitman, whose words he has so often set, would have thought about it'.[42] *A London Symphony* was thus a continuation of the 'visionary' Vaughan Williams of *Toward the Unknown Region* and *A Sea Symphony*, only this time the universal vision had a specifically national setting.

The reception of Vaughan Williams's pre-war works reveals increasing interest in a composer of whom much was expected but who, as yet, had realized little of his potential. The technical difficulty of some of his music, the lack of small-scale works for standard instrumental combinations (or of short piano works like those of Holbrooke and Scott) that would have led to repeated hearings, a compositional style not readily identified with modernity, and the double-edged sword of being closely associated with the folksong movement – all these contributed to his being eclipsed by composers whose music is seldom performed today. But with the end of the war came an attitudinal and, crucially, a generational shift in British music criticism. As we shall now see, music that seemed quirky and out of

step with modern British musical thinking in 1914 became wholly identified with it a decade later.

An English progressivist: writings on Vaughan Williams, 1918–25

The end of the First World War saw a number of significant changes to
British musical life that would have a lasting effect on the reception of
Vaughan Williams's music. Firstly, there was a conscious attempt to
improve the infrastructure of British music-making through the establishment of such bodies as the British Music Society (1918), which aimed to
co-ordinate musical events at a nationwide level under the presidency of
the editor of *Monthly Musical Record*, Arthur Eaglefield Hull. While the
Society lasted only fifteen years, it reflected a modern, centralized approach
to arts organization that was a departure from the more laissez-faire
approach that had existed before the war.[43] To this may be added the
establishment, in 1920, of *Music & Letters*, a quarterly periodical, edited
by A. H. Fox Strangways, the aims of which were more academic than
journalistic, and which from its very first number devoted some of its
coverage to British music and musicians.[44] In tandem with this was the
emergence of a new generation of writers on music, many of them composers who had graduated from the RCM or RAM, whose discourse was more
technical and less belletrist than that of their predecessors, reflecting something of the text-centred modernist spirit of New Criticism in literature.[45] A
consequence of this was that discussions of contemporary music, and
particularly the nature of modernism and modernity, were considerably
more nuanced than they had previously been.

An early example of this was a monograph by Hull entitled *Modern
Harmony* (1914), and a series of essays that he contributed to *Musical
Opinion* in 1917–18 about the nature of modernism more generally.
Unlike many of his British contemporaries, Hull realized that, in practice,
the main criterion for modern harmony should not be 'is it right?' but
rather 'does it work?', and that many of the traditional rules of harmony
were now largely irrelevant. *Modern Harmony* contains chapters on modality, the 'duodecuple' scale (Hull's term for freely chromatic, but still
ultimately tonal harmony), the whole-tone scale, and various other non-
traditional scales, thus explaining, and thereby legitimizing, the music of
such composers as Strauss, Debussy, Ravel and Scriabin (though not
Schoenberg, about whose Klavierstück Op. 11, No. 1, he was scathing).[46]
The same acknowledgement that the laws of composition were changing,
and that critics needed to refocus their horizons of expectation

accordingly, also underpinned Hull's articles on modernism, where he dwelt again on harmony, on sonority for its own sake in both piano and orchestral music, and on the most important practitioners of these techniques.[47] While he identified Debussy and, to a lesser extent, Scriabin as the leading innovators in these areas, Hull also mentioned a significant number of younger British composers, most notably Scott (on whom he would write a monograph in 1918), but also Vaughan Williams, whose use of modality linked him with Debussy, and whose unusual sonorities in *On Wenlock Edge* drew favourable comparison with Schoenberg's First Chamber Symphony.[48]

Hull followed up his articles on modernism in the autumn of 1918 with a three-part feature on Vaughan Williams: the longest that the composer had yet received in a major British periodical.[49] Based on a still narrow corpus of works, Hull not only identified Vaughan Williams's music as 'in many ways . . . the most distinctly English of any of our composers', based on Vaughan Williams's engagement with folk music as a collector and arranger, but also, more significantly, viewed him as 'one of the most engaging in the fine group of modern European composers'. Hull noted Vaughan Williams's engagement with the music of Debussy, whose influence he detected in a work as early as *Willow-Wood* (1903), and Ravel, from whom Vaughan Williams 'derived only what was good for himself, for he can never be charged with being a mere copyist'. While Hull held some reservations about *Toward the Unknown Region*, and made no reference at all to the Tallis Fantasia, he was sincere in his praise of *On Wenlock Edge* (which, presciently, he claimed would 'some day indisputably rank amongst the great musical classics'), *A Sea Symphony* and *A London Symphony*, where he identified Debussy, Ravel and (in the Scherzo) Whistler as significant influences.[50]

The prominence of *A London Symphony* in Hull's list of select works may have been a consequence of two performances of that work at Queen's Hall the previous spring under Adrian Boult. The first of these concerts took place on 18 February, and the symphony was sufficiently popular that it was repeated 'by desire' a month later, this time with cuts of about ten minutes (the first of three sets of alterations that Vaughan Williams would make to the piece). The changes seemed to work: *The Musical Times*, whose critic had complained at the earlier concert that the work 'broods too much and seems over long', described the March performance as 'very fine'.[51] These two concerts helped consolidate Vaughan Williams's position within the repertory after a war during which his music had been heard relatively infrequently. But it was the next performance of the symphony, revised once more, that perhaps did most to cement Vaughan Williams's reputation as one of the leaders of British music. The concert, given by the London Symphony Orchestra under Albert Coates on 4 May 1920, was part of the First Annual Congress of the British Music Society, and thus an important platform for modern British music. Alfred Kalisch, reviewing the work for *The Musical Times*, consciously ignored the other works in the programme, and instead focused solely on Vaughan Williams's symphony, which, he wrote, 'unless all competent judges are mistaken ... is destined to rank as one of the significant works of its generation'.[52]

Articles by other critics soon began to appear – and in abundance. In the first half of 1920 alone, Fox Strangways contributed a piece to the second number of *Music & Letters* that surveyed Vaughan Williams's works to date; Edwin Evans wrote a three-part essay for *The Musical Times*, part of a series of similar (but generally shorter) pieces on contemporary British composers; the pianist and composer Katharine Eggar wrote an article for *The Music Student*; and R. O. Morris (admittedly Vaughan Williams's brother-in-law) reviewed *A London Symphony* for *The Nation* (a short-lived journal that would merge with the *Athenaeum* in 1921).[53] Over the next few years there were journal articles and book chapters about the composer by Colles, Grew, Richard Capell (who would succeed Hull as editor of *Monthly Musical Record* following the latter's death in 1928), Holbrooke and others.[54] While not all these pieces were positive – Holbrooke, whose own star was waning, sniped that Vaughan Williams's music 'pleases the dull ones of our profession' (by which he meant academics) and was 'always severe, cold and noble' – most were strongly favourable, even those by critics, such as Cumberland, who had previously given Vaughan Williams short shrift.[55]

Three features recur in this literature. The first is that the critics increasingly distinguish between Vaughan Williams's folksong arrangements and the musical language that he derives from folk music. The importance of this lies in the fact that, far from Vaughan Williams's music becoming more popular in the 1920s because the use of folksong within art music had become more acceptable, the opposite is actually the case: Vaughan Williams's success lay in his development of a personal language that was qualitatively different from folksong. Several of the critics above were highly sceptical of the folksong movement: Eggar, for instance, viewed it as an 'indulgently regarded form of musical lunacy'; Evans, in expressing his doubts about Vaughan Williams's folksong accompaniments, distanced himself from the 'fanatics of the folksong world who arrogate to themselves the right of declaring how these old melodies should be set ... the example they give of exclusiveness is one to be avoided'; and Colles recalled that when he first heard the first *Norfolk Rhapsody* 'everyone who could not write new tunes was declaring that salvation lay in the dishing up of old ones. English music was becoming an Irish stew, a hotch-potch in which the scarcity of meat was compensated for by unlimited potatoes, fresh dug from the soil.'[56] There was a growing recognition, however, that for Vaughan Williams folksong was the means to an end (a mature, personal compositional style), not an end in itself; as Colles put it, 'Vaughan-Williams [*sic*] had found out through folk song how to say the thing he wanted to say'.[57] Quite when this stylistic change took place varied from critic to critic – Colles claimed to have detected it in *In the Fen Country* (a work originally completed in 1904, but not heard until 1909, by which time Vaughan Williams had made three revisions to it); Grew, writing in 1926, stated that Vaughan Williams's music 'ceased to reveal the *direct* influence of folk-song' from 1912 onwards – but its consequence was clear: Vaughan Williams's mature idiom was a perfect synthesis of the musical voice of the English people expressed through folksong, and the musical language of early modernism.[58]

The second point is that the austere, detached quality of Vaughan Williams's folk-derived musical language was attractive to younger critics whose mode of discourse was increasingly drawn towards discussions of technical processes and descriptions of sound for its own sake. In part, this may be seen as a reaction of a post-war generation to the perceived Romantic excess of some pre-war music. As Eggar observed, 'Vaughan Williams seems to have faced musical facts as we had to face social and economical facts over the war, and to have learnt to let superfluities go, to stop waste and to grip essentials in music, as the better part of the nation did in the things of daily life'; Capell contrasted the 'south wind' of Elgar's music with the 'if not north, at least the north-west' wind of Vaughan Williams's, and praised the 'music of coolness and sturdiness, with a new tartness in the taste of it' that arose from the latter's modal harmony.[59] But it may also reflect the adoption of a modernist aesthetic by some critics, for whom a more formalist type of analysis was an opportunity rather than a threat. A good example of this is Herbert Howells's account of *A Pastoral Symphony* in *Music & Letters*, in which Howells not only tries to explain the organic unity of the work through the interrelationship of themes and motives, but also explicitly defends this approach as appropriate for that genre:

> If it were possible to drive home the sense of [a piece] by the hackneyed means of work-a-day analogies, that were an easy task. But a Symphony which is purely musical thought from beginning to end, that shuts itself off from all definite outward images and familiar activities, cannot be so expounded.[60]

Similarly, a feature of Gerald Abraham's commentaries on the first three symphonies, which appeared in *The Musical Standard* in 1926 (when

Abraham was just 22 years old), is his focus on music *qua* music: 'the pictorial element, slight as it is in the "Sea Symphony", is thrust even further in the background of the "London"; in the "Pastoral" it disappears altogether'.[61] While this is hardly on a par with Stravinsky's claim that 'music is, by its very nature, essentially powerless to *express* anything at all' one can legitimately argue that the difference is one of degree, not of kind.[62]

The third point is the idea that Vaughan Williams's style represented a 'middle way' between conservative late Romanticism and an overly radical avant-garde. This position was first advocated by Fox Strangways in his *Music & Letters* article, when, while defending Vaughan Williams's use of triadic harmony, he asked:

> Does originality in music consist, as some think, in bringing more and more disonances [*sic*] into the provinces of the consonant, or not, rather, in exploiting the well-known chords and making them say new things. . .? Does progress lie in the direction of 'chromatic harmonies' or of 'chords in a key'? . . . It is worth noting that here is a modern who is not only broadening the outlook of key, but seems also to his contemporaries to be doing so.[63]

Fox Strangways's implication was that modernity in composition should be characterized by reconciliation with the past, not rejection of it, and that in this respect Vaughan Williams's music was a model for others to follow. In a similar vein, Colles wrote of Vaughan Williams's early works that

> the Frickas of music who liked 'wonted things' were inclined to regard him as dangerously modern; the cayenne-pepper school on the other hand found him deplorably archaic, but all recognized that he had a point of view of his own, and was speaking to the point with all the force of which he was capable.[64]

Vaughan Williams was thus less a musical modernist than a musical progressive: one whose work was the perfect synthesis of old and new. Indeed, in some ways 'progressivism', with its connotations of democratic reform rather than revolution and anarchy, is what Fox Strangways envisaged as an appropriate English alternative to modernism. In a review of Vaughan Williams's opera *Hugh the Drover*, he considered that 'the eventual English contribution to music would lie in a certain directness and all-roundness, pressing neither the logic [of the Germans] nor the fancy [of the French], but also neglecting neither', and that Vaughan Williams's 'imaginative use of diatonic harmonies' was 'the way in which Parry said the *progress* of music lay'.[65] Vaughan Williams, progressive in his politics and often characterized as blunt and direct by supporters and detractors alike, was thus not only representative of Fox Strangways's aesthetic ideal, but also the paradigm of what a modern English composer should be.[66]

A national composer: the reception of the early interwar works

A musical language derived from English folk music and an aesthetic congruent with the English character meant that by the early 1920s Vaughan Williams was identified increasingly as a 'national' composer. This impression was fortified by the premieres of two works that critics immediately connected with the geography and history of England: *A Pastoral Symphony* and the Mass in G minor. Both works are typical of what would later become known as Vaughan Williams's 'pastoral' style, which was characterized by tonal ambiguity (a result of Vaughan Williams's technique of combining major and minor scales with various modes, both in melody and harmony) and a certain restraint in dynamics and scoring. Recent research has suggested that the adoption by Vaughan Williams and other British composers of a self-consciously pastoral idiom may have been their response to the horrors of the First World War.[67] But there is little evidence that this is how the critics of the day saw either the Symphony or the Mass; instead, as we shall now see, both works were heard in the context of a discourse that emphasized English national identity, framed in strongly ruralist terms, above anything else.[68]

A Pastoral Symphony was premiered at Queen's Hall on 26 January 1922 by the orchestra of the Royal Philharmonic Society under Boult. The reaction of the audience that night seems to have been genuinely mixed, and this is reflected in contrasting reviews of the work in the musical press. Evans, writing for *Musical News*, acknowledged that some might find a work lacking 'the concert-room equivalent of the theatrical methods of showmanship' too uneventful, although he himself had enjoyed the 'poetic charm' of the symphony: 'I have spent months in a village without the slightest desire for contrast, and I did not feel that I needed it in this music'.[69] S. T. of *Monthly Musical Record*, however, was less convinced: 'despite many incontestable beauties there is a certain monotony in four successive movements in which the moods, and even the texture and thematic character, are similar'.[70] The symphony was soon discussed in the main music periodicals, both in concert reviews and in essays about its composer. Perhaps the most visceral response to the piece came from the composer and critic Rupert Erlebach, who, in an article for *Monthly Musical Record*, devised a programme for the work and its two symphonic predecessors that Eric Saylor has rightly called 'highly fanciful'.[71] The significance of Erlebach's interpretation is not its veracity, however, but the way that he connects the composer with his British predecessors, and asserts that the essential truthfulness of Vaughan Williams's art lies in its rurality. The first paragraph begins with Erlebach linking Vaughan Williams with Parry, Stanford and

Elgar, and ends with the claim that his ability to combine folksong colour with chromatic harmony is Purcellian. He then compares the *Pastoral Symphony* with the *London*, concluding that

> of these two Vaughan Williams is more at home in the country. He knows London, and knows it well, but he was not born there, and can never know what London means to a Londoner . . . But the English countryside he knows as well as did Wordsworth and Edward Thomas, and he lives in every scene of the 'Pastoral Symphony'.[72]

This is speculative at best, and misleading at worst – particularly in view of the composer's description of the earlier work as a 'symphony by a Londoner'.[73] Yet it is indicative of the way that Vaughan Williams's music was increasingly seen as a conflation of nationality, rurality, English musical history and a particular type of British modernism (Erlebach, in a manner reminiscent of Fox Strangways, notes that Vaughan Williams 'does not sacrifice progress to tradition, or tradition to progress').[74] Other less impressionistic reviews adopted a similar tone. At the Bournemouth Musical Festival in 1923, G. B. of *Musical News* observed that *The Lark Ascending* 'breathes the same essentially British atmosphere as the Pastoral Symphony' [*sic*].[75] Capell, writing in *Monthly Musical Record* in February 1924, was struck by the 'mysterious and serene beauty' of the work, which was 'not like any other . . . You might say that the symphony is the reappearance of a hidden stream of music that had gone underground with the Fantasies of Byrd'.[76] Later that year, Hull echoed Erlebach's elevation of country above city: 'To my mind the *Pastoral Symphony* infinitely surpasses the *London*, which has never yet obtained its satisfactory final movement', adding that '*To The Lark Ascending*' [*sic*] was 'one of the most exquisitely English things ever written'.[77] Colles gave his imprimatur to the symphony's essentially English rurality in a note quoted by Boult in *Musical News* in 1926:

> The wide spaces of the Wiltshire Downs, the part-coloured pastures of the Midlands, the heather-clad Yorkshire moors – take it where you will, with all its differences of detail, such country has a common spirit. It is country where the daily life of man and beast, of flower and tree, quietly persists. It is uneventful; some people think it dull to spend their holidays in it, because they are too active-minded to let it soak into them and take possession of them in its own way. . .
>
> It is of such country as this that Vaughan Williams sings in the 'Pastoral' Symphony.[78]

It was doubtless such comments that led Vaughan Williams to explain to Ursula Wood in 1938 that the work was actually inspired by French landscape; it was 'really war time music ... its [*sic*] not really Lambkins frisking at all as most people take for granted'.[79] For the critics above, however, one suspects that the idea that the work might *not* be about the English countryside would have been inconceivable.

The Mass was to time what *A Pastoral Symphony* was to place. Probably composed in 1920–1, it was first performed on 6 December 1922 in Birmingham by the City of Birmingham Choir under Joseph Lewis.[80] Even before then, however, it was hailed by W. G. Whittaker as one of the 'supreme examples of unaccompanied religious music of our decade, legitimate descendants of the great compositions of our sixteenth century forefathers'; and this view was quickly confirmed by others who heard the piece.[81] Sir Richard Runciman Terry, the Director of Music at Westminster Cathedral, while claiming that the piece 'copies no ancient technique, nor does it repeat ancient *cliché*', had no doubts about which music the Mass resembled spiritually: 'it shares with the works of the great Tudor composers all their aloof dignity, their atmosphere of mysticism and contemplation, their disciplined emotion, their grave sweetness'. The *Musical News* critic, who quoted Terry's remarks in his own coverage of the London premiere at Queen's Hall, agreed: 'Especially I felt that it was English music, yet only Vaughan Williams could have written it, and that is a sincere tribute'.[82] Grew also emphasized the national dimension to the work's historicism: the Mass, along with the Tallis Fantasia and the recently premiered 'O Vos Omnes' were the 'first-fruits' of the Tudor revival in England: 'His music in this style will be understood and appreciated exactly in proportion to our understanding and appreciation of the music of Dunstable, Tallis, Whyte, Byrd and Gibbons.'[83] Thus with the Mass, Vaughan Williams not only bridged the gap between the sixteenth and the twentieth centuries, but implicitly became the legitimate modern successor to the golden era of English music.

***

The transformation of Vaughan Williams from a relatively marginal figure within British composition to the embodiment of the national composer – progressive rather than radical, with a compositional style that combined the idioms of folksong, Tudor music and the harmonic techniques of Debussy and Ravel, and (seemingly) a geographical attachment to rural England – took place remarkably quickly: perhaps over a five-year period from Allen's performance of *A Sea Symphony* in December 1916 to the premiere of *A Pastoral Symphony* in January 1922. In this respect at least it recalls the sudden rise to fame of Elgar twenty years earlier, when the success of the 'Enigma' Variations in Britain and *The Dream of Gerontius* in Germany turned a little-known provincial composer of secular cantatas into a nationally and internationally renowned composer of large-scale symphonic music. Of course, the two cases are different in many respects, perhaps most notably the fact that, by 1920, Vaughan Williams was widely known and respected for his work in other areas (as an editor and folksong collector), something that was not the case with Elgar. But the suddenness of their rise in esteem is indicative of the fluidity of British musical life in this period: that a composer whose work reflected the national zeitgeist in some way could achieve instant and lasting recognition. And in Vaughan Williams's case that recognition was as much as anything else a consequence of the congruity between his stylistic blend of tradition and modernity and a new generation of critics who were capable of appreciating it.

Notes

1 Gerald Cumberland, 'The Present in the Eyes of the Future: A Chapter in Musical History', *MO* 37/438 (1 March 1914), 451–2 at 451.

2 London: Routledge, 1993, revised as *The English Musical Renaissance 1840–1940: Constructing a National Music* (Manchester University Press, 2001). Citations in this essay are from the revised edition.

3 *Ibid.*, 181–2. See also 164–212, in general, especially 168 (apropos *A Pastoral Symphony*) and 190–1 (apropos *The Lark Ascending*).

4 *The Times*, 12 October 1907, quoted in Stradling and Hughes, *The English Musical Renaissance*, 81; *ibid.*, 168. According to Stradling and Hughes, apropos Fuller Maitland's review, 'the [RCM-based] Renaissance had nominated its "coming man": the successor to Parry had been found, and found triumphantly, among its own' (*ibid.*, 82).

5 For background on these periodicals, see 'Early Reviews of *The Apostles* in British Periodicals', selected, introduced and annotated by Aidan J. Thomson, in Byron Adams (ed.), *Edward Elgar and His World* (Princeton University Press, 2007), 127–72 at 127–31. Essentially, *Monthly Musical Record* was a house journal of the publishers Augener, and aimed to provide scholarly writing – historical, analytical and critical – on music with the aim of educating the public; the other three journals all had a particular interest in church music, but their coverage extended considerably wider than that, to include concert life and opera, particularly in London, but also elsewhere in Britain.

6 See Aidan J. Thomson, 'Elgar's Critical Critics', in Adams (ed.), *Edward Elgar*, 193–222.

7 Edgar L. Bainton, 'Some British Composers: i. Hubert Bath', *MO* 34/399 (1 December 1910), 171–2.

8 Notable exceptions include W. Barclay Squire, 'On Some English Music', *The Pilot* 4/1 (21 March 1903); Edwin Evans, 'Modern British Composers VI', *MSt* 65/2034 (25 July 1903), 52–3, 55; 'Dr. R. Vaughan Williams', *The Musical Herald* (April 1913), 99–103 (the article is unattributed, but Sydney Grew admits responsibility for it when he quotes its conclusion verbatim in 'Ralph Vaughan Williams', in *Our Favourite Composers from Stanford to Holbrooke*, 2nd edn (London: Peter Davies, 1924), 159–75 at 174–5); H. A. Stuckey, 'The Music of Dr. Vaughan Williams', *MO* 37/440 (1 May 1914), 643–4.

9 'Music in 1909', *MN* 38/984 (8 January 1910), 37–40; 'Music in 1910', *MN* 40/1036 (7 January 1911), 15–16; 'The Year 1911', *MMR* 42/1 (1 January 1912), 1–4; 'The Year 1914', *MMR* 45/1 (1 January 1915), 2–5.

10 Ernest Newman, 'English Composers of To-day', *MSt* 80/2430 (25 February 1911), 117–18 at 117.

11 George Lowe, 'Holbrooke's "Pierrot & Pierrette"', *MO* 34/406 (1 July 1911), 683–4 at 683.

12 Sydney Grew, 'Bantock's "Atalanta"', *MO* 35/414 (1 March 1912), 419. Grew's review was perhaps far from disinterested: he had been appointed to a lectureship in music and poetry at the Birmingham and Midland Institute School of Music in 1902 while Bantock was the Institute's principal.

13 'Foreign Intelligence', *MN* 40/1059 (17 June 1911), 596–8 at 596; A. Eaglefield Hull, *Cyril Scott, Composer, Poet and Philosopher* (London: Kegan Paul, 1918), 96. During 1913, for instance, Scott's music was performed in Paris, Cologne and Vienna. See M.-D. Calvocoressi, 'Music in Paris', *MMR* 43/7 (1 July 1913), 177–8 at 178; and 'The Year 1913', *MMR* 44/1 (1 January 1914), 1–4 at 4.

14 'Cyril Scott's Recital at Bechstein Hall', *MMR* 43/5 (1 May 1913), 121.

15 M.-D. Calvocoressi, 'On Mr. Leo Ornstein', *MMR* 44/5 (1 May 1914), 118–19 at 118.

16 Howard Orsmond Anderton, *Granville Bantock* (London: John Lane, 1915); Hull, *Cyril Scott, Composer, Poet and Philosopher*; George Lowe, *Josef [sic] Holbrooke and His Work* (London: Kegan Paul, 1920).

17 Hubert Parry, 'Inaugural Address', *Journal of the Folk-Song Society* 1/1 (1899), 1–3.

18 Sydney Grew, 'English and Modern Ideas of Music', *MO* 33/386 (1 November 1909), 89–90 at 90.

19 J. H. G. B[aughan], 'Comments and Opinions: "Nationalism in Music"', *MSt* 80/2440 (6 May 1911), 271–2.

20 D[ouglas]. Donaldson, 'The Folk-Song Craze', *MSt* 80/2437 (15 April 1911), 229.

21 Gerald Cumberland, 'Twelve Heresies. ii. – The Folly of Folk Song', *MO* 35/415 (1 April 1912), 483–4 at 483. Cumberland's views were echoed a few months later in *The English Review* by Newman, which prompted a response from Sharp; see Ernest Newman, 'The Folk-Song Fallacy', *English Review* 11/10 (May 1912), 255–68; Cecil Sharp, '"The Folk-Song Fallacy": A Reply', *English Review* 11/12 (July 1912), 542–50; Ernest Newman, 'The Folk-Song Fallacy: A Rejoinder', *English Review* 12/1 (August 1912), 65–70.

22 *MSt* 79/2406 (10 September 1910), 169.

23 'Hereford Musical Festival', *MO* 36/421 (1 October 1912), 32–3 at 32.

24 'Midland Musical Competition Festival', *MO* 35/417 (1 June 1912), 638–9 at 639.

25 'Dr. R. Vaughan Williams', 99, 101.

26 *Ibid.*, 102.

27 E. H., 'London Concerts', *MN* 37/977 (20 November 1909), 470–2 at 472; 'Music in 1909', *MN* 38/984 (8 January 1910), 37–40. It is unclear whether 'E. H.' is Arthur Eaglefield Hull, who usually signed himself 'A. E. H.', under which initials he reviewed the premiere of *A Sea Symphony* for *MN*.

28 For instance, 'Autolycus', a columnist in *MO*, described *On Wenlock Edge* as 'one of the most moving of modern works' in a denunciation of Ernest Newman, who had recently written a negative analysis of the piece

in *The National News*; see 'Autolycus', 'Unconsidered Trifles', *MO* 41/486 (1 March 1918), 319–20.

29 'In the Concert Room', *MMR* 50/2 (1 February 1920), 39–40 at 39.

30 Sydney Grew, 'Leeds Festival Novelties', *MO* 34/397 (1 October 1910), 18.

31 Sydney Grew, 'Vaughan Williams' Sea Symphony', *MO* 34/398 (1 November 1910), 93–4 at 94.

32 Wm. Henry Caunt, 'Leeds Triennial Musical Festival', *MSt* 79/2412 (22 October 1910), 256–8 at 257; A. E. H., 'Leeds Musical Festival', *MN* 39/1025 (22 October 1910), 357–8 at 357.

33 C[yril] D. G[raham], 'In the Concert Room', *MMR* 47/2 (1 February 1917), 35–6. The concert took place at Queen's Hall on 12 December 1916, and was dedicated 'To the Memory of the Officers and Men of His Majesty's Fleet and the Mercantile Marine'. In a letter to Hubert Foss in 1941, Vaughan Williams wrote that Allen 'insisted on shoving the S. Symph down people's throats after it was a complete flop at Leeds' (6 November 1941; see *LRVW*, 326).

34 *The Daily Telegraph*, 8 September 1910; *The Times*, 7 September 1910; both quotations from Meirion Hughes, *The English Musical Renaissance and the Press 1850–1914: Watchmen of Music* (Aldershot: Ashgate, 2002), 62, 34.

35 G. H., 'Three Choirs Festival', *MN* 39/1019 (10 September 1910), 228; 'Gloucester Musical Festival', *MMR* 40/10 (1 October 1910), 220; Paul Seer, 'Three Choirs' Festival: Its Principal Features Discussed', *MSt* 79/2407 (17 September 1910), 177–8.

36 'The Gloucester Festival', *MO* 34/397 (1 October 1910), 30; 'The Year 1910', *MMR* 41/1 (1 January 1911), 1–4.

37 C[yril] D. G[raham], 'In the Concert Room', *MMR* 43/3 (1 March 1913), 65–6 at 66; 'Mr. Balfour Gardiner's Concert', 'London Concerts', *MT* 54/841 (1 March 1913), 174.

38 'Three Choirs Festival', *MN* 41/1072 (16 September 1911), 251–3 at 252; 'Worcester Musical Festival', *MMR* 41/10 (1 October 1911), 252–3.

39 'London Concerts', *MN* 41/1083 (2 December 1911), 494–6 at 494.

40 S. H. C. W., 'London Concerts', *MN* 46/1205 (4 April 1914), 318–20 at 319.

41 'Dr. Vaughan Williams's Symphony', *MT* 55/855 (1 May 1914), 310–11 at 310. The 'distractions' – Vaughan Williams's imitations of London street life – caused one critic, the pseudonymous 'Ripieno' of *MO*, to be strongly critical of the work, which he claimed seemed

'entirely lacking in humanity and red blood . . . truth to tell, [Vaughan Williams] is a trifle patronising in his manner and decidedly beside the mark in his musical soul-portraiture of that evanescent composite, the Cockney'. See 'Ripieno', 'Concert Notices', *MO* 37/440 (1 May 1914), 643–4.

42 S. H. C. W., 'London Concerts', 319; 'Dr. Vaughan Williams's Symphony', 311.

43 *KW*, 145–6.

44 For instance, the first issue contained an article on Elgar by George Bernard Shaw, and an article on the future of English song by Harry Plunket Greene.

45 For more on the relationship between music and New Criticism, specifically in the case of the F. R. Leavis-edited periodical, *Scrutiny*, see Stradling and Hughes, *The English Musical Renaissance*, 176–7.

46 A. Eaglefield Hull, *Modern Harmony* (London: Augener, 1914), 51.

47 A. Eaglefield Hull, 'Modernism in Music: An Enquiry into Its Rationale and Its Manifestations', *MO* 41/482 (1 November 1917), 85–6; 'Nationality and Modernism in Music', *MO* 41/483 (1 December 1917), 151–2; 'Modernism in Music: The Great Variety of Its Manifestations', *MO* 41/484 (1 January 1918), 213–14; 'Modernity and the Piano', *MO* 41/486 (1 March 1918), 329–30; 'Modernism and the Orchestra', *MO* 41/488 (1 May 1918), 443–4.

48 *Ibid.*, 443.

49 A. Eaglefield Hull, 'Vaughan-Williams and His Music', *MO* 42/493 (1 October 1918), 29–30; *MO* 42/494 (1 November 1918), 90–1; *MO* 42/495 (1 December 1918), 154–5.

50 *Ibid.*, 29, 30, 91, 155.

51 'Mr. Adrian C. Boult's Symphony Concerts', *MT* 59/902 (1 April 1918), 171.

52 Alfred Kalisch, 'British Music Society's Congress', *MT* 61/928 (1 June 1920), 387–90 at 389.

53 Editor [A. H. Fox Strangways], 'Ralph Vaughan Williams', *ML* 1/2 (March 1920), 78–86; Edwin Evans, 'Modern British Composers: IX. Ralph Vaughan Williams', *MT* 61/926 (1 April 1920), 232–4; Evans, 'Modern British Composers: X. Ralph Vaughan Williams (Contd.)', *MT* 61/927 (1 May 1920), 302–5; Evans, 'Modern British Composers: X. Ralph Vaughan Williams (Concluded.)', *MT* 61/928 (1 June 1920), 371–4; Katharine E. Eggar, 'Ralph Vaughan Williams: Some Reflections on His Work', *The Music Student* 12/9 (June 1920), 515–19; R. O. Morris, 'Music: Vaughan Williams' "London Symphony"', *The Nation* 27/7 (15 May 1920), 199–200.

54 Among the periodical articles are Gerald Cumberland, 'British Music in 1921',

The Bookman 59 (March 1921), 240–42; Rodney Bennett, 'The Songs of Ralph Vaughan Williams', *The Bookman* 61 (October 1921), 48–50; H. C. Colles, 'The Music of Vaughan-Williams', *The Chesterian* 21 (new series) (February 1922), 129–34; Richard Capell, 'Elgar and Vaughan Williams', *The Sackbut* 5/2 (September 1924), 40–2; Sydney Grew, 'Musicians. I. Ralph Vaughan Williams', *The Midland Musician* 1/1 (January 1926), 5–8; among the book chapters are Sydney Grew, 'Ralph Vaughan Williams', in *Our Favourite Composers from Stanford to Holbrooke*, 2nd edn (London: Peter Davies, 1924), 159–75; Joseph Holbrooke, 'Ralph Vaughan Williams', in *Contemporary British Composers* (London: Cecil Palmer, 1925), 94–107.

55 Holbrooke, *Contemporary British Composers*, 98, 100.

56 Eggar, 'Ralph Vaughan Williams', 515; Evans, 'Modern British Composers', 302; Colles, 'The Music of Vaughan-Williams', 130.

57 Colles, 'The Music of Vaughan-Williams', 130.

58 Colles, 'The Music of Vaughan-Williams', 130; Grew, 'Musicians. I. Ralph Vaughan Williams', 7.

59 Eggar, 'Ralph Vaughan Williams', 519; Capell, 'Elgar and Vaughan Williams', 42, 41.

60 Herbert Howells, 'Vaughan Williams's "Pastoral" Symphony', *ML* 3/2 (April 1922), 122–32 at 132.

61 Gerald E. H. Abraham, 'Vaughan Williams and His Symphonies', *MSt* 27 (new series)/481 (20 February 1926), 56.

62 Igor Stravinsky, *An Autobiography* (New York: Simon and Schuster, 1936), 83.

63 Fox Strangways, 'Ralph Vaughan Williams', 84.

64 Colles, 'The Music of Vaughan-Williams', 131.

65 Arthur Henry Fox Strangways, 'Music', 'Hugh the Drover', *The London Mercury* 10/60 (October 1924), 650–1 at 650 (italics added).

66 In a typically double-edged assessment of the composer, Gerald Cumberland referred to Vaughan Williams's 'essential British downrightness' in *Set Down in Malice: A Book of Reminiscence* (London: Grant Richards, 1919), 255. In a more sympathetic portrait of the composer, Sydney Grew described him as a 'man of simple, sincere, unsophisticated character' (*Our Favourite Composers*, 165).

67 See Eric Saylor, '"It's Not Lambkins Frisking At All": English Pastoral Music and the Great War', *MQ* 91 (2008), 39–59; Daniel M. Grimley, 'Landscape and Distance: Vaughan Williams, Modernism and the

Symphonic Pastoral', in Matthew Riley (ed.), *British Music and Modernism, 1895–1960* (Farnham: Ashgate, 2010), 147–74.

68 Alun Howkins has shown how the idea that the kernel of Englishness lay in the countryside, particularly that of southern England, was a notable feature of interwar British cultural politics; see Alun Howkins, 'The Discovery of Rural England', in Robert Colls and Philip Dodd (eds.), *Englishness: Politics and Culture 1880–1920* (London: Croom Helm, 1986), 62–88. See also Frank Trentmann, 'Civilization and Its Discontents: English Neo-Romanticism and the Transformation of Anti-Modernism in Twentieth-Century Western Culture', *Journal of Contemporary History* 29/4 (October 1994), 583–625; and Chapter 1 of this volume, 10–18.

69 E[dwin] E[vans], 'London Concerts', 'Royal Philharmonic Society', *MN* 62/1558 (4 February 1922), 148–9.

70 S. T., 'In the Concert Room', 'Royal Philharmonic Society', *MMR* 52/3 (1 March 1922), 58–62 at 58.

71 Saylor, '"It's Not Lambkins Frisking At All"', 48.

72 Rupert O. Erlebach, 'Vaughan Williams and His Three Symphonies', *MMR* 52/6 (1 June 1922), 127–8, 151, at 127.

73 See *VWOM*, 339.

74 Erlebach, 'Vaughan Williams and His Three Symphonies', 127.

75 G. B., 'Bournemouth Musical Festival', *MN* 64/1620 (14 April 1923), 373.

76 R[ichard] C[apell], 'In the Concert Room', *MMR* 54/2 (1 February 1924), 43–4 at 44.

77 A. Eaglefield Hull, 'On Dr. Walker's History of English Music: II', *MMR* 54/9 (1 September 1924), 258–9 at 258.

78 'Pastoral Symphony (Vaughan Williams) Analysed by Adrian C. Boult', *MN* 70/1763 (9 January 1926), 27–8 at 27.

79 Letter to Ursula Wood, 4 October 1938, *LRVW*, 264–5 at 265.

80 *KW*, 91.

81 W. G. Whittaker, 'Educational and Choral Pages', '"Mater Ora Filium"', *MN* 61/1553 (31 December 1921), 691–2 at 692.

82 J. C., 'A Choral Advance: Wolverhampton Comes to London', *MN* 64/1620 (April 1923), 358–9.

83 Grew, *Our Favourite Composers*, 168.

PART II

Works by genre

4 History and geography: the early orchestral works and the first three symphonies

ALAIN FROGLEY

Vaughan Williams's early development as a composer has been significantly obscured by three interrelated factors, all of which tend to set him off from major contemporaries. Firstly, by 1920, as he approached his fiftieth birthday, he had withdrawn almost twenty substantial works composed in the two decades leading up to 1914, works that with few exceptions had already been performed and had received broadly positive critical attention. Secondly, most of these works were written after the composer had turned thirty, and a number of them after he had already achieved some notable public successes, and thus could be considered to represent at least a first maturity (even if he did not necessarily see it in those terms). Thirdly, most of the withdrawn works are for orchestra or chamber ensembles: that is, not in the genres with which his early emergence as a composer has traditionally been most strongly associated, namely solo song and large-scale choral music (e.g. the *Songs of Travel*, *On Wenlock Edge* and *Toward the Unknown Region*). In fact, Vaughan Williams expended the greater part of his compositional energy during the period from the late 1890s up to 1914 in writing substantial chamber and orchestral works, especially the latter. It is well known that Vaughan Williams was a late developer, but this wide-ranging suppression of works that can hardly count as juvenilia is unusual among composers. The years 1898–1907 were especially rich in projects that were later withdrawn (see Table 4.1, which lists all the composer's orchestral works up to 1925).[1] In the case of the orchestral music, the impact of this cull on our understanding of the composer's development is partly mitigated by the retention in his public *oeuvre* of the *Norfolk Rhapsody* No. 1 and *In the Fen Country*, both composed before 1907 (albeit later revised), but these two pieces alone cannot represent an extremely varied body of music in its entirety. One other early orchestral work, the *Heroic Elegy and Triumphal Epilogue*, has now been published and recorded, and there are plans to revive some others; autograph scores survive, in the British Library in most cases, for nearly all the withdrawn orchestral works.

Table 4.1 *Vaughan Williams's orchestral works to 1925*

Work	Composition	First Performance	First Publication
Fantasia for Pianoforte and Orchestra*	1896–1902, rev. 1904	none	
Serenade in A minor*	1897–8	Bournemouth, 4 April 1901; Bournemouth Municipal Orchestra, cond. Dan Godfrey	
Bucolic Suite*	1900, rev. 1901	Bournemouth, 10 March 1902; Bournemouth Municipal Orchestra, cond. Dan Godfrey	
Heroic Elegy and Triumphal Epilogue*	1900–1, rev. 1902	Elegy only: London, RCM, 5 March 1901; RCM Orchestra, cond. Charles Stanford. Complete: Leeds, 21 January 1905; Leeds Municipal Orchestra, cond. RVW	
Symphonic Rhapsody*	1901–3; destroyed	Bournemouth, 7 March 1904; Bournemouth Municipal Orchestra, cond. Dan Godfrey	
The Solent: Impression*	1902–3	19 June 1903; location and performers unknown, probably private performance	
Burley Heath: Impression*	1903; incomplete	none	
Harnham Down: Impression*	1904–7	London, QH, 12 November 1907; New Symphony Orchestra, cond. Emil von Řezníček	
Boldre Wood: Impression*	?1904–7; lost	London, QH, 12 November 1907; New Symphony Orchestra, cond. Emil von Řezníček	
In the Fen Country: Symphonic Impression	1904, last rev. 1935	London, QH, 22 February 1909; Thomas Beecham, The Beecham Orchestra	1969
Norfolk Rhapsody No.1	1905–6, rev. ?1914	London, QH, 23 August 1906; Queen's Hall Orchestra, cond. Henry Wood	1925
Norfolk Rhapsody No.2*	1906	Cardiff, 27 September 1907; London Symphony Orchestra, cond. RVW	
Norfolk Rhapsody No.3*	1906; lost	Cardiff, 27 September 1907; London Symphony Orchestra, cond. RVW	
A Sea Symphony	1903–9, last rev. 1924	Leeds, 12 October 1910; Leeds Festival Chorus and Orchestra, cond. RVW	vocal score: 1909 full score: 1924
The Wasps: Aristophanic Suite [from incidental music to play]	1909	23 July 1912, RCM, London; New Symphony Orchestra, cond. RVW	1914
Fantasia on a Theme by Thomas Tallis	1910, last rev. 1919	Gloucester, 6 September 1910; London Symphony Orchestra, cond. RVW	1921
Fantasia on English Folk Song: Studies for an English Ballad Opera*	1910; lost	London, QH, 1 September 1910; Queen's Hall Orchestra, cond. Henry Wood	

Table 4.1 (*cont.*)

Work	Composition	First Performance	First Publication
A London Symphony	1911–13, main rev. 1918, last rev. 1933	London, QH, 27 March 1914; Queen's Hall Orchestra, cond. Geoffrey Toye	1920
A Pastoral Symphony	1916–21	London, QH, 26 January 1922; orchestra of the Royal Philharmonic Society, cond. Adrian Boult	1924

* – withdrawn
rev.– revised

QH Queen's Hall
RCM Royal College of Music
RVW Ralph Vaughan Williams
(Recent performances and publication of withdrawn works are not included.)

Our interest in Vaughan Williams's development in the orchestral field is rendered especially acute by his later emergence as arguably Britain's most important twentieth-century symphonist. This process began in the years before 1925 with the first three of the eventual corpus of nine symphonies: *A Sea Symphony*, *A London Symphony*, and *A Pastoral Symphony*, first performed in 1910, 1914 and 1922 respectively. Yet these unusual works further complicate the shape of the composer's career: with the partial exception of the *London*, none of them can be straightforwardly integrated into the symphonic tradition, as we shall see further below. For most commentators it was only in the mid-1930s, with his Fourth Symphony, that Vaughan Williams seemed finally to enter the symphonic mainstream. Indeed, all the composer's pre-1925 orchestral works reflect upon and engage with wider questions of genre facing composers of the period, and particular issues raised by the composer's own stylistic proclivities – challenges to which Vaughan Williams responded with a high degree of imagination, if not always with a consistent level of success. These works also reflect the composer's preoccupations with his particular identity as a British composer, and how the embodiment in his music of specific elements of geographical and historical situation – of place, space and time – could contribute to that identity. Indeed, it can be argued that during the period surveyed here Vaughan Williams engaged with such questions, especially those of geography, more intensively than at any other time in his career.

One implication of genre, or at least medium, was practical, specifically the place of the orchestra in British musical life of the early 1900s. Orchestral activities were on a healthier footing than when Elgar began his career, but conditions were still challenging compared to those in some

other nations, most notably in central Europe.[2] Performance opportunities remained sharply limited, publishing outlets even more so, to the
extent that only one of Vaughan Williams's strictly orchestral pieces, the
suite from his incidental music for Aristophanes' *The Wasps*, appeared in
print before the First World War, and this with the German publisher
Schott; several choral–orchestral works, including *A Sea Symphony*, were
published by Breitkopf & Härtel in Leipzig. Vocal and choral music
generally found a readier market, largely because of sales to amateur
performers, and so it is perhaps no surprise that the composer's first
published works of any kind were in these genres. Indeed, it seems doubtful that he would have been able to concentrate to the degree that he did on
orchestral music if he had not had a small private income to supplement
his compositional activities. In terms of securing performances he was
heavily reliant on connections from his days at the Royal College of Music,
his teacher Stanford in particular, and on the encouragement to younger
composers given by Dan Godfrey and the Bournemouth Symphony
Orchestra, and Henry Wood in his Promenade Concerts at Queen's Hall
in London, though Thomas Beecham and Emil von Řezníček also conducted his music on isolated occasions.[3]

Earliest works

Vaughan Williams's first sustained engagement with orchestral music
began in the second half of the 1890s and came to fruition initially with
a number of performances in 1901 and 1902. As can be seen from
Table 4.1, the first piece on which the composer embarked, the Fantasia
for Pianoforte and Orchestra, was in fact never performed, though he
worked on it on and off between 1896 and 1904. The Fantasia was one of a
number of early orchestral works that were revised (in some cases more
than once) after an initial phase of composition, and sometimes after a
first performance; this complicates an already patchy documentary record
of compositional and performance history, though we are at least helped
by the fact that at this stage of his career the composer often recorded dates
of composition and subsequent revision in his manuscripts, a practice
unfortunately abandoned in later life. Some works, for example the
Symphonic Rhapsody, were apparently withdrawn after a single performance, whereas others, such as the *Bucolic Suite* and the *Heroic Elegy and
Triumphal Epilogue*, received several. In most cases the works were not
withdrawn in a single and definitive act but simply allowed to lapse into
obscurity. The biggest obstacle to a full assessment of the pre-1908 works,
however, is the fact that for the most part we cannot hear them in

performance and must rely on the scores alone; this situation is beginning to change, as was noted above, but it will be some time before a fuller picture can be formed. This would be unfortunate with any composer, but in Vaughan Williams's case the real impact of his music is often especially difficult to imagine with any accuracy from the page alone.

Nevertheless, the scores alone can still tell us a great deal. The four works composed at the turn of the century show a thoughtful, and at times impressive, handling of late Romantic forms and orchestration, with attractive and at times compelling melodic and harmonic invention that, while not yet steeped in the fully developed modality that would characterize his later work, does contain flashes of the mature Vaughan Williams that would emerge over the next decade. The titles are abstract, or invoke generalized semantic associations rather than a specific programme; while all four works pre-date the composer's intensive involvement with folksong, they do partake of the kinds of generic pastoral elements well established in nineteenth-century music. Vaughan Williams's models for the *Bucolic Suite* and the Serenade seem to have been Brahms and Dvořák primarily (filtered in part through his RCM teachers, Stanford and Parry), along with Max Bruch, with whom Vaughan Williams studied in Berlin. In contrast, as Michael Vaillancourt has noted, the Piano Fantasia and the *Heroic Elegy and Triumphal Epilogue* suggest the more self-consciously 'progressive' central-European stream of Liszt, Strauss and Mahler, in terms particularly of development and thematic transformation within one-movement or cyclic formal structures (the Symphonic Rhapsody, whose manuscript the composer seems to have destroyed, may well have reflected similar influences).[4] In terms of orchestration, the composer used a variety of different ensembles, with an often deft and poetic handling of his resources; this is especially true of the *Bucolic Suite*, which includes a range of percussion, and wind and string exchanges in the second movement that bring to mind Tchaikovsky. Though Vaughan Williams would later write that by the end of 1907 he felt that his music was 'stodgy and lumpy', and that it was this that led him to take lessons with Ravel,[5] he was certainly capable of a light touch in these early works.

A more monumental tone is evident in the *Heroic Elegy and Triumphal Epilogue*, which uses the largest orchestral ensemble Vaughan Williams had yet mustered, with triple wind, a large complement of brass, and harps and organ *ad libitum* (the work was published by Faber Music in 2008 and has now been recorded).[6] It is the most obviously impressive of this group of four works, and it certainly received the warmest critical reception.[7] There are echoes of Wagner, Sibelius and Tchaikovsky, and several developmental passages call to mind Strauss and Elgar; the brass-heavy final pages in particular, building on earlier fanfare passages, suggest a new level of orchestral ambition. The two movements are separate but share thematic material; they were originally to have formed the second and third parts of a three-movement Symphonic Rhapsody, but it is unclear whether the first movement was even sketched (the title was revived, however, for the later work by that name).[8] The relatively unusual choice of B minor as tonic key for the *Elegy* brings to mind Tchaikovsky's Sixth Symphony, and the first movement of the Russian's Fourth Symphony may have inspired subsequent tonal motion through a chain of minor thirds, a feature found in several other early works by Vaughan Williams, including the *Bucolic Suite* and *Burley Heath*.[9] Yet the varied range of influences does not obscure an individual stamp; furthermore, the *Triumphal Epilogue* contains several striking adumbrations of the later and more consistently individual Vaughan Williams, in particular *A Sea Symphony*, on which he would begin work fairly soon afterwards. The developmental passages around rehearsal letter R look forward to the Scherzo of the symphony, while the D major melody that launches the *Triumphal Epilogue*, and returns in grandeur as its peroration (see Ex. 4.1), adumbrates the 'Token of all brave captains' theme of the symphony's first movement. And this latter element has a broader significance: aspiring, gapped D major melodies of this kind would go on to become a staple thematic archetype for Vaughan Williams throughout his career.

Landscapes with and without figures

As was noted above, the *Heroic Elegy and Triumphal Epilogue* received positive critical notices, and it was singled out by several critics familiar

Ex. 4.1. *Heroic Elegy and Triumphal Epilogue*, Epilogue, bars 256–63.

with other music by the composer as a landmark work confirming his potential.[10] But in 1902 Vaughan Williams began to move in new directions, producing over the next five years a series of one-movement pieces that carry programmatic titles specifying particular geographical locations. These works are relatively short, but a number of them seem to have been conceived with the idea of larger multi-movement cycles (in 1903 Vaughan Williams also began work on *A Sea Symphony*, of which more below).[11] Though they all share an intensified interest in modal harmony, combined with more chromatic elements in sometimes experimental ways, the eight pieces divide into two groups according to whether or not they make clear reference to English folksong. This is quoted explicitly, in the form of complete tunes, in the three Norfolk Rhapsodies, and is more loosely evoked in the principal thematic material of *In the Fen Country*. These four works were the earliest substantial creative fruits of Vaughan Williams's folksong conversion experience, as it were, of December 1903, when he first encountered this music in a personally compelling manner, and moved beyond scholarly appreciation to active engagement. This found expression not only in composition but in extensive activity as a collector.

The four other works, of which *Boldre Wood* is now lost and *Burley Heath* survives only incompletely, were all dubbed 'Impression' (the generic designation also of *In the Fen Country*) and relate to locations in and around the New Forest, the expanse of unenclosed heathland and forest between Southampton and Bournemouth. This was an area that Vaughan Williams knew well, from family holidays and other connections to the area, and he lectured in Bournemouth in 1902.[12] The manuscripts for the earliest pair of impressions, *Burley Heath* and *The Solent*, indicate that when he began work in 1902 the composer planned a set of four pieces, under the broader title of 'In the New Forest'; it is not at all clear, however, whether the later *Boldre Wood* and *Harnham Down* were originally related to this scheme in any way, or were instead a fresh start at representing this particular geographical locale in music. *The Solent* and *Harnham Down* are prefaced by poetic inscriptions, from Philip Marston and Matthew Arnold respectively, but these shed little interpretative light.[13] It is a great pity that so many unresolved questions surround these works, as musically they are of considerable interest. As Michael Vaillancourt has noted, they show a new structural compression, harmonic sophistication and subtle attention to orchestral sonority. Though the title 'Impression' hints at French influence, more striking in many respects is the anticipation in certain passages in *The Solent* of the kind of string-writing that the composer would a few years later develop with such distinction and originality in the *Fantasia on a Theme by Thomas Tallis*.

Of course, landscape, and the natural world in general, had a long history of inspiring composers to textural and other kinds of musical innovation, and it is perhaps no surprise that a composer becoming increasingly restless in his search for a style both individual and somehow rooted in a wider national identity should turn to such subject matter.

There is an experimental quality at times in these New Forest works, and the composer's broader restlessness during this period is reflected in the tally of works left incomplete, or discarded after a single performance, or (more commonly) subjected to multiple revisions. In the latter category is *In the Fen Country*, which has the distinction of being the composer's earliest orchestral work to be allowed eventually to form part of his public *oeuvre*. It was composed initially in 1904, but then subjected to multiple revisions over the next few years, with a final retouching of the orchestration in 1935. The work shares with much of the composer's music of this period a sometimes awkward combination of Wagnerian or Straussian chromaticism, fleeting echoes of Debussy, and fresher modal perspectives, and at times it relies too heavily on imitation or strained modulations to generate momentum from contemplative musical material. Nevertheless, it contains many compelling and beautiful passages and sustains its sense of musical direction overall. A glowing chordal passage heard at various points, in which high strings answer brass, strikingly anticipates *A Pastoral Symphony* of some fifteen years later. Although the opening cor anglais solo certainly suggests the kind of generic lonely shepherd heard as far back as Berlioz's *Symphonie Fantastique*, the contour of the melody is also undoubtedly shaped by the English folksongs that Vaughan Williams had recently begun to collect, as Elsie Payne has shown.[14]

A sense of the wide, flat vistas of the Fens, where land, water and sky blur together, is conjured once again in the *Norfolk Rhapsody* No. 1, the only other orchestral work from the period before the end of 1907, when the composer began his studies with Ravel, to have survived Vaughan Williams's severe self-criticism. Two further rhapsodies, the three together apparently intended eventually to form a Norfolk Symphony, with the second combining slow movement and scherzo, were eventually deemed unsatisfactory and not performed after 1912.[15] The third rhapsody is now lost, but the second survives in a largely complete manuscript and has been recorded.[16] All three rhapsodies drew on folksongs collected by the composer in East Anglia during 1905, and were designed in part to bring these tunes to a wider audience, though the composer also published vocal arrangements of a number of them. The rhapsodies are, in fact, the composer's only orchestral works to present complete folk tunes, with the exception of *Five Variants of 'Dives and Lazarus'* and some folk dance arrangements; indeed, in his later career Vaughan Williams would rarely quote even fragments of specific songs, but rather evolved a melodic language shaped by generic features of English folksong or of certain families of tunes.

The original manuscript of the first rhapsody is unfortunately lost, and so we are unable to reconstruct with any certainty the work as it existed before its publication in 1925, though it seems likely that it was in essentially its final form by the time of a performance in Bournemouth in May 1914. The programme note for the 1906 premiere, however, does indicate that at this date the piece ended rousingly, rather than with the return to the quiet opening stasis that we hear today, and that it originally contained the stirring song 'Ward the Pirate', which in the third rhapsody formed the basis of a climactic final section, functioning as a cyclic recall of the opening number.[17] The eventual withdrawal of the third rhapsody presumably played a part in the removal of 'Ward the Pirate' from the first. The songs that remain in the final version of the first rhapsody are memorable; this is especially true of the 'The Captain's Apprentice', whose elegiac mood opens and closes the work, and to an extent pervades it, despite the boisterous energy of the second main melody, 'On Board a 98' ('A Bold Young Sailor' is also included). The desolate opening, in which lonely birdcalls keening across a coastal landscape are eventually joined by the more human voice of a solo viola, which weaves an improvisatory solo around the 'The Captain's Apprentice', is truly haunting.[18] The rhapsody does not entirely avoid the endemic pitfalls of works of this kind, especially in occasional awkward changes of gear between songs, but it is much more than a medley; Ian Bates has pointed to a number of subtleties of modal treatment in the work, and to various levels of symmetrical structure that suggest a more careful compositional process than is often associated with the term 'rhapsody'.[19] The second rhapsody also begins and ends quietly; slow outer sections, based on the tunes 'Young Henry the Poacher' and 'All on Spurn Point', frame a central scherzo that focuses on 'The Saucy Bold Robber'. Though the third rhapsody is lost, reviews suggest that it was essentially a quick march with trio. Why Vaughan Williams withdrew all but the first rhapsody must remain a matter of speculation, though the second rhapsody does not seem to cohere as convincingly as the first (to this listener, at least).

Ravel and after

Vaughan Williams produced an impressive number of orchestral works in the period between 1902 and 1907, but he clearly remained deeply dissatisfied with his achievements (not only in the orchestral field, it should be noted), and it was at the end of 1907 that he travelled to Paris to begin his work with Maurice Ravel. As Byron Adams has discussed in Chapter 2 of this volume, despite a frustrating lack of concrete evidence as to the exact scope of his studies with Ravel, the time he spent with his younger French colleague was clearly transformative, at least judging by the compositional fruit of the next few years. Though this did not manifest itself immediately in the form of independent orchestral works, the substantial score (albeit for a 24-piece orchestra) that the composer wrote in 1909 for Aristophanes' play *The Wasps* does show the impact of Ravel's instruction in 'how to orchestrate in points of colour rather than in lines', as Vaughan Williams would later describe his teacher's primary lesson.[20] The suite that Vaughan Williams later drew from this incidental music, scored for a rather larger ensemble than the original, went on to be a successful concert work, and at its publication in 1914 was in fact the first of his orchestral works to appear in print; the Overture proved particularly popular, and in 1925 it was one of the two works that the composer chose for his first venture into the recording studio.[21]

But 1910 would bring what were ultimately more important landmarks. The autumn of that year saw within just over a month the premieres of two crucial works: the *Fantasia on a Theme by Thomas Tallis* at the Three Choirs Festival in September, and *A Sea Symphony* at the Leeds Festival in October, both conducted by the composer. At the end of 1911 Vaughan Williams wrote in a letter to Ernest Farrar that the *Fantasia* '[is] the best thing I have done',[22] and most commentators have endorsed that judgement. Indeed, its stature remains impressive even in the light of the composer's later accomplishments. The *Fantasia* is Vaughan Williams's most widely performed and recorded major work, achieving in particular an international currency that has so far eluded most of his other music – though it was some time before the work took hold in this way and even in England it would not become a staple until the 1930s. It has been widely regarded as the first work in which Vaughan Williams fully realized the individual stylistic synthesis that would form the basis of his mature compositional output. He apparently discovered Tallis's tune for Psalm 2 during work on *The English Hymnal* (1904–6), for which Vaughan Williams adapted it as 'When Rising from the Bed of Death'. Nathaniel Lew has plausibly suggested that the idea of using the tune as the basis of a longer work may have originated in 1906, in connection with the Reigate pageant based on John Bunyan's *The Pilgrim's Progress* (the composer's first engagement with the Bunyan work, which went on to become a lifelong fascination, of course).[23] This remarkable Phrygian-mode tune is certainly richly suggestive in terms of harmonic, rhythmic and other subtleties of construction, as a number of commentators have noted;[24] yet the process of revelation that Vaughan Williams drew from it nevertheless

Ex. 4.2. *Fantasia on a Theme by Thomas Tallis*, bars Q.17–21.

constitutes an extraordinary imaginative feat, for which the word 'visionary' is for once entirely free of hyperbole. Particularly striking is the manner in which a closed thematic model is daringly broken down to a condition of almost complete quietus, and then gradually reanimated, eventually culminating in a luminous climax. The climax itself, a passionate homorhythmic declamation, confirms the fact that harmonically the work is a profoundly original meditation on the power of unadorned triads: without a single appoggiatura, but instead juxtaposing triads riven by false relations that evoke sixteenth- and seventeenth-century English music, Vaughan Williams creates a climax as intense in its way as anything in Wagner or Tchaikovsky (see Ex. 4.2).

The rhythmic unison of the climax is especially dramatic because of the array of multifaceted textures that has preceded it. Indeed, perhaps the most immediately striking (and most influential) feature of the work is its new and spacious approach to string sonority. The composer describes the ensemble as 'double stringed orchestra with solo quartet'. Elgar's *Introduction and Allegro* of 1904 had employed the concerto-grosso-like contrast of a quartet with a larger body of strings, but Vaughan Williams adds an intermediary second orchestra, essentially a double-quartet with double-bass added (the two orchestras are thereby of unequal size). The second orchestra is to be placed apart from the first 'if possible'. These resources are exploited to the full, particularly to create spatially suggestive effects of light and shadow, with wide registral expanses evoking a vertical dimension that complements the recessed textural perspectives. This aspect of the work has understandably been linked by some writers to the experience of being within a Gothic cathedral such as that at Gloucester, where the work was premiered (though there is no direct evidence that the composer was thinking in these terms). Choral antiphony has also been suggested as a model, but the disparity in the size of the ensembles militates against this analogy, at least in terms of true double-choir music; the contrasts between different organ manuals offer a closer parallel. More precise architectural and spatial metaphors underpin the most recent re-examination of the work, in which Allan Atlas suggests that the structure of Gloucester Cathedral may have helped suggest a tension between two different proportional schemes in the Fantasia, between what Atlas identifies as a quarter-half-quarter (or 1:2:1) shape, and various manifestations of the so-called 'Golden Section' proportion.[25] Any spatial scheme has nonetheless to take into account (as does Atlas) the strong narrative thrust that develops during the work. Anthony Pople has conceived of this in part as an evolutionary historical account of musical style, invoking plainsong, folksong and organum before arriving at Tallis's polyphony.[26] As Pople notes, this particular narrative weakens as the work progresses and Vaughan Williams's own modern voice takes over; nevertheless, this is the composer's most self-consciously historicizing work up to this point in his career. One earlier model that Pople essentially dismisses, however, is that of the one-movement Jacobean fantasy, as promoted during this period by the wealthy musical amateur Walter Willson Cobbett through his prize for chamber music: as Pople points out, Vaughan Williams violates a number of the requirements set out by Cobbett.[27] Both Atlas and Pople take into account important differences between the original version of the work and the published score of 1921; by the time the latter appeared the composer had subjected the Fantasia to at least two rounds of revision, cutting a total of thirty-three bars from the score, which included a second statement of Tallis's theme at the end of the work where now there is only one.

Three symphonies

Though the Tallis Fantasia would ultimately eclipse it in fame, it was *A Sea Symphony*, for orchestra, chorus and soprano and baritone soloists, that established Vaughan Williams as a composer of large-scale works. It was first performed on 12 October 1910 – Vaughan Williams's thirty-eighth birthday – at the Leeds Festival, conducted by the composer (later in the programme Rachmaninov played his Piano Concerto No. 2). Its long gestation began in 1903 and thus straddles several important junctures in Vaughan Williams's early development. This is reflected in a disparate range of styles and influences, the latter including Brahms (*Ein deutsches Requiem* in particular), Parry, Stanford, Elgar, Wagner, Tchaikovsky and (to a lesser extent) Debussy and Ravel, along with folksong and hints of Tudor music. Though many aspects of its compositional chronology remain obscure, we do know that a short-score draft was complete by 1906; at this point the work contained an additional movement, 'The Steersman', placed between the Scherzo and the Finale.[28]

Vaughan Williams had begun to set Walt Whitman (1819–92) in 1902 and would remain preoccupied with his work for the next decade, and to some degree for the rest of his life; Stanford and Charles Wood had already made notable Whitman settings before him, but it was Vaughan Williams in the years before the First World War who would engage most deeply with the American's transcendent and universalist vision of the modern world.[29] In *A Sea Symphony* Whitman inspired a work of extraordinary originality and ambition. With a running time of around an hour and twenty minutes, it must surely have been the longest British symphony written to date. Its status as a true symphony has been disputed, and it is certainly a hybrid work in terms of genre, combining elements of symphony, oratorio and cantata. It is more fully choral than, say, Mahler's symphonies with voices, in that the choir or soloists are heard virtually throughout; this necessarily dilutes its ability to pursue some more traditionally symphonic processes, particularly in developmental sections, and the form is sometimes episodic, especially in the massive finale. Yet the tonal and thematic strategies across the work ensure that it is much more than a loose succession of character pieces, and the outer movements in particular generate passages of gripping symphonic momentum. The overall tonal scheme of the four movements, essentially D–E–G–Eb, is unconventional, but hardly unprecedented against the background of Mahler's 'progressive tonality'.[30] And despite the stylistic disparities, there are moments of dazzling audacity. The exhortation of 'Behold, the sea itself' that launches the first movement, 'A Song for All Seas, All Ships', is one of these: its dramatic shift from Bb minor to D major harmony at the word 'sea' conjures a visceral sense of space opening up before us, and surely constitutes one of the great opening gestures of musical history[31] – a gesture intensified further at its second appearance by the unexpected addition of a C bass note under the D harmony (see Ex. 4.3). In the finale, 'The Explorers', the build-up to the prophetic moment of revelation, when the 'Son of God shall come singing his songs', is similarly electrifying; the rugged diatonic dissonances here are original and bracing, with the explosive urgency of the bass line pushing it ahead of the upper-voice harmonies, a kind of disjunction that might almost suggest the influence of early

Ex. 4.3. *A Sea Symphony*, 'A Song for All Seas, All Ships', bars 42–50.

Stravinsky, were it not for the fact that it was composed before either *The Firebird* or *Petrushka*. The hushed and ambiguous ending, ostensibly in E♭ but with melodic emphasis on C and a low G in the bass undermining the stability of the tonality, is also striking.

The enormous last movement is certainly *sui generis*, and here Vaughan Williams's reach exceeds his grasp (even if the listener may remain grateful that he reached that far); despite certain recurring thematic and tonal elements that provide landmarks in the soul's cosmic journey of exploration, the structure remains relatively loose. The second

Ex. 4.3. (cont.)

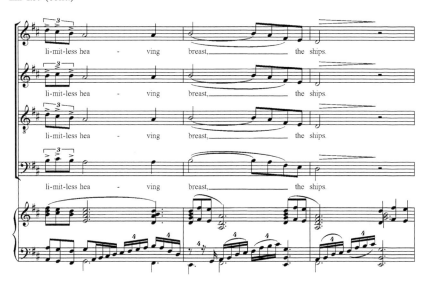

and third movements are more obviously in line with symphonic expectations: 'On the Beach at Night, Alone' is a slow ternary form, and the third movement, 'The Waves', is a scherzo. The third movement is the most impressionistic part of the symphony, replete with Debussy-like whole-tone passages among other elements. For the most part, however, the sea functions throughout the symphony as a spiritual metaphor rather than pictorial inspiration, reflecting the poet's own perspective. The sea was a common theme in British music at this time, with obvious nationalistic resonance, but Whitman's perspective is a universal one, reflecting his all-encompassing post-Christian sense of spiritual quest, his embrace of both the mystical and the mundane, and his visionary conception of global democracy. Such considerations, along with the poet's highly original and fluid approach to metre and diction, clearly influenced Vaughan Williams's choice of texts for the symphony; there is an almost palpable sense in a number of passages of an artist discovering the full extent of his powers for the first time, as Whitman's exaltation becomes the composer's own.

Though boldly innovative in a number of ways, *A London Symphony* is easier to place than its predecessor within the evolution of the symphonic genre since Beethoven, and it represents the culmination of Vaughan Williams's development as an orchestral composer before World War I. According to Vaughan Williams the work began as sketches for a symphonic poem about London,[32] but while it has important programmatic associations, these are subordinate to more traditional elements of musical coherence, including a unified tonal plan and cyclic returns of material in different movements. Nevertheless, one specific programmatic impetus was revealed in 1957, when, in correspondence about the symphony with Michael Kennedy, the composer remarked laconically: 'For actual coda see end of Wells's *Tono-Bungay*'.[33] This appears to refer to the final chapter of H. G. Wells's novel, which traces a journey taken by the protagonist down the River Thames, from some way upstream to the open sea, a progress that is framed in both geographical and historical terms, and which Wells describes as the three movements of 'a London symphony'. *Tono-Bungay* was first published in 1908; I have argued elsewhere that it was most likely the initial spur for the symphony, and surely influenced more than just its ending.[34] That said, it is not clear exactly when Vaughan Williams conceived of an orchestral work related to London, or made his initial sketches, though the symphony was apparently underway by mid-1911, and finished by the end of 1913.

The symphony made a strong impression at its premiere in March 1914, and confirmed for many Vaughan Williams's position as the leading figure in the cohort of British composers who had emerged since 1900. Though a more traditional work than *A Sea Symphony*, it is scarcely less ambitious or original, and lasted almost an hour in the version performed in 1914. Its full impact, however, was initially stifled by the outbreak of war, and it would not be heard in London again until 1918. Between 1918 and 1920, when the work was first published, the composer made draconian cuts, amounting to roughly 25–30 per cent of the original in terms of playing time; additional, though less severe, surgery would be performed before a revised version of the score appeared in 1936.[35] Vaughan Williams apparently agreed with those critics of the original version who had, despite generally positive reactions, expressed concerns about its length and prolixity. Of the four movements the first remained virtually intact in the revisions, but the slow second movement, the scherzo (which lost an extended subsidiary section), the finale and the long Epilogue that flows out of the finale were all heavily cut.

But the bold ambition of the work is represented more by breadth and depth of musical complexity than by sheer length, and these dimensions remain impressive even in the revised versions. Vaughan Williams created in this work a Mahlerian, at times almost Ivesian, range of stylistic and social reference.[36] Though the composer's own musical personality sounds strongly throughout, the clear imprint of Debussy, Wagner and even Stravinsky can be heard at various points. More significant in programmatic terms, however, are references to the urban street soundscape, including not only actual music – from modern ragtime inflections in the first movement and barrel-organ and harmonica in the scherzo, to the implicitly pre-modern lavender-seller's cry of the second movement – but also ambient sound, as it were, in the form of hansom-cab jingles, the chimes of Big Ben, or what seem to be the metallic shrieks and rumbles of trams and trains. And although the detail is intimately particular at times, the perspective is nevertheless implicitly global, not just local or national. The London that Vaughan Williams portrays, as centre of the British empire, is the capital of the modern world, a dimension emphasized by its status as a major port, intimately connected with the boundless sea. Nature, humanity of all classes, the technological challenges of modernity, and relationships with a multi-layered past are brought together in a heady mix. But they are not simply juxtaposed: Vaughan Williams confronts apparently irreconcilable contrasts and conflicts, but also seeks to integrate and reconcile. In this respect the work stands directly in the tradition of the Beethovenian symphonic paradigm, and indeed the grinding semi-tone dissonances at the beginning of the allegro section of the first movement, which are then taken up again in the finale, seem to evoke directly the opening of the finale of Beethoven's Ninth Symphony. A sense of strain, particularly in the last movement, is only fitting: if the symphony seems on the verge of collapsing under its own weight and self-contradiction at times, so did the city, nation and empire that it represents, riven as they were at this time by social and political turmoil (most notably widespread strikes and growing crisis in Ireland).

Programmatic interpretations of this kind must for the most part remain conjectural, since Vaughan Williams himself was ambivalent and inconsistent in shedding light on this aspect of the symphony (in common with most composers of programme music, it must be said). In 1925 he did tentatively acknowledge that the allegro of the first movement represented 'the noise and hurry of London, with always underlying calm', and that one might think of the slow movement in terms of Bloomsbury Square on a November afternoon, and of the Scherzo (subtitled 'Nocturne') as Westminster Embankment at night. He offered no such clues to the finale, however, or to the Epilogue into which the finale leads without a break. Nevertheless, the Epilogue, which is based on the slow introduction to the symphony, is clearly the 'coda' the composer mentions in reference to *Tono-Bungay*; the Wells connection confirms what is already strongly hinted at in the musical material itself, namely that both the beginning and the ending of the symphony evoke the Thames, and eventually the sea: the speed and turmoil of urban human modernity are thus framed by a mystical and implicitly timeless natural world. More broadly, Wells's novel portrays a society in decay, and a vision of London (one common at the time) as a vast and uncontrollable – almost unrepresentable – cancer of modern society, a mindlessly churning cauldron of capitalism engulfing its environs and its people. Though Vaughan Williams's view was surely not quite as bleak, there are many threatening shadows in the symphony, even moments suggesting nightmare, especially in the last movement and in a number of passages cut during the revision process. On the whole, the symphony darkens as it progresses, and the finale negates any notion of the kind of triumphal peroration beloved of many nineteenth-century symphonists, on the model of Beethoven's Fifth and Ninth symphonies (though of course Brahms's Fourth, Tchaikovsky's *Pathétique* and Mahler's Ninth all offered powerful precedents for such negation). The work is certainly much darker than Elgar's portrait of London in his *Cockaigne* overture of 1901, which is for the most part by turns exuberant and tender.[37]

Though the musical means by which Vaughan Williams expresses diversity and conflict are often original, the techniques by which he imposes coherence are for the most part well established in the symphonic tradition. Thus the interaction of tonal, modal and chromatic elements generates both dissonant conflicts, and the framework by which these are eventually absorbed into the overall G major tonality of the symphony.[38] Eb emerges early on as a chromatic alteration of the sixth degree of G, in the form of a keening D–Eb melodic figure in the slow introduction, and the interaction of scale-degrees 5 and 6, in a number of different tonal and modal contexts, looms large throughout the symphony. At the beginning of the allegro section of the first movement the D–Eb semitone is verticalized, as a shrill chromatic progression of parallel triads in the upper parts clashes with a thunderous bass line, suggesting the threatening and inhuman dimension of modern city life (see Ex. 4.4).

The bifurcation of the texture here into aggressively independent layers constitutes one of the most conspicuously modernist elements of the score, with clear parallels in the music of Stravinsky and Ives, and a powerful representation of the colliding simultaneities of urban experience. Such heterogeneity takes on a more positive aspect with the populist high spirits of the second-group material, which eventually brings the first movement to a rousing conclusion – a rarity in this composer's symphonies. But although this mood will return in parts of the deft Scherzo (especially the trio, which echoes *Petrushka*), the remainder of the symphony is mostly much darker. Twilit melancholy dominates the ternary second movement, and after the Scherzo itself burns out to end in ominous darkness, the finale embarks on an epic and ultimately tragic journey.[39] It is tempting to interpret this whole movement, not just the Epilogue into which it eventually leads, in terms of Wells's Thames progress, which travels through London's history as well as its geography; a solemn march gives way to more turbulent material, the hectic striving of

Ex. 4.4. *A London Symphony*, first movement, bars 34–44, transition from slow introduction to Allegro.

which fails to achieve closure, and eventually collapses into a return of the opening of the first movement allegro, before giving way to the Epilogue. The *niente* ending echoes that of *A Sea Symphony*, and despite its attempt to absorb the symphony's residual tonal conflicts, it offers more dissolution than resolution. As was suggested above, if the finale seems to strain too hard, and to fall short of the expectations and responsibilities generated by the preceding movements, such qualified failure is not inappropriate as a metaphor for the city and empire that inspired it – it may indeed have been inevitable, given the scale of the task that Vaughan Williams set himself in this work. The composer nevertheless retained an attachment to the symphony throughout his later life, and he conducted it more often than any of his other works.

Vaughan Williams made his first cuts to *A London Symphony* while on leave from active service in 1918 (he had enlisted in 1914). Though not obviously incapacitated, the composer was deeply marked by the war, not least through the loss of younger friends – most notably George Butterworth, to whom *A London Symphony* was dedicated upon publication. It is tempting to relate the removal of some of the work's most apparently subjective passages to the impact of war, representing perhaps a search for some objective, even stoical distance from a pre-war world irrevocably lost. Whether or not this was the case, such objectivity and emotional restraint is a striking feature of the composer's next symphony, made all the more telling there by isolated outbursts of anguish. *A Pastoral Symphony* was begun in 1916 and completed in 1921; it was the first major work that the composer completed after demobilization, and its unveiling in London in January 1922 was Vaughan Williams's first major premiere of the post-war period.

A Pastoral Symphony may lay claim to have been the composer's most misunderstood work, at least during his lifetime. While its reception cannot detain us here, insensitive critical reactions early on, including from some of the composer's friends, did much to forge the persistent image, which has only in recent years finally weakened its hold, of Vaughan Williams as a purveyor of insular pastoral nostalgia and meandering rhapsody. The composer himself was perhaps partly to blame (though his reticence was understandable), in that he failed to make clear until much later that the landscape evoked in the work was primarily that of wartime northern France, not the idyllic English vistas assumed by many commentators.[40] Yet a degree of musical incomprehension was understandable, not least on account of the genre expectations engaged by the work's title. Despite its imaginative orchestration – the deftly shifting and melding planes of sonority indicate a new and entirely individual absorption of the example of Debussy and Ravel – the symphony largely eschews traditional symphonic rhetoric. It is subdued in dynamic level for the most part, and employs almost unremittingly slow or slowish tempi; even the Scherzo has a relatively heavy tread for a movement of this kind.

In terms of deeper levels of construction, however, *A Pastoral Symphony* is in fact the composer's most rigorously disciplined symphony up to this point in his career. Several recent commentators have demonstrated the tightly knit motivic and formal coherence that underlies the apparently rhapsodic surface of the music; out of melodic material steeped in English folksong yet involving no direct quotation, the composer weaves a subtly compelling and evolving symphonic narrative.[41] Like its metropolitan predecessor, the symphony takes G as its fundamental point of departure (though in this case it will not return to end there); through subtle modal interplay, and the drawing-out of the implications of parallel triadic harmonization – a debt to the 'Nuages' movement of Debussy's orchestral *Nocturnes* is evident at the opening of the symphony – the composer introduces tonal tensions that impel the music forward (see Ex. 4.5).

A sense of teleological trajectory, in both the melodic and tonal dimensions, is pursued across the course of the work, even if it goes underground at times, as it were. An important element in this is the inconclusive

Ex. 4.5. *A Pastoral Symphony*, first movement, bars 1–12.

ending of the first movement, which leaves unresolved the tension between G and C♯ opened up early on in the movement, a tension bound up with the prominent role played by A major as a subsidiary tonal centre in the rotational sonata form.[42] In the finale it is D major that emerges as the strongest point of tonal arrival, and a belated resolution of earlier tensions. This coincides with a melodic fulfilment, in that for the first time in the symphony a fully fledged, rounded melodic statement is allowed to reach convincing closure. And yet this sense of arrival and completion is ultimately frustrated, in that the wordless and unaccompanied soprano solo that began the movement returns unchanged at the end, leaving the symphony floating ambiguously on an unharmonized A. The soprano solo is one of two elements in the symphony that seem to reach most obviously out towards a more programmatic level of meaning. It is not difficult to hear in wordless female keening a lament for the war dead; yet there is a remote and ritualized quality to the expression that might suggest instead a natural world oblivious to human suffering. The cadenza for natural trumpet in the second movement has a much clearer significance: it was suggested to the composer during the war by hearing an army bugler practise, and its realistic but gentle evocation of wrong notes has an almost unbearable poignancy – no surprise, perhaps, that the symphony flares into one of its rare moments of protesting anguish immediately following the cadenza. Michael Kennedy is surely right to argue that this symphony constitutes Vaughan Williams's 'war requiem'.[43]

***

In June 1922, a few months before his fiftieth birthday, Vaughan Williams made his first trip to the United States, having been invited to conduct the American premiere of *A Pastoral Symphony* at the Norfolk Music Festival in Connecticut, where Sibelius had premiered his tone poem *The Oceanides* in 1912. The invitation was probably made on the strength of *A London Symphony*, which was introduced to America in New York at the end of 1920 and was heard with some frequency there during the decade that followed. By the mid-1920s, Vaughan Williams had established himself as an orchestral composer of international standing. Through more than two decades of prolific, yet intensely self-critical, composition (and revision), he had succeeded in making the orchestra, that heavily freighted flagship of nineteenth-century musical culture, a flexible vehicle for his own profoundly original musical visions, including three extraordinarily contrasting symphonies. What no one could have predicted in 1922, however, is that this was just the beginning: that Vaughan Williams would go on to write six more symphonies that would help ensure the continued vitality and relevance of the genre for a tumultuous century and beyond.

Notes

1 Dates of composition and publication throughout this chapter are taken from *KC* except where otherwise indicated.
2 See Alain Frogley, 'The Symphony in Britain: Guardianship and Renewal', in Julian Horton (ed.), *The Cambridge*

Companion to the Symphony (Cambridge University Press, 2013), 376–95 at 378–9.
3 Writing after the Second World War, Hubert Foss recalled a performance of the *Norfolk Rhapsody* No. 1 in Berlin on 5 December 1906, conducted by Walter

Meyrowitz; though I have found no other record of the event, if it took place it was surely the first performance outside Britain of any of Vaughan Williams's orchestral works, and quite possibly of any music by the composer, as Foss suggests: see Hubert Foss, *Ralph Vaughan Williams: A Study* (London: George G. Harrap & Co., 1950), 111, n.1.

4 Michael Vaillancourt, 'Coming of Age: The Earliest Orchestral Music of Ralph Vaughan Williams', *VWS*, 23–46 at 33–6.

5 'Musical Autobiography', in Foss, *Vaughan Williams*, 18–38, at 34; see also Chapter 2 of the present volume. Vaughan Williams gives 1908 as the year in which he sought out Ravel; it was actually 1907, though most of their work together took place early in 1908.

6 By the BBC Concert Orchestra, conducted by John Wilson, on the Dutton Laboratories label, CDLX 7237[02], released in 2010.

7 See Vaillancourt, 'Coming of Age', 24–5, and *KW*, 55–7.

8 The inscription that heads the score, 'Terrible as an army with banners', is taken from the Song of Solomon, 6:10; its exact significance here, beyond reinforcing the general connotations of saluting a dead hero suggested by the work's title, remains obscure.

9 Andrew Herbert discusses a broader influence of Tchaikovsky's Fourth Symphony on the genesis of the first movement of *A Sea Symphony*: see 'The Genesis of Vaughan Williams's *Sea Symphony*: A Study of the Preliminary Material', PhD thesis, University of Birmingham, 1998, vol. I, 83–4.

10 As Vaillancourt points out, early praise for Vaughan Williams centred on his orchestral compositions, rather than the vocal music which later commentators would emphasize – in large part, no doubt, because so many of the orchestral works were subsequently withdrawn. The composer himself emphasized orchestral compositions when asked for information on his works by the critic Edwin Evans in 1903: see letter to Evans written about June 1903, *LRVW*, 43–4.

11 Writing his brief 'Musical Autobiography' around 1950, the composer recalled that before beginning work on *A London Symphony*, he had 'sketched three movements of one symphony and the first movement of another, all now happily lost' ('Musical Autobiography', 37). No sketches corresponding to this description would appear to have survived; one nevertheless wonders if the composer, half a century later, was thinking of some of the projects discussed here that advanced rather further than sketches, even if they did not achieve a definitive form.

12 On the Bournemouth lectures see Chapter 11, 231 and 240. It seems likely that a trip to the area in 1898 with Adeline Vaughan Williams played a part in the inspiration for these works. In a letter to his cousin Ralph Wedgwood written in early June of that year Vaughan Williams describes in some detail his reactions to the New Forest landscapes, and his preference at this time for 'soft scenery to stern uncomfortable scenery' (see *LRVW*, 30–1). His later fascination with the Fens and with Salisbury Plain suggests that this view of landscape evolved, or at least broadened to include other possibilities.

13 The main theme of *The Solent* seems to have haunted Vaughan Williams, cropping up again in *A Sea Symphony* and in two compositions from the last decade of his life, the music for the film *The England of Elizabeth* (1955) and, more importantly, the second movement of the Ninth Symphony (1956–8): see Alain Frogley, *Vaughan Williams's Ninth Symphony*, Studies in Musical Genesis and Structure (Oxford University Press, 2001), 272; and Herbert, 'The Genesis of Vaughan Williams's *Sea Symphony*', I, 164–79.

14 See Elsie Payne, 'Vaughan Williams and Folk-Song: The Relation between Folk-Song and Other Elements in His Comprehensive Style', *The Music Review* 15/2 (1954), 103–26 at 112.

15 See Edwin Evans, 'Modern British Composers. X. Ralph Vaughan Williams', *MT* 61/927 (May 1920), 302–5 at 305. The three rhapsodies were never in fact performed together before the composer abandoned the symphonic scheme, but they were integrated thematically in certain respects, as is discussed below.

16 By the London Symphony Orchestra, conducted by Richard Hickox, on the Chandos label, CHAN 10001 [01], released in 2002. Pages 15–16 of the manuscript are missing; they were speculatively reconstructed for this recording by Stephen Hogger.

17 See *KC*, 35–6.

18 James Day notes the similarity (one that has likely struck many listeners) between the opening of the *Norfolk Rhapsody* No. 1 and the 'Dawn' interlude from Britten's *Peter Grimes*, which uses strikingly similar textural and timbral effects to portray the same East Anglian coastline. See James Day, *Vaughan Williams*, 3rd edn (Oxford University Press, 1998), 176. Day does not mention, however, the extraordinary parallel between the text of the folksong, which comprises the confession of a sea captain on trial for his fatal abuse of a young boy taken from the workhouse, and the

almost identical story of Peter Grimes (though the captain of the folksong has been wilfully brutal, whereas Grimes's crimes, and the line between neglect and deliberate cruelty, remain shrouded in some obscurity).

19 Ian Bates, 'Generalized Diatonic Modality and Ralph Vaughan Williams' Compositional Practice', PhD dissertation, Yale University, 2008, Chapter 3.2.

20 In 'Musical Autobiography', 35.

21 The recording was released as Vocalion A0249; it has been reissued most recently on the Dutton Laboratories label, CDBP 9790 [01], in 2009.

22 Letter dated 31 December 1911, *LRVW*, 84.

23 Nathaniel G. Lew, '"Words and Music that are Forever England": *The Pilgrim's Progress* and the Pitfalls of Nostalgia', *VWE*, 182.

24 See in particular Lionel Pike, 'Tallis – Vaughan Williams – Howells: Reflections on Mode Three', *Tempo* 148 (1984), 2–13; and Anthony Pople, 'Vaughan Williams, Tallis, and the Phantasy Principle', *VWS*, 47–80.

25 Allan W. Atlas, 'On the Structure and Proportions of Vaughan Williams's *Fantasia on a Theme by Thomas Tallis*', *Journal of the Royal Musical Association* 135/1 (2010), 115–44.

26 See Pople, 'Vaughan Williams, Tallis, and the Phantasy Principle'.

27 *Ibid.*, 48–50. Vaughan Williams wrote another fantasia in 1910, this time for full orchestra, that seems to have hewn more closely to Cobbett's formal prescriptions; unfortunately nothing survives of the work, and our knowledge of it is based primarily on reviews of its first and only performance. The *Fantasia on English Folk Song: Studies for an English Ballad Opera* was performed at the Proms on 1 September 1910; it seems likely to have been an offshoot of the composer's work on his opera *Hugh the Drover*, and was in a single movement with three sections, fast–slow–fast. Michael Kennedy suggests that it may have been reworked for military band in the early 1920s as the suite *English Folk Songs*, which would go on, arranged for various ensembles, to be one of the composer's most popular works: see *KC*, 57–8.

28 For primary information on this and other Whitman settings referred to here, including poetic text sources, see *KC*. For a more detailed chronology of work on *A Sea Symphony* see Chapter 2 of Herbert, 'The Genesis of Vaughan Williams's *Sea Symphony*'.

29 See Byron Adams, 'No Armpits, Please, We're British', in Lawrence Kramer (ed.), *Walt Whitman and Modern Music: War, Desire, and the Trials of Nationhood*, Border Crossings

vol. 10 (New York: Garland Publishing, 2000), 25–42; and Alain Frogley, '"O Farther Sail": Vaughan Williams and Whitman', in Julian Rushton (ed.), *Let Beauty Awake: Vaughan Williams, Elgar and Literature* (London: Elgar Editions, 2010), 77–95.

30 Nuanced arguments *pro* and *contra* the symphonic status of the work have been advanced recently by Julian Onderdonk, 'Vaughan Williams and the Austro-German Tradition: Tonal Pairing and Directional Tonality in *A Sea Symphony*', paper presented at the annual national meeting of the American Musicological Society, Columbus, Ohio, 2002; and Charles Edward McGuire, 'Vaughan Williams and the English Music Festival: 1910', *VWE*, 235–68. Onderdonk argues in particular that the first movement cleaves more closely to sonata form than has often been taken to be the case.

31 The opening juxtaposition of B♭ minor and D major triads (a harmonic polarity that is recalled at several junctures of the symphony) creates a complete hexatonic collection; hexatonic relationships would go on to play a broader role in *A London Symphony*.

32 See 'Musical Autobiography', 37; here Vaughan Williams also credits George Butterworth, to whom the work was eventually dedicated, with the idea for beginning work on a symphony at this time, which was probably early in 1911. It is impossible to date the progress of the symphony with any precision, but in a letter to Cecil Sharp apparently written in July 1911 the composer refers to being 'in the middle of a great work', and Hugh Cobbe is surely right in suggesting that this refers to *A London Symphony*: see *LRVW*, 81–2.

33 Letter of 30 September 1957: see *KW*, 139–40.

34 See Alain Frogley, 'H. G. Wells and Vaughan Williams's *A London Symphony*: Politics and Culture in Fin-de-Siècle England', in Chris A. Banks, Arthur Searle and Malcolm Turner (eds.), *Sundry Sorts of Music Books: Essays on the British Library Collections. Presented to O. W. Neighbour on His 70th Birthday* (London: British Library, 1993), 299–308.

35 See Stephen Lloyd, 'Vaughan Williams's *A London Symphony*: The Original Version and Early Performances and Recordings', in *VWIP*, 91–117. The original version can be reconstructed from manuscript sources in the British Library (Add. MSS 50317A–D); it was recorded in 2000 by the London Symphony Orchestra, conducted by Richard Hickox (Chandos 9902). The first movement was left virtually untouched in later revisions, but the

other three movements were extensively altered.

36 Surprising though it may seem, this symphony has a strong claim to be the most ambitious musical representation of a modern metropolis composed before World War I. Its closest counterparts in the orchestral arena are Delius's tone poem *Paris: The Song of a Great City* (1899), Elgar's overture *Cockaigne: In London Town* (1901), and Ives's 'contemplation' (as he called it) *Central Park in the Dark* (1906); yet while all three works constitute important precedents they are much more modest in scope, with the longest of them, the Delius, lasting only about twenty minutes.

37 *Cockaigne* was the most significant orchestral portrait of London to have appeared before Vaughan Williams's symphony. While critical reception has largely taken at face value the work's undoubted energy and swagger, Aidan J. Thomson has recently suggested that darker undercurrents may be heard: see 'Elgar and the City: Some New Lines on *Cockaigne*', *MQ* 95/4 (Winter 2012). Such an interpretation may also be considered alongside Elgar's plans, albeit never realized, for a much darker companion piece, based on James Thomson's notorious poem 'The City of Dreadful Night': see Jerrold Northrop Moore, *Elgar: A Creative Life* (Oxford University Press, 1984), 349. The more positive side of Vaughan Williams's own response to city life is suggested by the composer's landmark 1912 essay entitled 'Who Wants the English Composer?' (*Royal College of Music Magazine* 9/1 (1912), 11–15; reprinted in *VWOM*, 39–42), written while he was working on the symphony. Here Vaughan Williams exhorted his composer peers to embrace all the rich

musical and sonic diversity of modern English life; he opens with a quotation from Walt Whitman, and seems to share with the poet a willingness, unusual at the time, to see in urban social diversity signs of hope as well as threat. *A London Symphony* certainly celebrates this aspect of the city, even as it also evokes more destructive forces.

38 See Alain Frogley, 'Tonality on the Town: Orchestrating the Metropolis in Vaughan Williams's *A London Symphony*', in Philip Rupprecht, Ulrike Scheidele and Felix Woerner (eds.), *Tonality 1900–1950: Concept and Practice* (Stuttgart: Franz Steiner Verlag, 2012), 187–202.

39 Both the Scherzo and the finale were heavily cut in the post-premiere revisions; the Scherzo lost an entire second trio, whose troubled character survives only in the menacing coda of the original version, and the finale (a complex and unorthodox structure even in its final form) originally contained additional episodes.

40 The wartime origins were revealed to Ursula Vaughan Williams (at that time Ursula Wood) in 1938: see *UVWB*, 121. On the initial critical reception of the work see *KW*, 155–6.

41 See in particular Michael Vaillancourt, 'Modal and Thematic Coherence in Vaughan Williams's *Pastoral Symphony*', *The Music Review* 52 (1991), 203–17; and Daniel M. Grimley, 'Landscape and Distance: Vaughan Williams, Modernism and the Symphonic Pastoral', in Matthew Riley (ed.), *British Music and Modernism, 1895–1960* (Farnham: Ashgate, 2010), 147–74.

42 See Grimley, 'Landscape and Distance', 150–2.

43 *KW*, 155.

5 The songs and shorter secular choral works

SOPHIE FULLER

Vaughan Williams clearly had a profound relationship with the voice. In an article published in 1902 he wrote that the voice 'can be made the medium of the best and deepest human emotion'.[1] Nearly forty years later, in an article published during the Second World War, he reiterated his belief in the primacy of the voice: 'One thing, I think, we can be sure of, no bombs or blockades can rob us of our vocal chords; there will always remain for us the oldest and greatest of musical instruments, the human voice.'[2] This belief in the fundamental role that the voice plays in expressing emotion through music is something Vaughan Williams was to exemplify throughout his career. His vocal music touches on every genre imaginable, from opera through cantatas, motets, anthems and other sacred works, to unaccompanied part-songs and choral music on a broader scale; from arrangements of folksongs and hymns to solo song, whether as individual songs or as sets of songs or song-cycles accompanied by a range of instruments from piano alone through to orchestra. Even some of his works in orchestral genres give a prominent role to the human voice, from the fully choral first symphony, *A Sea Symphony* (1909), through *A Pastoral Symphony* (1924), in which a wordless solo for soprano voice opens and closes the finale, and *Flos Campi* for viola, orchestra and wordless chorus (1928), to the *Sinfonia Antartica* (1953), which incorporates a female chorus and soprano solo, both wordless.

Yet in the first edition of his study of Vaughan Williams, published in the Master Musicians series shortly after the composer's death, James Day makes the somewhat surprising assertion that 'Vaughan Williams was not a great song-writer', going on to write: 'His melodic gift was fertile and original, and his ability to set words aptly and simply was undoubted, but his songs rarely rise above competence, and only very few of them are complete, rounded, successful works of art.'[3] This seems a strange way to assess the work of the composer of such well-loved and enduring songs as 'Linden Lea' (1902)[4] and 'Silent Noon' (1904), or the song-cycles *Songs of Travel* (1905, 1907) and *On Wenlock Edge* (1911). But such an assessment is perhaps best understood in the context of a recurring attitude not only to Vaughan Williams's song-writing but to

British song in general. Although Vaughan Williams composed solo song – the main focus of this chapter – throughout his life, until quite recently there has been a recurring tendency in literature on the composer to skirt over his small-scale vocal music and concentrate instead on works written for larger, primarily instrumental forces. Even Michael Kennedy's painstaking and thorough account of Vaughan Williams's music and its contexts manifests this tendency: rather than highlighting the composer's love of the voice, for instance, Kennedy explains the prominence of song in his early career as a response to the comparative difficulties of getting new orchestral works performed for British composers of his generation.[5] With the exception of Stephen Banfield's *Sensibility and English Song* (1985), which pays detailed attention to Vaughan Williams's song-writing,[6] this aspect of the composer's achievement has had to wait until the last few years to receive its due. *Vaughan Williams Essays*, edited by Byron Adams and Robin Wells in 2003, includes detailed explorations of *Songs of Travel* and *Four Last Songs*,[7] while a symposium at the British Library in 2008 explored Elgar, Vaughan Williams and literature, and featured a number of contributions on Vaughan Williams's songs and other settings of literary texts.[8] The re-evaluation of his song-writing has also benefited enormously from the Ralph Vaughan Williams Society's issue of two important recordings: *Kissing Her Hair: Twenty Early Songs of Ralph Vaughan Williams* and *Where Hope Is Shining: Songs for Mixed Chorus*.[9]

Whatever the state of critical opinion over the years, however, the songs have remained among the most widely performed and recorded of Vaughan Williams's works. Several general themes permeate the critical literature: that his best-known songs are early works and therefore primarily valuable in pointing the way to the large-scale music of his maturity; that he constantly chose highbrow texts by canonical poets; and that he had a particular aptitude for word setting.[10] But were these last two attributes unusual among English songwriters of his or earlier generations? What were the contexts in which songs were produced, particularly in the early years of the twentieth century, the time when Vaughan Williams's vocal music started to be published and performed beyond an immediate circle of friends or teachers? More generally, was song-writing really a genre in which Vaughan Williams rarely rose above the competent or seldom achieved complete, rounded, or successful works of art? In this chapter I will explore some of the misunderstandings surrounding turn-of-the-century British song culture and a continuing disregard for this genre, aiming to reach a deeper understanding of the context in which Vaughan Williams produced his songs in all their glorious diversity.

English song and the marketplace: royalty ballad and art song *c.* 1900

In 1902 Vaughan Williams wrote to his cousin Ralph Wedgwood:

> I've not much to chronicle except that I've sold my soul to a publisher – that
> is to say that I've agreed not to sell songs to any publisher but him for 5 years.
> And he is going to publish several pot-boiling songs of mine – that is to say
> not real pot boilers – that is to say they are quite good – I'm not ashamed of
> them – as they are more or less simple and popular in character. They are to
> come out in a magazine called 'The Vocalist' and then to be published at
> 1/0 – which is a new departure – and I'm to get a penny halfpenny on each
> copy – so you see I'm on the high road to a fortune.[11]

Vaughan Williams's typically self-deprecating attitude towards this publishing deal belies what was in fact a strongly held belief in what he was doing and
the music he was creating. Yet he is defiantly unashamed – as he was to
remain throughout his career – of simplicity and popularity. The extract also
says a good deal about contemporary attitudes to song publishing. For
decades there had been considerable press coverage of what were seen as
the iniquities of the 'royalty ballad' system, whereby publishers paid singers a
royalty every time they performed a certain song.[12] At the turn of the century,
the issue was still current. In 1901 *The Times* reported on an address by Frank
Sawyer to the Incorporated Society of Musicians. Sawyer talked about song
publishers and singers, explaining that

> there were, unfortunately, comparatively few singers who were also true
> artists, and the present condition of the song publishing trade intensified
> the evil. A song publisher was purely a tradesman. He accepted the copyright
> of a song, not because it was good music, but because he thought it would
> hit the more or less vulgar taste of a general audience. Having published
> it, he hired singers like so many sandwich-men to go round the country
> crying his wares.[13]

Often royalties were paid not only to singers but also to composers, who if
they did not sell their song outright, received a royalty for each copy sold,
as in Vaughan Williams's deal with *The Vocalist*.[14] *The Vocalist* had been
launched in April 1902 and was aimed at 'all those who consider themselves in the category of singers, whether they be elementary or advanced,
amateur or professional' as well as those 'interested in musical art, and. . .
"fond of singing"'.[15] Readers were promised 'four good new songs' in each
issue.[16] The first issue included Vaughan Williams's 'Linden Lea', a setting
of words by William Barnes described as 'a Dorset folksong'. This was
Vaughan Williams's first published work and he was to contribute several
articles and songs to the early issues of the magazine.[17]

In the late nineteenth and early twentieth centuries, songs were a part of the programme in every type of public concert, as well as sung in every kind of home – either to family and friends around the ubiquitous piano or, in high-class circles, to invited audiences in lavish music-rooms. Publishers promoted their songs through Ballad Concerts, such as Boosey's popular series at St James's Hall, which had started in the 1860s. Study of surviving programmes shows that Ballad Concerts could in fact provide a wide range of vocal music, including songs by canonical composers such as Schubert or Schumann as well as an array of ballads.[18] Nevertheless, the attitude in the musical press towards both the Ballad Concerts and the 'royalty ballad' remained consistently critical. Vaughan Williams joined in the criticism in his 'Sermon to Vocalists', published by *The Vocalist* in 1902. In this article he addresses amateur vocalists and implores them to use their intelligence when selecting songs, and to choose the sincere rather than the false. He describes the royalty ballad as possessing 'neither melody nor rhythm', and asks singers whether they really imagine that it is 'so called because it is patronized by Royalty?'[19]

What other songs were being published and heard in London's concert halls at the beginning of the twentieth century? Although by the turn of the century Vaughan Williams's teachers Charles Villiers Stanford (1852–1924) and Hubert Parry (1848–1918) were involved primarily with high-profile operatic, orchestral and choral works, they continued to publish songs. Stanford's *An Irish Idyll in Six Miniatures*, Op. 77, a collection of songs setting poetry by Moira O'Neill, appeared in 1901; and in 1902 Novello published the fifth set of Parry's *English Lyrics*, settings of various British authors, including Shakespeare, Scott and Julian Sturgis.[20] Another leading figure was Arthur Somervell (1863–1937), who, like Vaughan Williams, had studied at Cambridge and the Royal College of Music with Parry and Stanford. On 7 March 1901, at St James's Hall, he gave a concert of his own music that included the popular *Cycle of Songs from Maud* (Alfred, Lord Tennyson) and *Love in Spring Time*, which might aptly be termed an anthology, setting as it does poems by Tennyson, Dante Gabriel Rossetti and Charles Kingsley.[21]

Other composers active at this time were primarily songwriters. One of the best known today is Roger Quilter (1877–1953), remembered for his Tennyson setting 'Now Sleeps the Crimson Petal' (1904) and his many settings of sixteenth- and seventeenth-century English poets. In the summer of 1901 Quilter returned from studies in Frankfurt to accompany a performance of his *Four Songs of the Sea* (to his own words), at the Crystal Palace. This work was also published, as his Op. 1, in the same year. Quilter was a good friend of one of the most popular songwriters of the 1890s, Maude Valérie White (1855–1937). At the start of the century

White had moved to Taormina in Sicily, largely for the sake of her health, but returned regularly to England to organize concerts of her songs. On 20 May 1903, for example, she gave a concert of her 'tasteful and well-written songs' at St James's Hall.[22] The selection of songs, typical of White's diversity, included settings of German, French and English lyrics as well as arrangements of Sicilian tunes. The British poets represented included Burns, Swinburne, Herrick, Shelley and both the Brownings. White's friend Liza Lehmann (1862–1918) was another important songwriter of the time. Her song-cycle for four voices and piano, *In a Persian Garden* (1896), which sets parts of Omar Khayyám's *Rubáiyát*, in the then fashionable translation by Edward FitzGerald, remained popular far into the twentieth century. On 4 January 1902 it was performed at one of the 'Popular Concerts' at St James's Hall, a series that, despite its name, showcased the 'highbrow' end of the song spectrum.[23] Lehmann's songs, like those of White, were also heard at the lighter Ballad Concerts, and she herself clearly divided her compositions into ambitious or serious work, such as her Tennyson cycle *In Memoriam* (1899), and lighter, more popular and financially rewarding pieces.

The changing reception of Lehmann, White and their music highlights the difficulties of clearly defining the difference between the royalty or drawing-room ballad and the 'art song'.[24] Both these songwriters heard their work performed at a wide range of public and private venues. In their early careers both were regarded as raising the level of the English song and, particularly in the case of White, choosing a better class of lyric to set.[25] In 1903 Edwin Evans published an article on Lehmann in his series 'Modern British Music' for *The Musical Standard*, which showcased composers 'who actually are modern, breathe the modern spirit and write modern music'[26] (Vaughan Williams was featured in another article in the series). In these articles, Evans had decided 'to avoid the vortex of the English song world' but made an exception for Lehmann, feeling that there were several reasons, such as her introduction of the song-cycle, for writing about her 'apart from the artistic excellence of her work'.[27] Nevertheless, later in their careers both White and Lehmann came to be regarded only as ballad composers, and after their deaths their contribution to British song was almost entirely overlooked and forgotten. The reasons behind this neglect are complex; the fact that they were both women, and therefore not expected to be capable of producing 'great' music, undoubtedly played a significant part. But just as important is the fact that they were primarily songwriters, concentrating on a genre so consistently regarded as insignificant. The two issues of gender and genre are of course not unrelated: the prominence and success of female songwriters at the turn of the century undoubtedly contributed to the later downgrading of British song as a genre, despite the indisputable power and beauty of songs by composers as diverse as Parry, Quilter, White and Vaughan Williams.

The early songs: from Herrick to Housman

It is worth highlighting that Vaughan Williams was nearly 30 years old when 'Linden Lea' appeared in *The Vocalist* and he first stepped into this world of song production. 'Linden Lea' was, of course, not the first song he had written: there are several songs surviving in manuscript or published later that pre-date what was to become his best-selling song.[28] But what do we know about his experience of song in his first three decades? The answer is surprisingly little. Both Ursula Vaughan Williams's biography of the composer and Vaughan Williams's own brief 'Musical Autobiography' are curiously reticent about his early exposure to song.[29] Unfortunately, very few letters to or from Vaughan Williams survive from before the late 1890s, and even then they tend to be unforthcoming about his musical life and experiences.[30]

As a child at Leith Hill Place, Vaughan Williams learned the piano and harmony from his mother's sister, Sophy, who taught him theory from *The Child's Introduction to Thorough Bass in conversations of a Fortnight, between a Mother and her Daughter of Ten Years Old*, published in 1819.[31] When Ursula Vaughan Williams mentions this book, she gives only the first six words of the title, omitting the interesting fact that it was clearly aimed at educating female children. Neither Ursula nor Vaughan Williams himself mention singing as part of the family music-making, other than hymns on Sundays.[32] Vaughan Williams's childhood compositions included operas for his toy theatre, and it seems unlikely that he would have engaged in this genre with no experience of vocal music other than hymns. It is also unlikely that a family clearly interested in music would not have owned and enjoyed songs. Ursula Vaughan Williams records that the family went to the Three Choirs Festivals,[33] and here they would certainly have heard songs as well as orchestral and choral works.

At the age of seven Vaughan Williams started learning the violin, and he continued to be involved in music at both his preparatory school and then at Charterhouse, a fairly progressive school as far as teaching music to its male pupils was concerned. In his account of his childhood and schooldays Vaughan Williams emphasizes his exposure to canonical keyboard and chamber music, which included playing piano-duet arrangements of music by Handel, Haydn, Mozart and Schubert with his brother and sister. In his preference for the violin over the piano, he was, of course, moving away from the dangerously female world of piano-playing, an association reinforced by his first textbook and the largely female household in which he grew up. He does recall, however, that he had also been exposed to a more popular, less highbrow kind of music. Remembering an early composition for piano trio, he writes that he 'must have got the theme from one of the French or Belgian imitators of Franck whose salon music was popular in those days'.[34] We can only guess, but it seems likely that he would have heard this popular salon music in the homes of his music-loving relatives, alongside songs by composers such as Lehmann or White. Vaughan Williams was in his late seventies when he recorded these reminiscences, and it is only to be expected that he would have a selective memory of the musical experiences of his youth, ignoring the kind of music that had fallen so far from acceptance in the post-1945 musical world. But it is important not to overlook what must have been a significant aspect of Vaughan Williams's early musical experience. It seems unlikely that the composer of his earliest surviving songs, such as the Herrick setting 'To Daffodils' (1895) or the Tennyson setting 'Claribel' (*c.* 1896), was not aware of White's Herrick or Tennyson settings, not just for her choice of poets but also for her compelling, drawn-out melodies, finely judged sense of rhythmic propulsion, and subtly independent piano accompaniments that often avoid expected cadences or harmonies.

The songs through which Vaughan Williams first reached a wider audience included those published in *The Vocalist* between 1902 and 1905, his two Dante Gabriel Rossetti song-cycles, *The House of Life* (1904) and *Willow-Wood* (1909) and the *Songs of Travel*, in which he set poems from the collection of the same name by Robert Louis Stevenson.[35] The *Vocalist* songs were two Christina Rossetti settings ('If I Were a Queen' and 'Boy Johnny'); two Tennyson settings ('Tears, Idle Tears' and 'The Splendour Falls'); 'A Cradle Song' to a lyric by Coleridge; a setting of Robert Louis Stevenson's poem 'Whither Must I Wander?';[36] three settings of lyrics by William Barnes; and two arrangements of German folksongs.

The Barnes settings and German arrangements were written before Vaughan Williams had started collecting folksongs himself, and they represent a long-standing British and German tradition of folk-like settings and arrangements of folksongs from a variety of different cultures and countries.[37] Vaughan Williams's Tennyson settings reflect some of the approaches taken by other composers when choosing lyrics by this much-set poet. 'Tears, Idle Tears' (1903) is a sombre and substantial work that stands out among Vaughan Williams's early songs for its length. The weighty piano opening, and indeed the overall atmosphere and low tessitura of the song, recall Liza Lehmann's Tennyson cycle *In*

Memoriam.[38] Vaughan Williams turned to Christina Rossetti for several early songs for solo voice – the mournful 'When I Am Dead, My Dearest' (1903), for example – as well as in works for multiple voices, including 'Sound Sleep' (SSA, 1903) and 'Rest' (SSATB unaccompanied, *c.* 1904–5).

Vaughan Williams's ambitious song-cycles setting sonnets by Dante Gabriel Rossetti deserve to be better known. *Willow-Wood* was first performed in 1903 in a version for baritone and piano; an orchestral version was also made, and in 1909 the composer added a wordless female chorus, but following the first performance of the revised version he seems to have withdrawn the cycle. *The House of Life* appeared in 1904; one song from the cycle, 'Silent Noon', was performed and published before the rest, and went on to become a recital staple. The popularity of this evocative setting has not, unfortunately, led many singers to perform the cycle in its entirety. Michael Kennedy suggests that Vaughan Williams's interest in Pre-Raphaelite poetry was inspired by the example of Claude Debussy, who in 1887–8 had set Dante Gabriel Rossetti's poem 'The Blessed Damozel', as *La Damoiselle Elue.*[39] But there was a group of composers closer to home, and to Vaughan Williams's age, who were also drawn to such poetry. These were the men who came to be known as 'the Frankfurt group', because they had all spent time studying in that city: Norman O'Neill (1875–1934), H. Balfour Gardiner (1877–1950), Cyril Scott (1879–1970), Percy Grainger (1882–1961) and Quilter. Grainger felt that what set the group apart from other British composers was 'an excessive emotionality (& particularly a tragic or sentimental or wistful or pathetic emotionality)' and claimed: 'Perhaps it might be true to say we were all of us PRERAFAELITE [*sic*] composers'.[40] Yet while the Frankfurt group may have helped spur Vaughan Williams's interest in Rossetti, he took a very different approach: in *The House of Life* he expressed not an intense or excessive degree of emotion, but a measured and contemplative depiction of emotion that was perhaps closer in spirit and a certain ideal of beauty to the work of the Pre-Raphaelite brotherhood, as well as to the approach of earlier British songwriters. Some songs of the cycle, for example 'Heart's Haven', clearly echo the expressive expansiveness and harmonic colourings of White's song-writing. It is possibly this association with Victorian song-writing that has discouraged later singers from performing the whole cycle.

An unashamed sense of beauty can also be found in *Songs of Travel*, a song-cycle with a complex performance and publication history. The first eight songs of what is now regarded as the complete cycle were performed at Bechstein Hall on 2 December 1904. But Vaughan Williams's publishers in this case, Boosey, clearly did not feel that the complete cycle was commercially viable and insisted on publishing it instead as two collections, with songs 1, 3 and 8 as Book I (1905), and songs 2, 4, 5 and 6 as Book II (1907). The seventh song, 'Whither Must I Wander?', had been published earlier, in *The Vocalist* of 1902. The ninth and final song, thematically related to others in the cycle, was discovered posthumously.[41]

Songs of Travel, both Stevenson's poems and Vaughan Williams's songs, are usually taken as representing a particularly masculine breath of fresh air in their depiction of love in relation to the outdoor life of a wanderer. This quality is clearly a relief to commentators trying to find an escape from what they see as the hothouse femininity of a work such as *The House of Life*.[42] Kennedy, for example, writes of Stevenson's 'virile open-air verses', while Banfield describes the work as 'fertile in its Romantic wayfaring images'.[43] The first performance was sung by Walter Creighton and the cycle was taken up by Harry Plunket Greene, but it is perhaps surprising to note that other early performances were given by women. The cycle was, for example, sung 'very charmingly' by Norah Dawney at the opening concert of the 1905 Hovingham Music Festival,[44] and four years later the well-known Australian contralto Ada Crossley included 'The Roadside Fire' in a recital at Bechstein Hall.[45]

Like most songwriters Vaughan Williams relied on particular performers to promote his songs. In these early years, the bass-baritone Jack Francis Harford (1867–1948) and baritone James Campbell McInnes (1874–1945) gave important performances of Vaughan Williams's songs; neither was particularly well known, but both built reputations for promoting the work of young English composers. Harford gave the first performance of 'Tears, Idle Tears', which was dedicated to him, at St James's Hall in 1903, and sang Vaughan Williams's two arrangements of fifteenth-century French songs, 'Jean Renaud' and 'L'amour de moy', at the same hall in 1905.[46] In the early years of his career he was compared to Harry Plunket Greene, a singer who was also to become associated with Vaughan Williams's songs.[47] McInnes made his London debut in 1899.[48] 'Boy Johnny' (1902) was dedicated to him (although the first London performance was given by Harford), and McInnes gave the first performance of *Willow-Wood* in 1903. Both men were studying at the Royal College of Music when Vaughan Williams returned there in 1895, and their association with the composer may have started at that time. Much better known was the tenor Gervase Elwes (1866–1921), the other singer who regularly performed Vaughan Williams's early songs. Elwes is particularly associated with the song-cycle *On Wenlock Edge*, giving the first performance, with the Schwiller string quartet and pianist Frederick Kiddle, at Aeolian Hall on 15 November 1909. Elwes's wife recalled that 'Gervase was delighted at being asked . . . to give the first performance of the song-cycle, in which he discovered rare beauties'.[49]

Written after orchestration lessons with Ravel in Paris and famously described by the composer himself as 'a song cycle with several atmospheric effects', *On Wenlock Edge*, a setting of six poems from A. E. Housman's popular collection *A Shropshire Lad*, demonstrates a move away from the song world of Parry or White. The cycle has attracted attention from critics ever since its first performance. Edwin Evans and Ernest Newman had a notorious disagreement about it in the pages of *The Musical Times* in 1918. Evans felt that Vaughan Williams had realized 'the inner qualities of the poems' and summed up his achievement by saying:

> The musical sentiment of 'On Wenlock Edge' is as sincere and as unsophisticated as that of the poems themselves. Nowhere is it marred by the self-indulgence of excess, and nowhere does it show signs of being studied or self-conscious. It is fresh and spontaneous and therefore convincing. . . It expresses, as it were, in the colouring of his own climate, the clean faith of the healthy young Englishman.[50]

Newman retaliated by saying of Vaughan Williams's settings that 'they do not mate happily with the prosody of the poems', pointing to the importance of rhythm in this respect and claiming: 'We shall not get our great English song-writer until we get some one who can take up the rhythm of a poem into his music without distorting or mutilating it.'[51] He goes on to accuse Vaughan Williams of Wagnerian word-painting rather than conveying the sentiment at the heart of the poems, and in the song 'Bredon Hill' finds 'another of Dr. Vaughan Williams's disastrous attempts to imitate folk-song'. Later writers have been more inclined to agree with Evans, and in this work Vaughan Williams clearly found a distinctive and compelling voice.

It is curious that Vaughan Williams does not seem to have been associated with the upper-class music-making that played such an important role in the lives and careers of other British composers, such as Elgar, Grainger, Lehmann, Parry, Quilter or White.[52] It is perhaps not surprising that this is passed over by Michael Kennedy and Ursula Vaughan Williams, who were writing in the 1960s when biographers tended to stress the professionalism of musicians and to distance them from the tainted world of the Victorian and Edwardian drawing-room and salon culture, by then perceived as frivolous and unimportant. But there is very little mention of Vaughan Williams's participation in private musical worlds in his own letters or in the diaries, letters, or memoirs of others. He does not seem to have been involved in the private concerts or music-making of patrons and music-lovers such as Muriel Draper, Lady de Grey, Frank Schuster, or Edgar and Leonora Speyer, although both his class and his ability to play the viola would have made him very welcome at such gatherings, which in turn would have provided a significant venue for his music and a space in which to meet other composers and musicians.

Vaughan Williams did take part in musical gatherings at the Westminster home of his friend Lucy Broadwood (1858–1929), with whom he was, of course, also connected through their shared interest in folksong.[53] Another circle of private music-making with which he is known to have been involved is represented by parties held in Percy Grainger's rooms, at which Grainger's friends would try out part-songs,[54] and the musical 'jamborees' instigated by Gervase Elwes's brother-in law Everard Feilding, and held at the Elweses' Mayfair house in the winter of 1904.[55] Other participants at the 'jamborees' included Balfour Gardiner,[56] Grainger, W. Y. Hurlstone, Poldowski (Lady Dean Paul), Quilter and Scott, as well as Vaughan Williams's cousin Diana Montgomery-Massingberd and her sister-in-law Margaret Massingberd.

The Massingberds provided Vaughan Williams with other significant musical connections and opportunities. Diana was a member of the Magpie Madrigal Society, an amateur choir, organized by Lionel Benson, whose members included many prominent music-loving members of the upper classes. At one point Parry was its president.[57] The society sang contemporary music as well as English madrigals from the sixteenth and seventeenth centuries, and in 1902, at St James's Hall, gave the first performance of Vaughan Williams's Christina Rossetti setting, 'Rest', for unaccompanied voices in five parts. His lively madrigal 'Ring Out Your Bells' was also dedicated to the society, who doubtless sang it at one of their private gatherings.[58] Margaret Massingberd, married to a cousin of Vaughan Williams, was one of three musical sisters immortalized in the painting *The Home Quartet (Mrs. Vernon Lushington and Her Children)* (1882–3) by the Pre-Raphaelite artist Arthur Hughes. She ran the East Lincolnshire Musical Festival at Spilsby, near the Massingberd family home, Gunby Hall. Both McInnes and Elwes took part in the 1901 festival,[59] and Vaughan Williams wrote his Christina Rossetti setting 'Sound Sleep', a trio for female voices, as a test piece for the 1903 festival.[60]

Choral works and later songs

In general, much more is known about Vaughan Williams's involvement with choirs and choral singing than is known about his exposure to solo-song culture. Particularly at the start of his career, he was constantly involved in organizing and conducting choirs, many of which would have tried out and performed his choral works. As a student at Cambridge in the 1890s he conducted a small choral society, and in his first job, as organist at St Barnabas Church in South London from 1895, he was responsible for training the choir, and also founded a small choral society.[61] When the Leith Hill Festival was founded in 1905 by his sister Meggie and Lady Farrer, they turned to Vaughan Williams to conduct the Festival choirs, and during the First World War he formed a choir from the ranks of his fellow soldiers. From 1903 he had been a member of the Bach Choir, and in 1921 he became its conductor, having previously directed both the Palestrina Society (from 1912) and the Handel Society (from 1919).

Vaughan Williams's close connection to a variety of choral groups is reflected in the assurance of his part-songs and other choral music. Even a comparatively early work such as 'Rest' (1902) demonstrates his aware-ness of effective a cappella writing. The sense of concord and comradeship represented by a choir, whether of well-to-do Londoners or Lincolnshire villagers, was to have a lasting impact on Vaughan Williams's attitudes to the value of music-making. And this perhaps explains his avoidance of the 'At Home' aristocratic music culture. Like his close friend Gustav Holst, Vaughan Williams was a lifelong political radical, embracing socialist ideals from an early age. He may not have played the viola at high-society concerts, but he was happy to play at the Passmore Edwards Settlement, where Holst was musical director from 1904.[62] The Settlement, established in Bloomsbury by the novelist and campaigner Mary Ward, promoted 'equalisation in society' by offering opportunities for local people to learn skills and enjoy a variety of entertainment.[63]

Vaughan Williams's drive to write music for the voice had been firmly established by the end of the first decade of the twentieth century, and he continued to explore a variety of approaches to vocal writing in the years that followed. The rethinking of traditional accompaniment for song found in *On Wenlock Edge*, in which a string quartet is added to the standard pairing of voice and piano, was continued in works such as the *Four Hymns* (1920) for tenor, piano and viola, and the strikingly effective *Along the Field* (1927),[64] eight Housman settings for voice and violin. In 1940 he would write: 'Why should the voice always be accompanied by the pianoforte? There seem to me great possibilities in voices and instruments in combination.'[65]

Four Hymns was dedicated to and first performed by tenor Steuart Wilson, who was to become the principal exponent of Vaughan Williams's songs after the tragic early death of Gervase Elwes in 1921.[66] In 1925, for example, Wilson gave an all-Vaughan Williams recital at Aeolian Hall which included *On Wenlock Edge, Four Hymns, Merciless Beauty* (a 1922 setting of three Chaucer roundels for voice and string trio or piano), and several brand new works: *Three Poems by Walt Whitman, Three Songs from Shakespeare* and *Four Poems by Fredegond Shove*. The reviewer for *The Musical Times* was not impressed with the Whitman settings but found the Shakespeare songs 'admirable', and remarked that the Chaucer settings 'are surely among the best of modern English songs'.[67] Much has been written about Vaughan Williams's engagement with Whitman, realized most ambitiously in *A Sea Symphony*. Byron Adams has perceptively written of 'Vaughan Williams's search for a masculine but visionary poet [landing] him, metaphorically speaking, in the arms of Walt Whitman'.[68] But this 1925 collection of three songs is often overlooked by both critics and singers. 'Nocturne' is a sombre and poignant setting of the poem 'Whispers of Heavenly Death', underpinned by an ominous and relentless ground in the piano. A solemn equilibrium seems to be reached in the second song, 'A Clear Midnight', while the final song, 'Joy, Shipmate, Joy', is a reflection of a still sober and perhaps somewhat contemplative joy.

After several decades during which most of Vaughan Williams's work with the voice was on a larger scale (in opera, for example), he returned to solo song in the 1950s, most notably with the *Ten Blake Songs* (1958) for voice and oboe – perhaps the composer's most radical rethinking of song accompaniment – and the posthumously published *Four Last Songs* (1960), which set the poetry of his second wife, Ursula Vaughan Williams.

To claim that Vaughan Williams was not a 'great songwriter', as Day did in 1961, begs the question – what exactly is meant by the term 'great songwriter'? The history of British song, and the place of a variety of song genres within different musical cultures in the decades around 1900, is extremely rich, but also complex, and frequently misunderstood or misremembered, bound up as it is with a historical distrust of a feminized genre associated with feminized musical space. But Vaughan Williams certainly has a central place in the world of British song. He was a persistent and important songwriter who followed in the footsteps of composers who had gone before him and then, through the slow but determined maturing of a powerfully individual musical language, brought together his love of voice, and what it represented for him in terms of the human spirit, with a relentless belief in simple beauty, creating works of a profound and enduring impact.

Notes

1 Ralph Vaughan Williams, 'A Sermon to Vocalists', *The Vocalist* 1/8 (November 1902), 227–9, in *VWOM*, 28.
2 'The Composer in Wartime' (1940), in Ralph Vaughan Williams and Gustav Holst, *Heirs and Rebels: Letters Written to Each Other and Occasional Writings on Music* (London: Oxford University Press, 1959), 91.
3 James Day, *Vaughan Williams*, The Master Musicians Series, 1st edn (London: J. M. Dent, 1961), 87.

4 Dates of Vaughan Williams's works given are those of publication, as in *KC*.

5 *KW*, 62.

6 Stephen Banfield, *Sensibility and English Song* (Cambridge University Press, 1985).

7 Rufus Hallmark, 'Robert Louis Stevenson, Ralph Vaughan Williams and Their *Songs of Travel*', in *VWE*, 129–56; and Renée Chérie Clark, 'A Critical Appraisal of the *Four Last Songs*', in *VWE*, 157–74.

8 The proceedings of the symposium were published as Julian Rushton (ed.), *Let Beauty Awake: Elgar, Vaughan Williams and Literature* (London: Elgar Editions, 2010).

9 *Kissing Her Hair: Twenty Early Songs of Ralph Vaughan Williams*, Sarah Fox, Andrew Staples and Roderick Williams with Iain Burnside (Albion Records ALBCD002, 2007); *Where Hope Is Shining: Songs for Mixed Chorus*, the Joyful Company of Singers, conducted by Peter Broadbent (Albion Records ALBCD006, 2008).

10 See, for example, *KW*, 77–8.

11 *LRVW*, 41.

12 See, for example, the lengthy diatribe by an unsigned writer in 'Miscellaneous Intelligence', *MT* 13 (June 1867), 71–2.

13 Unsigned, 'The Incorporated Society of Musicians', *The Times*, 3 January 1901, 9.

14 See, for example, the records kept by Frances Allitsen in the 1880s and 90s: 'Book for entering Musical and Literary agreements', British Library Add. MS 50071.

15 Unsigned, 'From the Editor', *The Vocalist* 1/1 (April 1902), 2.

16 The songs were chosen by a committee who were asked to note '1) that the music is distinctly good i.e. neither trashy nor common-place; 2) that the melodic interest of the voice part shall be such as may appeal to any singer of average ability; 3) that the accompaniment is not too difficult; 4) and that the words are free from sentimental rubbish.' *Ibid*.

17 'Linden Lea' was also issued that year in the 'Vocalist Series of Songs and Ballads No. 2'.

18 See, for example, the programme of the 8th concert of the 31st season of Boosey's London Ballad Concerts, 3 February 1897, at Queen's Hall, in which most of the songs in the first half of the concert were by Schubert (British Library Add. MS d488b).

19 'A Sermon to Vocalists' (1902), in *VWOM*, 28–9.

20 Several of these songs had been written considerably earlier: 'Crabbed Age and Youth', for example, was composed in 1882.

21 Unsigned, 'Mr. Arthur Somervell's Concert', *MT* 42 (1 April 1901), 247.

22 *The Athenaeum* (23 May 1903), 67.

23 *The Times*, 6 January 1902, 7.

24 On the hazy boundary between 'ballad' and 'art song' see also 'The Condition of English Song in 1900', in Banfield, *Sensibility and English Song*, 1–14.

25 See, for example, unsigned, *The Musical Review* (3 March 1883), 142; *The Times*, 23 February 1883, 10; or *MT* (March 1883), 136.

26 Edwin Evans, 'Modern British Composers I', *MSt* 64/2025 (23 May 1903), 321.

27 Edwin Evans, 'Modern British Composers xI', *MSt* 65/2046 (17 October 1903), 242.

28 *KW*, 51.

29 Ralph Vaughan Williams, 'Musical Autobiography', in Hubert Foss, *Ralph Vaughan Williams: A Study* (London: George G. Harrap, 1950), 18–38.

30 See *LRVW*, 8.

31 Vaughan Williams, 'Musical Autobiography', 18.

32 *UVWB*, 19.

33 *UVWB*, 21.

34 Vaughan Williams, 'Musical Autobiography', 21.

35 Although published five years later, *Willow-Wood* was written at the same time as *House of Life*. It was first performed in 1903. *KC*, 17.

36 Later published as one of the *Songs of Travel*.

37 See for example Maude Valérie White's 'Prayer for Mary' (Robert Burns), 'Adapted to a Livonian Volkslied and arranged' (Stanley, Lucas Weber & Co., 1886), or 6 *Volkslieder* (Robert Cocks, 1893).

38 Liza Lehmann, *In Memoriam* for baritone or mezzo-soprano and piano (J. Church, 1899).

39 *KW*, 78.

40 Quoted in Stephen Lloyd, *H. Balfour Gardiner* (Cambridge University Press, 1984), 16.

41 See *KC*, 25–7 and Hallmark, 'Robert Louis Stevenson, Ralph Vaughan Williams and Their *Songs of Travel*' in *VWE*, 129–56.

42 In this respect Stevenson is closer than Rossetti to the composer's main literary preoccupation of the period, the poetry of Walt Whitman, which first took compositional form when he began work on *A Sea Symphony* in 1903. For now Whitman inspired Vaughan Williams to think primarily on an orchestral scale: it was not until the 1920s that he set any texts by the American as solo songs with piano accompaniment. Two Whitman settings from 1904, for soprano, baritone, violin, piano and

(optional) string quartet, were performed but
then withdrawn. On the composer's
unpublished Whitman settings, see Alain
Frogley, '"O Farther Sail": Vaughan Williams
and Whitman', in Rushton (ed.), *Let Beauty
Awake*, 77–95; for more on the preoccupation
of early twentieth-century British composers
with setting masculine verse, see Byron Adams,
'"No Armpits, Please, We're British":
Whitman and English Music', in
Lawrence Kramer (ed.), *Walt Whitman and
Modern Music: War, Desire, and the Trials of
Nationhood* (New York and London: Garland,
2000), 25–42.
43 Banfield, *Sensibility and English Song*, 83.
44 *The Times*, 22 October 1905, 3. The Hon.
Norah Dawney (1874–1947), who performed
throughout the United Kingdom, had been a
student at the Royal College of Music in the
late 1890s. It is not clear whether she sang the
entire cycle: the reviewer simply refers to *Songs
of Travel*.
45 Unsigned, 'Mme Ada Crossley's Recital',
The Times, 20 October 1909, 13. In the 'English
section' of her recital, as well as 'Roadside Fire',
Crossley (1874–1929) also sang songs by
Lehmann and Quilter.
46 *KC*, 16–17 and 21.
47 See, for example, Harford's advertisement
in *MT* 38 (October 1897), 653.
48 On McInnes, see Margot Strickland, *Angela
Thirkell: Portrait of a Lady Novelist* (London:
Duckworth, 1977), 22–39.
49 *KC*, 43; Winifried and Richard Elwes,
Gervase Elwes: His Life Story (London:
Grayson & Grayson, 1935), 195–7. Elwes also
gave the first performance of 'Dreamland'
(Christina Rossetti) in 1905. *KC*, 29.
50 Edwin Evans, 'English Song and "On
Wenlock Edge"', *MT* 59 (June 1918), 247, 248.
51 Ernest Newman, 'Concerning "A
Shropshire Lad" and Other Matters', *MT* 59
(September 1918), 394.
52 See, for example, Sophie Fuller, 'Elgar and
the Salons: The Significance of a Private
Musical World', in Byron Adams (ed.), *Edward
Elgar and His World* (Princeton University
Press, 2007), 223–47.
53 See 'Lucy E Broadwood: Diaries and
Notebooks, 1882–1929', http://www.

exploringsurreyspast.org.uk/GetRecord/
SHCOL_6782 (accessed 7 October 2012).
54 John Bird, *Percy Grainger* (London: Elek
Books, 1976), 99. Bird describes Vaughan
Williams as making 'rare appearances'.
55 Elwes and Elwes, *Gervase Elwes*, 156–7.
Elwes and Grainger were also involved in
collecting folksong.
56 Balfour Gardiner programmed Vaughan
Williams's music at the important concerts he
organized in 1912 and 1913. Recalling these
events, however, Cyril Scott remarked that 'it
was strange that Vaughan Williams was never
of the number'. Quoted in Lloyd, *H. Balfour
Gardiner*, 86.
57 Percy Scholes, *The Mirror of Music
1844–1944*, vol. i (London: Novello and
Oxford University Press, 1947), 52. See also
British Library Add. MSS g.1760 and g.1760.a.
58 No record of a public performance has
survived. *KC*, 15.
59 Elwes and Elwes, *Gervase Elwes*, 111.
60 *KC*, 18.
61 Vaughan Williams, 'A Musical
Autobiography', 143 and 146.
62 Imogen Holst, *Gustav Holst: A Biography*,
2nd edn (London: Oxford University Press,
1969), 25.
63 See 'Mary Ward Centre', www.
marywardcentre.ac.uk/Welcome/Welcome.
asp (accessed 7 October 2012).
64 Although not published until 1954, these
songs were first performed in 1927. *KC*,
116–17.
65 'The Composer in Wartime' (1940) in
Vaughan Williams and Holst, *Heirs and
Rebels*, 92.
66 The *Four Hymns* were written in 1914 but
not published or publicly performed until after
the First World War. *KC*, 74.
67 Unsigned, 'London Concerts', *MT* 66 (1
May 1925), 448. In this review the Whitman
settings were called 'Three Whitman Songs (on
a Ground)', not the title under which they were
eventually published. *KC* does not indicate that
the Whitman settings were sung at this
concert.
68 Adams, '"No Armpits, Please, We're
British"', 33. See also Frogley, '"O Farther Sail",
77–95.

6 'An Englishman and a democrat': Vaughan Williams, large choral works, and the British festival tradition

CHARLES EDWARD McGUIRE

Large choral works were a major part of the repertoire for a musician of Vaughan Williams's generation. He began composing at the peak of the British love of the oratorio and musical festivals, and though Great Britain's infrastructure – if not its enthusiasm – for choral music diminished in the decades after the First World War, Vaughan Williams continued to compose ambitious works for chorus and orchestra throughout his career. His experience with choral music was varied and fluid. It included major narrative works for, or performed at, the major musical festivals; smaller compositions written for competition festivals, and conducting and adjudicating at such events; and sacred and secular compositions taken up by many choral societies, church choirs, school organizations and the like. Such experience brought Vaughan Williams his first major professional opportunities, in which he honed the crafts of composition and conducting, and gave him great solace in the closing years of his life. In the course of this chapter, we will locate the large-scale choral music of Vaughan Williams within this wider context.

When Vaughan Williams was a student, his teacher, Hubert Parry, gave him a famous charge: 'Write choral music as befits an Englishman and a democrat.'[1] Within the works studied in this chapter, Vaughan Williams did precisely this. His democratic beliefs led him to compose music that was at once didactic (introducing singers and audiences to folk traditions and techniques from older English church and concert music) and progressive (through his use of advanced harmony and dissonance control), while still maintaining a style that was both accessible and palatable to the amateur singer. For music that 'befits an Englishman', Vaughan Williams sometimes challenged the status quo of Victorian festival genres such as oratorio and cantata, but he also composed music that quickly became just as important to the festivals, including pieces that served double duty as both festival works and music appropriate for Anglican rite and ritual. Even so, Vaughan Williams was not content to let his own music alone fulfil Parry's charge. As a public musician, and an increasingly eminent one, Vaughan Williams took an active role in promoting what he considered to be 'good' music of all kinds to the British people. This he did through his conducting and steward-ship of the Leith Hill Musical Competition. Even when his own composi-tions were not cast in the traditional genres of the cantata and the oratorio, he promoted such works by other composers to the amateur choirs vouch-safed to him.

The discussion that follows is divided into three parts, based on Vaughan Williams's own experience with larger choral works and festivals. The first part addresses Vaughan Williams's initial engagement, as a young and learning composer, with the middle-class choral infrastructure he inherited (1906–14). The second traces his consolidation of both style and fame within the remnants of the structure that existed after the First World War, noting his progression from a composer who occasionally contributed to the festivals to a national figure who could be counted on as a festival presence (1920–38). The final section reveals Vaughan Williams as the pre-eminent choral and festival composer of his generation, someone who would be included in any sort of celebratory or traditional occasion, and often the only living composer to be so included (1939–58). Certain traits in his composition and his music-making are common to all of these periods: a suspicion, only rarely transcended, of traditional genres for festival music; a predilection to mix texts from diverse sources, especially the sacred and the profane; but above all, a respect for the choral institutions and singers of his day – perhaps the reason why he remains the most important English (and Anglophone) choral composer of the twentieth century.

Crafting a choral tradition: 1906 to 1914

Over the course of eight years, Vaughan Williams exploited much of what the British choral tradition he inherited had to offer. For most of the nineteenth century, festivals were the focus of music-making in areas outside of London; they were also the location of many choral premieres.[2] Repertoire at these festivals consisted of choral works, predominantly oratorios and cantatas in the mould of Handel's *Messiah* and Mendelssohn's *Elijah*, though in the last decades of the nineteenth century the importance of producing excellent instrumental works, such as sym-phonies, increased.[3] But Vaughan Williams's inheritance (and that of his contemporaries) was greater than the few festivals still known and cele-brated today: the last quarter of the nineteenth century witnessed a revolution in choral music, and music festivals and choral societies were founded at an amazing rate. The music for festivals and choral societies was further disseminated to more parts of British society through the introduction of sight-singing methods, such as Tonic Sol-fa, which aided the middle and working classes in both reading and appreciating music.[4] Such democratizing trends were general tenets of the so-called English Musical Renaissance, which promoted better training for British musicians – for professionals at institutions such as the Royal College of Music (hereafter RCM), and for amateurs at ordinary schools because of the inclusion of singing classes – and strengthened the infrastructure in which both professionals and amateurs could make music. This in turn led to more potential commissions for compositions. Vocal music publishing, both for the newly founded festivals and for smaller choral societies, also greatly increased during this time.[5]

Between 1906 and 1914, seven festivals performed Vaughan Williams's compositions (see Table 6.1). These included smaller festivals like Hovingham; younger ones like that at Cardiff; the venerable major festivals of Leeds and the Three Choirs (which rotated among Worcester, Hereford and Gloucester); and the Music League Festival, meant to celebrate new foreign and domestic compositions.[6]

How important was a premiere at a choral festival to the young Vaughan Williams? The money given for a premiere, while not excessively generous, was certainly not inconsequential. Vaughan Williams was paid 10 guineas for the premiere of *Toward the Unknown Region* at the Leeds Musical Festival in 1907; three years later, the Festival Management Committee considered paying him between 25 and 30 guineas for the premiere of *A Sea Symphony*.[7] For a virtually unknown composer (as Vaughan Williams was at this point), the offer of a premiere was provisional, based on whether or not the Committee and the festival conductor liked the completed work; fortunately for Vaughan Williams he had an

Table 6.1 *Music by Vaughan Williams at major British choral festivals: 1906–14*

Date	Venue	Compositions	Remarks
1906	Hovingham	*Songs of Travel*	
1907	Leeds	*Toward the Unknown Region*	P; C
	Cardiff	*Norfolk Rhapsody* No. 2	P; C
		Norfolk Rhapsody No. 3	
1909	Music League Festival	*Willow-Wood*	P (revised version)
1910	Three Choirs (G)	*Fantasia on a Theme by Thomas Tallis*	P; C
	Leeds	*A Sea Symphony*	P; C
1911	Three Choirs (W)	*Five Mystical Songs*	P; C
1912	Three Choirs (H)	*Fantasia on Christmas Carols*	P; C
1914	Sheffield	*A Sea Symphony*	

P = premiere of composition
C = conducted by Vaughan Williams
(G) = Gloucester
(H) = Hereford
(W) = Worcester

ally at Leeds, as the festival conductor in both 1907 and 1910 was his old teacher from the RCM, Charles Villiers Stanford.[8] Once a festival accepted a work from a composer, though, it meant additional royalties (the Leeds Musical Festival bought 400 copies of the vocal score of *A Sea Symphony* from Breitkopf & Härtel), and a great deal of publicity (the festival placed advertisements in 27 provincial newspapers, 7 London papers and specialist journals like *The Musical Times*).[9] Advance columns in most of the papers gave the entire festival programme.[10]

Vaughan Williams's offerings to these festivals were a mixture of standard fare and innovative ideas. *A Sea Symphony* and *Five Mystical Songs* were such works, in that they blended genres. *A Sea Symphony* is in practice less a symphony than a secular cantata cast into the four-movement form of a symphony, with a structure that is almost narrative at points. Vaughan Williams refuses to promote a nationalistic ideal or even a triumphant one within this work: it ends with the listener cast out into the infinite, and without any sense of harmonic assurance.[11] Similarly, *Five Mystical Songs* – an orchestrated song-cycle on sacred texts with *ad libitum* choral accompaniment in four of the songs – was not the developed religious composition expected in a venue such as Worcester Cathedral. The genre itself was new to the musical festival. By contrast, *Toward the Unknown Region* and the cantata *Willow-Wood* were, in spite of their unusual texts (Walt Whitman and Dante Gabriel Rossetti respectively), exactly what festival audiences of the time expected for shorter choral works: non-narrative compositions that balanced orchestral textures with easy choral declamation. Each sets its text carefully, with the orchestral accompaniment emphasizing structural divisions. In *Toward the Unknown Region*, the care Vaughan Williams took with the text is particularly evident. The first four of Whitman's five verses are separate syntactical units, with Vaughan Williams providing a sense of closure for each before moving to the next. At the end of the first verse, for instance, the composer returns to the three motives which opened the piece, though in reverse order (a horn fanfare, pizzicato lower strings, and a falling pentatonic gesture, now in a stripped-down orchestration), before presenting a new, arch-like chromatic motive to introduce the second verse. To end the piece with a greater sense of drama, Vaughan Williams avoids such an obvious structural break between the fourth and the fifth verses. After establishing continued motion into the fifth verse, Vaughan Williams sets this segment as an exercise in triumphant rhetoric, including several climaxes, a grand pause before a homorhythmic choral declaration, and a copious use of exclamatory brass and percussion.

Vaughan Williams's choral experience before the First World War also included competition festivals. Whereas the charity and civic festivals described above brought music to middle-class individuals, the competition festivals in general were open to members of all classes, and frequently aimed paternalistically towards the working classes.[12] Such was the case with the Leith Hill Musical Competition, founded in 1905 in part by Vaughan Williams's sister, Margaret Vaughan Williams (she was Leith Hill's first Honorary Secretary). A feature of this festival was a massed concert of the choral forces at the conclusion of the competition. In 1905 Vaughan Williams became the conductor of this massed concert, a position he would hold (aside from his years of service during the First World War) until 1953.

Vaughan Williams worked assiduously and benevolently for Leith Hill. While he refused payment for his services to the festival, the strength of his commitment and the energy he gave to the institution were extraordinary.[13] He was for many years part of the Musical Committee that decided not only the repertoire for the massed concert, but also the competition test pieces. His duties as conductor, especially in the early years of the festival, included rearranging music as needed to suit the amateur voices, occasionally improving translations of the texts (as he did in 1907 with the Novello scores to J. S. Bach's Cantata No. 140, 'Wachet auf'), and even reassigning trombone parts to the strings to save money by slimming the ensemble (he saved the Festival £5 10s. this way in 1909).[14] Such work with Leith Hill gave Vaughan Williams both experience with amateur singers (which improved his own composition for such groups) and an outlet to explore what he came increasingly to call 'good music' from the choral tradition, such as works by Handel and Bach.

While the early part of Vaughan Williams's career saw his reputation as a composer grow through the performance of his works at the major festivals, his immersion in the realm of the competition festival provides evidence of a desire to improve standards in music-making at a local, community level. Thus he exploited the traditional infrastructure of British music while at the same time attempting, through his pedagogical work, to preserve and enhance it.

Celebration and consolidation: 1920–38

If the period before the First World War was a time during which Vaughan Williams used the musical festival to introduce himself to British audiences, during the interwar years he consolidated his position vis-à-vis the festivals to become one of the most important working composers in Great Britain. When the festivals resumed after the war, they brought Vaughan Williams's music into a new prominence (see Table 6.2). For instance, the only interwar year without a Vaughan

Table 6.2 *Music by Vaughan Williams at major British choral festivals:
1920–38* [abbreviations as in Table 6.1]

Date	Venue	Compositions	Remarks
1920	Three Choirs (W)	*Four Hymns* for Tenor and Strings	C
1921	Three Choirs (H)	*Fantasia on a Theme by Thomas Tallis*	C
1922	Festival of English Music, Bournemouth	*A Pastoral Symphony*	C
1923	Three Choirs (W)	'Lord, Thou Hast Been Our Refuge'	
	Festival of British Music, Bournemouth	*A London Symphony*	
		Fantasia on a Theme by Thomas Tallis	
		The Lark Ascending	
1924	Three Choirs (H)	*On Wenlock Edge*	
	Norwich	*A Sea Symphony*	
1925	Three Choirs (G)	*A Sea Symphony*	
	Leeds	*A Sea Symphony*	
	Bournemouth	*A London Symphony*	
1926	Three Choirs (W)	*A Pastoral Symphony*	C
		Overture to *The Wasps*	
1927	Three Choirs (H)	*Shepherds of the Delectable Mountains*	
		A Pastoral Symphony	
1928	Three Choirs (G)	*Charterhouse Suite*	C
		The Lark Ascending	
	Leeds	*A Pastoral Symphony*	
1929	Three Choirs (W)	*Sancta Civitas*	C
		Overture to *The Wasps*	
1930	Three Choirs (H)	*Sancta Civitas*	C
		Prelude and Fugue in C minor for Orchestra	C
1931	Three Choirs (G)	Suite from *Job: A Masque for Dancing*	C
		The Lark Ascending	C
		On Wenlock Edge	
	Leeds	*Toward the Unknown Region*	
1932	Three Choirs (W)	*Benedicite*	
		Magnificat	
1933	Three Choirs (H)	*Six Choral Songs*	Selections
		Shepherds of the Delectable Mountains	
		Songs of Travel	
1934	Three Choirs (G)	*Magnificat*	
		A Pastoral Symphony	
		Norfolk Rhapsody No. 1	
	Leeds	*Benedicite*	
1935	Three Choirs (W)	*Sancta Civitas*	C
		Fantasia on 'Greensleeves'	C
		Suite from *Job: A Masque for Dancing*	C
		The Running Set	C
1936	Three Choirs (H)	*A Sea Symphony*	'The Explorers' only
		Suite for Viola and Orchestra	C
		Two Hymn-Tune Preludes for Orchestra	P; C
	Norwich	*Five Tudor Portraits*	P; C
	Sheffield	*A Sea Symphony*	
1937	Three Choirs (G)	Overture and Songs from *The Poisoned Kiss*	C
		Dona Nobis Pacem	C
	Leeds	*Dona Nobis Pacem*	
1938	Three Choirs (W)	Overture to *The Wasps*	C
		Fantasia on a Theme by Thomas Tallis	C
		Dona Nobis Pacem	C

Williams composition at the Three Choirs Festival was 1922. Some years featured several (three in 1931, 1933, 1934, 1936 and 1938, four in 1935), with Vaughan Williams frequently conducting his own compositions. And if the Three Choirs Festival still did not enlist Vaughan Williams to compose a major new choral work during the era, smaller commissions did come from his pen: Four Hymns for tenor and strings (originally written for Worcester in 1914, but not performed there until the first Three Choirs Festival after World War I, in October 1920, a few months after it had received its premiere in Cardiff) and *Two Hymn-Tune Preludes for Orchestra* (1936). In addition, the festivals at Leeds and Norwich regularly featured his music, and Norwich commissioned a major choral work, *Five Tudor Portraits*, for the 1936 festival.

Aside from the festival performances, commissions for commemorations also signalled Vaughan Williams's arrival as a composer. *Sancta Civitas* was premiered in 1926 at the so-called 'Heather Festival' in Oxford, which was a commemoration of the 300th anniversary of the establishment of a chair of music there; the concerts featured both new and old music, with a decidedly English bent for the former.[15] *Dona Nobis Pacem* was premiered in 1936 as part of a series of concerts to celebrate the centenary of the Huddersfield Choral Society, while *Serenade to Music* was written in 1938 for the concert celebrating Henry Wood's golden jubilee (fiftieth anniversary) as a conductor.

This consolidation of Vaughan Williams's position at the forefront of the musical festival and within British celebratory music meant that there was a shift in his compositional output. His works became more deliberately cultivated for such performance settings, and began using somewhat more 'traditional' genres and texts. His festival compositions during this time included an oratorio (*Sancta Civitas*) and a secular cantata (*Five Tudor Portraits*); and he set major English literary figures, such as John Skelton in *Five Tudor Portraits* and William Shakespeare in *Serenade to Music* (which is largely reworked from Act v of *The Merchant of Venice*). Although his compositions increasingly acquired a more modernist bent, their musical language remained accessible to the choral singer.[16] While his earlier, experimental works continued to be programmed at the musical festivals – *A Sea Symphony*, in particular, was a perennial favourite, and performed more often at interwar festivals than any of his other compositions – and even his non-choral symphonies found a space within them, it was these more traditionalist compositions of the interwar years that usually garnered the most critical attention in contemporary reviews.

Such a nod to tradition may also be seen in Vaughan Williams's continued work with Leith Hill. After the First World War, the competition's importance to the composer grew, especially because of the didactic 'massing' of the choirs. Increasingly, Vaughan Williams took advantage of this venue to present even more 'good music' to the people of Dorking and the surrounding area. One highlight was the festival's 1931 anniversary concert, which featured a performance of Bach's *St Matthew Passion*, with a force of 800 performers. The performance was planned as a special event, beyond the competitions themselves, and subsequent performances of this work (1938 and 1942–58, with Vaughan Williams conducting them until his death) showed the educational and taste-making (or taste-raising) component that Vaughan Williams believed should be a part of Leith Hill. In the 1930s, Vaughan Williams introduced many other large and important works to the massed choirs, including excerpts from Brahms's *Ein deutsches Requiem* (1933), Elgar's *The Dream of Gerontius* (1934), Dvořák's Te Deum (1938) and his own *Dona Nobis Pacem* (1938).[17]

Choral music at this time also provided Vaughan Williams with an opportunity to respond to the horrors of the First World War. In this, he was not unique: many creative veterans directly or indirectly shared their battlefield experiences within a more artistic space in the decades that followed the war.[18] Eric Saylor notes that the difference between Vaughan Williams and many of his contemporaries was that instead of dwelling entirely on the ravages of war, Vaughan Williams always left room for hope, 'if not in this world or at this time, then in a time and place yet to come'.[19] Within *Sancta Civitas*, this hope may be seen in the quick juxtaposition of the rhetoric for the Angel of the Lord descending on his white horse (the forces of righteousness; rehearsal figures 9–17) versus the armies of earthly kings (the forces of despair; figures 17–21). Vaughan Williams uses the same primary rhythmic motive in each segment: a grouping of dotted crotchet – quaver – crotchet. Furthermore, each segment is also introduced by the baritone soloist in a quasi-recitative style. But the first segment is rhetorically more insistent and triumphant, as a homorhythmic choir narrates the Angel's appearance, skill and power; this section is further emphasized by fanfare-like flourishes in the brass. The armies of the worldly kings, in contrast, have no coherent organization. The chorus here only supports the baritone recitation, instead of driving the entire segment, as it does for the Angel. The chorus also does not unify itself into a homorhythmic structure, instead attempting imitative points, and even these Vaughan Williams destabilizes. In the first point of imitation the bass, tenor and alto parts enter at a rhythmic interval of five beats (beginning one bar after rehearsal figure 19). The soprano entrance (three bars later) is at an interval of four beats, and Vaughan Williams further undermines the metre by shifting from 5/4 to

3/4. The second point of imitation is even more disorganized: the five beats between the bass and tenor parts contract to three between the tenors and altos and the altos and sopranos, and the entry loses the energetic force of the 5/4 metre after only one bar, flattened instead quickly into 3/4.

The battle of good and evil in *Sancta Civitas* has a clear outcome of victory for the righteous. Not so for *Dona Nobis Pacem*, which is often seen as a presage of the Second World War. In the fifth movement of this work there is also an angel, but this is the Angel of Death, and the choir responds in a pleading *fortissimo* explosion in the second bar after rehearsal figure 30, before the soprano soloist cries out for peace over almost her entire range: from a high A♭ down to a middle C. There is hope here, too, but it is a hope that is distinctly qualified: the soprano solo that begins the work, chromatically asking God to grant peace using the verbal formula from the Mass Ordinary ('Agnus Dei, qui tollis peccata mundi, dona nobis pacem'), becomes the mostly diatonic final plea at the end of the work (five bars after rehearsal figure 44). The ending also features a 27-bar structural decrescendo, removing first all of the instruments from the texture, then the chorus, finally leaving only the soprano soloist. While the choir articulates a solid C major chord for almost four bars, it is so low within the range of all of the voices that at a *ppp* dynamic, it is almost inaudible. Further, the ending is not reached from a dominant–tonic resolution, with that progression's traditional connotations of finality. Instead, Vaughan Williams presents a third relationship, in a final harmonic progression of vi^7–I in C major. Thus when the soprano articulates her final pitch of E, it does not bring a sense of completion or resolution: peace may be present, and it may be possible, but it is a tentative, fragile thing. While *Sancta Civitas* drew its vision of war's horror and resolution mostly from biblical texts, *Dona Nobis Pacem* saw Vaughan Williams using an admixture of texts, including poems by Walt Whitman, a parliamentary speech by John Bright and texts from the Mass Ordinary, the Old Testament and the Gospel of St Luke. One contemporary critic thought this juxtaposition to be 'peculiar',[20] but the Whitman and Bright texts are used throughout the composition to focus on human tragedy, while the biblical ones engage with its reconciliation in peace.

Both these works became staples of the musical festivals in the years that followed. *Five Tudor Portraits*, with its premiere at the Norwich Musical Festival (1936), should have had a similar reception, but was not presented at the Three Choirs during the composer's lifetime. It was popular enough, though, that in the 1938–9 season, British choral societies programmed it no fewer than nine times – the same number of performances as there were that year of Elgar's *Dream of Gerontius*.[21] In *Five Tudor Portraits*, Vaughan Williams presented a large choral work incorporating elements of his folksong style – something absent for the most part from both *Sancta Civitas* and *Dona Nobis Pacem*. The folksong style works better within *Five Tudor Portraits*, perhaps, because of its subject: what Jennifer Oates has called a 'tonal genre-picture' of John Skelton's early sixteenth-century English poetry, in contrast to the biblical Armageddon of *Sancta Civitas* or the prayers of *Dona Nobis Pacem*.[22] Indications for the soloist to emphasize a nasal quality (just after rehearsal figure 24), as well as spatial effects such as the placement of a few solo choral voices at the backs of their sections (figure 28), add some twists to the modal melodies and occasional rhetorical riffs, like the sea-shanty sound at figure 17. A genial roughness and modern tonal fluidity, with movements sometimes ending far from where they began, differentiates the Skelton settings from the ravishing *Serenade to Music*, which followed two years later. The *Serenade* is a tonally self-contained work, beginning and ending in D major, and prominently rearticulating motives and rhetorical devices (such as passages featuring the solo violin) from the beginning of the work to its end. A cinematic rhetoric inhabits this composition, whether it be fanfare-like figures for an evocation of Diana, the Huntress between rehearsal letters H and K, or moving to much more chromatic material when discussing those who do not appreciate music (letter M and following). The work has a clearly audible structure, and is sweet enough that it purportedly brought Sergei Rachmaninov to tears at the first performance.[23]

Indeed, all of the compositions written for festivals or celebrations that Vaughan Williams composed during the interwar period are accessible, both to choral singers and to audiences. As he ascended to become the most important living composer in Britain, Vaughan Williams took the promotion of a choral heritage for British music extremely seriously. He did so with the understanding that he would not be considered a revolutionary, and that critics might even value his work less on account of that: 'I think, sometimes, that I ought not to try to do the greatest thing on earth, which no fellow will understand, but to use my skill, such as I have, for doing useful work. E.g. things for Div:2 kind of people to sing & enjoy.'[24] The choral institutions were only too happy to accept such compositions from him, and responded through occasional commissions, by inviting him to conduct, and by drawing on his compositions to emphasize the important festal moments in interwar British music and culture.

Eminence and pre-eminence: 1939–58

The period from 1939 to 1958 saw Vaughan Williams become the acknowledged master of both festivals and choirs. Though the major festivals ceased for the duration of the war in 1939, not to return until 1946, Vaughan Williams's music and choral activities took on a greater importance than ever before. By 1943, as the tide of the war was turning in favour of the Allies, the BBC commissioned him to compose a celebratory piece that would become *Thanksgiving for Victory*, a composition for soprano, full SATB chorus, children's chorus, orchestra, organ and speaker. The work was recorded to be ready when Allied victory was assured. The execution of the premiere left a great deal to be desired. The composition was effectively hidden from public hearing, as the BBC did not announce or advertise the performance, and presented it at 9.30 a.m. on 13 May 1945. Yet it was Vaughan Williams, not another composer, whom the BBC had approached for this task.[25] As Edward Lockspeiser noted in his review of the work for *Music & Letters*, 'Vaughan Williams was the right composer to choose [for this commission], not so much because of his acknowledged place among English composers, but because no one would have been so sure to avoid any suggestion of rhetorical pompousness.'[26] The competitions at Leith Hill also ceased during the war. Vaughan Williams, though, ensured that music – and good music – continued, to provide recreation for those soldiers, refugees, evacuees and townspeople in the area around Dorking. The massed choir concert continued each year, and in 1942 Vaughan Williams began conducting Bach's *St Matthew Passion* annually.

In the years after the war, Leith Hill was a good friend to Vaughan Williams, and he to it. He continued his duties as director of the massed choirs there, finding them to be amenable to his pet projects, including a 1947 performance of Bach's Mass in B minor in English. To commemorate the composer in 1949, Leith Hill organized a concert by the London Symphony Orchestra for a 'birthday present' performance of *A London Symphony*, the Sixth Symphony, *Fantasia on 'Greensleeves'* and *Five Variants of 'Dives and Lazarus'*.[27] Vaughan Williams officially retired from conducting the festival in 1953; as a tribute, every concert in the 1954 festival included one of his compositions.

When the larger music festivals resumed after the war, Vaughan Williams's music was again a central feature (see Table 6.3). Each year from 1946 until his death in 1958, the Three Choirs Festival included at least one major work by him, and in most years included several. Between 1946 and 1951, such festival programming focused on the performance of one of the symphonies (Nos. 3, 5 and 6); after 1951, the major works included both vocal and instrumental compositions. And with 1954 came the landmark of Vaughan Williams's first and only major choral commission from the Three Choirs, for the Christmas cantata *Hodie*.

Table 6.3 *Music by Vaughan Williams at major British choral festivals: 1946–58* [abbreviations as in Table 6.1]

Date	Venue	Compositions	Remarks
1946	Three Choirs (H)	*Benedicite*	
		A Pastoral Symphony	
1947	Three Choirs (G)	*Magnificat*	C
		Symphony No. 5	
	Leeds	*A Sea Symphony*	
1948	Three Choirs (W)	*Fantasia on a Theme by Thomas Tallis*	C
		Suite from *Job: A Masque for Dancing*	C
1949	Three Choirs (H)	*A Pastoral Symphony*	
1950	Three Choirs (G)	*Fantasia on the Old 104th*	C
		Psalm 100	
		Symphony No. 6	
	Leeds	Symphony No. 6	
1951	Three Choirs (W)	*Sancta Civitas*	C
		Symphony No. 5	C
		Overture to *The Wasps*	C
1952	Three Choirs (H)	*Five Mystical Songs*	
		Sancta Civitas	
1953	Three Choirs (G)	Suite from *Job: A Masque for Dancing*	C
		Dona Nobis Pacem	C
	Leeds	*Fantasia on a Theme by Thomas Tallis*	
		Sancta Civitas	
1954	Three Choirs (W)	*Hodie*	P; C
		Flos Campi	
1955	Three Choirs (H)	*Fantasia on a Theme by Thomas Tallis*	
1956	Three Choirs (G)	*Hodie*	C
		The Lark Ascending	
1957	Three Choirs (W)	Suite from *Job: A Masque for Dancing*	
		Five Variants of 'Dives and Lazarus'	
		An Oxford Elegy	
1958	Three Choirs (H)	*Psalm 100*	
		'Lord, Thou Hast Been Our Refuge'	

Hodie was premiered on 8 September 1954 in Worcester Cathedral. The review in *The Musical Times* noted that it 'was found to be easy on the ear and quickly acceptable'.[28] The work has had its detractors, including Donald Mitchell, who found it 'grossly over-praised', primitive and even simply 'downright unacceptable'; but James Day found the work to be wholly approachable, even almost familiar because it is 'childlike, not childish, for *Hodie* is a wide-eyed "once-upon-a-time" child's view of the Nativity told with all the wit and understanding of what lies behind the story, even if he does not believe it literally'.[29] As a Christmas cantata, there is no need for the work to be dramatic. Instead, Vaughan Williams concentrates on the evocative, and this he does with an easy fluency. The texts chosen are a mélange of the sacred (passages from the Gospels of Luke, Matthew and John together with snippets of the Mass and the Christmas Vespers, as well as hymns by William Drummond, Martin Luther, John Milton and Ursula Vaughan Williams) and the profane (poetry of William Ballet, Thomas Hardy, George Herbert and Ursula

Vaughan Williams). As Eric Saylor notes, '*Hodie* ... follows the textual layout of Bach's [St Matthew] Passion by alternating between scripture and meditative poetry'.[30] The assignment of much of the narration to a boys' choir singing in unison underscores this alternation, and the Bach connection is reinforced by the inclusion of four-part chorales at two points in the work (even though the style of the chorales is unmistakably that of Vaughan Williams).

The chorales and the narration, however, pale in comparison to the stand-alone movements, such as 'The March of the Three Kings'. Like most of the movements within *Hodie*, this is compelling and wholly evocative of its subject. The text (from a poem by Ursula Vaughan Williams) has two separate subjects: the three kings from 'kingdoms secret and far' seeking Christ, and the 'star of morning', the sign of Christ himself. Vaughan Williams alternates two basic styles of music to capture the shifting moods of the text. The three kings march into and out of the texture over an ostinato of three crotchets (D, C, A), which is metrically dissonant with the 4/4 metre of the passage. The scoring includes a good deal of percussion, which accompanies a brass melody and fanfare that is mostly in D Aeolian, with an overlying pentatonic figure. When the first strain of the star music is heard (four bars following rehearsal figure 2), Vaughan Williams removes the percussion, creating instead an organ-like texture out of a choir of woodwinds, horns and tuba. He also shifts from Aeolian modality to a freer, more chromatic scale that generates cross-relations in the harmony,[31] and carefully structures the exchange of solo and choral writing to provide a natural climax within the movement. The initial narration of the three kings' march is given to tenors and basses alone. When each of the three kings in turn explains his gift (rehearsal figure 6 to four bars after figure 10), there is a response by the full chorus. The gift solos are built up from the lowest voice, baritone (gold), through the tenor (frankincense) and finally to the soprano (myrrh). Only at the climax of the movement (figure 12) do the three soloists sing together, and they do so to an immediate response by the choir. The vocalists reach to the highest points of their ranges in this exultant moment (the solo soprano, for instance, hits a high A in the bar after figure 13). The entire movement closes with a return to the instrumental ostinato, presumably as the three kings march home.

By far the largest festival in this last period of Vaughan Williams's life was the Festival of Britain in 1951, a post-war multi-disciplinary event meant to promote British culture and raise morale (in addition to the arts, design was featured prominently). The *Serenade to Music* was heard at the ceremonial opening concert at the Royal Festival Hall, on

3 May, alongside compositions by Handel, Arne, Parry, Purcell and Elgar, making it the only piece on the programme by a living composer. A few days later (6 May), the Schools' Music Association of Great Britain premiered the choral work *The Sons of Light*, to a text by Ursula Vaughan Williams, with 1,100 children's voices accompanied by the London Philharmonic Orchestra.

If the period between the wars was one of consolidation for Vaughan Williams, where he settled into his role as one of the most eminent British composers of his generation, in the years between the onset of the Second World War and his death he became *the* eminent composer of his generation. This, to be sure, led to his being castigated by some younger composers and critics – those with something to prove – and because of the narrative of 'progressive revolution' required by the modernist enterprise, these individuals were often suspicious of compositions and composers that forwarded discernable didactic aims. But it was precisely these didactic aims – to promote good music, to write music that was at once modern and comprehensible by the amateur performer and the casual listener, to compose as 'befits an Englishman and a democrat' – that make these compositions by Vaughan Williams so valuable to the festival and choral tradition, in their own time, and today.

Notes

1 Ralph Vaughan Williams, 'A Musical Autobiography', in *NM*, 182.

2 For a brief discussion of the history of music festivals in Great Britain, see Charles Edward McGuire, *Elgar's Oratorios: The Creation of an Epic Narrative* (Aldershot: Ashgate Press, 2002), 9–17.

3 See Charles Edward McGuire, 'Vaughan Williams and the English Music Festival: 1910', in *VWE*, 235–68 for a discussion of this repertoire change.

4 See Charles Edward McGuire, *Music and Victorian Philanthropy: The Tonic Sol-fa Movement* (Cambridge University Press, 2009), especially 13–42.

5 See McGuire, *Elgar's Oratorios*, especially 30–4, for a detailed discussion.

6 'Musical League Festival at Liverpool', *MT* 50 (1909), 724.

7 Leeds Musical Festival Management Committee Minutes, 19 July 1909, TMF Records (WYL 201) West Yorkshire Archives Service, Leeds. The Committee at Leeds were generous in their payment to Vaughan Williams, but not overly so; for the 1907 festival, Elgar received 100 guineas for conducting his oratorio *The Kingdom*, which

was not even a premiere; it had previously been heard in Birmingham in 1906.

8 Vaughan Williams's journeyman status is apparent in the discussions leading up to the 1910 festival at Leeds. The Committee initially asked Stanford and Elgar outright for new works, with a promise that they would be accepted; Vaughan Williams, along with Basil Harwood, was asked to submit a work for the Committee's consideration, with no guarantee of a performance (Leeds Musical Festival Management Committee Minutes, 1 March 1909).

9 Leeds Musical Festival Management Committee Minutes, 28 May 1910.

10 See, for instance, the 'Occasional Notes' column in *MT* 51 (1910), 157, which notes both the presence of *A Sea Symphony* on the Leeds Musical Festival programme, and that it was the composition's premiere.

11 See Eric Saylor, 'The Significance of Nation in the Music of Ralph Vaughan Williams' (PhD dissertation, University of Michigan, 2003), 57–8 and McGuire, 'Vaughan Williams and the English Music Festival: 1910', especially 245–6.

12 The first of the English musical competition festivals – those of John Spencer

Curwen in East London and Mary Wakefield at Kendal – were patterned after the Welsh Eisteddfod. The history of competition festivals has yet to be written. For a brief discussion see Percy A. Scholes, *The Mirror of Music, 1844–1944: A Century of Musical Life in Britain as Reflected in the Pages of the Musical Times*, 2 vols. (London: Novello; Oxford University Press, 1947), ɪɪ, 635–48. A short history of the Leith Hill Musical Competition (renamed the Leith Hill Musical Festival in 1950) may be found in *Music Won the Cause: 100 Years of the Leith Hill Musical Festival, 1905–2005* (Dorking: Published by the Leith Hill Musical Festival, 2005).

13 After the second festival in 1906, the Steering Committee offered him a payment of five guineas for his services; he refused this, stating that 'He was very grateful to them for their kind thought, but if they would allow him, he would ask a still greater favour – i.e. to be considered as part of the organization, in which case he could not receive a present, as it would be like giving a present to himself.' Leith Hill Musical Competition Minute Book 1, minutes from 26 September 1906.

14 Leith Hill Musical Competition Minute Book 1, minutes from 22 August 1907, 29 October 1907, 5 February 1909 and 23 July 1909.

15 For a longer description of this festival and its import, see Charles Edward McGuire, 'From *The Apostles* to *Sancta Civitas*: The Oratorios of Elgar and Vaughan Williams', in John Norris and Andrew Ward (eds.), *A Special Flame: The Music of Elgar and Vaughan Williams* (Rickmansworth: Elgar Editions, 2004), especially 100–3.

16 For a discussion of Vaughan Williams's modernist musical language during this period, see Saylor, 'The Significance of Nation', especially 115–22 and 153.

17 For a complete listing of the larger choral works presented by the massed choirs at the Leith Hill Musical Festival, see *Music Won the Cause*, 148–50.

18 See Leonard V. Smith, *The Embattled Self: French Soldiers' Testimony of the Great War* (Ithaca and London: Cornell University Press, 2007), especially 1–19.

19 Saylor, 'The Significance of Nation', 140.

20 R[ichard] C[apell], 'Three Choirs Festival – Gloucester, September 5–10', *MT* 78 (1937), 910.

21 Anthony Boden, *Three Choirs: A History of the Festival* (Stroud: Alan Sutton, 1992), 279 and 'Notes and News', *MT* 79 (1938), 220; the only works scheduled for more choral society performances in that season were Bach's *St Matthew Passion* (10), Mendelssohn's *Elijah* (10), Brahms's *A German Requiem* (12), Samuel Coleridge-Taylor's *Hiawatha's Wedding Feast* (15), and Handel's *Messiah* (38). Vaughan Williams's *Dona Nobis Pacem* was also scheduled for two performances that season.

22 Jennifer Oates, '*Five Tudor Portraits*: A "Tonal Genre-Picture" of Sixteenth-Century England or an Encapsulation of Vaughan Williams's Musical Style?', paper presented at the Second Biennial Conference of the North American British Music Studies Association, St Michael's College, Vermont, August 2006.

23 Reginald Pound, *Sir Henry Wood: A Biography* (London: Cassell, 1969), 236.

24 Letter of Vaughan Williams to Robert Longman, [December 1937], transcribed as letter No. 287 in *LRVW*, 255.

25 *LRVW*, 285 and letter No. 445 (from Vaughan Williams to Victor Hely-Hutchinson, 14 May 1945), 385–6. After this broadcast, the piece was first performed live at the London Promenade Concerts on 14 September 1945.

26 Edward Lockspeiser, review of *Thanksgiving for Victory*, *ML* 26 (1945), 243–44. A similarly enthusiastic review may be found in *MT* 86 (1945), 315.

27 *The Times*, Friday, 11 November 1949, 7.

28 Scott Goddard, 'Three Choirs Festival', *MT* 95 (1954), 615–16.

29 See Donald Mitchell, 'Contemporary Chronicle', *MO* (April 1958), 409, and James Day, *Vaughan Williams*, 3rd edn (Oxford University Press, 1998), 142.

30 Saylor, 'The Significance of Nation', 166–7.

31 In his analysis of the composition, Paul James Etter states that this section is built on two tetrachords in a G scale: 'a lower Phrygian tetrachord while the upper tetrachord is Dorian or Mixolydian'. See Paul James Etter, 'Ralph Vaughan Williams's *Hodie*: An Analysis and Performance Guide for the Choral Conductor' (DMA dissertation, Texas Tech University, 2002), 104.

7 Folksong arrangements, hymn tunes and church music

JULIAN ONDERDONK

In his 1934 essay 'The Influence of Folk-song on the Music of the Church', Vaughan Williams argues for an alternative history of church music, one in which the long-standing influence of folk and popular traditions on church musicians and their compositions is given its due. In his view, the impulse to attribute musical works to the authorship of known composers had obscured general knowledge of this influence, and he sets out in the essay to put the record straight. At one point, observing that the famous Passion Chorale 'O Haupt voll Blut und Wunden' originated as a parody of the early seventeenth-century German love-song 'Mein G'müth ist mir verwirret', he challenges Franz Böhme's opinion that the original song was composed by Hans Leo Hassler in 1601. Noting that Hassler's version 'has all the appearance of a folk-song', he asserts that 'it is quite possible that Hasler [sic] only arranged it. Such things were quite usual in those days before the modern craze for personality set in.'[1]

The remark neatly encapsulates beliefs that the composer held dear – the idea that art and popular musical traditions have long been interdependent, and the related notion that composers throughout the centuries have drawn on local popular musics as a source of artistic inspiration, and should do so again. Somewhat unexpected, though, is the implied criticism of Romanticism and the cult of the individual genius – 'the modern craze for personality' – which he insinuates did much to damage this healthy state of affairs. To a Renaissance composer like Hassler, untouched by Romantic canons of creativity, it was evidently all the same whether he wrote the tune in question or merely arranged it; not so to Böhme, who as a nineteenth-century musicologist and editor of the *Altdeutsches Liederbuch* (1877) presumably felt the need to ascribe the tune to Hassler's personal invention.

We do not normally think of Vaughan Williams as an 'anti-Romantic' composer. Holding music to be 'the vehicle of emotional expression and nothing else', he took lifelong inspiration from nineteenth-century poets like Whitman and Arnold and drew, perhaps more consistently than any

My thanks to Hugh Cobbe, Marc B. Meacy, Paul Emmons, Mark Rimple, Danton Arlotto, Tracie Meloy, Gail Dotson and especially Oliver Neighbour, to whom this essay is dedicated, for the loan of materials and for much help and advice in the preparation of this essay.

other twentieth-century symphonist, on Beethoven and the heroic tradition.[2] Sharing the nineteenth-century belief in a nation's unique cultural characteristics, he turned to native folksong and to models of early English composition in order to craft a personal and highly idiosyncratic style. But embedded in this project of self-creation was a suspicion of the unbridled individualism associated with Romanticism. While reflective of national pride, his turn to Tallis, Gibbons and Purcell was equally driven by an attraction to musical 'historicism' and the compositional and emotional discipline it imposed on the musician. Folksong, similarly, brought its own welcome restraints. Passed down orally from singer to singer over generations, it reflected 'feelings and tastes that are communal rather than personal'.[3] In these terms, folksong offered opportunities for self-discovery, paradoxically, by freeing the composer from the intolerable pressure, unrealizable in itself, always to be original.

On one level, anti-Romantic sentiment must always have a place in so 'collective' an endeavour as establishing a national school of composition. Yet it is clear that Vaughan Williams's opposition went deeper than mere logistical calculation and touched on core values that he retained throughout his life. Chief among these was the social utility of the artist – the idea, as he famously put it, that the 'composer must not shut himself up and think about art, he must live with his fellows and make his art an expression of the whole life of the community'.[4] It was in this spirit that he entered into the musical life of his time not just as a composer, but also as a conductor, lecturer, competition adjudicator, and much else. In these capacities, he worked with young and old, professional and amateur, alike, and saw himself as a practical musician whose job it was to help others engage with music actively and meaningfully. Hence his avoidance, in his own music, of the most extreme 'modernistic' (and potentially alienating) devices of the day; hence also the delight he took in writing music to fit different circumstances. Viewing himself as a facilitator of 'national' (i.e. local and community-based) music-making, he was a craftsman on the model (as he saw it) of Hassler, less concerned about the aesthetic sources of his creativity than its social effects.

That these ideas permeate Vaughan Williams's life and work is amply demonstrated by even the most casual survey of his *oeuvre*. The simplified arrangements he frequently made of his works – by means of cueing in alternative instruments or recasting works for reduced forces – are oft-cited examples of this emphasis. Another is the astonishing amount of 'functional' music he produced – smaller works intended chiefly for amateur performance or written for religious services and commemorative occasions. This *Gebrauchsmusik* amounts to more than half of his published and unpublished catalogue. These works do not, of course, come close to matching the large-scale compositions in intensity or expressive significance (and, being smaller and often very short, they represent far less than half of his total output in terms of actual playing time). But it is a remarkable percentage nonetheless, one that testifies to the depth of the composer's social idealism and that demonstrates with unexpected force the importance of 'secondary' compositional work to his nationalist vision.

What follows, then, is a first attempt to provide a survey of Vaughan Williams's 'functional' music for amateurs, or at least that portion of it covered by folksong arrangements, hymn tunes and church music.[5] Admittedly, not all of the church music falls neatly into the 'amateur' category, but the small scale of these works, their specific purpose, and the manifest influence of folksong and popular hymnody that they display, clearly justify their inclusion here. The discussion will take up the three groups in turn, surveying the composer's engagement with each, identifying key works, and, where possible, noting stylistic traits that parallel developments in his musical language as a whole.

Folksong arrangements

Vaughan Williams's arrangements of English folk music take many forms. They are scored for small orchestra, chamber ensemble, military and brass band, solo piano, chorus (mostly mixed but also women's and men's) and solo voice (usually accompanied by piano); are intended for home, school, concert and church use; and are included as incidental, dancing, occasionally even diegetic, music for plays, masques, pageants, ballets and operas. So numerous are his settings, indeed, that a final reckoning is virtually impossible, especially as the more ambitious arrangements (like those found in the suite *English Folk Songs* (1923) and other borderline 'free compositions') typically quote tunes piecemeal or as a kind of contrapuntal quodlibet. Arrangements of individual folksongs (i.e. arrangements identified as such and not intended as part of a larger musical design) are somewhat easier to tabulate, though even here we need to differentiate between folksongs (i.e. tunes with mostly secular texts), folk carols (tunes with religious texts) and folk dances (tunes without texts). Collating these, we arrive at 47 separate publications containing 260 distinct arrangements (at least 12 more are unpublished). Settings of Scottish, Welsh and Irish as well as continental folksongs and carols also appear in these and other sources, adding a further 31 individual arrangements to this total.[6]

There were of course long-term compositional benefits to be gained from this work. Crafting so many different arrangements in so many different formats had the potential to bring folksong within reach of a wide segment of the population, and thus deepen public appreciation of native musical traditions. This, it was hoped, would help solve the perennial problem of generating an audience for the English composer who had long been passed over in favour of continental musicians. (A cornerstone of this strategy, pursued by Cecil Sharp and enthusiastically supported by Vaughan Williams, was to introduce folksongs to the populace at an early age by including folksongs in the school curriculum.)[7] But social and humanitarian concerns were a possibly more important motivation, for folksong was held up as a cultural artifact common to the experience of all English men and women; its dissemination throughout society as a whole would thus serve as a reminder of a shared cultural heritage and help forge connections between social classes. It would also transfer to a new, literate class of performers long-standing oral traditions of making music 'for yourself'.

It was an ambitious agenda, especially since not everyone shared the composer's belief in folksong's contemporary relevance. The ingrained prejudice against folksong as antiquated and extraneous to the modern world was strong, and countering it required careful presentation. One approach was to focus primarily on those songs that seemed relevant by virtue of their recent collection. Vaughan Williams occasionally arranged folksongs that he found in antiquarian sources like William Chappell's *Popular Music of the Olden Time* (1853–9), but by far the great majority of his settings are of songs collected by Cecil Sharp, Lucy Broadwood, H. E. D. Hammond and others, himself included, active in the contemporaneous Folk Revival. A second, and more important, strategy was to select the most attractive folksongs for publication – those, as he put it, that possessed 'beauty and vitality'[8] – and clothe them in equally attractive arrangements. 'Beauty and vitality' are subjective values, and while Vaughan Williams dropped occasional hints about what made one folksong better than another,[9] he refrained from identifying a specific method for arranging them. It was essential to focus on the melody – the arranger must be 'in the grip of the tune' so that the setting 'flows naturally from it', he wrote[10] – but beyond that his own tendency was to pursue a wide range of compositional solutions, tailoring his arrangements to the abilities of those who would probably perform them. As a result, simple piano and choral arrangements, derived from parlour-music and popular choral traditions, stand alongside more elaborately 'worked' settings that draw on art-song and choral part-song repertories. The separation between styles is never absolute, however, as even the simplest arrangements show the traces of the skilled composer.

Ex. 7.1. 'I Will Give My Love An Apple'.

I Will Give My Love An Apple
(Folk-Song)

Collected by H. E. D. Hammond
Arranged by R. Vaughan Williams

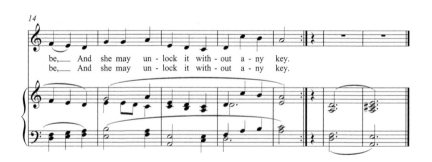

'I Will Give My Love An Apple', from *Folk Songs for Schools* (1912), for unison singing and piano accompaniment, offers a case in point (see Ex. 7.1). Vaughan Williams always reserved his 'simplest' manner for children, on whose musical tastes and preferences much of the hope for the future evidently depended, and the setting is clearly designed with their inexperience in mind. The tune in the vocal line is doubled throughout by the pianist's right hand, while the steady three- (occasionally four-) part texture, with its unvarying crotchet rhythm, provides further encouragement. The Aeolian melody, with its occasional tricky skips, might seem to represent a challenge for children, but Vaughan Williams's strict modal diatonicism and careful placement of each chord lend it an inevitable air.

Carrying this off successfully is harder than it looks and is in fact rooted in part-writing techniques taken from the 'learned' tradition. The many chord voicings and inversions, the careful control of suspensions and other diatonic dissonances, the well-conceived bass that moves mostly by step and usually in contrary motion to the melody – these sustain a sense of forward motion that splendidly enhances the tune. Contributing to the overall effect are the unexpected move to the F (VI) chord in bar 15, the late (and once-only) employment of which lends extra weight to the end of the strophe, and the careful integration of the tune's frequent quaver-quaver-crotchet rhythm throughout the accompaniment. Such concern for the overall architecture of the setting demonstrates the degree of 'composerly' skill that Vaughan Williams was prepared to bring to even his most modest folksong settings.

The settings for adult vocal groups, by contrast, run the gamut from simple to more complex in tone and construction. To some extent, the level of difficulty or elaboration is a function of the specific choral subgenre drawn on in each case. Thus a dozen settings for unaccompanied men's voices (TTBB), largely homophonic and with the melody principally in the 1st Tenors, invite comparison with the eighteenth-century glee and especially (given the folksong material on which they are based) the early nineteenth-century German *Männerchöre* repertory. 'The Jolly Ploughboy' (1908), 'The Ploughman' (1934) and the old English air 'The Farmer's Boy' (1921) are exemplary. Other TTBB arrangements, however, combine this 'direct' style with the varied textures and more intricate part-writing of the contemporaneous part-song. Thus 'Bushes and Briars' (1908) and 'Dives and Lazarus' (1942, from *Nine Carols for Male Voices*) – to take two widely separated publications – pass the tune engagingly between different voices and use overlapping suspensions to create piquant harmonies that express the text. The striking polychords at the final cadence of the former, in particular – parallel $\frac{6}{4}$ chords sounding against a dissonant pedal – convey the despair of the final verse while also briefly anticipating the bitonal effects of the composer's music of the 1920s. Timbral contrast between texted soloist and wordless choir, first essayed in 'The Winter Is Gone' (1912) and incorporated into the *Fantasia on Christmas Carols* of the same year, becomes an especially favoured device, and contributes much to the appeal of celebrated arrangements like 'The Turtle Dove' (1919) and the Scottish 'Loch Lomond' (1921).

Elaboration is especially pronounced in the twenty-six settings whose scoring for unaccompanied mixed voices (SATB and its variants) draws even more firmly on the part-song tradition. Shifting textures and thoroughgoing counterpoint are the very lifeblood of arrangements like 'A Farmer's Son So Sweet' (1926) and the SATB versions of 'Bushes and Briars' and 'The Turtle Dove' (both 1924), as well as of a number of non-English settings like the Manx 'Mannin Veen' (1913) and the Scottish 'Alister McAlpine's Lament' (1912) and 'Ca' the Yowes' (1922). The timbral innovations of this last, in particular – wordless female voices 'distanced' from the texted lower voices by means of their high register and parallel motion – resemble those found in Vaughan Williams's purely original compositions from the period. Similar effects inform the *Five English Folk Songs* (1913), probably the composer's most famous folksong settings, in any medium, and still frequently heard today. The vocal virtuosity demanded by these arrangements is unsurpassed in his output (Michael Kennedy surmises that they were composed for a choral competition).[11] Frequent vocal divisi results in as many as six different parts (in 'The Spring Time of the Year') while rapid-fire voice exchange ('The Dark-Eyed Sailor', 'Just as the Tide Was Flowing') creates a dizzying effect. In 'The Lover's Ghost', folksong material combines with techniques drawn from the sixteenth-century madrigal, a distant forebear of the part-song. Textural contrasts and points of imitation punctuate the structure while, in verse 3, competing melodic fragments of the tune are presented in both 'real' and 'tonal' contexts (and in original and inverted forms) to create Elizabethan false relations.

Other mixed-voice settings display a similar thematic integration. The 'derived' counter-melody of the 1924 'Bushes and Briars' increasingly dominates the setting as it proceeds, culminating in the anguished clash of descending lines in the final verse. The rocking tertian progressions of the whimsical SATB 'An Acre of Land' (1934), themselves drawn from the skipping thirds of the melody, inform the tonal plan, which ambles no less whimsically between tonic and relative minor. Even the opening modal mixture (E♯ in the soprano vs. E♮ in the tenor) that 'summarizes' the tune in the celebrated SATB 'Greensleeves' (1945) turns out on closer inspection to encapsulate the harmonic conflict between tonal and modal forms of the dominant and ultimately between the setting's principal keys of F♯ and A. Similar links between modal inflection and tonal argument are found in the *Serenade to Music* (1938) and the Sixth Symphony (1944–7) from the same period.

No obvious stylistic divide between subgenres emerges when it comes to the ninety-five settings for solo voice and piano accompaniment. The dominance of the late Victorian royalty ballad and parlour song, already a problem for those who would establish an art-song tradition in England, was keenly felt by those seeking to disseminate folksongs through arrangements for the domestic market. For a high-minded composer like Vaughan Williams, contemptuous of the commercial music industry[12] but cognizant of its popularizing potential, compromise was inevitable. Not that his arrangements merely duplicate the stereotyped arpeggiations and simplistic harmonies of the parlour ballad (a few of the twelve French and German folksong settings from 1902–3 come close, but are saved by the tasteful manner in which the formulae are applied). Rather, his tendency is to combine Victorian elements with the more sophisticated techniques of the solo art song. Sometimes the competing styles are kept separate – as in 'The Lost Lady Found' and 'As I Walked Out', Nos. 4 and 5 of *Folk Songs from the Eastern Counties* (1908), where uniformly simple triads and textures in one setting give way to melting diatonic dissonances and an elegantly shifting formal arrangement in the next. More typically, the two styles are combined in the same setting, as with 'Tarry Trowsers' (No. 2 from the same collection), in which popular 'oompah' rhythms mix with Bachian counterpoint, and 'The Lincolnshire Farmer' (No. 12), where broken-chord vamps are clothed in Debussian harmony. 'The Saucy Bold Robber' (No. 10), likewise, begins with simple crotchet rhythms in the accompaniment, only to pick up speed in later verses and conclude with chromatic runs worthy of Liszt.

Folk Songs from Sussex (1912), comprising fourteen arrangements of folksongs collected by W. P. Merrick, offers a stronger dose of art song. The continental styles that were mostly hinted at in the 1908 collection are more prominent here; in some cases, they form the core of the setting. The atmospheric effects and passionately descending parallel seventh chords of 'Low Down in the Broom' (No. 2) are deeply indebted to Debussy, for example, while Wagner stalks the wildly chromatic passages of the carol 'Come All You Worthy Christians' (No. 9). Fauré, too, permeates 'The Seeds of Love' (No. 11, with violin *ad lib.*), where lush harmonies, richly arpeggiated, reveal a side of the composer glimpsed virtually nowhere else. By no means are these and other settings from the collection pale imitations of their models, however: integrating continental styles with the strong diatonic lines of folksong, they embody the hard-won eclecticism of Vaughan Williams's first maturity. 'O Who Is That That Raps at My Window' (No. 5) virtually summarizes this in its tremolo effects, static polychords and shifting pentatonic pitch collections – elements that contribute to a dramatic intensity not unlike that of *On Wenlock Edge* (see Ex. 7.2). The gapped head-motive, a Vaughan Williams fingerprint here drawn from the first phrase of the tune and presented in a variety of timbral and harmonic contexts, anchors the setting formally, while the motive's rhapsodic extensions in bars 10 and 14–16 anticipate those of *The Lark Ascending*, begun two years later. The non-functional juxtaposition of triads, observable beneath the surface activity in bars 10–15, is another mark of the mature style; their return during the dramatic final verse, *forte* and spaced out over as many as four octaves, is in the manner of the

Ex. 7.2. 'O Who Is That That Raps at My Window', bars 1–16.

Fantasia on a Theme by Thomas Tallis and other works that reserve purely triadic harmony for climactic moments.

Whatever pressure he felt to conform to Edwardian song culture, 'O Who Is That That Raps at My Window' shows that Vaughan Williams believed that there was room for innovation so long as it was properly balanced by an awareness of the needs and expectations of amateurs.[13] Thus we find the same mixture of novelty and convention, elaboration and simplification, throughout all his later arrangements for voice and piano – in the *Eight Traditional English Carols* (1919) and *Twelve Traditional Carols from Herefordshire* (1920), notable for their frequent modal mixture, as well as in *Folk Songs from Newfoundland* (1934) and *Nine English Folk Songs from the Southern Appalachian Mountains* (*c.* 1938; published 1967). Here, as before, idiosyncratic and 'uncomplicated' settings stand side by side, while more than a few combine elements of both. Reduced textures – slighter chords, single-line accompaniments, etc. – increasingly characterize the last two publications, but this is less a concession to routine than a reflection of the relative austerity of Vaughan Williams's interwar manner. Like the Shove and Whitman settings of the mid-1920s, the reduction of means results in concentration of material, as pithy head-motives and rhythmic figures, even the occasional counter-melody, distil the essence of the vocal line. An outwardly simple arrangement like 'The Ploughman', from *Six English Folk-Songs* (1935), packs all this and more into its sixteen bars, making it a small masterpiece of structural integration.

After 1945, Vaughan Williams turned almost exclusively to choral settings. The choice is partly explained by the fact that twenty-two of the thirty-seven arrangements from this period were written for *Folk Songs of the Four Seasons* (1949) and *The First Nowell* (1958), two large-scale choral works based around the idea of the folksong 'anthology'. The retrospective aura surrounding these works – reinforced by the familiarity of most of the tunes selected – is not, however, matched by the arrangements themselves, which offer much to surprise. The unusual scoring (for women's voices with orchestral or piano accompaniment) and striking modal innovations of the 1949 work, in particular, closely parallel the timbral and tonal experiments of the composer's last decade. No two settings are quite alike – even the 'unison' settings vary in the forces used for accompanying descants – while the synthetic modal scales and contrapuntal knottiness of a cappella two- and three-part settings like 'The Sheep Shearing' and 'The Unquiet Grave' make them among the most interesting of his entire career.

Hymn tunes

Among Vaughan Williams's best-known – and certainly most widely disseminated – folksong arrangements are the seventy or so that he adapted as hymn tunes and published in *The English Hymnal* (1906; revised edition, 1933) and its later offshoot *Songs of Praise* (1925; enlarged edition, 1931).[14] Tunes like 'Monks Gate' (adapted from 'Our Captain Calls'), 'Kingsfold' ('Dives and Lazarus') and 'Forest Green' ('O Little Town of Bethlehem', adapted from 'The Ploughboy's Dream') have spread well beyond the Church of England to occupy a permanent place in the repertories of Catholic and Reformed congregations alike. But the composer's involvement with hymnody went much deeper than mere folksong campaigning, for he served as music editor of these hymn books,[15] an enormous undertaking that brought him into close contact with a wide range of musical traditions, many from outside his native shores. These volumes have been much praised for their editorial discernment and clarity – he exhumed old versions of tunes and greatly improved on contemporary practices of source identification – and for the quality of their musicianship. Arrangements by Vaughan Williams (and his adaptations of others' arrangements) are among the most common versions of tunes like 'Helmsley' and 'Winchester Old', met with in the hymn books of many different faiths, while his redaction of 'Lasst Uns Erfreuen' ('Ye Watchers and Ye Holy Ones'), used for the doxology in many English-speaking churches and homes to this day, is possibly one of the best-known melodies in Christendom. His eighteen original hymn tunes, likewise, are among the most popular written in the twentieth century; 'Sine Nomine' ('For All the Saints'), 'Salve Festa Dies' ('Hail Thee, Festival Day') and 'Down Ampney' ('Come Down, O Love Divine'), among others, have spread across the globe, lodging themselves within many hymnodic traditions, and show no signs of disappearing.[16]

Much has been written about the apparent incongruity of a self-proclaimed atheist – one who 'drifted into a cheerful agnosticism' later in life – devoting so much time and energy to religious music.[17] Whatever the precise nature of his beliefs, there can be little doubt that writing for the Church of England provided for Vaughan Williams the opportunity to put his deepest artistic beliefs into action. Recognizing that for most people, church attendance represented their only regular opportunity for music-making, he set aside any theological scruples in order to focus on this crucial venue for amateur singing. Placing the needs of the congregation before those of the trained choir, he pitched tunes as low as possible, insisted on slower tempi and unison singing, and provided a wide variety of accompanimental patterns and arrangements, including various methods of combining congregation and choir.[18] He also introduced much unfamiliar English material, notably folksongs but also early psalm tunes by Tallis, Gibbons and Henry Lawes. Exposure to these 'bracing and stimulating' melodies would, he believed, help create a demand for the music of contemporary English composers who were inspired by this same source material. It would also improve a debased musical taste by weaning congregations from the 'languishing and sentimental' hymn tunes of the Victorian church, and ultimately ease the grip of the commercial interests that had foisted these tunes, unwanted, upon them. Replacing what was essentially an alien and repugnant musical style with one that more truly 'represent[ed] the people', his reforms would improve the musical health of the nation.[19]

The mixture of paternalism and progressivism will be familiar from Chapter 1. On the one hand, he assumed the insufficiency of the people to make good musical choices for themselves, especially in the face of commercial pressures, and worked to 'improve' their taste. On the other, by insisting on unison singing and suggesting new methods of performance, he effectively elevated the congregation to a status of artistic equality with the choir. The unlikely combination of aesthetism and populism was one he shared with other early twentieth-century hymnodic reformers, notably the Poet Laureate, Robert Bridges, whose *Yattendon Hymnal* (1899) may be said to have initiated the trend, as well as the left-leaning Anglo-Catholics making up *The English Hymnal* committee, and the founders of the 'Hymn Festival' movement, Hugh Allen, Walford Davies and Martin Shaw among them.[20] But it was Vaughan Williams who did most to mainstream these ideas, with the result that he has been singled out by critics who question how a self-styled 'populist' could dismiss an entire repertory of Victorian 'favourites'.[21] Close examination of the sources shows, however, that, whatever he may have said about them, Vaughan Williams was surprisingly indulgent towards Victorian hymns, retaining 118 tunes by Victorian composers in the 1906 *English Hymnal*, where (by his own admission) he felt some pressure to do so, and more than 70 in *Songs of Praise Enlarged*, where he was under no such obligation.[22] It is true that he generally viewed the strong diatonic outlines of folksong and the relative austerity of early English psalmody as a salutary antidote to nineteenth-century emotionality. But then this was the attitude of many Victorian editors, particularly those of High Church leanings, who maintained earlier traditions of adapting hymn tunes from folksong and who did much to infuse the English hymn-tune repertory with music taken from older non-English sources.[23] Indeed, it was their example that inspired Vaughan Williams to expand his hymn books' offerings even beyond theirs, so that English tunes new and old now coexisted with an unprecedented number of Scottish, Welsh, Irish, continental European and even American tunes of all periods. As he later wrote of his *English Hymnal* experiences, 'I determined to do the work thoroughly' so that the book might be 'a thesaurus of all the finest hymn tunes in the world'.[24]

The eclecticism of Vaughan Williams's editorial work is often overlooked, a casualty of the insularity that often characterizes the reception of his music, and yet it holds the key to one of the meanings of his nationalism. For what he really sought with hymn tunes was not the propagation of a specifically 'English' musical style but rather the consolidation of a repertory of tunes, native or otherwise, that reflected English musical practice. Basing hymn tunes on early English music and folksong was only one way to achieve this; drawing on 'outside' sources that had made their way into English tradition was another. In these terms, the Genevan psalter, brought to England by sixteenth-century Protestants returning home after the Marian Exile, counted as 'national music', as did those Lutheran chorales, harmonized plainchant melodies and continental folk-songs and carols (notably those adapted from the 1582 *Piae Cantiones*) that had entered into English usage, largely at the hands of Victorian editors. He was interested not only in retaining well-known tunes, however, but also in introducing those that might *become* popular. Hence his striking out into French Diocesan and American revivalist repertories as well as his digging yet deeper into sources first tapped by the Victorians. (Here, his introduction of recently collected folksongs, not just those taken from antiquarian publications, was a real innovation.) If these efforts to expand the repertory conveniently coincided with his weeding out of Victoriana, it is important to stress again his deliberate retention of a large number of these tunes. Taken to the hearts of the people, Victorian hymnody had unquestionably become part of the nation's cultural heritage and could not be ignored.

Thus was Vaughan Williams's approach to hymnody closer to Victorian practice than his words might suggest. The similarities extend to his own original hymn tunes which, if they carefully avoid the 'sickly harmonies of Spohr' and the 'operatic sensationalism of Gounod', still partake of the 'grand effects' of nineteenth-century art music that Nicholas Temperley has identified as the overriding characteristic of the Victorian hymn tune.[25] This is the case with 'Sine Nomine' and 'Salve Festa Dies', with their 'orchestral' organ parts and 'symphonic' treatment of vocal forces, no less than with 'Down Ampney' and 'Magda', whose lyrical warmth and intricate part-writing clearly emulate tunes by John Bacchus Dykes and Samuel Sebastian Wesley. Even the composer's concern for a tune's 'singability' – its accessibility to congregations of limited musical experience – seems to have been anticipated by the Victorians. It is no coincidence that all of the tunes mentioned here are firmly tonal, nor that his folksong adaptations tend to blunt the idiosyncrasies of the source melody by harmonizing modal and gapped scales in a tonal context and by ironing out irregular rhythms and phrase lengths. Such alterations were an inevitable consequence of the need to match tunes with metrical texts; even so, it is plain that he took extra care to bring 'unorthodox' tunes into line with Victorian norms.[26]

Not that innovation was lacking. The slower tempi, lower pitching and varied arrangement offerings were all radically new, as was the insistence on unison congregational singing. Indeed, one of the most striking features of *The English Hymnal* was the adaptation of the 'unison song' to the hymn-tune format. This very English choral subgenre, whereby harmony is relegated to the accompaniment while all voices (here, congregation *and* choir) crowd on to the melody line, had been adapted to church hymnody by Stanford and Parry but not to the extent that Vaughan Williams used it. Meanwhile, his revival of psalm-tune settings by Ravenscroft and others, in which the congregation was directed to sing the tune (in the tenor) against the choir's four-part harmony, contributed to the emergence of the popular 'descant' style of Anglican hymnody after 1915.[27] Purely stylistic innovation, by contrast, was slower to emerge. Possibly the success of 'Kingsfold' and 'Kings Lynn', two adapted folksongs whose modal eccentricities were *not* 'edited out' of the 1906 *English Hymnal*, convinced him that congregations could sing such music; whatever the inspiration, *Songs of Praise* introduced a spate of original hymn tunes that emphasized the 'characteristic' features of folksong and early English music. Tunes like 'Mantegna', rooted in the Phrygian scale and with wildly unpredictable harmonies throughout, and 'Oakley', whose sudden turn to Elizabethan dance rhythms halfway through makes for a striking formal experiment, drink deep at the well of native tradition and unabashedly proclaim a 'national' style.

These tunes represent the extreme, however. By far the more common procedure in the later hymn books was to combine native elements with mainstream techniques, as in the celebrated 'King's Weston' from 1925 (see Ex. 7.3). The rugged Dorian melody and repeated VII–i progression (occurring in bars 1–2, 6, 10 and 15–16) announce a boldly modal music, while a descending stream of parallel $^6_3$ chords in bar 13 – concluded, after an interruption, on the third beat of bar 14 – introduces a taste of fauxbourdon. Yet these 'characteristic' features are carefully blended with traditional methods of part-writing, dissonance treatment and long-range formal planning whereby an insistent melodic pattern of rising pitches and repeated rhythms mounts until its sudden reversal in bar 13. So dramatic a trajectory is enhanced by the infiltration of the modal E minor tonic by its relative G major, a competing 'tonal' key area that reinterprets the crucial D major chord (VII in E) as a dominant (note its strong reinforcement by the secondary dominant in bars 11–12). The 'true' key is ambiguous because the composer carefully refrains from directly emphasizing either tonic – here the parallel $^6_3$ chords at precisely the moment we anticipate resolution are a stroke of genius – and it is only with the arrival at the E minor chord in the last bar, at once surprising and expected, that harmonic tension is released.

In its mixing of native materials and common-practice techniques 'King's Weston' embodies a kind of synthetic 'middle ground' between innovation and convention, ideological commitment and broad-minded

Ex. 7.3. 'King's Weston'.

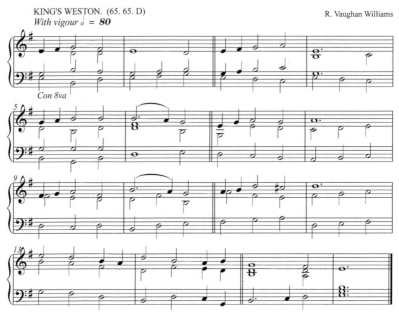

1. At the name of Jesus
   Every knee shall bow,
   Every tongue confess him
   King of glory now;
   'Tis the Father's pleasure
   We should call him Lord,
   Who from the beginning
   Was the mighty word.

3. Humbled for a season,
   To receive a name
   From the lips of sinners
   Unto whom he came,
   Faithfully he bore it
   Spotless to the last,
   Brought it back victorious
   When from death he passed:

6. In your hearts enthrone him;
   There let him subdue
   All that is not holy,
   All that is not true:
   Crown him as your captain
   In temptation's hour;
   Let his will enfold you
   In its light and power.

7. Brothers, this Lord Jesus
   Shall return again,
   With his Father's glory,
   With his Angel train;
   For all wreaths of empire
   Meet upon his brow,
   And our hearts confess him
   King of glory now.

inclusiveness, that we find in Vaughan Williams's engagement with hymnody as a whole. Even the details of the arrangement reflect this blended approach, for the massed voices and unconventional three-part accompaniment draw both on the 'unison song' format of the reformers and on the Victorian practice of giving 'orchestral' weight to the organ part. The forceful tone and 'Sine Nomine'-like march tread, meanwhile, conform to the 'muscular Christianity' of Caroline Noel's very Victorian text, with its militant references to 'captains', 'empires' and 'victory'.

Church music

Vaughan Williams's early atheism appears to have affected his attitude towards other forms of liturgical music for, apart from hymn tunes and a few student works, he wrote no music for the church until 1913. This was the isolated anthem 'O Praise the Lord of Heaven', composed for the fortieth anniversary of the London Church Choir Association. Music appropriate to Anglican worship does begin to appear with greater frequency after World War I; still, many of the works from this period were either commissioned or written with specific performers in mind. Altogether, only eight of the composer's twenty-seven mature liturgical works (comprising small-scale anthems, motets, canticles and organ preludes, as well as a small clutch of simple prayer settings for children) were composed entirely 'on spec'.

Like his hymn-tune arrangements, in other words, Vaughan Williams's church music would seem chiefly to be an outgrowth of his philosophy of musical citizenship. A number of these works – the Te Deum in G (written for the enthronement of the Archbishop of Canterbury, 1928), the Festival Te Deum 'founded on traditional themes' (for the coronation of George VI, 1937), 'The Souls of the Righteous' (for the dedication of the 'Battle of Britain' Chapel, Westminster Abbey, 1947), *O Taste and See* and the *The Old Hundredth Psalm Tune* (for the coronation of Elizabeth II, 1953) – were specially composed for state occasions. Others, like the Magnificat and Nunc Dimittis ('The Village Service', 1925) and the simple Anglican-chant setting of Psalm 67 that he wrote for St Martin's Church, Dorking in 1945, were explicitly geared to the limited resources of the parish choir. Taken together, these works display an extraordinary disparity in their intended audience and venue, and yet are united in a shared focus on filling a specific need. Moreover, many of them can be performed using 'alternative' forces, while some are even suitable for non-liturgical performance at outdoor festivals, public ceremonies and concerts.

The use of popular hymn tunes in many of these works confirms this broadly democratic approach. 'St Anne' ('O God Our Help in Ages Past') appears in both 'Lord, Thou Hast Been Our Refuge' (1921) and 'O How Amiable' (1934), while the entire text of the 1954 Te Deum and Benedictus is grafted, somewhat bizarrely, on to a series of well-known psalm tunes. This last choral work has a part for the congregation, as do the four so-called 'hymn-anthems', of which the *The Old Hundredth Psalm Tune*, mentioned above, is the best known. This genre, popularized by the interwar Hymn Festival but appropriate to worship services, combined congregation and choir by presenting the different verses of popular hymns in varied forms of arrangement (a descant was obligatory), sometimes with brief instrumental interludes linking the strophes.[28] A more striking experiment involving untrained voices is the complete set of Services (Morning, Communion, Evening) in D minor written for performance at Christ's Hospital boarding school in 1939. No hymn tunes are employed, but an ingenious arrangement – a unison congregational part, seldom rising above d'', combines with more complex music for SATB choir – allows (as the score states) for 'a large body of voices [to] share in the musical settings of the service'. Here, the 'unison song' of the school assembly joins with the traditional forms of Anglican church music to create a work in which all can take part.

About a third of Vaughan Williams's church music invites congregational participation; the remainder is for the trained choir alone and occupies a sliding scale from relatively easy to extremely difficult – further proof of his determination to provide music for every situation. Whatever the difficulty, liturgical and musical tradition is closely observed. Thus the Te Deum settings provide cuts for the authorized 'shortened form' of that canticle, while the D minor Communion Service follows the Prayer Book's sequence of movements to the letter, with the Gloria placed last (Some Responses are also included). It is true that motets (only one of them in Latin) outnumber anthems, the more strictly Anglican genre, but this may reflect the development of a late nineteenth-century type of cathedral anthem, pioneered by Stanford, to which the name 'motet' was generally affixed.[29] Stanford's stylistic innovations, indeed, are palpable in the prominent organ parts (often quite independent of the voices) of several works as well as in the tight construction of 'O Clap Your Hands' (1920), the Te Deum in G and others. The Irish composer's application of cyclical elements to all the movements of a service, thus creating a unified musical experience spanning a whole day, is actually carried further in the D minor Services, as nearly all the material can be traced back to the first two themes (bars 1 and 36) of the opening Te Deum. Finally, the antiphonal effects of the cathedral tradition are prominent in many works, achieved through the juxtaposition of *decani* and *cantoris* choral groups (or their equivalents) and by the playing of soloists off against the full choir in the manner of verse anthems and services.

The selection and handling of texts, likewise, show an impressive familiarity with church history and tradition. Most are taken from The Book of Common Prayer and the Authorized (King James) Version of the Bible, though the composer pushes past Anglican orthodoxy by also setting the dissenting prose of Bunyan ('Valiant for Truth', 1940) and mysterious Catholic texts by Skelton ('Prayer to the Father of Heaven', 1948) and the Office of Tenebrae for Maundy Thursday ('O Vos Omnes', 1922). Hymns and metrical psalm texts are also prominent – in the 'hymn-anthems', of course, but also in the remarkable 'Lord, Thou Hast Been Our Refuge', which interleaves the Prayer-Book version of Psalm 90 with the first verse of Isaac Watts's metrical paraphrase of the same. Critics who complain of the work's stylistic incongruities – Watts's poem is set to the sturdily diatonic 'St Anne', its 'proper' melody, while the Prayer-Book words are set to a rhythmically and modally flexible plainchant – have possibly overlooked this textual nuance.

So intimate a knowledge of the liturgy, texts and music of the Established Church speaks strongly of the composer's cultural nationalism – his love for the words of the Authorized Version, his respect for patterns of worship that have prevailed in England for centuries, even his 'inclusive' embrace of the range of religious traditions (Puritan, Catholic, centrist) making up the Anglican compromise. (The works pointedly based on English folksong – the 1937 Te Deum, and the Benedictus and Agnus Dei that he contributed to J. H. Arnold's *Oxford Liturgical Settings* (1938) – clearly also embody this 'cultural' view of the Church.) And yet, the intensity of expression in certain works suggests the possibility of an added personal motivation. It seems hardly coincidental that the stream of Vaughan Williams's liturgical choral works effectively began with his return from the Great War, an experience that most commentators now agree triggered in him some kind of emotional if not metaphysical crisis. In particular, the immediate post-war works – 'Lord, Thou Hast Been Our Refuge', 'O Vos Omnes' and the Mass in G minor (1922) – communicate a sense of spiritual urgency that is conveyed by texts that emphasize human weakness and by settings that are predominantly sombre, occasionally anguished, but also flecked with unmistakable moments of radiance. The mysterious, even devotional mood of these works, one of which was directly inspired by Catholic ritual,[30] is decidedly private, not public, in expression, and may well mark a shift from the composer's early atheism to a mature agnosticism or possibly to something approaching orthodox Christian belief. For the charged atmosphere of these works is not exclusive to the immediate post-war period. It resurfaces in 'Valiant for Truth' and in 'Prayer to the Father of Heaven', as well as in 'The Voice out of the Whirlwind' (1947) and 'A Vision of Aeroplanes' (1956), works whose harrowing Old Testament imagery asserts the base inadequacies of human beings.

We should be wary of interpreting these works too securely in conventional religious terms, however. They may acknowledge human fallibility and insignificance but this does not mean that Vaughan Williams necessarily addressed himself to a specifically Christian God. He was certainly drawn to the ethical teachings of Christ and found solace in the Christian focus on the life of the spirit. But he would never have asserted that Christianity had a monopoly on what he called the 'ultimate realities': in the tradition of philosophical idealism, no religious faith had exclusive access to the realm that lay 'beyond sense and knowledge'.[31] Indeed, the inscrutability of these regions prepared him for a stoical acceptance of the possibility that the spirit did not exist at all. Whatever his uncertainty, the aspiration remained, and he viewed it as the role of the artist to share intimations of spirit with others in a language that they could understand. Hence his adoption of the ready-made frameworks of Christian ritual, and hence his focus on the everyday needs of the human community around him. The anguished cry that concludes the Agnus Dei and thus the Mass is a plea for peace directed not merely to the Divine but to all of humanity in the wake of World War I. The triumphal entry of the hymn tune 'St Anne', sweeping away all doubts at the conclusion of 'Lord, Thou Hast Been Our Refuge', celebrates God's role as protector even as it proclaims the power of a shared musical culture to comfort and sustain us.

Like the folksong settings but unlike the hymn tunes, the church music roughly follows the mainstream of Vaughan Williams's stylistic development. Thus the antiphonal forces of 'O Praise the Lord of Heaven' – two full choirs and semi-chorus – employ the textural and dynamic contrasts of the *Fantasia on a Theme by Thomas Tallis*, written three years earlier, while the blatant root-position parallel triads of 'O Clap Your Hands' announce the new simplification of means of the 1920s. The stylistic possibilities of retrenchment, meanwhile, are explored in 'O Vos Omnes', where chromatic parallel chord streams (at 'desolatam', for example) anticipate the bitonality and localized atonality of the large-scale experimental works of the interwar years. Expressive devices peculiar to the post-1945 music are observable as well – the shadings of light and dark resulting from subtle shifts of mode and tonality ('The Souls of the Righteous', 'Prayer to the Father of Heaven') and the captivation with new timbres and scales ('A Vision of Aeroplanes'). Even works written in his patented 'public' vein – remarkably consistent across his entire career – echo more distinctive compositions from the same period. The melismatic jubilations of the 1928 Te Deum resemble those heard in the *Benedicite*, while the Jubilate from the D minor Morning Service shares material with the finale of the Fifth Symphony.

But it is the personal synthesis of elements taken from a wide variety of historical styles and periods that most strongly links the church music with Vaughan Williams's output as a whole. This can be observed anywhere but is perhaps best illustrated by the Mass, a work whose neo-Tudor associations have obscured awareness of a wider eclecticism. Techniques favoured by sixteenth-century English church musicians – false relations, fauxbourdon-like textures, contrasts between soloist(s) and the full choir – are indeed present, but they are combined with others – canon and points of imitation, sectional division of the text (articulated by textural contrasts), emphasis on the church modes – that were the *lingua franca* of the period, common to English and continental music alike. Even these Renaissance techniques are but a 'starting-point'[32] for what is clearly a highly personal essay, however. The false relations derive less from contrapuntal logic than from Vaughan Williams's idiosyncratic modal harmony (itself adapted from Debussy), while the traditional 'sectional' organization is cross-cut by nineteenth-century methods of thematic recall, both within and across movements. The striking employment of two SATB choirs, 'answering' one another and often combining into eight parts, likewise, would seem to derive less from Renaissance models than from the imaginative reconstructions of the nineteenth-century Cecilian movement.[33] (Extreme dynamic markings – reaching *pppp* in the Credo – suggest this as well.) Folksong plays a role too, not merely in the frequent pentatonic gestures (as at 'Gratias' in the Gloria) but also in the way those gestures contribute to localized and even long-range motivic argument.

✳✳✳

Though not lengthy, the Mass is undeniably a major work, a masterful utterance that the composer never sought to duplicate. The same cannot be said of the other works discussed in this chapter: small-scale 'functional' works chiefly intended for amateurs that for the most part trace well-worn patterns of genre, performance and style. What is remarkable is that, within this limited framework, Vaughan Williams produced such interesting music, much of it paralleling (and in some cases even anticipating) developments in his musical language. In the final analysis, though, innovation was secondary to the overarching social goals that he conceived for this music. With it, he sought to familiarize generations with a wealth of beautiful melody, raise awareness of a common cultural heritage, and above all inspire individuals to make music for themselves.

Notes

1 *NM*, 78.

2 Quotation from *NM*, 12. See Oliver Neighbour, 'The Place of the Eighth among Vaughan Williams's Symphonies', in *VWS*, 213–33, and Lewis Foreman, 'Restless Explorations: Articulating Many Visions', in *VWIP*, 1–24, for discussion of the composer's place in the Romantic tradition.

3 Cecil Sharp, quoted in *NM*, 32.

4 *VWOM*, 42.

5 Frank Howes, *The Music of Ralph Vaughan Williams* (Oxford University Press, 1954), 242–4, and A. E. F. Dickinson, *Vaughan Williams* (London: Faber and Faber, 1963), 117–20, 123–42,

devote sections of their books to these repertories but their treatments are generally very brief. Richard Wienhorst, 'The Church Music of Ralph Vaughan Williams', *Journal of Church Music* 3/7 (July–August 1961), 2–5, offers a similarly short critical introduction.

6 There are an additional eighteen arrangements of 'old English' songs and carols, anonymous compositions that (in his view) bordered on folksong. For the rationale used in arriving at these numbers, see the series of checklists by the present author appearing in *RVW Society Journal* 49–51 (October 2010– June 2011).

7 Maud Karpeles, *Cecil Sharp: His Life and Work* (London: Routledge and Kegan Paul, 1967), 58–67; see also *VWOM*, 270.

8 *VWOM*, 249.

9 See *NM*, 19–20; *VWOM*, 205–13. An unstated but nonetheless clear preference for modal (as opposed to tonal) folksongs emerges from his fieldwork practices and his selection of songs for publication. See Julian Onderdonk, 'Vaughan Williams and the Modes', *Folk Music Journal* 7/5 (1999), 609–26.

10 R. V[aughan] W[illiams], 'Review of *Six Suffolk Folk-Songs*, collected and arranged by E. J. Moeran', *Journal of the English Folk Dance and Song Society* 1/3 (1934), 173.

11 *KC*, 66.

12 *VWOM*, 25–30.

13 This may be why, in the course of an otherwise positive review of his folksong arrangements, Vaughan Williams criticized Cecil Sharp for his 'fear of the harmony professor' and timidity generally. See *VWOM*, 233–4. Certainly, modern settings by 'such fiery young steeds' (as he called them) as Benjamin Britten and E. J. Moeran met with his whole-hearted approval. See his reviews of folksong settings by these and others in *Journal of the English Folk Dance and Song Society* 1/3 (1934), 173–4, and 4/4 (1943), 164.

14 There were also many spin-off publications of these two volumes, of which *Hymns Selected from The English Hymnal* (1921) and *Songs of Praise for Boys and Girls* (1929) are representative. *The Oxford Book of Carols* (1928), co-edited with Percy Dearmer and Martin Shaw, also includes many hymn-like settings of folk carols.

15 *Songs of Praise* was co-edited with Martin Shaw.

16 Dickinson, *Vaughan Williams*, 488–93, provides a concordance of hymn tunes composed or arranged by Vaughan Williams that were reprinted in other twentieth-century hymn books. A complete list of the composer's original hymn tunes will appear in a forthcoming article by the present author in the periodical *The Hymn*.

17 *UVWB*, 29. Byron Adams, 'Scripture, Church and Culture: Biblical Texts in the Works of Ralph Vaughan Williams', in *VWS*, 99–117, and Eric Seddon, 'Beyond Wishful Thinking: A Re-Evaluation of Vaughan Williams and Religion', *Ralph Vaughan Williams Society Journal* 36 (June 2006), 14–23, provide differing views of the composer's religious beliefs.

18 John Bawden, 'The Music of *The English Hymnal*' in Alan Luff (ed.), *Strengthen for Service: 100 Years of The English Hymnal*

1906–2006 (Norwich: Canterbury Press, 2005), 133–54, provides an overview of Vaughan Williams's editorial methods.

19 Quotations from *KW*, 33–4, and *VWOM*, 32.

20 For the social and political views of the committee members, see Donald Gray, *Percy Dearmer: A Parson's Pilgrimage* (Norwich: Canterbury Press, 2000), esp. 62–3. The 'Hymn Festival' was a non-liturgical 'service', popular between the wars, in which members of the congregation met for the sole purpose of singing – and practising – hymns. See Erik Routley, *Twentieth Century Church Music* (Oxford University Press, 1964), 99–100.

21 Nicholas Temperley, *The Music of the English Parish Church* (Cambridge University Press, 1979), vol. I, 319–30.

22 See Ian Bradley, 'Vaughan Williams' "Chamber of Horrors" – Changing Attitudes towards Victorian Hymns', in Luff (ed.), *Strengthen for Service*, 231–43 at 236–9, and Julian Onderdonk, 'Folk-Songs in *The English Hymnal*', in *ibid.*, 191–216 at 205–10, for discussion of the composer's selection of sources. Also significant in this context are the composer's fourteen chorale preludes, eleven of which are based on nineteenth-century British hymn tunes.

23 Erik Routley, *The Music of Christian Hymnody* (London: Independent Press, 1957), 115–21.

24 *VWOM*, 116.

25 Temperley, *Parish Church*, 303–10. Other quotations from *KW*, 33.

26 Onderdonk, 'Folk-Songs'.

27 Temperley, *Parish Church*, 324–5; Clark Kimberling, 'Hymn Tune Descants, Part I: 1915–1934', *The Hymn* 54/3 (July 2003), 20–7.

28 Routley, *Twentieth Century Church Music*, 105–6.

29 Watkins Shaw, 'Church Music in England from the Reformation to the Present Day' in Friedrich Blume (ed.), *Protestant Church Music: A History* (New York: W. W. Norton, 1974), 729.

30 *UVWB*, 142.

31 *VWOM*, 101; *NM*, 122.

32 James Day, *Vaughan Williams*, 3rd edn (Oxford University Press, 1998), 128.

33 In most sixteenth-century English antiphonal writing, the *decani* and *cantoris* sides are kept strictly separate; when combined, they nearly always double the same parts. Expansion of parts in tutti passages does characterize the polychoral writing of sixteenth-century Venetian composers like Willaert and the Gabrielis, but it is doubtful that Vaughan Williams was familiar with this repertory.

8 Music for stage and film

ERIC SAYLOR

Of all the genres in which Vaughan Williams composed, his dramatic works typically receive the least recognition or respect. There are several possible reasons for this, foremost among them that Vaughan Williams wrote for the stage at a time when such efforts by English composers were largely unappreciated. But Vaughan Williams also faced problems of his own making: his tendencies to write without commissions, to allow amateur or student groups to mount premieres of his works, to engage operatic neophytes as his librettists, and to resist any attempts – even from his fellow collaborators – to compromise his artistic vision have elicited questions about his basic dramaturgical competency.[1]

Still, any man who penned the scores for *The Wasps*, *Riders to the Sea* and *Job* cannot be dismissed as a mere dilettante. In fact, Vaughan Williams's contributions to dramatic music were substantial, comprising half a dozen operas, another six ballets and masques, almost thirty pieces of incidental music for films and plays (for both stage and radio) and a handful of pageants and occasional pieces. His works for the stage present a deeply idiosyncratic vision of the relationship between music and drama, one that attempts to employ musical beauty as a means of achieving a purely dramatic end. I will explore this issue by surveying the major dramatic genres to which he contributed music, concluding with an overview of his multiple settings of John Bunyan's *The Pilgrim's Progress*.

Operas

With the possible exception of Tchaikovsky, no composer's operatic career was less emblematic of his success elsewhere than Vaughan Williams's. An avid opera-goer who loved the works of Mozart, Verdi and Wagner, he was well-versed in the genre's conventions, as revealed in his first letter to his librettist for *Hugh the Drover*, Harold Child: 'I have no objection to the structure being more or less formal & conventional – as I like duets, trios, quartets or even quintets – I think all opera has to be conventional (or perhaps I should say *not* realistic)'.[2] But he then used the 'not realistic' qualifier to make a more radical assertion: 'Slow – long tableaux – or long dramatic pauses are always good, as the music takes a long time to speak, much longer than words by themselves – in fact, one wants purely musical effects in an opera just as one wants purely poetical effects in a drama.'[3] Indeed, Vaughan Williams repeatedly turned to dramatic scenarios that were inspired by, conceived as, or offered opportunities for static tableaux – not just in his operas, but in his masques and pageants as well. Such an attitude may explain the inconsistency of his libretti, implying that he was less interested in the literary quality of texts *per se* than in the potential he saw in individual scenes for eliciting effective emotional (and therefore musical) responses.[4]

His first attempt to put these principles into practice came in the form of his 'Romantic ballad opera' *Hugh the Drover*. He began composing the work in 1910, had largely completed the vocal score by the time he volunteered for military duty in 1914, and finished scoring it in 1920. Soon after, representatives from the short-lived British National Opera Company approached him about arranging a performance, which took place at His Majesty's Theatre in London on 14 July 1924. Since then, *Hugh* has proved remarkably resilient, its tunefulness and local colour appealing to generations of amateur and student performers. Its emphasis on English music and imagery – ballad opera, English folk tunes, West Country villages, Maying festivities – reflected the composer's advocacy for a distinctively English approach to opera, which he felt could be achieved by presenting clear alternatives to established continental traditions. This was his goal from the outset, as he wrote to Child – 'I have an idea for an opera written to *real* English words, with a certain amount of *real* English music and also a real English subject [which] might just hit the right nail on the head'[5] – but it deviated from most mainstream attitudes about opera in England, undoubtedly colouring critical opinions towards its reception.[6]

In letters to Child, Vaughan Williams expressed strong views about the characters' portrayals – specifically, that the members of the English peasantry should be treated as sympathetic figures rather than comedy rustics – but in the attempt to avoid one set of stereotypes, he fell into another. The characters occupy generic roles: the mysterious outsider (Hugh), the star-crossed heroine (Mary), the dastardly villain (John the Butcher), the stern authority figure (the Constable), the sympathetic matron (Aunt Jane) and so on. This might have lent itself quite well to a light comic setting, but the characters' earnestness – and the general lack of humour in the libretto – reduce them to stock character types rather than fully fledged personalities. None of the revisions Vaughan Williams made to the opera over the next three decades overcame this initial shortcoming, but despite the dramatic problems, there is much to enjoy in the music.[7] As with most of his operas, the vocal lines are delivered in a flexible arioso style occasionally interrupted with more conventional numbers. Some of these are in fact arrangements of traditional English songs, which the characters usually perceive as diegetic music, but non-folkish arias occupy the usual expressive space reserved for such tunes in more conventional operas.[8] Here the composer finds a vein of almost Puccinian passion that transcends the more narrowly parochial aspects of the story, foreshadowing similar effects in works to come.

Vaughan Williams's next opera, and the only dramatic work he classified as such, was *Sir John in Love* (1924–8). Based on Shakespeare's *The Merry Wives of Windsor*, *Sir John in Love* demonstrates that Otto Nicolai, Gustav Holst and even Verdi did not exhaust the tale's possibilities. With a large and engaging cast, a well-crafted libretto (adapted by the composer), and a ravishingly tuneful score, *Sir John* stands as Vaughan Williams's finest full-length opera, possessing a musical and dramatic range far beyond *Hugh the Drover*. Folk music is present once again, but much more subtly and effectively employed than in *Hugh* – no longer mere musical display, it can indicate characters' emotional states, or help facilitate or foreshadow dramatic developments.[9]

The musical idiom Vaughan Williams employed in *Sir John* is somewhat more conservative than in contemporaneous works, but its emphasis on lyric vocal modality – encompassing a wide expressive range, from Falstaff's cocksureness to Ford's jealousy to Anne's and Fenton's tenderness – plays to one of Vaughan Williams's greatest strengths as a composer, and his admiration for Shakespeare comes through in the exquisite text setting. That is not to say that productions of this work lack challenges. Whereas Verdi's *Falstaff* has only ten principal parts (plus chorus), *Sir John* has twice that number; it also demands considerable acting skills, and the emphasis on small groups and ensembles limits the opportunities to showcase individual performers. Nonetheless, following its revival by English National Opera in 2006, *Sir John in Love* is ripe for reconsideration. Far from being second-rate Verdi, it is first-rate Vaughan Williams, and would be a welcome addition to the standard repertory.

If *Sir John* is Vaughan Williams's best full-length opera, then his best one-act work – and one of his finest works in any genre – is *Riders to the Sea* (1925–32), a setting of the eponymous text by J. M. Synge. This introspective and fatalistic tale ('a tragedy in undertones', as Frank Howes put it)[10] was well suited for Vaughan Williams: its unpretentious vernacular language supports a nearly actionless plot, thus allowing many opportunities for musical narrative. Naturalistic declamation dominates the vocal lines, underscored by octatonic harmonies that several writers have compared to those of Mussorgsky's *Boris Godunov* or Debussy's *Pelléas et Mélisande*. It is equally likely, however, that Vaughan Williams was following the example of his former tutor, Ravel, who was similarly obsessed with symmetrical scales and capturing the cadence and inflection of the spoken word.[11]

Riders to the Sea was composed simultaneously with *Sir John in Love* in the late 1920s, a period when Vaughan Williams began expanding his compositional idiom into previously unexplored regions (not just octatonicism, but polytonality and polymodality).[12] In some ways, *Riders* could be *Sir John's* tragic reflection. Synge's tale, like Shakespeare's, is populated by realistic characters with clear and plausible emotions; yet in *Riders*, as Howes observed, the characters 'are real but oppressed and overwhelmed' by the forces of the world, a profoundly modernist conceit.[13] While 'modernist' is not often a term applied to Vaughan Williams's works, *Riders to the Sea* expresses the same unflinching view of modernity as the Fourth Symphony, the vision of a man deeply engaged with the cultural and political challenges of his own era. Hugh Ottaway recognized this after hearing a radio broadcast of the work in 1952: 'If, for a moment, the composer be substituted for Synge's islanders and the sea taken as a symbol of the overwhelming forces in the modern world, then the work will assume its true proportions as a remarkably complete expression of Vaughan Williams's character and outlook'.[14]

Walter Aaron Clark also observes that the characters of Synge's play find no solace in religion, which he points to as another factor that may have attracted the agnostic composer to the work.[15] Certainly there is no overt reference to organized religion, but Maurya's stoic acceptance of her son Bartley's death ('They are all gone now, and there isn't anything more the sea can do to me . . . it's a great rest I'll have now, and it's time surely') parallels the passage in *The Pilgrim's Progress* when Christian, his burden having finally dropped from his back, says 'He has given me rest by his sorrow, and life by his death'.[16] Vaughan Williams emphasizes this theme of redemption through loss in several works, but despite its decidedly Christian overtones, the sacrifice that ultimately redeems the protagonist in *Riders* (as well as in *The Pilgrim's Progress*, *Job*, and other works) is caused by indifferent Nature or an inscrutable God, not by another person of their own free will. (This may account for the opera's harmonic ambiguity, appropriate for a work with such an unsettling dramatic resolution.) This dark echo of the Wagnerian tenet of redemption through love is a distinctly modernist phenomenon, and is perhaps understandable coming from a veteran whose memories of the dead and dying he encountered on the fields of France – and the apparent senselessness of their deaths – must have haunted him for years.

One other opera had its genesis during the late 1920s: *The Poisoned Kiss; or The Empress and the Necromancer*. Begun in 1927, the plot for *The Poisoned Kiss* was derived from two short stories: Nathaniel Hawthorne's *Rappaccini's Daughter* (1846) and Richard Garnett's *The Poison Maid* (1888), itself based on Hawthorne's tale. Vaughan Williams thought Garnett's story 'had the makings of a light opera',[17] and it shows considerable potential as a comic fairy-tale that could live up to its billing as a 'Romantic Extravaganza'; by the end, all of the characters pair off in the best tradition of mannered comedies by Oscar Wilde or W. S. Gilbert. And with its discrete numbers separated by spoken dialogue, *The Poisoned Kiss* outdoes even *Hugh the Drover* in its resemblance to conventional ballad opera. Unfortunately, as with its predecessor, the libretto is highly problematic (which may explain why the opera was not recorded until 2003). Librettist Evelyn Sharp – journalist, author, suffragette and the sister of Vaughan Williams's late colleague and fellow folksong advocate Cecil Sharp – simply was not up to the task, and the composer ended up doing much of the work himself.[18] By the time he died, Vaughan Williams had substantially revised Sharp's text three times, ultimately replacing the prose dialogue with rhymed couplets by his second wife, Ursula.[19] As with any patient subjected to multiple operations, however, these continual revisions weakened the work as much as they strengthened it. Flawed from the start by not committing either to a frothy romantic comedy or to a satirical fairy-tale, Vaughan Williams tried to split the difference between the two, and failed at both.

But again, as with *Hugh the Drover*, the poor libretto belies the considerable beauty of the music. Indeed, this may be part of the problem Vaughan Williams faced when composing: the balance between lyrical romanticism and light comedy skews heavily towards the romantic side. Consider Tormentilla's touching lullaby for her pet cobra in Act I, and the duet that follows with Amaryllus ('Blue larkspur in a garden'), Amaryllus's own 'Dear love, behold for good or ill' from Act II, or the gorgeous duet between Tormentilla and the Empress from Act III ('Love breaks all rules'). Even minor characters, such as Tormentilla's attending trio of Mediums, receive such delights as the tango-inflected 'Behold our mystic exercises' in Act III. However, when it came to patter songs or deliberately humorous texts, Vaughan Williams simply could not adopt a Sullivanian manner. Musical humour was never the composer's strongest suit; on those occasions that he succeeds, it is when he uses long-breathed, lyrical tunes as parodies (e.g., the lovely 'O, who would be unhappy me' at the end of Act I, as a takeoff on the standard lover's complaint), a technique also employed in Jane Scroop's Lament from the contemporaneous *Five Tudor Portraits*.

Masques, ballets and pageants

With one exception, Vaughan Williams's masques and ballets are not particularly well known, perhaps because he eschewed most balletic conventions. Several of his dance works have no significant female lead; he also shunned the use of classical techniques (in *Job*, he went so far as to stipulate that there should be no dancing *en pointe*), had little interest in Diaghilev's wildly popular productions for the Ballets Russes, and even avoided referring to his own works as 'ballets'.[20] This parallels his disinclination to use the term 'opera', and perhaps for the same reason; in both cases, he wanted to create something distinct from continental models, and his idiosyncratic descriptors hint at the sources of his inspiration.

His first effort, *Pan's Anniversary* (1905), was written with Gustav Holst for a performance of Ben Jonson's eponymous masque at Stratford-upon-Avon. Comprising a series of hymns, fanfares and dances (the latter arranged by Holst from various folk tunes and Elizabethan keyboard works), it is more notable for being Vaughan Williams's first attempt at writing for the stage than for any of the actual music.[21] Most of the original numbers he wrote are both tuneful and diatonically tonal – perhaps surprisingly, given that the presence of shepherds, nymphs, and other quintessentially pastoral figures might imply a strong gravitation towards modality. The tunes are not especially distinctive (although the closing half of Hymn II, 'Pan Is Our All', recalls the final two phrases of Vaughan Williams's own 'Sine Nomine'), and exploit standard dramatic choral effects, such as echo choruses in Hymn III.

Nearly two decades passed before his next contribution to the field, *Old King Cole* (1923), the only work that Vaughan Williams designated a ballet rather than a masque. It re-enacts an embellished version of the nursery rhyme: King Cole of Colchester is visited by his daughter, Helena, who has brought him an elaborate hookah pipe as a gift. When it breaks, the King calls for a drink – brought forth in a bowl – and then presides over a contest among his fiddlers three. He awards the prize to the third fiddler (although his daughter preferred the romantic tune of the second), and all march off to dinner in a general dance. Unsurprisingly, given his interest in English folk customs, Vaughan Williams chose to showcase morris dances in this work, while the three fiddlers' solos also featured traditional tunes ('Go And List For A Sailor', 'A Bold Young Farmer' and 'The Jolly Thresherman', respectively), though only the first and third Fiddlers' tunes are danced – the first to a morris jig, and the third to a sword dance.

As was typical for Vaughan Williams's dramatic works, *Old King Cole*'s debut was mounted by amateurs (on this occasion, musicians from the

Cambridge University Musical Society, and dancers from the English Folk Dance Society), and presumably very nervous amateurs at that, since the composer apparently continued making corrections to the score following the dress rehearsal. That Vaughan Williams countenanced, even encouraged, such performances may seem odd, but he strongly supported amateur musicians; without them, he argued, there could be no artistic environment in which professionals could thrive.[22] This may explain why, even as an elder statesman of English music, he deigned to compose such comparatively humble works as a folk tune medley for a masque mounted by the English Folk Dance Society (*An EFDS Medley*, 1937), or a short passage of *Solemn Music for the Masque of Charterhouse* (1950) as a gift to his old public school.

On Christmas Night (1926) was the first work that Vaughan Williams specifically referred to as a masque. Adolph Bolm, a former dancer with Diaghilev, proposed a scenario based on Dickens's *A Christmas Carol* (the original name of the work); by 1935, the composer had revised it for a performance at Cecil Sharp House with Douglas Kennedy providing new choreography.[23] The work is a quodlibet of Christmas tunes, primarily traditional English carols and dances, awkwardly shoehorned into a free-wheeling adaptation of Dickens's story: only one spirit visits Scrooge; there are no visions of Christmases yet to come; and the lively closing feast has been replaced, rather oddly, with a tableau of the Nativity in the manner of 'an Italian "Sancta Famiglia"'.[24] Vaughan Williams was aware of the thematic conflicts that this engendered, and considered jettisoning all references to *A Christmas Carol* altogether in the revisions of 1935. Yet he did not, and the resulting dramatic hodgepodge probably discouraged later performers' interest. (Vaughan Williams did undertake a more straightforwardly religious Christmas piece when he composed and arranged the music for *The First Nowell* (1958), a nativity play that turned out to be his final work.)

Given that Vaughan Williams's early contributions to dance literature were not especially noteworthy, the depth and sophistication of *Job: A Masque for Dancing* (1930) comes as something of a shock. Unlike most of Vaughan Williams's other dance works, *Job* eschews folk dances in favour of more formal Tudor-era genres, such as pavanes, galliards and sarabands, which may go some way towards justifying its classification as a masque. *Job* was the brainchild of surgeon and scholar Geoffrey Keynes, who approached his sister-in-law, Gwen Raverat, about designing the sets and costumes for a ballet based on the scenes in William Blake's *Illustrations of the Book of Job*. She in turn recommended that Keynes approach Vaughan Williams – her cousin – to provide the music. As Alison McFarland has explained, each of the participants brought their own interpretation of Blake with them, but 'by the end of the project [Vaughan Williams] had become the dominant voice, and the finished drama bore little resemblance to what Keynes and Raverat initially had written' – and for that matter, to what Blake himself had drawn.[25]

Vaughan Williams's facility in composing *Job* may have stemmed from his interest in dramatic tableaux. Keynes originally selected only eight of Blake's twenty-one illustrations as the basis for the ballet, but Vaughan Williams refers to seventeen of them in his scenario and stage instructions. He also reordered several illustrations (sometimes over the strong objections of his collaborators), though he provided instructions in the published score on how to restage Scenes 4 and 5 if producers wished to retain the original order of Blake's images.[26] In some cases, Vaughan Williams undermined or even contradicted Blake's own pictures. He pointed to paintings by Rubens and Botticelli as useful models for the blocking,[27] and insisted that Job not be seen to play an instrument at the ballet's end, despite Blake's depiction of him playing a harp in celebration. Once again, Vaughan Williams sees Job's acceptance of his loss as the primary vehicle for his redemption: following his ordeals, Blake's Job is raised up and made prosperous by God once more, but Vaughan Williams's Job is left, as the stage directions indicate, an old and humbled man content to gaze upon his cornfields and bless his daughters as the curtain falls. He has accepted the punishment that he believes to be his due, and in this understanding of his own shortcomings, achieves some measure of spiritual tranquillity and inner peace.[28]

In spite of the tensions with his colleagues, it seems that Vaughan Williams tried to find musical analogues for the work's visual components. Keynes and Raverat were impressed by Joseph Wicksteed's analysis of Blake's pictures, in which he argues that Blake represents 'good and evil by the use of pervasive symbolism regarding spiritual and corporeal, that corresponds to right and left in the illustrations'.[29] Vaughan Williams read Wicksteed's book at the urging of his collaborators, but told Raverat 'I'm not going to worry about the left foot and the right foot'.[30] In terms of the choreography and set design, this is true; however, perhaps taking a cue from Stravinsky, he did employ contrasting musical systems to represent the opposing forces at work in the ballet. McFarland points out that the music associated with Satan (or his influence) emphasizes minor thirds and tritones, short and metrically ambiguous motives organized contrapuntally, and extensive dissonance. The music of God and heaven, by contrast, features lyrical modal melodies with restrained accompaniment, homophonic textures, and generally diatonic harmonies. Job, appropriately, lies between: his main themes are long-breathed and either modal or pentatonic (i.e. heavenly), but often receive contrapuntal settings and may return in fragments (i.e. satanic).[31] Thus while professing his lack of interest in systems of symbolic interpretation, Vaughan Williams apparently gleaned enough from them to imagine a way of applying the visual imagery within a purely aural context.

Vaughan Williams's last masque was *The Bridal Day*, which he originally wrote for the English Folk Dance and Song Society. It was his first collaboration with Ursula Wood – later Ursula Vaughan Williams – whose transformative effect on Vaughan Williams's life is well documented.[32] Their deeply passionate love affair helped the composer break through his professional crisis of the mid-1930s, and *The Bridal Day* was the first fruit of this relationship. Scored for strings, flute and piano, its first performance was scheduled for the autumn of 1939, but was cancelled because of the war; after fourteen years and some revision, it received a television broadcast by the BBC in June 1953, though both Wood and Vaughan Williams found the production unsatisfactory. More extensive revisions took place in 1957, when the composer recast the work as a cantata titled *Epithalamion*, the name of the poem by Edmund Spenser featured in both pieces.[33]

The masque celebrates the marriage of a Bridegroom and his Bride; nymphs, gods and the Graces participate in the festivities alongside the couple's family and friends. The guests take their leave as the couple, serenaded by musicians and blessed by the goddess Juno, enters the bridal chamber. Although choral singing, ritualistic gesture and mime play important parts in this work, many of the short scenes are organized as dances, and most are separated by monologues delivered by a Speaker; according to the stage instructions, whenever the Speaker delivers his verses, 'everyone on the stage should be still, forming a tableau'.[34] The use of scenic tableaux and ceremonial gestures is applied in a more Dionysian context here than in some of his earlier compositions (appropriately, considering the presence of the god Bacchus in the masque). The solemnity of the event notwithstanding, this joyous and festive work uses dance to celebrate physical love as much as spiritual, and does so without either prurience or prissiness. The emphasis on the solo flute and viola signals this context, as these instruments were closely associated with two of Vaughan Williams's most sensual works: the viola with *Flos Campi* (1925), inspired by erotic texts from the Song of Solomon, and the *Magnificat* (1932), in which he 'thought of the flute as the disembodied, visiting spirit and the alto solo as the voice of a girl yielding to her lover for the first time'.[35]

The least familiar of the composer's dramatic works – and destined to remain so because of their occasional origins – are the three pageants: the *London Pageant* (1911), the *Abinger Pageant* (or *The Pageant of*

Abinger, 1934) and *England's Pleasant Land* (1938). Pageants are episodic historical plays (usually affiliated with a particular locale) intended for outdoor performance. Of the three in which Vaughan Williams was involved, the London Pageant was unquestionably the most audacious. It engaged some 15,000 participants on the grounds of the Crystal Palace, and was one of the high points of the festivities surrounding the coronation of King George V and the accompanying Festival of Empire.[36] Vaughan Williams was one of several composers recruited by the musical organizer, W. H. Bell, to write the music, and was assigned the fifth scene of Part II, a setting of sixteenth-century May-Day Revels entitled 'The London of Merrie England'. Roger Savage describes the scenario as 'standard Victorian antiquarian picturesque stuff', that is to say, a warmly nostalgic view of England's supposed golden age 'before Puritans, Satanic mills, and suburban sprawl'.[37] Vaughan Williams arranged a medley of English folk and traditional music for the scene's twelve short movements.[38]

The Pageant of Abinger and *England's Pleasant Land* were smaller affairs, and involved collaboration with E. M. Forster (who wrote the scenarios) and Tom Harrison (who produced the performances). The three men all lived near each other in rural Surrey, and conceived the works as benefits for the local communities: the *Abinger Pageant* was designed to aid the Abinger Church Preservation Fund, while the proceeds of *England's Pleasant Land* went to the Dorking and Leith Hill District Preservation Society.[39] Vaughan Williams's own contributions consisted primarily of folksong and hymn-tune arrangements, although he did compose a few short pieces of new music; among these was the anthem 'O How Amiable' for the *Abinger Pageant*, which went on to enjoy an independent existence.[40] For *England's Pleasant Land* he recruited several composers to contribute new works and arrangements along with his own,[41] and also borrowed some pre-existing pieces, among them Holst's 'I Vow to Thee, My Country' and Parry's 'Jerusalem', along with several traditional tunes.[42] Although much of the music Vaughan Williams composed for the pageant has been lost, what remains includes two passages (a procession for the Ghosts of the Past and a funeral march set to poetry by Horace) that have connections to the Fifth Symphony, work on which began in the same year (though exactly when is not clear). The Exit of Ghosts resembles the chorale-like tune heard in the Scherzo of the symphony, while much of the music accompanying the setting of Horace foreshadows the oscillating and palindromic figures associated with the opening of the first movement. Ironically, these seeds were planted at a time when Vaughan Williams feared that he was creatively 'dried up'.[43]

Incidental music

A simple inventory reveals that most of Vaughan Williams's dramatic works can be broadly classified as 'incidental music' (whether for stage plays, radio dramas, or film); however, in terms of their aggregate length, such works constitute less than half of his dramatic output. With a handful of exceptions, this music is not particularly well known. Much of it has never been recorded (or, as with much of the film music, has not been widely available until recently), and performances or broadcasts are rare. Nonetheless, these works are significant not just on their compositional merits, but for what they reveal about Vaughan Williams's interest in artistic collaboration and his own personal creative growth.

His earliest (and one of his finest) efforts in this field came in the form of incidental music for Aristophanes' *The Wasps* (1909), which he wrote for the Cambridge Greek Play Series. *The Wasps* is a bawdy political satire that criticizes the Athenian legal system via the protagonist, Philocleon (or Procleon), and his antagonistic son, Bdelycleon (or Anticleon). It was performed in Greek (although the vocal score published by the Cambridge Greek Play Committee featured English translations of the songs and choruses), required a relatively large, all-male cast,[44] and featured a wide array of comic styles, from lowbrow puns to sophisticated social parody to a surrealistic dream sequence featuring enormous dancing crabs.[45]

Although the overture to *The Wasps* is one of Vaughan Williams's most popular instrumental works, the score is rarely heard in its entirety. This is a great shame, for as he had recently completed his tutelage with Ravel, Vaughan Williams displays in the work a level of confidence that he had hitherto lacked. To describe it merely as 'incidental music' does not do it justice: while there are entr'actes and other passages for orchestra alone, there are also nine choruses (including a twenty-minute Parabasis) and several passages of melodrama in which the orchestra plays a critical role. It is also quite witty – much more so than *Hugh the Drover* or *The Poisoned Kiss*. For example, No. 17a in the full autograph score (the dream sequence with the Sons of Carcinus) features quotations from Mendelssohn (the famous *Frühlingslied*, Op. 62, No. 6), Offenbach (the 'Apache Dance' from the ballet *Le Papillon* and the opera *Le Roi Carotte*) and Lehár (a much-slowed and ominous-sounding version of the waltz from *The Merry Widow*), though none of these are present in the published vocal score. Instead, there is a note at the end of No. 17: 'Here follows the entry music of the "sons of Carcinus" which will vary according to season'.[46] This statement not only implies that Vaughan Williams fully expected *The Wasps* to be revived, but that future producers should not feel obligated to use the music he provided for this scene if they did not find it suitable or topical. This practice of suggesting possible performing modifications within the score became a hallmark of his later compositions, but the latitude he provided here is exceptional.

In 1911, Vaughan Williams continued his forays into Attic drama by turning to three plays by Euripides – *The Bacchae, Iphegenia in Tauris* and *Electra* – that had been translated by Gilbert Murray, then Regius Professor of Greek at Oxford. Dancer and choreographer Isadora Duncan had proposed using parts of these plays as the basis for a larger collaborative project involving other creative luminaries such as Vaughan Williams, Murray and the actor Gordon Craig; unfortunately, Duncan soon lost interest in the idea, and so productions were never staged. Nonetheless, Vaughan Williams set several choruses from the three plays to music (and as three independent works, rather than as a single Euripidean cantata), and may have conducted performances of them with the Palestrina Society.[47] They consist almost exclusively of extended choral monologues, but are interspersed with passages for soloists and by different configurations of semi-chorus. The declamation is more evocative of Greek theatre than is the music from *The Wasps*, in part because of the strong emphasis on unison choral textures. A footnote in 'Dark of the Sea' from *Iphegenia* makes clear the effect that Vaughan Williams sought: 'In this and similar passages the note values are only approximate – the passage should be declaimed freely as in good reciting'.[48]

Not long after completing the Euripides choruses, Vaughan Williams was invited to serve as music director for the Shakespeare Memorial Theatre Festival at Stratford-upon-Avon for the autumn and spring seasons of 1912 and 1913, respectively. Archibald Flower, Chairman of the Theatre Board, engaged him 'to conduct the Theatre orchestra, to rearrange music for *Richard the Second* and *Henry the Fifth*, and eventually to reconsider music for all the Histories', although this daunting final request did not come to fruition.[49] Despite Vaughan Williams's initial enthusiasm for the task – probably because it gave him practical stage experience as he worked on *Hugh the Drover* – his efforts met with indifference from the festival's long-time manager, Frank Benson, and lackadaisical musical attitudes from the performers. This must have frustrated him no end; for one performance of *Richard III*, he had to sing an offstage passage of plainchant himself because no singers were available.[50] Nonetheless, his efforts were singled out for praise in the *Stratford-upon-Avon Herald*, and he was presented with a 'silver-mounted baton of ebony and ivory' by a group of long-time festival attendees as a token of their esteem.[51]

The number of Stratford productions for which he completed music was impressive for such a short period: these included *The Merry Wives of Windsor, Richard II, Henry IV Part 2, Richard III, Henry V* and *Twelfth*

Night; he may also have written music for *Much Ado About Nothing* and *Romeo and Juliet*.[52] Benson's company also mounted a performance of Shaw's *The Devil's Disciple*, for which Vaughan Williams also contributed three arrangements. All of these works emphasize simple, short musical numbers, mainly fanfares and entrance music carefully timed to suit the actors' needs. While the scores themselves are not particularly distinctive or significant, the challenges of working to deadlines and the opportunity to observe production techniques were unquestionably of long-term benefit to the composer.

Some other incidental music from this period serves a very different kind of drama: the plays of Maurice Maeterlinck. Vaughan Williams composed scores for both *The Death of Tintagiles* and *The Blue Bird* in 1913; the former was performed privately the same year, but it is unclear if the music for *The Blue Bird* ever received a performance.[53] Unusually for one of Vaughan Williams's early works, the music for *Tintagiles* was privately commissioned; Philip Sassoon asked Vaughan Williams to write the music on the strength of a recommendation from Cecil Sharp.[54] Although the dark, mysterious music is perfectly suited to Maeterlinck's symbolist text, the first performance met with an unreceptive audience. The surviving music for *The Blue Bird* is considerably different, to judge from the piano score; much of it is dancelike in character, but echoes of Debussy, Tchaikovsky and Wagner's 'Loge' motif evoke the magical events taking place on stage.

Later in his career Vaughan Williams had the chance to write music for a handful of radio plays, two of which allowed him to revisit earlier works. His first effort was for a version of *The Pilgrim's Progress* (1942), which will be discussed later. He also returned to Shakespeare in 1944, composing an entirely new score of *Richard II* for a BBC radio performance.[55] Although in the end it was not in fact used for the production, its incorporation of reminiscence themes (for Richard, John of Gaunt, Bolingbroke and 'Impending Tragedy') and longer, more chromatically complex numbers marked a significant advance from the music he wrote for the same play at the Stratford Festival. His last radio work was on a new subject, Thomas Hardy's *The Mayor of Casterbridge* (1950). This is very brief compared to the other two, consisting of only three movements ('Casterbridge', 'Intermezzo' and 'Weyhill Fair'), though the last is divided into five subsections. The first two movements feature a broadly pastoral idiom and are rather longer than most of the movements of incidental music he wrote (nearly three minutes each). 'Casterbridge' also features an arrangement of the carol 'On Christmas Night the Joy-Bells Ring', published separately in 1953 as *Prelude on an Old Carol Tune*.

This practice – arranging and renaming individual numbers from incidental music scores – was even more conspicuous in the case of Vaughan Williams's film music, his involvement with which began in 1940 when he was asked to write the score for the Oscar-winning *49th Parallel*. Some arrangements were fairly conventional: he fashioned a concert suite out of the film score for *The Flemish Farm* (retitled *Story of a Flemish Farm*, 1945), a song-cycle from *The Vision of William Blake* (the *Ten Blake Songs*, 1957) and, in perhaps the most famous and complex example of such activity, drew liberally upon the music he wrote for *Scott of the Antarctic* in composing *Sinfonia Antartica* (1949–52). But he also allowed others to make such arrangements, most notably Muir Mathieson, musical director for several films in which Vaughan Williams participated, who crafted suites out of the scores for *Coastal Command* (1942) and *The England of Elizabeth* (1957).[56]

As Daniel Goldmark rightly points out, however, it would be wrong to assume that Vaughan Williams simply viewed his film scores as 'the starting-point for larger and greater (and more utilitarian) chamber and orchestral pieces', even if that was the prevailing critical response to them during the composer's own lifetime.[57] In fact, Vaughan Williams was powerfully attracted to the medium of film composition, claiming it 'contained potentialities for the combination of all the arts such as Wagner never dreamt of'.[58] And while the creative possibilities drew him to the genre in the first place – it is perhaps worth noting that one of Vaughan Williams's only extended descriptions of his own compositional processes came in his essay 'Composing for the Films' (1945) – he was also impressed by the discipline that it imposed, viewing it as a particularly apposite craft for young composers 'apt to be dawdling in their ideas, or whose every bar is sacred and must not be cut or altered'.[59]

Most of the films he worked on were either quasi-documentaries or propaganda efforts, often under Mathieson's musical direction; these included *49th Parallel* (1941), *Coastal Command* (1942), *The Flemish Farm* and *The People's Land* (both 1943), *Stricken Peninsula* (1945), *Dim Little Island* (1949), *The England of Elizabeth* (1957) and *The Vision of William Blake* (1958). He also received more conventional studio commissions from Ernest Irving – the music director for Ealing Studios and eventual dedicatee of *Sinfonia Antartica* – including *The Loves of Joanna Godden* (1946), *Scott of the Antarctic* (1948) and *Bitter Springs* (1950).[60] As the titles suggest, many of these films celebrated English cultural, historical and political accomplishments, either overtly or implicitly. Given Vaughan Williams's close association with such markers of Englishness in his own music, it is unsurprising that Mathieson thought he might be a suitable recruit for similarly evocative cinematic works.

His approach to writing for films was idiosyncratic. Rather than compose the soundtrack in post-production or after viewing a rough cut of the film (the most typical practice), he would start writing the music based on the scripts and cues provided to him before shooting actually started, then collaborate with the musical director after the film was complete to adjust it as necessary.[61] He was less inclined to use musical stingers or short, evocative motives to punctuate 'every action, word, gesture or incident' than to 'ignore the details and . . . intensify the spirit of the whole situation by a continuous stream of music' – that is, to create a self-contained number that would evoke a general mood or atmosphere rather than reflect a specific image on screen, a practice well in keeping with his established approach in writing for the stage.[62] Jeffrey Richards and Daniel Goldmark have both made admirable assessments of the style, function and larger cultural significance of Vaughan Williams's film music – particularly those scores written during wartime – which reveal considerable dramatic sophistication residing in music intended for mass consumption.

The Pilgrim's Progress

The reasons for Vaughan Williams's fascination with John Bunyan's allegorical novel remain obscure; after all, one would hardly expect that a wealthy, intellectual, agnostic artist of the twentieth century would find much common ground with a working-class, unschooled, evangelical Puritan of the seventeenth. Yet Vaughan Williams kept returning to Bunyan's writing for nearly half a century, setting it in part and in whole, in small and large forms alike, despite its limited dramatic potential. While full of sharply defined settings and characters, the story's allegorical nature does not encourage naturalistic behaviour. Vaughan Williams's various truncations of the story only heightened this condition, as he eliminated many of the confrontational challenges that Christian/ Pilgrim faced in favour of ritualistic and/or transcendently religious scenes, yet another reflection of his penchant for scenic tableaux. The result was that the pilgrimage often came off less as a quest for redemption and more as a watered-down paean to the values of the spiritual life, 'attended by a few obstacles but nothing that a mildly proper spiritual exercise and ritual action could not overcome'.[63]

Vaughan Williams's first setting of *The Pilgrim's Progress* (1906) came at the request of Evelyn Ouless and Joanna Hadley, who produced an adaptation of the story for a community performance in Reigate, Surrey. Of Vaughan Williams's four versions of this work, the Reigate production is the most iconoclastic: it has a larger cast than any of the others (featuring major figures such as Faithful, Hopeful and Christiana); the opening is set not 'in the similitude of a dream', but in the City of Destruction itself; Christian's and Faithful's trial in Vanity Fair is much longer; and the tune 'Monks Gate' – one of several folk and traditional tunes the composer set in this production, including Tallis's Third Mode Melody and the hymn tune 'York' – is sung to the words 'Who would true valour see', which received a different melody in later settings.

Nathaniel Lew's analysis of the Reigate performance provides an invaluable description of how the story was adapted to suit the needs of a small, amateur company.[64] In particular, he points out the producers' frequent recourse to tableaux, which constitute fully half of the play's twelve scenes.[65] This is a less eccentric decision than it may seem at first glance, as *tableaux vivants* were familiar nineteenth-century dramatic staples, and would have effectively circumvented any major limitations of the amateur actors involved. More importantly, the tableaux allowed the music to proceed without significant dramatic distractions, emphasizing an aural rather than a visual focus. Lew argues that this formative experience powerfully shaped Vaughan Williams's approach to later settings of Bunyan's work, though not always advantageously.[66]

Vaughan Williams's next major setting came in 1922, when he completed a one-act 'pastoral episode' entitled *The Shepherds of the Delectable Mountains*, based on the concluding section of *The Pilgrim's Progress*. It is a very compact work, with a twenty-minute duration and a cast of five (though it also calls for the 'Voice of a Bird' and a small chorus offstage). Although not a tableau in the strict sense, the dramatic climax (Pilgrim's crossing of the River of Death) takes place offstage as the Shepherds watch, a technique recalling the epilogue of Glinka's *A Life for the Tsar*. The action on stage is decidedly understated, as is much of the music; as with the *Pastoral Symphony* of the same year, the musical efficacy of *The Shepherds* comes from the quiet intensity of its expression rather than though large, demonstrative gestures, which would have ill fit the tranquillity of the hills overlooking the Celestial City.

While Vaughan Williams's libretto closely follows Bunyan's prose, the composer excised and reordered several scenes, and borrowed additional passages from Christiana's arrival at the Delectable Mountains from the second part of the story.[67] This version was also the first one where Vaughan Williams used the name 'Pilgrim' for his protagonist, a choice he explained many years later to Rutland Boughton: 'I, on purpose, did not call the Pilgrim "Christian" because I want the work to be universal and apply to any body who aims at the spiritual life whether he is Xtian, Jew, Buddhist, Shintoist or 5th [*sic*] day Adventist'.[68] Vaughan Williams also chose not to include Pilgrim's companion, Hopeful, even though the two reached the Delectable Mountains together in Bunyan's original. This seems a dramatically sensible choice for a work of this length, but may have shaped his more questionable decision not to include a companion in the 'morality' of 1951, the final act of which assimilated much of the music and text from *The Shepherds*.

Twenty years after the premiere of *The Shepherds of the Delectable Mountains*, Vaughan Williams composed incidental music for a radio play of *The Pilgrim's Progress*. Adapted by Edward Sackville-West and starring John Gielgud, it was first broadcast in 1943. The score features thirty-eight discrete musical numbers, though some of them feature sub-entries while others simply reprise earlier passages from the play.[69] As a whole, the score marks a considerable advancement over the incidental music he wrote for Reigate; in fact, much like his radio score for *Richard II*, its use of reminiscence themes and confident scoring resembles the compositional practices associated with his film music.

That is not to suggest the radio play completely broke with the past. Like the Reigate production, the radio play prominently features the hymn tune 'York' in the prologue and epilogue; unlike Reigate, however, it greatly expanded the use of Tallis's Third Mode Melody – better known as the theme from *Fantasia on a Theme by Thomas Tallis* – which was heard only at the end of the Reigate production.[70] The score of the radio version reproduces the arrangement from the Tallis Fantasia at its first appearance in the prologue, and the tune returns in scenes evoking the Celestial City or its representatives (as when Christian arrives at the House Beautiful, again after the death of Faithful, and several times throughout the scene at the Delectable Mountains). A third tune, replacing 'Monks Gate' from Reigate and accompanying Bunyan's text 'Who would true valour see', is equally persistent. Foreshadowed by a trumpet fanfare as Christian arrives at the Wicket Gate, it is associated with Christian himself. It returns in a triumphant brass arrangement following the defeat of Apollyon, and again throughout the scene in the Delectable Mountains. All three tunes are heard in sequence at the end of this scene, a marvellous point of culmination.

In some ways, this may be Vaughan Williams's most effective setting of Bunyan precisely because the visual element is removed. Deprived of the scenic tableaux he felt were so critical to staged performances, Vaughan Williams could allow the music to carry more dramatic weight without any concomitant loss of interest on the part of the audience, now primed to accept the story as a purely aural performance. With the dramatic expectations thus adjusted, the music can accompany audience members' inner visions of Vanity Fair, the House Beautiful, the confrontation with Apollyon in the Valley of Humiliation, or the Delectable Mountains – visions undoubtedly more sumptuous and magical than the stage could allow.

With his four-act morality of 1951, Vaughan Williams came full circle in his personal pilgrimage with Bunyan's work – quite literally so. As already noted, the dramatic and scenic organization of this opera closely resembled that of the Reigate production.[71] This is somewhat unusual, as one might expect that the larger budget and scale of a full-length Covent Garden performance – not to mention the passage of several decades – would have inspired Vaughan Williams to new heights, leading him to introduce characters or scenes absent from the earlier version (say, 'failed pilgrims' like Talkative, Pliable, or Ignorance; tempters like Mr Worldly Wiseman; or obstacles such as the Slough of Despond, or Giant Despair and Doubting Castle). In fact, the opposite was the case: removing Faithful and Hopeful, for instance, eliminated opportunities for Pilgrim to commiserate or celebrate with others, and in so doing reveal his humanity to the audience. Instead, the ritualistic and static aspects of the drama were thrown into even sharper relief, leading several critics to suggest that performances of the work might be better suited to cathedrals than concert halls.

Despite these problems – heightened by the questionable direction and design of the first performance – the music is beautiful, if something of a stylistic jumble. Most of the music from *The Shepherds of the Delectable Mountains* was incorporated into the final act, and, as is well known, portions of the Romanza from the Fifth Symphony accompany the loss of Pilgrim's burden from his back. Such ethereal sounds contrast with Apollyon's doleful monotone, the oleaginous huckstering of Lord Lechery in Vanity Fair – a later addition set to a text by Ursula Vaughan Williams – or the cheerfully vacuous duet for Mr and Mrs By-Ends, though these more evocative passages are in the minority. Vaughan Williams retains a certain degree of dramatic consistency in all versions of the story, however, by once more returning to the theme of redemption through loss. True, Christian/Pilgrim achieves life everlasting in the Celestial City, but does so at the cost of his mortal existence; moreover, in order to demonstrate his worthiness to an allegedly all-loving and all-forgiving God, he is obliged to abandon his family, friends and way of life for a lonely and dangerous quest, and will be condemned to everlasting torment should he fail to surmount all of the obstacles placed before him. This, of course, reflects Bunyan's own uncompromising Puritanism, but also the tropes of abandonment and divine caprice seen in several of Vaughan Williams's other dramatic works.

Conclusion

Vaughan Williams's dramatic music spans an enormous range, encompassing everything from deadline-driven hackwork to the inspired heights of sublimity only attainable by great artists. Taken as a whole, the quality of his output in the field is inconsistent, and this unevenness has almost certainly led to the underestimation of his abilities. But this is not surprising, considering the array of performers, settings and occasions for which he wrote: rushed schedules, amateur performances and works of brief topicality are not conducive to legacy-building. Still, many of the shortcomings in Vaughan Williams's writing for the stage stem more from his musical reach exceeding his dramatic grasp than from an absence of inspiration or compositional facility. Nowhere is this more evident than in his various settings of *The Pilgrim's Progress*. Although the music is often transcendently lovely, and well suited to the more meditative and reflective portions of the story, it seems to come at the expense of similarly effective music for passages driven more by action or character study. While it is perhaps unfair to criticize the composer for not adhering to dramatic goals that he did not set for himself (after all, he was quite open about his preference for letting the music carry the story rather than the text), his disinclination to follow established stage conventions more closely, for whatever reason – a desire to establish an independent 'English' musical identity within a particular genre, personal dislike for current musical trends, limitations of time or resources or collaborators – opens the door for such critiques. Several of his attempts to establish new (and, in many cases, specifically English) models and subjects for the stage may have confused or alienated critics and audiences alike, thus rendering them less viable for adoption by larger, more well-established performing organizations.

Yet for all his idiosyncrasies in writing for the stage, Vaughan Williams did create several works of great power and beauty. Given the degree to which he refused to compromise his artistic vision, and the long odds most English composers of his generation faced in having their stage works realized – not to mention the lack of encouragement from the English musical world in general – the fact that he met with any success at all is remarkable. But if the time has come to stop dismissing Vaughan Williams's dramatic works out of hand, then it is also time to forgo special pleading for their value. That not all of his stage works were triumphs is no mark of shame. It is to posterity's discredit, however, if received wisdom about the nature and quality of his efforts in the field is allowed to blind us to his very real and significant accomplishments within it.[72]

Notes

1 For examples of his collaborative relationships, see Alison Sanders McFarland, 'A Deconstruction of William Blake's Vision: Vaughan Williams and *Job*' in *VWE*, 34–5; also exchanges between Vaughan Williams and Edward Dent following the premiere of *The*

Pilgrim's Progress in 1951 (reprinted in *KC*, 196–206).

2 Ralph Vaughan Williams to Harold Child, 15 July (?) 1910, quoted in *LRVW*, 73.

3 *Ibid.*

4 See, for example, Vaughan Williams, 'The Words of Wagner's Music Dramas', *The Vocalist* 1/3 and 1/5 (1902), 94–6 and 156–9, quoted in *VWOM*, 142, 145.

5 Ralph Vaughan Williams to Harold Child, July 1915, in *LRVW*, 71. Vaughan Williams was not alone in his advocacy for a 'national school' of British opera; see, for instance, W. Johnson Galloway's *The Operatic Problem* (London: J. Long, 1902); C. V. Stanford's 'The Case for National Opera', in *Studies and Memories* (London: A. Constable, 1908), 3–23; and Cecil Forsyth's *Music and Nationalism: A Study of English Opera* (London: Macmillan, 1911). However, the lack of any widespread agreement of what constituted a distinctively British approach to opera (not to mention the lack of state subsidies or permanent facilities for such an enterprise) meant that such calls to action went largely unheeded.

6 See Ernest Newman, 'This Week's Music', *The Sunday Times*, 20 July 1924, 7; Anonymous (poss. Robin Legge), 'Hugh the Drover', *The Daily Telegraph*, 15 July 1924, 16; and Hubert Foss, *Ralph Vaughan Williams: A Study* (London: George G. Harrap and Co., Ltd., 1950), 177.

7 See *KC*, 101 for a summary of those revisions. The composer's final revision serves today as the definitive score.

8 For more on the treatment of folksongs in this opera, see Eric Saylor, 'Dramatic Applications of Folksong in Vaughan Williams's Operas *Hugh the Drover* and *Sir John in Love*', *Journal of the Royal Musical Association* 134/1 (2009), 47–58 *passim*.

9 See *ibid.*, 66ff.

10 Frank Howes, *The Music of Ralph Vaughan Williams* (London: Oxford University Press, 1954), 316.

11 See Walter Aaron Clark, 'Vaughan Williams and the "night Side of Nature": Octatonicism in *Riders to the Sea*', in *VWE*, 60–1.

12 For more on Vaughan Williams's exploration of octatonicism, see Chapter 2 of this volume, esp. 44–52.

13 Howes, *The Music of Ralph Vaughan Williams*, 317.

14 D. Hugh Ottaway, 'Riders to the Sea', *MT* 93/1314 (August 1952): 359.

15 Clark, 'Vaughan Williams and the "Night Side of nature"', 56.

16 John Bunyan, *The Pilgrim's Progress*, Everyman's Library No. 204 (London: J. M. Dent and Sons, 1907; reprint, 1916), 42.

17 *UVWB*, 209.

18 See *KW*, 199–200.

19 This final revision took place following Sharp's death in 1955, at which point Vaughan Williams suggested to Oxford University Press's Alan Frank that the Press purchase the rights to the text from her executors, thus freeing him to make the alterations he desired; see Stephen Connock, '"It Will Be Alright in the End": The Complex Evolution of the Libretto', *Journal of the RVW Society*, No. 26 (February 2003): 6.

20 See McFarland, 'A Deconstruction of William Blake's Vision', 29.

21 For a list of the tunes Holst arranged, see 'Pan's Anniversary', in *VWOM*, 333; for more on the work, see Deborah Heckert, 'Composing History: National Identity and the Uses of the Past in the English Masque, 1860–1918', PhD dissertation, Stony Brook University (December 2003), 28–36 and 203–215.

22 As noted in his essays 'Who Wants the English Composer?' (*VWOM*, 39–42); 'The Foundations of a National Art' (*VWOM*, 43–7); and 'Nationalism and Internationalism', in *NM*, 154–9.

23 For a comparison of the two scenarios, see *KC*, 114–15.

24 Quoted in *KC*, 115.

25 McFarland, 'A Deconstruction of William Blake's Vision', 30. A comparison of all three scenarios may be found in *ibid.*, 45–50.

26 See *ibid.*, 35.

27 *KC*, 132–3.

28 See also McFarland, 'A Deconstruction of William Blake's Vision', 44.

29 *Ibid.*, 31.

30 Ralph Vaughan Williams to Gwen Raverat, August 1927, quoted in *LRVW*, 158.

31 See McFarland, 'A Deconstruction of William Blake's Vision', 37–43. O. Alan Weltzien also points to the duality inherent in the masque as appropriate for a story about a struggle between God and Satan; see his 'Notes and Lineaments: Vaughan Williams's "Job: A Masque for Dancing" and Blake's "Illustrations"', *MQ* 76/3 (Autumn 1992): 304.

32 See Oliver Neighbour, 'Ralph, Adeline, and Ursula Vaughan Williams: Some Facts and Speculation (With a Note About Tippett)', *ML* 89/3 (2008): 337–45.

33 A chart comparing the two works may be found in A. E. F. Dickinson, *Vaughan Williams* (London: Faber and Faber, 1963), 468–9. Apparently *Epithalamion* was also the working

title for *The Bridal Day*, but was changed late in the creative process.

34 Ralph Vaughan Williams, *The Bridal Day*, vocal score (London: Oxford University Press, 1956), 12.

35 *UVWB*, 191–2.

36 The Festival of Empire was originally scheduled for the summer of 1910, but the death of Edward VII in May of that year necessitated its postponement. For more on the background of the pageant itself, see Roger Savage, 'Vaughan Williams Brings in the May: Sydenham, 1911', in *Journal of the RVW Society*, No. 28 (October 2003): 12–14. Michael Kennedy misidentifies the *London Pageant* in his *Catalogue*, describing it as possibly having 'been written for some kind of EFDS festivity associated with the coronation of King George V' (see *KC*, 56).

37 Savage, 'Sydenham, 1911', 13.

38 For a complete list of the songs Vaughan Williams included, see *KC*, 56.

39 Celia Newbery (ed.), *Vaughan Williams in Dorking: A Collection of Personal Reminiscences of the Composer Dr. Ralph Vaughan Williams O.M.* (Dorking, Surrey: The Local History Group of the Dorking and Leith Hill District Preservation Society, 1979), 9–10.

40 For a list of the tunes Vaughan Williams arranged for this work, see *KC*, 145.

41 The other composers included William Cole, David Moule Evans, Julian Gardiner and John Ticehurst. See E. M. Forster, *England's Pleasant Land: A Pageant Play* (London: The Hogarth Press), 11; Newbery (ed.), *Vaughan Williams in Dorking*, 11; and Ralph Vaughan Williams, *England's Pleasant Land*, autograph score, London, BL Add. MS 57290, folio 5.

42 See Newbery (ed.), *Vaughan Williams in Dorking*, 10, and Ralph Vaughan Williams, *England's Pleasant Land*, autograph score, London, BL Add. MS 57290. Folios 41–3 of the latter list the musical cuts, cues and repeats (in Vaughan Williams's hand) used for the pageant.

43 See Ralph Vaughan Williams to Mary Fletcher [?], 10 July 1938, in *LRVW*, 262; and *UVWB*, 216 and 222.

44 In an audio recording of *The Wasps* made in 2006 (Hallé CD HLD 7510), David Pountney provided an edited and newly translated version of the play that featured a single actor playing both Procleon and Anticleon, and eliminated nearly all other speaking parts (aside from the priest and the chorus leader).

45 In the script, the crabs are referred to as 'the sons of Carcinus', a Latinized version of 'Karkinos', which means 'crab'. Karkinos was a contemporary of Aristophanes, and also a tragedian, but he and his three sons were better known as dancers. See H. F. Hose, 'Personalities in Aristophanes', *Greece and Rome* 9/26 (February 1940): 94; also S. Douglas Olson, 'We Didn't Know whether to Laugh or Cry: The Case of Karkinos', in David Harvey and John Wilkins (eds.), *The Rivals of Aristophanes: Studies in Athenian Old Comedy* (London: Duckworth and the Classical Press of Wales, 2000), 65–70 *passim*.

46 Ralph Vaughan Williams, *The Music to The Wasps of Aristophanes*, vocal score, trans. H. J. Edwards (Cambridge: The Greek Play Committee, 1909), 100.

47 Evidence of performances actually having taken place is suggested by the fact that parts were copied out and performing times were indicated in the score. For more on the origins of these works, see Duncan Wilson, *Gilbert Murray O.M. 1866–1957* (Oxford: Clarendon Press, 1987), 169–71; *UVWB*, 94 and 105; and Roger Savage, 'Vaughan Williams, the Romany Ryes, and the Cambridge Ritualists', *ML* 83/3 (August 2002): 398.

48 Ralph Vaughan Williams, *Incidental Music for Iphigenia in Tauris*, vocal manuscript score, BL Add. MS 71483, folio 4 verso.

49 J. C. Trewin, *Benson and the Bensonians* (London: Barrie and Rockliff, 1960), 193.

50 See *UVWB*, 104; and Trewin, *Benson and the Bensonians*, 194.

51 Trewin, *Benson and the Bensonians*, 194.

52 These last two plays are not accounted for in Kennedy's *Catalogue*; however, both were performed by the company during the North American tour of 1913–14 (see Trewin, *Benson and the Bensonians*, 276–7), and there are passages of music written for these plays in archives held at the Shakespeare Memorial Library in Stratford-upon-Avon. The copyists vary from one score to another (and even within the scores of a single work), but there are passages in all three that resemble Vaughan Williams's handwriting. More can be seen in *Much Ado About Nothing*, manuscript short score, 208–17, O. S. 55 BEN 9142-i; *Much Ado About Nothing*, parts, MS 55 (9232); *Romeo and Juliet*, manuscript vocal score, O. S. 55 BEN 9142-i, 219–21. Additionally, there are supplemental materials for *Twelfth Night* also held at Stratford; see *Twelfth Night*, manuscript vocal score, O. S. 55 BEN 9142-i, 218ff.

53 Some of the MS pages included with the score of *The Blue Bird* actually belong with *The Death of Tintagiles*; Kennedy notes that the MS for *Tintagiles* also has a 'full score of prelude. . .and four numbers of unidentified

play containing character "Ygraine"', who is one of the characters in *Tintagiles* (*KC*, 73).

54 See *LRVW*, 89–91.

55 There is a misprint in Kennedy's *Catalogue* for the fair copy of the piano score to this work; it should be Add. MS. 63597 rather than 63647.

56 Mathieson arranged two separate suites, both of which were published in 1964: *Three Portraits from 'The England of Elizabeth' Suite* and *Two Shakespeare Sketches from 'The England of Elizabeth'*.

57 Daniel Goldmark, 'Music, Film and Vaughan Williams', in *VWE*, 207.

58 Ralph Vaughan Williams, 'Composing for the Films', in *NM*, 162.

59 *Ibid.*, 160.

60 See also Vaughan Williams's charming remembrance, 'Ernest Irving (1878–1953)', in *NM*, 258–60.

61 See Goldmark, 'Music, Film and Vaughan Williams', 209–11; and Jeffrey Richards, 'Vaughan Williams and British Wartime Cinema', in *VWS*, 142. An expanded version of the latter essay ('Vaughan Williams, the Cinema, and England') appears in Jeffrey Richards, *Films and British National Identity: From Dickens to Dad's Army, Studies in Popular Culture* (Manchester University Press, 1997), 283–325.

62 Vaughan Williams, 'Composing for the Films', 161. Richards indicates that Vaughan Williams employed this method for *Coastal Command*, *The Loves of Joanna Godden* (1946), and *Scott of the Antarctic*, which meant that they were easily adaptable as concert suites (see Richards, 'Vaughan Williams and British Wartime Cinema', 142).

63 Nathaniel G. Lew, '"Words and Music that are Forever England": *The Pilgrim's Progress* and the Pitfalls of Nostalgia', in *VWE*, 196.

64 *Ibid.*, 175–84.

65 *Ibid.*, 177.

66 *Ibid.*, 195–200.

67 Vaughan Williams, personal copy of John Bunyan's *The Pilgrim's Progress*, BL Add. MS 71123, 368–69, 377. Vaughan Williams also included text not in Bunyan, such as the setting of Psalm 23 sung by the offstage Voice of a Bird.

68 Ralph Vaughan Williams to Rutland Boughton, 21 (?) May 1951, quoted in *LRVW*, 485.

69 Ralph Vaughan Williams, *Incidental Music for The Pilgrim's Progress*, MS score, BL Add. MS 50419. Christopher Palmer has produced an edited version of this work, which he has called 'A Bunyan Sequence' (originally released in 1991 as Hyperion CDA66511; reissued in 2008 as Hyperion CDS44323), which retains only the bare minimum of spoken text necessary to preserve basic continuity. This also led to the elimination of some of the musical passages, but the bulk of the music still remains.

70 Lew, 'Words and Music', 182.

71 Lew, 'Words and Music', 185 (see Table 9.3).

72 The recent revival of *The Pilgrim's Progress* at the London Coliseum (2012) suggests that twenty-first-century critics are perhaps less inclined than their predecessors to throw out the musical baby with the dramatic bathwater. Moreover, Yoshi Oida's production effectively shows how Bunyan's tale can be adapted to address the concerns and tastes of modern audiences in the developed world. See, for instance, http://www.guardian.co.uk/music/2012/nov/06/the-pilgrims-progress-review; http://www.independent.co.uk/arts-entertainment/classical/reviews/ios-classical-review-the-pilgrims-progress-coliseum-londontotal-immersion-oliver-knussen-at-60-barbican-london-8303694.html?origin=internalSearch (both accessed 29 May 2013).

9 Chamber music and works for soloist with orchestra

CHRISTOPHER MARK

Of Vaughan Williams's works that fall within the categories discussed in this chapter, only *The Lark Ascending* is widely known.[1] The general listener might also have come across the Tuba Concerto: as a rare instance of a serious virtuoso work for that instrument, this has the occasional airing. But the rest of the composer's works for chamber ensembles or for a soloist with orchestra are probably known only to specialist performers, Vaughan Williams scholars, CD completists (most of the chamber music, even the earliest, exists in recordings, as do all the concertos) and audiences who have come across them at concerts they have attended primarily in order to hear other works on the programme. Yet there is much of interest in this music: the stylistic characteristics by which Vaughan Williams is generally recognized are as much on display as in better-known works, as are his music's strengths and weaknesses, and the broad lines of his development. With the possible exception of *The Lark Ascending*, it would require a good deal of special pleading to place any of the works I am considering within the highest reaches of his output. But some of the invention is highly imaginative and there are moments, too, of that quality of 'vision' for which the composer is renowned.

While the pairing of categories in this chapter represents to some degree a marriage of convenience, a compromise inevitable in a volume of this kind, there are, in fact, interesting common concerns as well as illuminating differences of approach that can be traced between the two groups of works (as there are, of course, with the rest of Vaughan Williams's output). As it happens, with the exception of the work for tuba, the concertos were written between the periods of composition of the main chamber pieces. Approaching the task chronologically, my narrative therefore begins with chamber music, moves to four of the concertos, and ends by contrasting the contemporaneous Violin Sonata and Tuba Concerto.[2]

The early chamber music: finding a voice

Vaughan Williams's first acknowledged chamber work is the String Quartet No. 1 in G minor (1908–9; revised 1921). A number of earlier pieces were withdrawn by the composer, and remained in manuscript until his widow, Ursula, lifted the embargo forty years after his death, and allowed a number to be published by Faber Music. The earliest of these is effectively Vaughan Williams's first completed attempt at an extended original composition, the String Quartet in C minor (1898). This shows some flair for string-writing, even though the textures never exceed the conventional. Particularly impressive is the fleet, scherzo-like music in the Trio, which derives much of its impetus from rhythmic disruption. If the liking for (and, in some ways, the manner of) development suggests a Beethovenian model, the minuet-like Intermezzo suggests Haydn in its asymmetrical phrasing. Meanwhile the modality for which the mature Vaughan Williams is known is incipient at most. The opening of the first movement is consistently Aeolian up to bar 28, the only harmonic deflection from the tonic C minor triad being the Neapolitan in bar 15. More varied colours, in both timbre and harmony, are found in the expansive Quintet in D major for clarinet, horn, violin, cello and piano of the same year.[3]

Breadth of utterance is another characteristic of the mature composer and is a notable feature, too, of the Piano Quintet in C minor (1903), which comprises three big, ambitious movements, each lasting around ten minutes. These movements are, generally speaking, impressively paced, suggesting an embryonic symphonist. A sense of trajectory across the span of the work is achieved by inserting pre-echoes of the finale's main theme in the first two movements (from bars 186 and 277 in the first movement, and from bars 55, 99 and 171 in the second). The style is post-Brahmsian, nowhere more so than in the bold opening gesture. But the music also shows the influence of Parry in its investment in the expressive potential of diatonic dissonance (see, for example, bars 1–7 in the second movement)[4] – though non-dissonant diatonic contexts such as from bar 139 in the first movement also make their mark. Indeed, it is these moments – mostly wistful, often slightly pained – that make the biggest impression, rather than the chromatic working-out. All three movements end quietly, with melodic descents and a sense of withdrawal – precursors of the 'niente' endings for which Vaughan Williams was later to become famous. There is a tendency towards over-writing, and his writing for piano (for which he was criticized throughout his career) has more than a few awkward moments, especially when he is attempting to forge his own manner of modal harmony and voice-leading (in, for example, the harmonized repeats of the final movement theme).

Three years later, in the Nocturne and Scherzo (1906), the problem of how to integrate separate and radically different resources (a vein of late Romantic chromaticism that is more reminiscent of Bridge, and two kinds of diatonicism – the appoggiatura-laden version inherited from Samuel Sebastian Wesley and Parry noted in the Piano Quintet (see n. 4), and the modality of the folksongs in which he had an increasing interest) seems to come to a head. As Kennedy observes of the contemporaneous *In the Fen Country*: 'The harmonic idiom is a curious mixture of the chromaticism of Strauss and his imitators, the pure diatonic style in which Butterworth was to write, and occasional glimpses of the Vaughan Williams of a few years later'.[5] While there is no hint of folksong in the Nocturne movement, various moments of melancholic yearning convey an English tone. See, for example, the events from bar 91 to the end – the long descent from the climax, the nostalgic return to the opening bars and the listless cadence on to an added-sixth chord. Folksong does play a part in the Scherzo movement (which is actually subtitled 'founded on an English Folk-song': Vaughan Williams had started collecting folksong three years earlier in 1903), principally in the Lento section towards the end, though elements of the song do also appear in the Scherzo section proper.

When the String Quartet No. 1 in G minor received its first performance in 1909, the purportedly specialist audience was, if the report in *The Musical Times* is accurate, if not hostile then certainly dismissive:

SOCIETY OF BRITISH COMPOSERS.
A meeting of this Society was held at Messrs. Novello's Rooms on
November 8. String quartets by Dr. Vaughan Williams and Dr. James Lyon
were performed by the Schwiller Quartet. There were passages in
Dr. Vaughan Williams's work which, on the assumption that the composer's
aims were fully carried out by the executants, represented the extreme
development of modernism, so much so that not even the advanced tastes of
an audience of British composers could find everything in them acceptable.[6]

To the audience of today, cognizant, say, of Schoenberg's works of 1909 (*Erwartung* Op. 17, Five Orchestral Pieces Op. 16, *Das Buch der hängenden Gärten* Op. 15 and Drei Klavierstücke Op. 11), the notion of Vaughan Williams's music representing 'the extreme development of modernism' seems absurd. Indeed, despite the modal resources (the quartet begins with a theme in G Dorian, and the main material of all four movements is modal) and a classicizing tendency at certain points (perhaps the result of studying with Ravel in Paris the previous year), much of the work is conservatively Romantic. It is possibly these elements that the *Grove* writers are thinking of when they say that the 'traces of former ways, usually involving a chromatic expressiveness' constitute 'a serious handicap'.[7] Peter Evans observes that 'A sonata plan can be read into the first movement, but the progress is desultory and quartet dialogue minimal; the surprisingly *grazioso* minuet and the jiggish rondo-finale are more successful'.[8] He does not mention the third, slow movement. Entitled 'Romance', it is notable for its obliquity: no cadence is other than equivocal, while the opening theme suggests several possible 'tonics' (the proper modal term would be 'final'), none of which is confirmed by supporting harmony. The coda is characterized by the unexpected 'discovery' of the C major triad, one of very few pure triads in the movement; even this is presented in its least stable $^6_4$ position, and has the seventh, B, pitted against it. Nevertheless, it is a moment of 'revelation' that is perhaps the most Vaughan Williams-ish aspect of the movement. Particularly uncharacteristic of the mature composer is the Romantic subjectivity: he adopts a personal, if not actually confessional, utterance, especially in the outer sections, rather than the 'communal' tone found in later movements titled 'Romance' or 'Romanza' (those, for example, in Symphony No. 5, the Piano and Tuba Concertos, String Quartet No. 2 and indeed in *The Lark Ascending*, which is subtitled 'Romance').

In both the Minuet and Trio and the Finale (Rondo capriccioso) a structural role is accorded to modal elements. Some of the elaborating chromaticism derives from the extension of modal qualities: for example, the parallel whole-tone scales in the violins in the Minuet at two bars after rehearsal letter C are readily heard as an extension of the whole-tone step at the top of E Mixolydian scale, E–D♮. This is a far more convincing use of the whole-tone scale than at the end of the first paragraph of the Romance, where it seems unmotivated. The whole-tone scale is also generated in this way in the Finale (see the three bars before rehearsal letter B and from five bars after rehearsal letter E to letter F). It is presumably these (relatively short) examples of whole-tonery that caused one of Vaughan Williams's friends to say that he 'must have been having tea with Debussy' when he wrote the work.[9]

Writing the year before String Quartet No. 1 was revised and again saw the light of day, Edwin Evans noted that it

> has been lost apparently beyond recall, and there remains only the Phantasy Quintet for two violins, two violas, and violoncello. This has had several performances, and has made a lasting impression on those who heard it . . . in my recollection it is one of the most characteristic works of its author, and one which makes lovers of chamber music regret that his contribution to their repertoire should not be more voluminous.[10]

The Phantasy Quintet was actually composed in 1912, two years after the *Fantasia on a Theme by Thomas Tallis*, Vaughan Williams's 'breakthrough' work (in technique if not in terms of initial public recognition). So it is not surprising that there should be a much clearer sense of identity. Some of the *Fantasia*'s technical means of achieving rapt contemplation are on show in the Prelude, while the lento Alla sarabanda foreshadows the luminous, diatonic hymnic tone of the final movement of *A Pastoral Symphony* and the slow movement of Symphony No. 5. The work was commissioned by W. W. Cobbett, presumably to exemplify his chamber-music ideal of a one-movement, multi-sectional composition, though this particular piece is in essence divided into four separate movements (each linked to the next by an 'attacca').[11] Vaughan Williams does, though, employ an integrative strategy he had essayed on a much larger scale in *A London Symphony*, on which he was concurrently working – the return of the opening melodic material in a 'window' near the end of the fourth movement (Burlesca). Material from the Prelude also returns in the development section of the Scherzo.

The success of the Prelude results in large measure from the simplicity of both materials and structure. The movement begins with a pentatonic melody rising from the bottom of the viola's range. The pentatonic scale is devoid of semitones, with the consequence that, firstly, there is no inherent hierarchy: it is the metrical and rhythmic emphasis of the notes F and C that creates the sense of F as tonic. Secondly, there is no inherent sense of tension and release (there is no leading note demanding to be resolved to the tonic). It is primarily the latter that engenders the atmosphere of contemplation. After the second of the two types of material – triads moving in parallel – is brought into play, a second melody is introduced, employing the same pentatonic scale but this time descending from an f″ on violin I. The shape of the movement arises from the disposition and combination of this material. In the first section, the F centre is elaborated by shifts to the flattened mediant, A♭. The second section, meanwhile, starts with a shift to A♮: the harmony focuses on the A major triad (though this subsequently alternates with, and is supplanted by, the C that provides the route back to F), while both melodies are transposed to A: see Ex. 9.1. One could say that the melodies are counterpointed against each other, except that there is none of the propulsion normally associated with counterpoint: they are simply allowed to unfurl in the same modal 'field'. The third section is the most exploratory harmonically, visiting as before first the flat, then the sharp side, but extending a little deeper into both. The movement is then rounded off with a literal repeat of the first melody. It is partly the recognition that regions of experience have been explored but 'things remain the same' that lends this short movement such a profound sense of melancholy. The *Grove* writers observe that in the Tallis Fantasia 'hidden depths' are revealed 'contemplatively and obliquely rather than through direct dialectic'. The Prelude demonstrates this in miniature. It is a world immediately recognizable as Vaughan Williams's own. It is not without dissonance (a ninth results

Ex. 9.1. Phantasy Quintet: shift to A, 5 bars before rehearsal letter C.

from the voice-leading at four bars after rehearsal letter B, for instance, and the exact parallelisms after letter D result in a succession of false relations), but this enhances the contemplative state rather than supplying a destabilizing element.

It would be a mistake to view this as representing Vaughan Williams's only authentic mode of utterance, however. As we have already seen, some of his finest apprentice music is to be found in scherzos, and the Scherzo in this Quintet strengthens the notion that he has a particular affinity for the genre. It is cast in sonata form, and it is in the development section that the material from the Prelude makes its reappearance: the initial harmonic succession recurs from five to seven bars after rehearsal letter E and the first melody from seven bars after letter F. Like the latter, the main theme of the third movement, Alla sarabanda, is pentatonic, and because of this a kinship with the Prelude may well be felt; but there is no actual thematic connection (at least, I cannot detect one, despite Vaughan Williams's own statement that 'There is one principal theme . . . which runs through every movement'[12]). The Burlesca, which starts on the cello (that instrument having been silent in the sarabanda) confirms the overall centre as D, though the final cadence in the subdued closing section is preceded by an alternative harmonization of the violin's serene a''' by F major, the tonic triad of the first movement.

The Phantasy is evidence that Vaughan Williams had purged himself of the stylistic traits of nineteenth-century musical Romanticism, even if his world-view remained in at least some sense Romantic.[13] It could be argued that his voice was yet to emerge fully (the revision of *A London Symphony* in 1918 shows that he was tussling with how to respond to aspects of modernism), but the quality of lyricism was fully established. As I have suggested above, this is characterized by a sense of the collective: both the folksong resonances in the Phantasy, and derivations from English Renaissance music in the Tallis Fantasia, conjure up a repository of experience suspended outside time and evoke an authorial voice that is representative rather than personal and individualistic, even though the music is of course both of those things. This is consolidated in *The Lark Ascending*, which was initially completed in 1914, the year in which, in an article entitled 'British Music', Vaughan Williams discusses (however sketchily) the relationship between compositional individuality and communal utterance.[14]

Modality and melancholy: *The Lark Ascending*

Though composed just before the First World War, *The Lark Ascending* was not performed until 1920, by which time the composer had revised it. Subtitled 'Romance for violin and orchestra', it might be called a meditation on George Meredith's sentimental (and, at best, third-rate) poem of the same name, extracts from which are reproduced at the beginning of the score. Vaughan Williams's response is also often dismissed as sentimental, and too slight to be accorded serious scholarly attention.[15] It seems likely to have been one of the works that provoked the epithet 'cowpat music'.[16] Yet it is a work of greater subtlety than has been generally acknowledged.

The term 'Romance' signals lyricism, of course, and, on this occasion at least, an essentially non-dialectical approach to form, as Table. 9.1, a précis after David Manning, shows.[17] The *Grove* writers describe the work as 'wholly idyllic, and therefore different in feeling from the post-war pastoral works'.[18] It must be questioned, though, whether a 'wholly idyllic' scene is possible. As other writers have noted, only the outer sections are representational, the violin's cadenzas enacting the lark's song and ascending flight. I would suggest that a distinction between representation and commentary leads to an undermining of the idyllic – a distancing from the scene depicted that creates a powerful sense of loss.

The opening of the work is reproduced as Ex. 9.2. The orchestral 'introduction', as Manning labels it, provides a frame that allows the

Table 9.1 *Formal summary of* The Lark Ascending*

Bar	Section	Theme	Mode
1	Introduction 1		E Dorian
3	Cadenza 1	Cad. 1	D Pentatonic (D, E, F♯, A, B)
4		A1	(G, A, B, D) then D Pentatonic
5	A	A1, A2, A3	E Dorian
C.10		A4	modulating
D.10		A2, A1	E Aeolian
F.4	Introduction 2		E Dorian
F.7	Cadenza 2	Cad. 1	D Pentatonic
F.8	B	B1	E Aeolian
L.6		B2	D Dorian
R.1		B1	E Aeolian
T.10	A'	A1, A2, A3	modulating, E Aeolian
V.9		A4	modulating
W.4		A2, A1	E Aeolian
Y.1	Introduction 3		E Aeolian
Y.6	Cadenza 3	Cad. 1	E Pentatonic, B Pentatonic, E Pentatonic

*adapted from David Manning, 'Harmony, Tonality and Structure in Vaughan Williams's Music', II, 79

Ex. 9.2. *The Lark Ascending*, opening.

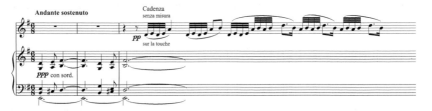

representational world to come into being. Modality does some crucial work here. Firstly, for the listener used to common-practice tonality as the norm (arguably all of us in the industrialized West) it offers something 'other'. Secondly, Vaughan Williams's particular construction of modality here allows the underpinning major ninth chord to be dissonant without needing resolution, creating a symbol of time suspended. The pentatonicism of the cadenza similarly symbolizes effortlessness. However, when the orchestra becomes a mobile accompaniment in section A (see Table 9.1), and begins to introduce melodic material derived from the soloist, it takes on a commentating role that develops with the introduction of solos from four bars before rehearsal letter B. The passage for full orchestra at letter D is the first move away from the established modal field. Initially, this proceeds without the solo violin for the first time, and with a more forceful tone (a fuller sonority), but then the soloist joins in and actually effects the climax. In so doing, the soloist moves decisively away itself from representation into commentary;[19] though the climax quickly subsides, it is not until the return of the opening material at four bars after rehearsal letter F that the initial point of view is recaptured, and it could be argued that even here the presentation is more of a reminiscence than 'the thing itself' (the reprise is, after all, truncated).

Section B begins with a new, folk-like melody in the flute, shifting the focus from the sky to ground-level and human activity: the cadenza heard earlier contained folk-like shapes, but these point towards the environment rather than connoting, as now, a community. The soloist's music is essentially decorative in the first two of the three subsections, B1 and B2. Indeed, at the end of B2, from five bars after rehearsal letter Q, it becomes pure decoration once it has jettisoned the thematic oscillating minor third. This process of liquidation has the effect of emphasizing the soloist's taking up of the flute melody in the return of B1 at letter R. In some ways this section can claim to be the linchpin of the work, in that the various reworkings create the clearest sense of nostalgia: the soloist's assumption of the flute melody, the repeated cadences supporting the soloist's languorous double-stopped descents, and the gently yearning suspensions in the soloist's subsidiary line from six to ten bars after letter R (one of only two times the soloist has them[20]) all support the effect. After this the second return of the cadenza material is imbued with an even greater sense of loss, the ambivalent modal final and *niente* ending intensifying the melancholy as an already distant vision vanishes.

The importance of endings: three concertos and a quartet

The Lark Ascending is obviously a virtuoso work, even though the virtuosity most memorably consists in being still and quiet rather than loud and flashy. But it is also the relationship between the soloist and the orchestra that marks this as essentially a concerto – the clear differentiation of roles if not the outright opposition that is commonly viewed as the essence of Romantic manifestations of the genre. The Concerto in D minor for violin and strings (1924–5), written for the Hungarian-born but London-based virtuoso Jelly d'Aranyi at around the time she gave the first performance of Ravel's *Tzigane* (1924),[21] is cast in a more traditional mould. It was originally entitled 'Concerto Accademico', though exactly why has been a source of debate. Hubert Foss sees a hearkening back to pre-Romantic approaches: 'The implication is not derogatory, as "academic" (a word of different meaning in our modern world) is used in England: only that the form derives from the eighteenth-century concertos of Bach and his fellows'.[22] A. E. F. Dickinson wonders whether 'the ulterior motive is surely some jape, some desire to avoid the burden of a full-blown concerto, by a mock reference to the earlier type'.[23] The *Grove* writers, meanwhile, see the work as 'Vaughan Williams's nearest approach to a

Bachian "neo-classicism"', and Kennedy observes a 'tightly-wrought synthesis of neo-classicism, folk-dance rhythms and triadic harmony'.[24] But it would be misleading to imply that the work represents a serious engagement with neoclassical principles. The structural organization derives from Vaughan Williams's modal practice, and the neoclassical elements are largely surface phenomena, particularly in the second and third movements. In the first, the debt of the first-group material to baroque shapes and rhythms gives a certain degree of impetus, but has the effect of depriving the music of much sense of personality; and the more folky material, such as the new pentatonic theme that initiates the second half of the development at rehearsal letter L, has the 'all-purpose' air to which Vaughan Williams's thematic invention is sometimes prone. But even if it is recognized that, like many composers who have a natural bent for symphonic composition, Vaughan Williams is generally more impressive for what he does with his material than for the quality of the material itself, the first movement is insufficiently inventive at the formal/ structural level to make much impact.

One aspect worth noting, though, is the technique of planing. Ex. 9.3 shows two instances: (a) is the beginning of the pentatonic theme mentioned above, in which the soloist and lower strings, which inhabit the same mode, are pitted against a sustained E♭ in the bass; the more protracted (b), which begins at rehearsal letter R, sees an f″-based layer pitted against a lower G♭-based layer. Both dissonances are quickly

Ex. 9.3. Violin Concerto, first movement, instances of planing: **(a)** rehearsal letter L; **(b)** rehearsal letter R.

Ex. 9.4. Violin Concerto, second movement, coda, instance of planing.

resolved, but planing (or bitonality, as it is usually called in the Vaughan Williams literature) takes on greater structural significance in later works, most famously in *Flos Campi*, completed in the same year as the concerto.[25] It is employed in the second movement, too. Ex. 9.4 shows the coda, in which the upper strings elaborate a G triad (with the parallel triadic movement that was firmly established as a Vaughan Williams fingerprint by this stage) while the lower strings descend by step until there results a clash of E♭ against G that is sustained for three bars. As in the first-movement examples, the tension is relatively local, almost colouristic: the E♭ level simply drops away to leave G unchallenged.

Tovey says of the ending of the Presto finale that it is the 'most poetically fantastic and convincing end imaginable'.[26] It is certainly the most impressive movement, and again shows Vaughan Williams's facility for the control of fast music. It is, though, the introduction of a broader melody from rehearsal letter U (a slowed-down version of the theme first stated at a bar after letter B) that sets up the 'fantastic' effect. The melody's alternation between two versions, one in the acoustic mode[27] and one in the Dorian, focuses increasingly on the equivocation between major and minor mediants that is fully crystallized at the very end of the movement. This concentration on the play of modal alternatives is possible because of the emergence of a strong tonic: a long dominant pedal beginning at two bars before rehearsal letter U is followed by a stepwise bass descent to D via A♭, G, G♭, F and E.

It can be debated whether the ending of the Piano Concerto (1926–31) is equally effective. The work underwent various revisions in 1933 and 1934, and a version for two pianos was made in 1946, before the revised ending emerged in 1947, changing the closing key from G to B.[28] B is the key of a long piano solo that precedes the coda. As discussed further below, this solo passage prefigures the ending of Symphony No. 5 in its diatonic purity and ethereal ascent. But while the closing pages of the symphony complete a work-length trajectory, there is a patchwork quality about the Piano Concerto. This is epitomized by the first of the three movements,[29] Toccata, which for all its energy gives an overall impression of being rather static. This is partly due to transitions often being engineered over the last bar or even last couple of beats of a section. But it is mostly to do with the handling of the form. Vaughan Williams's own rather terse programme note, with its use of the terms 'development' and 'recapitulation', implies a sonata-form background.[30] His listing of the thematic material suggests that the second group occurs at rehearsal figure 3, with a theme in B Aeolian. But this is not accorded the rhetorical force of a traditional second group, or indeed the length one would expect: whereas the work begins with twenty-four bars of C, the transition to the second subject group lasts just three bars; and the second subject group itself lasts only eleven bars (two short sentences of six and five bars in B Aeolian and F Aeolian respectively), before a further transition to the opening material in the tonic. Rather than setting up the traditional tonal dichotomy, Vaughan Williams's purpose seems to be to set up a solid block of C major from which the rest of the music struggles to move away. The opening is sonically massive, the soloist playing a *martellato* semiquaver figuration over octave Cs supported by the brass, while the strings have a unison rising *marcato* line. It is the latter that embodies the straining against C, with a move from C Dorian to more dissonant Locrian inflections. In reference to the traditional expositional repeat, this music returns at rehearsal figure 5 with roles swapped. The hegemony of C is epitomized by the long C pedal in the development from figure 10, but also by the ease with which C returns after the 'shortened recapitulation' (as Vaughan Williams describes it) in A♭ for the final, Largamente section: the transition is effected in just three notes.

The Romanza is in ternary form. The opening of section A, which is itself ternary, is notable for its use of planing, the pentatonic tune being placed against various elaborated triads: see Ex. 9.5, which also shows the tune's chromatic 'tail'. In the central part of section A, E major emerges as

Ex. 9.5. Piano Concerto, second movement, bars 7–13.

the first clear key to support the initial melodic pivot, B. Such clarity, though, turns out to be fugitive: the harmonic underpinning of the next two phrases returns to ambiguity – a minor seventh built on C♯ major and the overlaying of E major and A minor triads. Section B, meanwhile, is largely diatonic and notable for chains of luminous suspensions: a putatively idyllic foil to the less stable outer sections.

The final movement takes elements from the chromatic tail of Ex. 9.5 – in particular the pattern of a semitone followed by a minor third (e.g. C–B–G♯) amplified by the oboe and solo viola in the coda of the Romanza – as the basis for a chromatic fugue subject. This pattern, appearing in the bass, is the chief means of transition back to the tonic C in the first movement: see the bar before rehearsal figure 5 and the bar before figure 13 (this suggests a greater degree of unity across the work than the *Grove* writers allow). It is this fragmentary use of the hexatonic scale (so called because the replication of the interval pattern semitone–minor third across the octave results in six pitch classes), and the fugal writing itself, that most clearly marks the Concerto as 'an interesting transition to the Fourth Symphony'.[31] But it is the final section of the last of the three cadenzas, a reminiscence of section B of the Romanza, that is the most interesting music not only of the movement but also of the whole work. Cast in pure B major, it could be viewed, according to mood, as inspired or as a frankly lazy piece of composition. Ex. 9.6 shows the end of the section. As is the case throughout all of the section, there are three lines, each of which is filled out with parallel triads. The lines have to be arranged so that they are playable with only two hands, but the details of incidence are, I would suggest, otherwise inconsequential. Any dissonance is acceptable in this world so long as the tonic chord arrives at the end: the broad effect is what counts.

The Oboe Concerto of 1944 (which, like the Violin Concerto, is for soloist and strings) can be heard as a satellite of Symphony No. 5,

Ex. 9.6. Piano Concerto, third movement, end of final piano section.

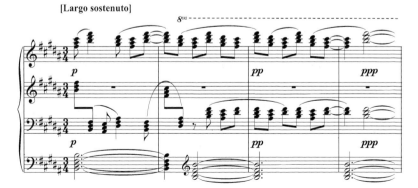

Table 9.2 *Formal summary of Oboe Concerto, first movement*

Bar	Section	Mode
1	A	A Dorian
A.7	B	G major[†]
B	A'	A Dorian
C	C	F♯ Aeolian
D	D	C Dorian
		A Dorian at letter E
F	B'	A major
		A Dorian at 5 bars after letter F
		C Lydian at 8 bars after letter F[‡]
		C Dorian at 2 bars after letter G
H	A'	mostly A Dorian

Notes:

[†] G major is the same collection as the preceding A Dorian.
[‡] C Lydian is the same collection as the preceding A Dorian.

completed the year before. The most obvious connection with the larger work is the pastoralism: the first movement of the concerto is actually entitled Rondo Pastorale, and double-reed instruments have long been associated with rural contexts. And the concerto, too, has a cyclic element: a pentatonic theme spanning an octave marks the beginning and end of each movement.

The form of the first movement is outlined in Table 9.2. The movement opens ruminatively, with a gesture not unlike the opening of *The Lark Ascending*, and the main theme is supported by the relaxed rotation of three chords (i, VII and IV); even the ensuing short cadenza seems to be taking it easy. Momentum picks up in section B, though the varied return of section A at rehearsal letter B eases down before section C picks up the pace again. Section D is quasi-developmental, drawing on the dotted rhythm that characterizes section C; section A themes emerge from rehearsal letter E onwards, literally underneath section D material. It could be claimed that the events in Ex. 9.7, which open a 'window' into the return of section B, are the key moments of the movement, ensuring that it ends with disquiet rather than the cosy glow in which it begins: when the window opens, it is on to a very different kind of stasis. C is not a new centre (it underpins much of section D), but the mode, the Lydian, is new (and relatively rare in Vaughan Williams), producing slightly more tension than the Dorian and Aeolian patterns that have prevailed up to this point, especially when the line leaps to F♯ and thus highlights the tritonal and semitonal dissonances with the underlying C triad. The subsequent juxtaposition of C major and C minor furthers the tension, and the alternation of E and E♭ returns to colour the coda, which finally settles on a rather despairing A minor.

Ex. 9.7. Oboe Concerto, first movement, C-Lydian 'window' during return of material from section B, 4 bars after rehearsal letter F.

The journey of the final movement, the longest, is rather different. The main material is of scherzo character,[32] but the form is essentially sonata form, with a development from six bars before rehearsal letter L and the recapitulation from thirteen bars after letter R after the interpolation of what is in effect a slow movement based on material from the second group. There is a greater sense of melodic expansiveness in this movement, culminating in a broad theme from nine bars after letter V. Kennedy refers to this as a 'passionate and regretful episode'. Dickinson, in a highly dismissive commentary, sees 'the penultimate resort to a new tune in G major, traditional in style if not in fact' as 'desperate'; furthermore, 'the abandonment of the original E modal minor is quite unpersuasive'.[33] In fact, the 'new tune' is adumbrated at the end of the exposition, and

E Dorian is little more than a starting point. It makes more sense to see the shape of this particular movement as being formed by balancing different characters of material and harmonic pacing rather than through tonal structure. The 'new tune' has some kinship with the hymnic music of the slow movement of Symphony No. 5, and as in that work the appoggiatura-laden diatonicism is indeed, despite the major mode, tinged with the sadness that Kennedy hears.

The last page of the contemporaneous String Quartet No. 2 in A minor (1942–4) also settles into pure diatonicism, though of the more serenely uplifting kind found in the closing pages of Symphony No. 5 (the correspondence is underlined by the use of the same key, D major, to which the music shifts from the F major of the first part of the movement). The final melodic utterance is given to the viola, which has a particular presence throughout because the work is dedicated to the violist Jean Stewart. The instrument also initiates all four movements. As Jeffrey Richards notes, 'the main theme of the movement comes from the composer's sketches for a score to a film about St Joan that never materialized'.[34] Regarding overall shape, it is with some justification that Evans writes of a 'suite-like succession'.[35] Dickinson, too, says it is 'Almost a short suite', but he is surely wrong to say that it is 'light-weight'.[36] The slow movement, which is the longest (it is the length of the others put together) and one of Vaughan Williams's least romantic 'Romances', is serious in mood, its contrapuntal *senza vibrato* opening and the ecclesiastical chordal chanting of the contrasting idea and eventual climax suggesting an aspiration towards the tone of Beethoven's late quartets. And both the first and third movements display a degree of angst not encountered in any of the other works in this chapter. As Richards observes,

> The Second String Quartet is a product of the same period of musical development as the Sixth Symphony and can be seen to share the same mood. The first three movements are bleak, anguished and jagged, and the scherzo repeats over and over again the stabbing motif that accompanies the Nazis in [the 1941 film] *49th Parallel*, the title of which Vaughan Williams marked in his score against this movement.[37]

The first movement (another bearing the title 'Prelude') is in fact the only one that has anything to do with the titular A minor, and this only unambiguously at the end, where it emerges more to articulate the moment of the music's withdrawal than to celebrate a point of arrival. This moment represents the dissolution of the considerable amount of energy generated at the beginning from a dichotomy between E minor and F minor triads (an opposition also crucial to the Sixth Symphony). Embedded within their oscillation is the semitone–minor third pattern, and this plays an increasing role, leading to several statements of a complete hexatonic scale, A–A, in Violin I towards the end of the development section (from five bars after rehearsal letter G to one bar before letter H). Whilst this does not yet fully focus A as a tonal centre, as the passage includes all twelve pitch classes of the chromatic collection, it does prepare for the eventual outcome; the middle stage in the process is the A minor triad that underpins the G#-based reprise of the second subject at the beginning of the reverse recapitulation (from nine bars after rehearsal letter H).

The beginning of the third movement is also ambiguous, but in a different way. It begins with a whole-tone motif on viola, G–F–Eb–Db (Richards's 'stabbing motif'), and during the opening section either G or Db can be regarded as the 'tonic'. Initially, because the rest of the ensemble emphasizes it, it seems that G is the tonic and that the mode is G Locrian. When the violins and cello have the motif and the viola sustains the Db, that note appears to be the tonic and the mode Db Lydian. Both of these pitch classes are later asserted as key centres: G Dorian at the climax at rehearsal letter E, then Db at eight bars after letter G before the shift to F minor for the close.

Envoi: Violin Sonata and Tuba Concerto

String Quartet No. 2 received its first performance on Vaughan Williams's seventy-second birthday. On his eighty-second birthday he was present at the first performance of a work with the same titular key, the Sonata for Violin and Pianoforte in A minor (1954). The role of the titular centre is this time more traditional: the first movement, Fantasia, begins and ends in some form of A (Aeolian at the start; more chromaticized but closing on the A minor triad at the end), and the work concludes with an A major triad. The middle movement, another scherzo, begins and ends in a relatively traditional related area, the subdominant, D. While the quartet is compact and highly focused, and one of the most impressive works discussed in this chapter, the Violin Sonata seems (certainly in the outer movements) diffuse and often routine: Evans's complaint about the late symphonies that 'the habits of composition have outlasted the impulse' is perhaps appropriate here.[38] He notes of the Sonata that the Fantasia 'is in fact a sonata movement, propelled by those minor 3rd shifts prominent in the Fourth Symphony',[39] but the rather episodic – if frequently energetic – approach suggests that 'Fantasia' is indeed a more appropriate title. The Scherzo, driven by unpredictable accentuation and harmonic deflection, compels more sustained concentration. While there are moments of comparative quiet – at rehearsal figure 10, for example, and in the coda from figure 14 – rhythmic or harmonic tension is maintained. The Variations of the final movement are based on the theme from the last movement of the 1903 Piano Quintet, delivered at the outset in octaves by the piano. This is representative of the utilitarian aspect that frequently mars Vaughan Williams's writing for the piano, whose part here often seems like an orchestral reduction: there is little attempt (apart from a few moments in the Scherzo) to explore the instrument's characteristic sonorities.

The Tuba Concerto (1954) is much shorter (under fourteen minutes in contrast to the twenty-seven or so of the Violin Sonata), presumably in deference to the physical demands of the instrument, whose capabilities Vaughan Williams took 'great pains' to explore.[40] The work benefits greatly from the reduced dimensions: there is a tighter structure, more sharply etched material, and it is much clearer what the composer is setting out to achieve. There is an obvious danger in writing a serious work for an instrument that, because of its size and perceived lack of agility, has often been characterized as comic, but Vaughan Williams takes the tuba into territory far away from caricature, especially in the second movement, Romanza. The music here perhaps risks sentimentality, particularly when the orchestra 'corrects' the tuba's F♮ of the penultimate bar so that the movement ends on a tonic major triad that can seem a little too sweet, but otherwise the composer demonstrates once again the nostalgic, melancholic potential in pure diatonicism (see, for example, the tuba's appoggiatura-laden descents from its second bar, and in particular the descent to low B, supported by a move from D major to B Aeolian, at the end of the first paragraph).

The outer movements may not be emotionally searching, but they sustain the listener's interest in simple but effective ways: as Vaughan Williams's own programme note announces, 'The music is fairly simple and obvious and can probably be listened to without much previous explanation'.[41] The first movement is an inventive sonata-form hybrid in which the development is concurrent with the recapitulation, such is the degree of reworking in the latter. The rumbustious finale – Rondo alla tedesca – relies on Vaughan Williams's trademark alternative scale-degrees and chromatic sideslips to generate tension: see in particular the *poco animato* from five bars before rehearsal figure 9 that leads to the final cadenza. Set alongside the symphonies – including Symphony No. 9 (1956–8), which is relatively compact in comparison with all the others except No. 8 – the Tuba Concerto clearly has reduced ambitions. But it epitomizes Vaughan Williams's (decidedly unmodernistic) desire, even to the end of his career, to meet the need for a broad range of musical experiences for performer and listener alike. And if it can be said that there is an aspect of 'lateness' about Symphony No. 9, the final works in both the chamber and concerto genres have nothing of this about them.

Notes

1 Its popularity in the UK can be gauged by its being voted 'the top piece of classical music' in the Classic FM Hall of Fame four years running between 2007 and 2010 (see www.classicfm. com/hall-of-fame/, accessed 30 May 2013; the website proclaims the work to be 'No.1 for a 3rd year'). The work was also chosen as the focus of the BBC's populist *Culture Show*, in a commemoration of the 50th anniversary of Vaughan Williams's death broadcast on 8 July 2008: see www.bbc.co.uk/cultureshow/videos/ 2008/07/s5_e6_williams/index.shtml, accessed 30 May 2013.

2 Several of the works examined here were revised, sometimes more than once; a more expansive study would find considerable interest in comparisons, but here I address only the final versions. I will also not attempt to discuss here the Concerto for Cello and Orchestra that Vaughan Williams completed in short-score draft form in the early 1940s but never brought to full fruition.

3 All the recently published early chamber works have been recorded by the Nash Ensemble, on Hyperion CDA67381/2, released in 2002. Another early work relevant to this chapter is the Fantasia for Piano and Orchestra, on which Vaughan Williams laboured intermittently between 1896 and 1904, after which it appears to have been set aside; though completed, it was never performed.

4 This is derived, ultimately, from Samuel Sebastian Wesley and other nineteenth-century ecclesiastical composers: see Jeremy C. Dibble, 'Parry and Elgar: A New Perspective', *MT* 125 (1984), 639–43.

5 *KW*, 83.

6 *MT* 50 (1909), 797.

7 Hugh Ottaway and Alain Frogley, 'Vaughan Williams, Ralph', in *Grove Music Online, Oxford Music Online*, www. oxfordmusiconline.com/subscriber/article/ grove/music/42507 (accessed 30 May 2013).

8 Peter Evans, 'Instrumental Music I', in Stephen Banfield (ed.), *The Blackwell History of Music in Britain: The Twentieth Century* (Oxford: Blackwell, 1995), 245.

9 *KW*, 90.

10 Edwin Evans, 'Modern British Composers: Ralph Vaughan Williams', *MT* 61 (1920), 232–4, 302–5, 371–4, at 373.

11 Cobbett established a chamber-music prize in 1905, originally for a Phantasy Quartet. As *Grove* explains, 'There followed numerous other awards for such "phantasies", a name Cobbett chose as a modern analogue of the Elizabethan viol fancies, in which a single movement includes a number of sections in different rhythms – or as Stanford defined the genre, a condensation of the three or four movements of a sonata into a single movement of moderate dimensions.' Frank Howes and Christina Bashford, 'Cobbett, Walter Willson', in *Grove Music Online, Oxford Music Online*, www.oxfordmusiconline.com/subscriber/ article/grove/music/06006 (accessed 30 May 2013).

12 Programme note for the first performance reproduced in *VWOM*, 337.

13 Julian Onderdonk suggests Vaughan Williams 'never rid himself of certain romanticized notions about traditional music', for example (Julian Onderdonk, 'Vaughan Williams's Folksong Transcriptions', in *VWS*, 138).

14 *VWOM*, 43–56.

15 An exception can be found in the second chapter of David Manning, 'Harmony, Tonality and Structure in Vaughan Williams's Music' (PhD dissertation, Cardiff University, 2003).

16 The term was coined by Elisabeth Lutyens: see 'Cowpat Music', in *The Oxford Dictionary of Music, Oxford Music Online*, www. oxfordmusiconline.com/subscriber/article/ opr/t237/e2526 (accessed 30 May 2013).

17 Manning, 'Harmony, Tonality and Structure in Vaughan Williams's Music', 79.

18 Ottaway and Frogley, *Grove Music Online*.

19 This new role is briefly pre-echoed at two to three bars after rehearsal letter C.

20 The other is from three bars after rehearsal letter V.

21 Bartók's two Violin Sonatas were also written for her, in 1921 and 1922.

22 Hubert Foss, *Ralph Vaughan Williams: A Study* (London: Harrap, 1950), 170.

23 A. E. F. Dickinson, *Vaughan Williams* (London: Faber and Faber, 1963), 412.

24 Ottaway and Frogley, *Grove Music Online*; *KW*, 216.

25 *Flos Campi* is discussed in detail in Chapter 2, 48–9.

26 Donald Francis Tovey, *Essays in Musical Analysis*, vol. 11 (London: Oxford University Press, 1935), 208.

27 The acoustic mode is the major scale with sharpened fourth and flattened seventh.

28 Duncan Hinnells, 'Vaughan Williams's Piano Concerto: The First Seventy Years', in *VWIP*, 132–4.

29 The track listing on some of the commercially available recordings lists four movements, regarding the 'alla Tedesca' part of the third movement, Fuga chromatica con Finale alla Tedesca, as separate. The published score (out of print at the date of writing) is clear that there are three movements.

30 *VWOM*, 352.

31 Ottaway and Frogley, *Grove Music Online*.

32 Kennedy writes that 'A discarded scherzo of the [Fifth] symphony was turned into part of an Oboe Concerto for Léon Goossens' (*KW*, 285), and presumably he is referring to the final movement. The prominence of fourths (see, for example, the four bars before rehearsal letter A) is reminiscent of the published Scherzo of Symphony No. 5.

33 *KW*, 347; Dickinson, *Vaughan Williams*, 422.

34 Jeffrey Richards, 'Vaughan Williams and British Wartime Cinema', in *VWS*, 151.

35 Evans, 'Instrumental Music 1', 245.

36 Dickinson, *Vaughan Williams*, 474.

37 Richards, 'Vaughan Williams and British Wartime Cinema', 150.

38 Evans, 'Instrumental Music 1', 187. I do not agree, however, with his assessment of Symphony No. 9, in particular, which seems to me rather harsh.

39 *Ibid.*, 245–6.

40 *KW*, 362.

41 *VWOM*, 379.

10 The later symphonies

JULIAN HORTON

Contexts for the later symphonies

One of the most striking aspects of Vaughan Williams's long career is his late flowering as a symphonist. When the composer turned sixty in 1932, he had three symphonic works to his name: *A Sea Symphony*, completed in 1909; *A London Symphony*, which dates from 1910–14; and *A Pastoral Symphony*, composed during and after the First World War. Between 1934 and 1957, Vaughan Williams completed six further essays in the genre, establishing himself as one of the great twentieth-century symphonists and contributing vitally both to the consolidation of British symphonism and to the reorientation of the genre after Mahler away from central Europe and towards the Slavic, Scandinavian, Francophone and Anglophone contexts.

Charting this progression is, however, neither historically nor analytically straightforward. The direction the symphonic cycle would eventually take is, for instance, not easily inferred from the first three symphonies. As a multi-movement cantata, *A Sea Symphony* is closer in conception to Mahler's Symphony No. 8 or Rachmaninov's *The Bells* than to any of Vaughan Williams's subsequent essays in the genre; *A London Symphony* prefigures the programmatic aspirations of the *Sinfonia Antartica*, but not its technical means; and although many features of *A Pastoral Symphony* are carried forward in later works, as a whole it gives only a sketchy indication of the later symphonic idiom's expressive and technical range.

Moreover, the division into earlier and later symphonic phases is itself problematic. I have assumed throughout that Symphony No. 4 should be regarded as the first work of a second phase, but this view has not received multilateral endorsement. Writing before the completion of Symphonies Nos. 8 and 9, Frank Howes divided Nos. 1–6 into three groups of two, thereby attaching No. 4 to its predecessor, notwithstanding their chronological distance: as he phrased it, 'two are pre-war, two inter-war, and two in-war'.[1] *Sinfonia Antartica* by these terms stands alone as 'a symphonic poem cast into a formal mould as a symphony'.[2] Michael Kennedy also distinguishes between a pre-war or 'Edwardian' manner in *A Sea*

Symphony and *A London Symphony* and a more ascetic, Ravelian style in *A Pastoral Symphony*: however, he then groups *A Pastoral Symphony* with Nos. 4 and 5 as 'inter-war' works; and having the benefit of access to the complete cycle, he attaches No. 6 to Nos. 7–9 as 'post-war' symphonies, characterized by their shared debt to the composer's wartime film scores, most overt in the relationship between the score for *Scott of the Antarctic* and the *Sinfonia Antartica*.[3] Alain Frogley, by contrast, discriminates between the first two symphonies and a central cycle of four, which he further divides into two non-consecutive groups: Symphonies Nos. 4 and 6 emphasize 'chromaticism, dissonance, and rhythmic turbulence', while *A Pastoral Symphony* and Symphony No. 5 betray 'a mode of expression shaped by the influence of English folksong, Tudor music and the works of Debussy and Ravel'.[4] Unlike Kennedy, Frogley treats the last three symphonies separately, noting that 'Although each of the final group of symphonies has its own particular character, all three works share a tendency to synthesize elements from the two polarized worlds of the symphonies from the "Pastoral" to the Sixth'.[5] All these perspectives have merit; however, I will argue here for the subdivision advocated by James Day, Elliott S. Schwartz and Hugh Ottaway into early, middle and late trilogies respectively.[6] *Pace* Frogley, I perceive a critical shift in technique and concept separating *A Pastoral Symphony* and Symphony No. 4; and *pace* Kennedy, I regard Symphony No. 6 as belonging to a line of development initiated with No. 4, apparent in a commonality of technical, formal and expressive means.

This partitioning is supported by contextual factors. Symphony No. 4, completed in 1934, not only occupies a key position in Vaughan Williams's *oeuvre*, but is also his pivotal contribution to the interwar rejuvenation of British symphonism. The primary influence for this notion of symphonic modernism was Sibelius, whose music was advocated as a compositional model by a number of influential commentators, notably Cecil Gray and Constant Lambert;[7] as J. P. E. Harper-Scott has recently observed, Sibelius was 'the post-war influence of choice for British composers'.[8] A substantial corpus of works flowed from this context, among them William Walton's Symphony No. 1 (1934), the seven symphonies of Arnold Bax (1922–39) and the first five of Havergal Brian (1919–37). Vaughan Williams's identification of Symphony No. 4 with the aspiration to compose a 'modern' symphony consequently implied above all a post-Sibelian symphony.

The larger context for Anglo-Sibelian symphonic modernism is the consolidation of what is often termed the 'nationalist' symphony, or the types of symphonism emerging outside of the Austro-German sphere in the late nineteenth and early twentieth centuries. If Sibelius and Nielsen furnished the dominant Scandinavian paradigms, coeval interwar strands of development can also be identified in Russia, where a version of symphonic modernism coalesced in Shostakovich's symphonies Nos. 1–4 of 1926–36, and in the works of expatriate Russian composers, of which the most well-known examples are Prokofiev's Symphonies Nos. 2–4 (1924–5, 1928 and 1929–30 respectively), Rachmaninov's No. 3 (1935–6) and Stravinsky's Symphony in C (1938–40).[9] To this we must also add Francophone contributions in the wake of Saint-Saëns, Franck and D'Indy, notably Roussel's Symphonies Nos. 2–4 (1919–34) and Honegger's Symphony No. 1 (1930),[10] as well as American symphonism in the aftermath of Charles Ives, primarily Copland's three symphonies (1926–46) and Roy Harris's Symphonies Nos. 1–6 (1933–44).[11] If Vaughan Williams's Symphony No. 4 adopts an Anglo-Sibelian pose, it also responds to an international symphonic currency, the presence of which is markedly stronger after the First World War.

The following offers a broad analytical commentary on the six later symphonies, isolating salient structural characteristics and pursuing their extra-musical connotations. I have for the most part resisted the temptation to ground this commentary in a single theory or methodology, but instead draw out thematic, formal, tonal and post-tonal processes in each work, relating them where pertinent to commonly averred extra-musical meanings. The distinction between dynamic and static conceptions of form is a central concern, being vital to both the technical and extra-musical dimensions of Vaughan Williams's evolving symphonic attitude.

Symphonies Nos. 4, 5 and 6

Symphonies Nos. 4–6 are most overtly Sibelian in their address on problems of formal integration.[12] A preoccupation with thematicism pervades Symphony No. 4 especially, both at an intra- and inter-movement level. Vaughan Williams himself identified two themes that, as he put it, 'run through this Symphony' (see Ex. 10.1), and also pointed out the derivation of the Finale's main subject from the flute theme entering in bar 61 of the slow movement, and the reprise of the Symphony's opening in the Finale's coda.[13]

Ex. 10.1. Symphony No. 4, two main themes.

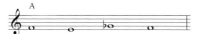

The composer's analytical commentaries are notoriously cursory; here, as elsewhere, the situation is more complex than he suggests. In fact, the work is overlaid with a dense web of thematic links, clarified in Exx. 10.2a–d. As Ex. 10.2a shows, theme 'A' is a variant of its precursor ('a') from bar 1. 'A' recurs in three successively diminished forms in the Scherzo's introduction, in the Finale's development (bar 189), and as the first subject of the fugal epilogue. Variant 'a' reasserts itself in the coda's recall of the symphony's opening. The Scherzo introduction's third variant of 'A' also supplies the accompaniment to a main theme derived from 'B', which as Ex. 10.2b shows, is adumbrated at the movement's opening. Theme 'B' is also a critical ancillary idea in the slow movement, forming the substance of the introduction and recurring as a marker of each major climax. In the

Ex. 10.2(a). Symphony No. 4, examples of theme 'A' in first, third and fourth movements.

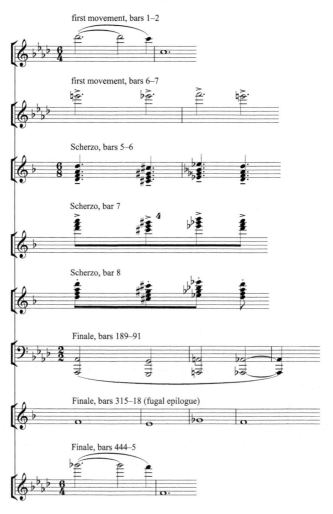

Ex. 10.2(b). Symphony No. 4, examples of theme 'B' in first, second, third and fourth movements.

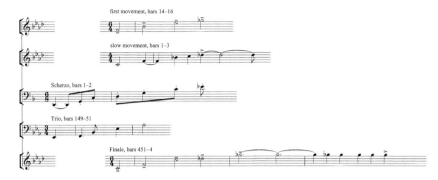

Ex. 10.2(c). Symphony No. 4, recurrence of first movement 'C' theme in the fourth movement.

Ex. 10.2(d). Symphony No. 4, recurrence of second movement flute theme in the fourth movement.

Finale, bar 177 in the development core supplies a shadowy reminiscence of the first movement's closing-section theme (labelled 'C' in Ex. 10.2c). Lastly, the Finale's main theme (Ex. 10.2d) retrieves the slow-movement flute theme.

The work's most blatant cyclical device is, however, the Finale's fugal epilogue, the complexities of which are hardly conveyed by Vaughan Williams's bland observation that it combines 'A' with the movement's other subjects. Table 10.1 summarizes its entry structure and the origins of the themes.

Table 10.1 *Symphony No. 4, fourth movement, fugal epilogue*

Bars:	309	354	379	424	444
Fugue:	1	2	3	4	Coda
Material:	A stretto	A dimin.; Finale A2; B	A stretto, dimin.; Finale B1	A aug.; Finale A1	first-movement reprise (A and B)
Pitch level of entries (/ indicates counterpoint of A and one or more themes):	F, C	Gb/Bb, Fb/Eb, G/Bb/Eb	D, A, F#/D, C	F, C, C/F	–

The table reveals that the epilogue more specifically consists of four fugues, each pitting 'A' against a different counter-subject. The first is a stretto fugue, in which 'A' is its own counter-subject, combined both as a whole-note subject and in diminution. The second pits 'A' against the Finale's second main-theme-group idea, labelled 'A2', as well as a variant of 'B'. In the third fugue, 'A' confronts the Finale's second theme, labelled B1, combined from bar 385 with 'A' in stretto. The fourth fugue crowns the structure with the combination of 'A' in augmentation and the Finale's main theme, labelled 'A1'. Fugues three and four are linked by an extended episode, based on the Finale's closing-section material, labelled C, given in dialogue with numerous variants of 'A', as *rectus, inversus* and (loosely) *per arsis et thesis*. As Table 10.1 explains, each fugue is organized into subject-answer pairings around a specific complex of pitch levels: fugue 1 is centred on F and C; fugue 2 on Gb, Bb and Eb; fugue 3 primarily around A and D, with additional entries on F#, C and E; fugue 4 returns to F and C, culminating on the tonic F.

Although neither Symphony No. 5 nor No. 6 matches No. 4's dense cyclical logic, inter-movement relationships are nevertheless present. Symphony No. 5 has one clear cyclical event (Ex. 10.3): the first movement's initial material interrupts the Passacaglia's variation sequence four bars before rehearsal figure 14, pitting three of the first movement's main-theme ideas against the *Hauptmotiv* of the finale's ground bass. The latter occurs five times as an elaboration of the bass pedal C, above which the work's initial horn call, labelled 'a1', appears seven times in complete or incomplete forms, counterpointed against the first movement's principal subject from rehearsal figure 14.8 (labelled 'a3'), and prefacing the response to the horn call (labelled 'a2') in figure 14.14.[14] There are, additionally, three more generalized first-movement correspondences. Firstly, the passage also invokes the first-movement main theme's accompanimental texture, evident in the consistent dotted figures. Secondly, the C pedal itself recalls the symphony's opening; its embellishment with the Passacaglia *Hauptmotiv* is consequently also a cyclical

Ex. 10.3. Symphony No. 5, fourth movement, 4 bars before rehearsal number 14.

synthesis, through which the harmonic milieu of the first-movement subject incorporates finale material. Thirdly, the first-movement material's underlying progression from D major to D minor over a C pedal is also retrieved, a recollection having critical structural consequences.

Several issues converge in this passage. In one respect, it constitutes a 'breakthrough' in the Adornian sense, influentially defined by James Hepokoski as an 'unforeseen in-breaking of a seemingly new (although normally motivically related) event'.[15] The Preludio material descends on the finale from outside, interrupting the form's flow (it interjects between the twenty-seventh and twenty-eighth variations) and imposing an unprepared harmonic event. The bass pedal is emblematic of this char-acteristic: because the form is driven by the repetition of a bass line, the pedal freezes its structural agent on a single pitch. The passage also elaborates a formal characteristic of the first movement: the Preludio's analogous material (as far as rehearsal figure 2) establishes a recursive model as the basis of an additive process of varied recurrence acting against the implied sonata context. Because the reprise of this model in the Finale recovers all its elements, and (despite revisions) in the same twenty-bar span, it effectively continues the first movement's formal process, as if Vaughan Williams had simply deferred its completion in order to accommodate the intervening movements. The 'breakthrough' consequently both interjects within the Finale, and reframes the material of the second, third and fourth movements as an interjection suspending the first movement's formal action.

Symphony No. 6 forsakes No. 4's dense thematicism and No. 5's large-scale cyclical recall for more elusive cross-references. The epilogue's opening retrieves three first-movement elements in a radically altered context (see Ex. 10.4). The implied clash between E minor and F minor in the first move-ment's main theme is also skeletally reprised here, the bass settling on an E pedal while the first violins intone the rising trichord F–G –A♭. As Ex. 10.4 demonstrates, the violins' continuation takes up and inverts the second motivic element of the first movement's theme. These two ideas saturate

Ex. 10.4. Symphony No. 6, relationship between opening themes of first and fourth movements.

the movement: instead of working synthetically with thematic combination (as in Symphony No. 4) or large-scale reprise (as in Symphony No. 5), Vaughan Williams trades in fragmentation: the Epilogue functions as an exhaustive, if understated, liquidation of first-movement material.

The E–F semitonal clash mobilizes a structural principle, which is basic to all three works and further differentiates them from the three earlier symphonies, namely the generative use of harmonic and modal duality. In Symphony No. 4, themes 'A' and 'B' are related by their common origin in the work's opening gesture, a semitonal dyad projected both horizontally and vertically, which proves crucial to the entire structural narrative: the motive Db–C in the violins and winds in bar 1, labelled 'a', is its own harmonic context, since Db also clashes with the bass C on the first beat of the bar (Ex. 10.5). Transposed, this ninth also forms the end-point of theme 'B', which peaks in bar 15 on a Gb supported by F in the bass; the quartal ascent with which B begins is thus really a prefix to a harmonic variant of 'a'. As if to clarify the relationship, Vaughan Williams reprises the initial material from bar 20, transposed so that the Gb–F dyad is reiterated.

As the symphony progresses, 'a' is accorded greater harmonic substance (see Ex. 10.6). The first-theme return initiating the first movement's development section transposes 'a' as Eb–D, the latter harmonized within a second-inversion D minor triad. At the start of the recapitulation, 'a' acquires a harmonic character with which it is associated for the rest of the piece: the Gb participates in a Gb minor triad, the third admittedly spelled enharmonically as A♮; and the dissonant ninth is now the frame for a clash between an F minor triad and a chromatic neighbouring chord. The slow movement's twin introductory statements of 'B' harmonize its final pitch in a similar way, as Ex. 10.6 indicates: each statement peaks on a Db minor chord supported by a bass C. This in effect summarizes the movement's gestural trajectory: its two pivotal climaxes (bars 56–7 and 90–1) are both signalled by the return of 'B' untransposed, bringing successive processes of melodic intensification to a point of culmination on the same critical sonority.

Ex. 10.5. Symphony No. 4, first movement, semitonal clashes in themes A and B.

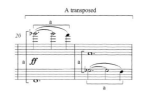

Ex. 10.6. Symphony No. 4, transformations of themes A and B.

In fact, the dissonant neighbouring chord is never allowed fully to resolve. The reprise of the symphony's opening from bar 444 of the Finale retrieves the first movement's grating Gb minor–F minor clash. The work's last harmonic gesture, in bars 451–5, categorically refutes the possibility of any smooth accommodation of Gb within the tonic context. Theme 'B' builds in the brass towards a tutti, *fortissimo* reiteration of the F/Gb sonority. Rather than a smooth descent of Gb on to the tonic, Vaughan Williams isolates this dissonance with an abrupt caesura, and the final chord brutally enforces F at the expense of its modally defining third.

Arnold Whittall has noted a similar 'destabilizing contrast' in the opening paragraph of Symphony No. 5, albeit clothed in a very different

Ex. 10.7. Symphony No. 5, first movement, opening, and alternative modal analyses.

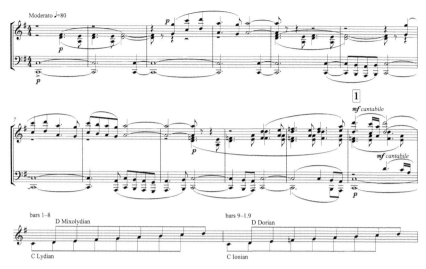

expressive garb. The critical ambiguity here is between C as tonic and C as neighbour to D. Whittall pursues this as a basic structural device;[16] elaborating on this reading, we can identify two successive ambiguities in the Preludio, both arising from the conflict between C and D as potential final tones. In bars 1–8, this is expressed as a tension between Lydian C and Mixolydian D: if we orientate our hearing around the bass C, then the music projects the former; if we orientate it around the horn call, then C behaves as the bass of a D$^4_2$ chord, and the music projects the latter (Ex. 10.7).

The exchange of F♯ for F♮ in bar 9 introduces the second duality: we now have to choose between Ionian C and Dorian D. In both cases, the fundamental relationship is the major second C–D. At the end of the first movement, this tension is left unresolved. There is no convergence on a stable tonic; instead, the C–D dyad persists in the final bars without harmonic elaboration. The catalyst for resolution comes with the finale's 'breakthrough' reprise of the symphony's opening, in the wake of which the bass C is dispelled in favour of a grounding D pedal.

In Symphony No. 6, the question of modal conflict gains complexity, because the work's initial material implies at least four possible modal origins, all of which the work exploits (see Ex. 10.8). At the start, the notation posits a conflict between semitonally distant minor modes (F and E) that is redolent of Symphony No. 4. Towards the end of bar 1, however, a contrary impression emerges of modal mixture over the same root: respelled enharmonically, the soprano A♭ could also be the raised third of E major. The material in bar 1 also implies two

Ex. 10.8. Symphony No. 6, first movement, opening, and alternative modal analyses.

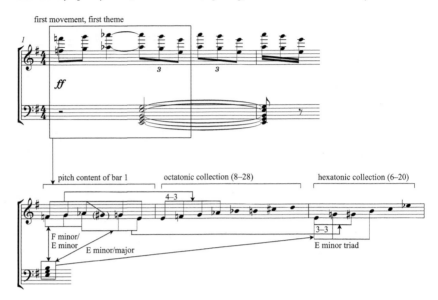

symmetrical pitch collections: altogether, it forms a tetrachord of the octatonic collection (4–3 in set-theoretical notation); the A♭–G–E tail suggests a hexatonic origin (3–3 being a subset of the hexatonic set 6–20), a context into which the underlying E minor triad also fits.

Vaughan Williams deploys these contrasting implications strategically throughout the symphony. The sense of modal mixture comes to the fore in the first movement's coda. From bar 159, the reprise of the subordinate theme first heard from bar 82 exchanges E minor for E major, but the harmony moves freely between the two modes, and the climactic return of the opening in bars 187–190 respells A♭ as G♯, temporarily dispelling the incipient E minor/F minor duality. Later on, the hexatonic trichord gains harmonic significance. The climax in bars 117–29 of the slow movement alternates G♭ major and G minor triads over a B♭ pedal, anticipating in transposition the oscillating D♯ major–E minor progression with which the symphony ends. This arises from the pairing of two inversionally related forms of the trichord 3–3 around an 'axial' central pitch (Ex. 10.9). G♭ major and G minor hold the pitch B♭ in common; the pitch content of the two chords laid out in succession produces the five-note set 5–2.[17]

In addition to their structural significance, these techniques are also programmatically suggestive, being deployed in the service of symphonic narratives, which, despite Vaughan Williams's tight-lipped responses to such suggestions, resonate irresistibly with their cultural and political circumstances: for No. 4, the looming European crisis of the 1930s; for No. 5, written between 1938 and 1943, the war itself; and for No. 6, completed in 1947, its atomic aftermath.[18]

Ex. 10.9. Symphony No. 6, second and fourth movements, transformations of pairs of inversionally related 3–3 trichords.

Symphony No. 5's crucial interpretative associations have been, firstly, its apparent withdrawal from No. 4's aggression, and secondly, its relationship with the contemporaneous opera on John Bunyan's *The Pilgrim's Progress*, completed in 1949. The former characteristic habitually licences interpretation as a plea for peace in the midst of war, the latter as a journey towards a musical analogy of Bunyan's 'Celestial City', attained in the work's valedictory coda.[19] Attractive though these readings are, they conceal other, less pointedly metaphysical agendas. Symphony No. 5 for instance projects a suggestive music-historical narrative, evinced in the Preludio by the mediation of pre- and post-tonal idioms. The dualism of the opening is founded on pre-tonal modality, albeit projected as an interpretative simultaneity rather than a unitary resource. In contrast, the middle section exploits pentatonic heterophony: linear projections of the pentatonic collection are overlaid contrapuntally, such that the collection is also expressed as a vertical sonority, most forcefully in the climax in rehearsal figure 10.5–11. Between these extremes, Vaughan Williams introduces sequential and cadential progressions mingling archaism with post-tonal triadic harmony. We first encounter this in rehearsal figure 6.3–6.5, which establishes a 10–5 linear intervallic pattern followed by a modal v^7–I cadence, which echoes the so-called 'English' cadence in its use of a lowered leading note. Shortly afterwards, a variant of this progression closes the section in rehearsal figure 6.10–6a.1; the cadence subsequently appears in G in rehearsal figure 13.4–13.5, and the whole progression recurs in its most expansive form as the substance of the climax in rehearsal figure 13.15–14.1.

The dialogue of these dimensions is rich in interpretative possibilities. The contrivance of a post-tonal medium from pre-tonal materials narrates the revivification of English music through recovery of its pre-tonal ancestry, a theme explicit in Vaughan Williams's music at least from the Tallis Fantasia onwards. In the Preludio, this dialectic of tradition and innovation is marshalled as an agent of nostalgia: the modal cadences emerge as glimpses of a lost musical order, the subsequent dissipation of which is each time as pronounced as its mounting presentational force. The cadences invoke not simply a pre-war world, but more accurately a pre-modern one, antedating the tortuous conditions of musical modernism and political catastrophe.

Yet because it is caught between modal dualism and heterophony, the sequence–cadence model also cohabits with the arbiters of its own salvation, made most explicit at the end of the finale. The quiet resolution of the C/D duality on to a D pedal in rehearsal figure 15.2 ushers in a coda that projects a synthesis of the three dimensions introduced successively in the Preludio. The modal dualisms are dispelled, because the diatonic D modality is entirely consistent with the D pedal in the bass, but the harmony is modal-heterophonic rather than tonal, the various lines combining so as persistently to create diatonic pitch clusters, which only clarify to triadic harmony in the final D major chord. Vaughan Williams's 'Celestial City' is a new musical order, in which there is no contradiction between modal and post-tonal harmonic means.

Although sharing Symphony No. 5's mediation of pre- and post-tonality, Symphonies Nos. 4 and 6 by contrast suggest narratives of negation and resignation. Symphony No. 4 mobilizes the high-classical summative finale – apparent in the Beethovenian elision of Scherzo and Finale and the contrapuntal coda after Mozart's 'Jupiter' Symphony – but in order to deny its potential for synthesis.[20] Vaughan Williams's forcefully end-directed structure decisively rejects transcendental affirmation by dissociating thematic combination and resolution of the symphony's

Ex. 10.10. Symphony No. 6, third movement, opening.

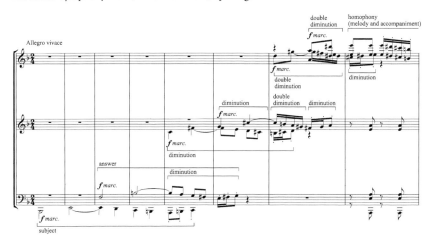

propulsive structural dissonance. The synthetic efforts of the finale's fugal epilogue come to nothing, because, at the end, the work's generative modal duality remains starkly exposed; as Wilfrid Mellers writes, 'Fugal unity fails; it cannot engulf, or gobble up, the contradictions'.[21]

Symphony No. 6 reformulates the same narrative of failure in valedictory terms. As with Symphony No. 4, so here also the narrative's expressive core is the failure to attain the synthesis of modal duality through counterpoint. The Scherzo, for instance, narrates an unstable dialogue between a counterpoint that persistently congeals into melody and accompaniment, and a thematic homophony that persistently dissolves into counterpoint. The movement's opening, analysed in Ex. 10.10, clearly reveals this. In bars 1–7, Vaughan Williams piles up successively diminished forms of the movement's principal motive, but the entry structure and the diminution process are irregular: the 'answer' in bar 3 is initially literal, but the subject's note values are diminished from bar 5; the entry in bar 5 is a strict diminution; and the entry in bar 6 shifts between diminution and double diminution. Bars 1–8, in brief, initiate a contrapuntal form, which they cannot sustain. The Shostakovichian music in bars 8–19 contrastingly comprises two themes (in bars 8–15 and 16–19) presented against syncopated chords, which fail to maintain their simple melody-and-accompaniment texture, instead tending increasingly towards counterpoint.[22]

The Epilogue is not, as is sometimes suggested, a 'subjectless' fugue; rather, each entry cultivates a tension between stable and variable contrapuntal features, which, as we have already seen, are derived from the first movement. In one sense, the Scherzo's contrapuntal impulse is fulfilled here, because the fugal entry structure is unchallenged as the Epilogue's guiding formal principle. Yet we are still a long way from genuine counterpoint: fugal writing is made to serve a textural rather than a contrapuntal end. The oft-noted tonal ambivalence of the closing bars again signifies an abyss-like distance between the synthetic aspirations of contrapuntal forms and their ultimate impotence in the face of an irreparable rift in the music's tonal fabric. Whereas in Symphony No. 4 this rift is formulated as violence, in Symphony No. 6 it informs a symphonic 'farewell', to which the oscillating closing triads furnish a gestural vanishing point. The parallel with Mahler's Symphony No. 9, the Rondo Burleske and Adagio of which also contrast dissonant counterpoint and valedictory leave-taking, is striking.[23]

Symphonies Nos. 7, 8 and 9

Although Symphony No. 6 and the *Sinfonia Antartica* are both coloured by Vaughan Williams's wartime turn to film composition and hold technical characteristics in common, they are in many respects radically different, diverging particularly in their conceptions of large-scale symphonic process. Notwithstanding numerous inter-movement links, *Sinfonia Antartica* conveys a much weaker sense of dynamic trajectory, replacing linear narrative with a more episodic manner and a frequent concentration on static structures.[24] In truth, the last three symphonies are all in various ways imbued with these qualities, suggesting that the dialogue with modernism evident in Symphonies Nos. 4–6 has here ceded to a rather different perspective.

The genesis of the *Sinfonia Antartica* (1949–52) in the sketches for the music to the film *Scott of the Antarctic* (1948) moreover points to an overtly programmatic agenda, which locates the *Sinfonia* in a different symphonic subgenre. If Symphonies Nos. 4–6 engage with the 'absolute' symphonic model from Beethoven's Fifth to Sibelius's Seventh, then the *Sinfonia* is a programme symphony in the vein of Liszt's *Dante*, Tchaikovsky's *Manfred* and Rimsky-Korsakov's *Antar*; but it embodies a uniquely twentieth-century take on this subgenre, supplanting the nineteenth-century affiliation of symphony and literary or poetic sources with a debt to filmic narrative.[25] The *Sinfonia* remains true to its genealogy in its looser attitude towards generic markers: it has five movements rather than four; and although the internal movements expand upon the traditional scheme – two dance movements ('Scherzo' and 'Intermezzo') frame a slow movement ('Landscape') – the outer movements pay no more than lip service to sonata and rondo forms. The programmatic lineage is also underscored by the provision of literary epigrams for each movement, from Shelley's *Prometheus Unbound*, Psalm 140, Coleridge's *Hymn before Sunrise in the Vale of Chamouni*, Donne's *The Sun Rising* and Scott's last journal respectively.

The composer's programme note indicates four specific associations between film and *Sinfonia*.[26] Vaughan Williams explains that a 'theme accompanied by deep bells' in the first movement (rehearsal figure 12.9–12.16) 'was supposed in the film to be "menacing"'. Two ideas in the Scherzo are then curtly related to more specific references: the first is associated with 'whales'; the second 'was used in the film to suggest penguins' (the latter first appearing at rehearsal figure 5.4). Finally, the music 'connected in the film with the death of Oates' appears in the fourth movement at figure 7, following a recurrence of the Prelude's 'menacing' theme.

Thanks to the work of Daniel M. Grimley and others, we now know that the links between film and *Sinfonia* run somewhat deeper.[27] Most obviously, Vaughan Williams fails to mention that the first movement's opening theme is used, in an abbreviated form, to accompany the film's opening credits; this material recurs both as the film's postlude and in the last section of the *Sinfonia*'s Epilogue. Other relationships include the nature music accompanying the shots of the Antarctic wilderness in the film's Scene 1, which became the second section of the Prelude and the closing music of the Epilogue; the accompaniment to the ascent of the Beardmore Glacier in Scene 6, which is used twice in the 'Landscape' movement from rehearsal figures 3.13 and 8.4 respectively; a brief fragment of the Intermezzo's second section (figures 2.7–6.1) used in the conversation between Scott and his wife Kathleen in Scene 2; and the theme forming the basis of figures 5.6–5.9 in the Epilogue, which first appears in the film's Scene 7 to depict the arduous process Scott describes as 'manhauling', the transporting of sleds and equipment on foot. Grimley's study of the film score's sketches reveals that Vaughan Williams gave the germinal forms of many of these ideas extra-musical tags. The music opening both film and *Sinfonia* is, for example, labelled 'Heroism', whilst the 'nature music' that follows it (from figure 5.6) represented the 'terror and fascination of the S. [*sic*] Pole', and the music with which the Intermezzo opens was conceived as a *valse triste* depicting Wilson's wife Oriana.

The *Sinfonia*'s movement scheme is balanced by two means: the work as a whole is framed by the 'heroism' music, perhaps the most overt debt to the structure of the film; and a number of key motives are recycled at critical junctures, affording if not large-scale integration, then at least a degree of narrative continuity. Ex. 10.11 shows three variants of a pivotal

Ex. 10.11. *Sinfonia Antartica*, transformations of 'a' theme.

idea drawn from the 'heroism' theme, marked 'a': its presentation in the Prelude's main theme; the variant heard after the 'death of Oates' music in the Intermezzo; and its first appearance in the Epilogue.

Taken together, these occurrences chart a process of dissolution. In the Intermezzo, Vaughan Williams detaches the theme's tail and varies its rhythmic design, metrical character (3/4 becomes 4/4) and pitch content. The crisis of metrical identity becomes more acute in the Epilogue: despite the 4/4 context, the theme initially retains its 3/4 groupings, but this soon becomes displaced against both the notated and implied metres, eventually forcing a temporary shift to 3/2. The gradual weakening of the theme's stability reflects its programmatic contexts: heroism is expressed straightforwardly at the start, in the shadow of death in the Intermezzo and of tragic failure in the Epilogue, under which conditions the theme's identity starts to buckle.

A pervasive technique in the *Sinfonia* is the composer's habit of opposing post-tonal triadic harmony with a sort of collection-based heterophony. Typically, the former is associated with the human themes of heroism, adversity and death, while the latter underpins much of the work's nature music. The 'heroism' theme, quoted in Ex. 10.12, gives the clearest example of the first type.

Ex. 10.12. *Sinfonia Antartica*, first movement, opening; chord transformations; bitonal projections.

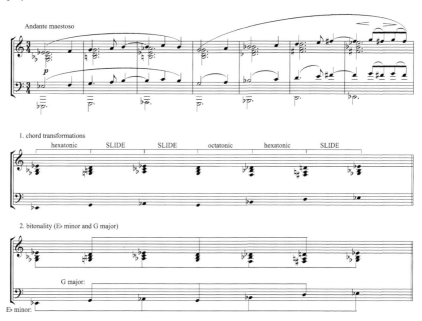

In one sense, the harmony here can be understood as employing three kinds of chord transformation: eb–G and bb–D are fragments of major-third cycles, and as such have hexatonic origins; G–bb is a minor-third transformation, having an octatonic basis; and G–ab–G is a semitonal shift, which David Lewin has termed a 'SLIDE' transformation.[28] At the same time, the passage also projects a kind of bitonality, alternating between Eb minor and G major. This has large-scale ramifications: the *Sinfonia*'s framing tonality is G; but Eb and its relations often intrude as a counter-pole. Tellingly, and in a manner redolent of the end of Symphony No. 5's Preludio, the work ends not by confirming G, but by juxtaposing a G bass pedal and a melody that comes to rest on an Eb.

In the Prelude, the 'heroism' music is followed from rehearsal figure 5.6 by the first 'nature' music, which clearly demonstrates the turn to a collection-based mentality (see Ex. 10.13). The basis of the passage is the alternation of a C_5^{b6} chord with its tritone transposition, redolent of the 'Chez Pétrouchka' scene of Stravinsky's *Petruschka*. The underlying collection here, however, is not the octatonic set 8–28, but as Ex. 10.13 shows, set 8–25, expanded to set 9–8 at rehearsal figure 6.1, where the strings introduce an Eb. Unlike the opening, where melodic material elaborates a triadic scheme, here harmony results from the vertical projection of a pitch collection.

These two harmonic attitudes play a fundamental role in supporting the work's programme, embodying not just the opposition of the human

Ex. 10.13. *Sinfonia Antartica*, first movement, 'nature' music.

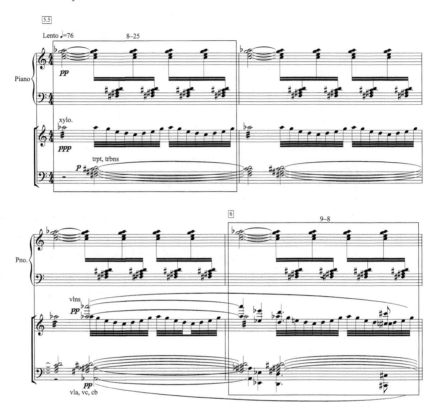

and the natural, but also that of symphonism and a repertoire of ecological 'noises', which, as Grimley explains, 'are essentially unsymphonic, in that they are almost entirely static and resist any attempt at development or change'.[29] For Grimley, this juxtaposition functions symbolically, aligning the futile heroism of Scott's expedition and the tragic heroism of the Great War, an affiliation that was prominent in the public consciousness. He thereby reads the *Sinfonia* as 'a monument to the war dead'.[30]

Each movement formulates the polarization of humanity and nature in a different way; and each perspective is clarified by Vaughan Williams's prefatory poetic and literary epigrams. Thus the Prelude's pitting of human endeavour against impassive nature is reflected in Shelley's 'woes which hope thinks infinite' in the face of 'power which seems omnipotent', whilst Shelley's conclusion that such struggle 'is alone life, joy, empire and victory' is embodied in the prematurely triumphal coda. The Scherzo and the 'Landscape' movement are both broadly naturalistic, reflecting scenes 3 and 6 of the film, which respectively portray life at the coastal base camp and the ascent of the Beardmore Glacier. In the second movement, the quotation from Psalm 104 succinctly appraises both the Scherzo material, which marshals a barcarolle topic to underscore the nautical context ('There go the ships'), and the whales and penguins of the Trio ('And there is that Leviathan'). Similarly, the transfer of the film's glacier music into the 'Landscape' movement suggestively parallels the 'Motionless torrents' and 'Silent cataracts' of Coleridge's poem.

The Intermezzo's juxtaposition of love and death attends instead to a dichotomy within the human pole. It comprises a loose ternary form in which the A and A^1 sections employ material designed to represent Wilson's wife Oriana and Scott's wife Kathleen, contrasting a B section built from the 'menacing' theme and the music for Oates's death. The sectional contrast here stresses a physical distance between the protagonists' wives in England and Oates's Antarctic demise, which, however, Donne's poem transcends ('Love, all alike, no season knows, nor clime'). Finally, the Epilogue retrieves the heroic theme, here couched as a tragic march. The ultimate collapse back into the Prelude's main theme and vocalise nature music confirms a tragic circularity, which circumscribes human endeavour: Scott's failure does nothing to quell human folly and has no effect on impassive nature. In symphonic terms, there is ultimately no teleological fulfilment, simply the reassertion of the germinal dichotomy.

If the retreat from 'dynamic' form in the *Sinfonia Antartica* results from its programmatic affiliations, in Symphony No. 8 (1953–6) it arises from an abstract preoccupation with subverting the teleological processes of the post-classical symphony. The outer movements, entitled 'Fantasia' and 'Toccata' respectively, both declare a baroque genealogy, which sidesteps classical and post-classical attitudes. And although the Scherzo and Cavatina seem more generically conventional, Vaughan Williams isolates them within the overall design as showcases for the winds and strings respectively ('per stromenti a fiato' and 'per stromenti ad arco'). The symphony as a whole consequently projects a textural strategy, in which the tutti is established in the Fantasia, dismantled in the inner movements, and then re-assembled in the Toccata. The resulting instrumental differentiation resembles a stretching-out of the baroque concerto grosso's ripieno/concertante distinction, to the point where it conditions an entire symphonic movement cycle. The baroque atmosphere is reinforced by various material allusions, most blatant of which is the quotation of the first strain of the chorale 'O Haupt voll Blut und Wunden' from Bach's *St Matthew Passion*, which comprises the Cavatina's main theme.[31] Cyclical thematic connections are present (the flourish at the start of the Scherzo is, for example, a variant of the Fantasia's initial motive), but they act as passing allusions rather than supplying a consistent, overarching process.

Ex. 10.14. Symphony No. 8, first movement, motives 'a', 'b' and 'c'.

The design of the individual movements reinforces the withdrawal from teleology. The Fantasia's 'Variazioni senza Tema' engineer a twofold structural displacement. The professed absence of a theme deprives the variations of their normal frame of reference, thereby removing the customary sense of the accumulation of variants around a fixed melodic-harmonic framework. Instead, Vaughan Williams exploits the developmental potential of three germinal motives stated in the first variation, quoted in Ex. 10.14 as 'a', 'b' and 'c', which are developed freely in the six subsequent variations, before being revisited in the brief coda. This produces a comparable displacement at the level of the movement cycle: the variations replace the generically normal sonata form and in so doing abandon the teleological impulse that sonata form customarily installs as a symphonic starting point.

The sense of goal-directedness is never recovered. The Scherzo is both self-contained and yet curiously provisional. It falls into six sections: sections 1–3 (rehearsal figures 0.1–2.12, 2.13–3.8 and 4.1–6.7) present four themes in succession, two in sections 1 and 2 and two in section 3, all couched in a simple melody-and-accompaniment context. Section 4 (figures 6.7–10.10), in contrast, is an increasingly dense fugato on theme 4, curtailed at its point of maximum density by section 5 (figure 10.11), which in its metrical, topical and textural character resembles a trio. Section 6 (figure 13.8) functions both as a coda and a heavily truncated reprise, retrieving first the opening and then the fugato. The result is an unbalanced implied ternary design, reflecting Vaughan Williams's predilection for truncated reprises: B and A^1 together occupy the last 55 bars of a 181-bar structure. This scheme is weakened further by the tonal plot, which is not discretely correlated with the regions of the ternary form: sections 1, 5 and 6 are all centred on a Phrygian C minor; sections 2–4 are orientated around D minor. Altogether, the movement is understood better as projecting two formal ideas, which are mutually negating: an additive, sectional design, which is brought to a halt by the trio and has no time to reassert itself; and a ternary scheme, which is initially swamped by the sectional form and reasserts itself too late to balance the movement's proportions. The sense of imbalance is compounded by the coda's last-minute contrapuntal gymnastics, through which prime and augmented forms of theme 4 pile up in stretto and combine with theme 1, and by the elusive ending, which undermines any sense that closure is synonymous with the attainment of a structural goal.

The symphony comes closest to retrieving a sonata dynamic in the Cavatina, in which two contrasted sections (rehearsal figures 1–3.3 and 3.4–5.6) are reprised (from figure 8.14), following a rhapsodic intervening development. Yet this hardly compensates for the form's absence in the outer movements; rather, any sense of an emergent sonata process is constrained by the material's expressive intimacy. The Toccata embraces a greater sense of continuity, but again this is not grounded in structural conflict. It has the character of a loose rondo, in which contrasted episodes alternate with freely varied returns to the triumphant main theme first proposed in bar 9. The movement exploits two generic implications: it transfers the properties of the ostinato-based keyboard piece into an orchestral context; and it references the genre's older usage as an operatic *intrada*, most famously in Monteverdi's *Orfeo*, an expressive sense that the Finale paradoxically projects.

Symphony No. 9 occupies a middle ground between the extremes of programmatic depiction and abstraction evident in its two predecessors. Its form is if anything more conventional than that of No. 8, comprising a four-movement scheme, with an (admittedly idiosyncratic) sonata-type first movement, Andante, Scherzo and Finale. At the same time, as Alain Frogley has identified, its genesis is bound up with programmatic ambitions more obviously redolent of the *Sinfonia*.[32]

The types of stasis evident in Nos. 7 and 8 play a central role in Symphony No. 9. The first movement's engagement with sonata form is calculated to undermine key features of its structural dynamic, the operative technique being '[t]ension between the static tendencies of juxtaposition and the dynamism of expansion and development', as Frogley puts it.[33] In the exposition, this is evident in the relationship between first and second themes. Vaughan Williams makes no clear distinction between a closed first theme and a modulating transition, instead framing the whole passage within a Phrygian E minor. The second group, following in a mixed mediant minor/major from rehearsal figure 4, is by contrast formally and tonally open-ended. Sectional divisions ensue at figures 8 and 10, but neither demarcates an obvious closing section, either tonally or gesturally. The music at figure 11 is at least grounded on a G pedal, and so as Frogley suggests potentially rounds off the group, and with it the exposition; the melodic momentum of figure 11.8, however, pushes into figure 12, which is harmonically mobile.[34] In the recapitulation, the relationship between stasis and mobility is reversed: the first group is now mobile and the second is framed by the tonic. A putative first-theme reprise enters at rehearsal figure 15, where its diminution appears in the tonic in the strings. This does not settle, but rather moves rapidly through a succession of key centres, attaining D minor by figure 16 and reaching a climax on a modally mixed C tonality by bar 17.5. The stability of this recapitulation is further challenged, retrospectively, by the coda, beginning at figure 23, which recovers the first theme's initial form, key and orchestral texture, thereby fostering the impression that the coda is in fact a first-theme return in a reversed recapitulation. Despite localized chromaticism, the second theme's reprise from figure 19 is altogether more secure, being circumscribed by the tonic and projecting the character of an enclosed formal episode.

The tendency to juxtapose dynamic strategies and episodic designs comes to the fore in the Finale. The movement begins with a large expository phase consisting of three main sections (rehearsal figures 0.1–2.5, 2.6–5.6 and 6.1–7.5), which is immediately reprised in varied form (figures 8.1–14.3). Rehearsal figures 16–31 are then cast as a single developmental span, culminating in the C major climax at figure 29.1 (the score contains no figure 15, thanks to a cut the composer made before publication). This music, however, is based almost exclusively on a new theme, presented in quasi-fugal fashion from figure 16.1. The result is that the functions of presentation and development are separated out, such that the latter does not flow from the former: excepting the return from figure 27 of elements of the post-cadential idea first appearing at figure 13, the development undertakes a self-contained process, which does not draw upon the first half of the movement. Rehearsal figures 32–35 then furnish a broad coda, which returns to the Prelude's main theme and pulls the music back towards E major. The form seems purposely to isolate episodic and developmental ways of organizing material, such that each is denied the support of the other: the developmental potential of the initial material is not realized; and the development is also of necessity presentational, evolving out of its own initial thematic statement.

At the same time, Symphony No. 9 revisits thematic strategies more readily associated with Symphonies Nos. 4 and 6. The first movement's ostensibly rhapsodic second theme is linked to the first theme by the motive in its second bar, identified in Ex. 10.15 as 'b'.[35] This idea makes its first appearance in the saxophones in rehearsal figures 1.3–1.6, thereafter infusing the first group. Subsequently, Vaughan Williams subjects 'b' to a variety of transformations, the most dramatically effective of which is that employed at the climax of the first-theme reprise.

The first theme's Phrygian inflection furthermore supplies a cyclical device that recalls Symphony No. 6. Ex. 10.16 displays the theme and a

Ex. 10.15. Symphony No. 9, first movement, relationship between first and second themes.

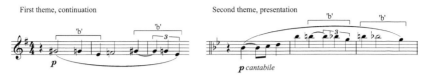

Ex. 10.16. Symphony No. 9, appearances of 'a' in first, third and fourth movements.

number of critical relationships within and between movements, isolating the germinal Phrygian second as 'a'. In a manner redolent of Symphony No. 4, 'a' is given harmonic substance from rehearsal figure 1.1 by the saxophones' e–f–e triadic succession. As Frogley observes, the Scherzo's initial gesture relocates 'a' around an F tonic, and its main theme develops out of this in its compound-melodic conflation of two chromatic neighbour-note patterns.[36] Frogley has also noted the debt the Finale's first theme owes to 'a';[37] and the symphony's opening is recalled directly in the coda, both in the recovery of a variant of 'a' from bar 32.3 and in the saxophones' neighbour-note figure in bar 34.3.

In contrast with the *Sinfonia Antartica*'s mediation of film, symphony and historical narrative, Symphony No. 9 adopts a more straightforward

Ex. 10.17. Symphony No. 9, second movement, opening and 'Tess' theme.

literary affiliation. The association with Thomas Hardy's *Tess of the D'Urbervilles* has been understood at least since Michael Kennedy drew attention to it in 1964, but has been given its most substantial formulation by Frogley.[38] His investigation of the sources reveals numerous connections between the material and Hardy's novel, ranging from the generalized description of the first movement as a 'Wessex Prelude' (the domain of Hardy's novels in general), through various links with associated locations (Stonehenge, Salisbury, Salisbury Plain) and characters (Tess herself) to the narration of parts of the novel.

The most sustained engagement with *Tess* takes place in the second movement, which Frogley identifies as tracing the action of chapters 58 and 59, from the flight of Tess and Angel Clare to Stonehenge after the murder of Alec D'Urberville, to Tess's capture and execution. Ex. 10.17 shows the themes to which Vaughan Williams gave specific programmatic tags. This material is arranged into a ternary design with coda, such that the 'Stonehenge' and 'barbaric march' themes form the A and A^1 sections and the 'Tess' theme sustains B and the coda. For Frogley, this scheme shifts between specific narrative and character portrait: section A depicts Tess's and Angel's night-time arrival at Stonehenge and her arrest at dawn; A^1 describes Tess's execution at Winchester (Wintoncester in the novel), the eight deep-bell strokes between rehearsal figures 14 and 19 signifying the town clocks chiming the hour of execution; the B section rather constitutes a 'character study' of Tess herself. The coda then has a transcendental function mirroring the end of the novel, Tess finally being released from the 'sport' of the gods.

This by no means exhausts the symphony's extra-musical associations. Frogley identifies numerous tangible allusions in other movements, including links between the Finale's development theme, Elgar's *The Apostles* and plainsong, the opening of the Prelude and the first chorus of the *St Matthew Passion*, and the main theme of the Scherzo with *The Sorcerer's Apprentice*, as well as numerous inter-opus connections within Vaughan Williams's *oeuvre*.[39] Drawing all of this together, he proffers a programme for the symphony that returns again to the problem of wartime sacrifice and the futility of heroism:

> If Vaughan Williams does intend to situate the sacrifices of the Great War, and of war in general, within a Hardyesque view of the universe, [Symphony No. 9] puts forward a much darker vision than in the Eighth Symphony: it seems to pose the question, does it ultimately count for anything that we mortals – who must by definition die – love and mourn one another, if the President of the Immortals [Hardy's phrase] cares nothing for us or our suffering? The suggestion of transcendence at the end of the second movement . . . may point to nothing more than the cessation of suffering in oblivion.[40]

At a broader level of formal process, the agent of Vaughan Williams's struggle with such existential questions is, in Symphony No. 9 and in the last three symphonies generally, surely the conflict between dynamic and static modes of symphonic discourse. In the Beethovenian tradition, the dynamic model of form is intimately related to the possibility of transcendence, or 'utopian semiosis' in Michael Spitzer's apt phrase.[41] But in Vaughan Williams's late symphonies, this impulse is repeatedly halted by episodic structures: the nature music and the ultimate circularity of the 'heroic' music in the *Sinfonia Antartica*; the evasion of post-classical symphonic forms in Symphony No. 8; and the dissociation of presentation and development in the Finale of Symphony No. 9. Whereas Beethovenian dynamism still drives Symphonies Nos. 4–6, even as a negative presence, in the final three symphonies a more pessimistic, pointedly postmodern vision emerges, which suggests that the utopian aspirations of modernity are enslaved by a futile, goalless circularity.

Conclusions

In 1955, Donald Mitchell published two articles spearheading a critical reaction against Vaughan Williams, which have fundamentally coloured the composer's subsequent reception.[42] Where earlier critics marshalled superlatives, Mitchell sought to expose Vaughan Williams's art as flawed and transient. Vaughan Williams's music has of course endured this critique, and recent scholarship has done much to balance the Oedipal hostility it engendered. Nevertheless, its lingering consequence has been an *ex post facto* alignment with a kind of establishment conservatism, contrasting the modernism of a generation of post-war British composers who looked towards central Europe rather than England and Scandinavia for their model of musical modernity (what Dai Griffiths has acerbically called 'grammar schoolboy music').[43]

The myopia of the post-war critique is nowhere more forcefully exposed than in the later symphonies. Even cursory engagement reveals a post-tonal vocabulary, which is no less progressive than that employed by Bartók, Stravinsky, Prokofiev or Shostakovich. Neither is this one isolated facet of Vaughan Williams's compositional personality: indeed, a remarkable characteristic of this music is its derivation of post-tonal chromaticism and luminous modality as possibilities within an integrated mode of expression. Symphonies Nos. 4 and 5 demonstrate this very clearly: the semitonal bitonality of the former and pre-tonal modality of the latter both stem from the same underlying concept. There are, moreover, practices in these works that run considerably ahead of their time. The collection-based textures of the *Sinfonia Antartica*'s nature music, for instance, prefigure heterophonic techniques exploited by the second generation of the post-war avant-garde, most obviously in the spatial works of Ligeti's first maturity (*Lontano*, for example).

Yet perhaps the most compelling argument for the relevance of these works is the ways in which they not only absorb, but also critique twentieth-century modernism. Symphonies Nos. 4–6 engage directly with the ideal of the teleological symphony, responding with narratives of brutal negation, valediction and leave-taking respectively. In the last three symphonies, the tendency to replace goal-directed processes with static, episodic or circular structures suggests more than an Adornian pessimism; it locates these works in a territory more readily associated with postmodern thought. This is given narrative immediacy in the *Sinfonia Antartica*, where progressive human ideals are not only seen to fail, but are more bleakly revealed as circling helplessly in the face of an impassive, purposeless wilderness. Consequently, although Vaughan Williams's later symphonies tell us much about the development of the

British symphony, about the European symphony in the twilight of the Austro-German tradition, and about how modes of musical expression change under the impact of the two world wars, they resonate at least as strongly with the present, expressing *in nuce* sentiments that came to dominate Western culture at the end of the twentieth century.

Notes

1 See Frank Howes, *The Music of Ralph Vaughan Williams* (London: Oxford University Press, 1954), 1–3.

2 *Ibid.*, 3.

3 See Michael Kennedy, 'Vaughan Williams and His Symphonies', accompanying booklet to *Vaughan Williams: Symphonies 1–9, Fantasia on a Theme by Thomas Tallis, Norfolk Rhapsody* No. 1, *The Lark Ascending, In the Fen Country* and *On Wenlock Edge*, LPO, Bernard Haitink *et al.* (EMI Classics, 2004), and also *KW*, for example at 305, where Kennedy states that 'The *Scott* music and the Finale of the Sixth Symphony inaugurate an "experimental" phase in Vaughan Williams's compositions'.

4 See Alain Frogley, *Vaughan Williams's Ninth Symphony* (New York and Oxford University Press, 2001), 15.

5 *Ibid.*

6 See James Day, *The Master Musicians: Vaughan Williams* (3rd edn, Oxford and New York: Oxford University Press, 1998), Elliott S. Schwartz, *The Symphonies of Ralph Vaughan Williams* (Amherst: University of Massachusetts Press, 1964) and Hugh Ottaway, *Vaughan Williams Symphonies* (London: BBC, 1972).

7 See Cecil Gray, *Sibelius* (London, 1931) and *Sibelius: The Symphonies* (London, 1935), and most famously Constant Lambert, *Music Ho! A Study of Music in Decline* (London: Faber, 1934). For a general survey of British Sibelius reception, see Peter Franklin, 'Sibelius in Britain', in Daniel M. Grimley (ed.), *The Cambridge Companion to Sibelius* (Cambridge University Press, 2004), 182–95; and Byron Adams, '"Thor's Hammer": Sibelius and British Music Critics, 1905–1957', in Daniel M. Grimley (ed.), *Jean Sibelius and His World* (Princeton University Press, 2010), 125–57.

8 See J. P. E. Harper-Scott, '"Our True North": Walton's First Symphony, Sibelianism, and the Nationalization of Modernism in England', *ML* 89/4 (2008), 562–89 at 563.

9 It should be noted that the English view of Shostakovich became notably more favourable after the Second World War; on this subject,

see Pauline Fairclough, 'The Old Shostakovich: Reception in the British Press', *ML* 88/2 (2007), 266–98.

10 On French symphonism after D'Indy, see Brian Hart, 'Vincent D'Indy and the Development of the French Symphony', *ML* 87/2 (2006), 237–61.

11 A large-scale reorientation of the twentieth-century symphony towards Russia and North America is attempted in Richard Taruskin, *The Oxford History of Western Music*, vol. v (Oxford and New York: Oxford University Press, 2005).

12 For an attempt to develop a narrative of symphonism from Beethoven to Sibelius predicated on the concept of thematic logic, see Lionel Pike, *Beethoven, Sibelius and 'the Profound Logic': Studies in Symphonic Analysis* (London: Athlone Press, 1978).

13 See 'Fourth Symphony' in *VWOM*, 355–60.

14 The horn call also reveals Vaughan Williams's debt to Debussy and Ravel, occurring both in the third of Debussy's *Nocturnes*, 'Sirènes', and as the 'kiss' motive in Ravel's *Daphnis et Chloe*. It also furnishes a link with the *Sinfonia Antartica*, where it is used in the vocalise material first heard in the Prelude from bars 7.3–7.5.

15 See Theodor W. Adorno, *Mahler: A Musical Physiognomy*, trans. Edmund Jephcott (Chicago University Press, 1992) and James Hepokoski, *Sibelius: Symphony No. 5* (Cambridge University Press, 1993), 6.

16 See Arnold Whittall, '"Symphony in D Major": Models and Mutations' in *VWS*, 187–212.

17 The use of this set at the end of Symphony No. 6 and in the *Sinfonia Antartica* is noted in Daniel M. Grimley, 'Music, Ice, and the Geometry of Fear: Vaughan Williams's *Sinfonia Antartica*', *MQ* 91 (2008), 116–50, especially 129–30. Grimley in turn acknowledges Sebastian Forbes's unpublished identification of it in Symphony No. 6.

18 Vaughan Williams's hostility to other commentators' hermeneutics has been frequently noted; see for example *KW*, 301–2, referring specifically to Frank Howes's views

on Symphony No. 6. Unfortunately, Vaughan Williams's own opinions on the composer's wartime role offer little help. See for instance his remarks in 'The Composer in Wartime', in *VWOM*, 83–6.

19 See for example *KW*, 280–3; Whittall, '"Symphony in D Major"'; and Wilfrid Mellers, *Vaughan Williams and the Vision of Albion* (London: Barrie & Jenkins, 1989), 176–86.

20 I use the term 'summative' in the sense intended by Michael Talbot; see *The Finale in Western Instrumental Music* (Oxford and New York: Oxford University Press, 2001).

21 See Mellers, *Vaughan Williams and the Vision of Albion*, 169.

22 The 'Russianness' of this music resonates with Vaughan Williams's description of the work as 'The Big Three', a reference to the post-War allied powers of Russia, Britain and the USA. See Oliver Neighbour, 'The Place of the Eighth among Vaughan Williams's Symphonies', in *VWS*, 213–33, especially at 224.

23 Vaughan Williams's suggestion that the meaning of the Epilogue could be more closely captured by a quotation from Prospero's speech in Act IV, Scene 1 of *The Tempest* ('We are such stuff as dreams are made on, and our little life is rounded by a sleep') is entirely consonant both with a narrative of farewell and a post-apocalyptic reading, as the context of the quotation makes clear:

> These our actors,
> As I foretold you, were all spirits and
> Are melted into air, into thin air:
> And, like the baseless fabric of this vision,
> The cloud-capp'd towers, the gorgeous
>   palaces,
> The solemn temples, the great globe
>   itself,
> Yea, all which it inherit, shall dissolve
> And, like this insubstantial pageant faded,
> Leave not a rack behind. We are such stuff
> As dreams are made on, and our little life
> Is rounded with a sleep.

See W. J. Craig (ed.), *The Complete Works of William Shakespeare* (London: Oxford University Press, 1962) 17, and *KW*, 302.

24 The early critical reception of the *Sinfonia* sometimes construed this episodic character as a flaw. For an account of the work's reception, see Grimley, 'Music, Ice, and the Geometry of Fear', 124–5.

25 Vaughan Williams was familiar with *Antar* from his period of study with Ravel; see Chapter 2, 45–6.

26 See '*Sinfonia Antartica*' in *VWOM*, 371–6.

27 See Grimley, 'Music, Ice, and the Geometry of Fear', and also Michael Beckerman, 'The Composer as Pole Seeker: Reading Vaughan Williams's *Sinfonia Antartica*', *Current Musicology* 69 (2000), 42–67.

28 See for example David Lewin, *Generalized Musical Intervals and Transformations* (New Haven: Yale University Press, 1987), 178.

29 See Grimley, 'Music, Ice, and the Geometry of Fear', 132.

30 *Ibid.*, 120.

31 This quotation was spotted by Paul Henry Lang after the work's American premiere, and verified by the composer in a letter to Lang; see Oliver Neighbour, 'The Place of the Eighth among Vaughan Williams's Symphonies', 228–30.

32 See Frogley, *Vaughan Williams's Ninth Symphony* and also 'Vaughan Williams and Thomas Hardy: "Tess" and the Slow Movement of the Ninth Symphony', *ML* 68/1 (1987), 42–59.

33 See Frogley, *Vaughan Williams's Ninth Symphony*, 59.

34 See *ibid.*, 60.

35 This figure, it should be noted, is ubiquitous in Vaughan Williams's mature music. The opening theme of Symphony No. 6 offers another example among many.

36 See Frogley, *Vaughan Williams's Ninth Symphony*, 151.

37 *Ibid.*, 195.

38 See *KW*, 370 and Frogley, *Vaughan Williams's Ninth Symphony*, 257–94.

39 See Frogley, *Vaughan Williams's Ninth Symphony*, 277–94.

40 *Ibid.*, 287.

41 See Michael Spitzer, *Music as Philosophy: Adorno and Beethoven's Late Style* (Bloomington: Indiana University Press, 2006), 209.

42 See Donald Mitchell, 'Contemporary Chronicle: Revaluations: Vaughan Williams', *MO* 78 (1955), 409–11 and 471.

43 See Dai Griffiths, 'On Grammar Schoolboy Music' in Derek B. Scott (ed.), *Music, Culture and Society: A Reader* (Oxford and New York: Oxford University Press, 2000), 143–5 and also Ben Earle, 'Taste, Power and Trying to Understand Op. 36: British Attempts to Popularise Schoenberg', *ML* 84/4 (2003), 608–43.

Activism, reception and influence

PART III

Activism, reception and influence

11 The public figure: Vaughan Williams as writer and activist

DAVID MANNING

In 1902, Vaughan Williams gave a series of Oxford University extension lectures, advertised under the title of 'The History of Folk Song', at Pokesdown Technical School, Bournemouth. During these lectures he offered a public critique of musical life in Britain at the beginning of the twentieth century, which he viewed with some dissatisfaction. Among his complaints was the familiar one that native composers of repute were few in number ('occasionally a Purcell, a Parry or an Elgar has come along . . . and has given us some real music'); but, as Vaughan Williams pointed out, these figures were the exceptions in 250 years of British music history, not the rule.[1] Yet during this same period active participation in music-making had been widespread in Britain, and had grown significantly during the nineteenth century.[2] So why, Vaughan Williams asked, were there not more musicians emerging from the numerous amateur orchestras and choirs to become composers in their own right? The problem, from Vaughan Williams's perspective, lay in the nature and quality of musical life in Britain, and it manifested itself in three ways: firstly, the oral tradition of folksong singing was in an advanced stage of terminal decline and as a result a whole musical culture, barely known by a wider audience, was on the verge of being lost forever; secondly, many of the hymn tunes sung in church (from *Hymns Ancient and Modern*) were sentimental and not fit for purpose; and thirdly, the music sung by choral societies was too often of poor quality. In this unpromising environment it was unsurprising to Vaughan Williams that native composers had not emerged with greater frequency. Addressing these three weaknesses became a personal challenge that he pursued with great tenacity in the following decades. As Vaughan Williams's stature as a composer grew, he used the public platform he was granted to campaign on a broad range of musical issues, while remaining passionately committed to his own practical involvement in music-making, particularly among amateurs. Though other British composers, most notably Benjamin Britten and Sir Peter Maxwell Davies, have adopted high public profiles in this manner, particularly in the arena of performance with amateurs, Vaughan Williams was unique in the range of activities that he embraced, which included a substantial corpus of published writing about music.

This chapter, which considers Vaughan Williams's attempt to remake Britain's musical culture, is in two parts. The first provides a broadly chronological survey of his practical activities, such as conducting, editing and committee work, through which he pursued this musical campaign. The second part turns to the vision of a musical nation, complete with its own 'national music', which Vaughan Williams sets out in his lectures and published writings. These ideas form an essential, if sometimes problematic, context in which the practical work to revitalize musical life in Britain may be more fully understood.

Vaughan Williams: the activist

By the time he came to give the lectures discussed above, Vaughan Williams had already developed a personal appreciation of folksong. In his final lecture, he conveyed his sense of frustration that this music was not more widely known:

> [Folksongs] are hardly sung at all by the people nowadays. They are only to be heard from some oldest inhabitant in an out-of-the-way district. That precious legacy had slipped out of the hands of those whose it was by right and passed into the hands of enthusiastic connoisseurs . . . Will they not, perhaps, once more make their way back to the mouths of the people?[3]

At the time he made this plea, Vaughan Williams was not an active participant in the folksong movement. This all changed in 1903 after another lecture on folksong that Vaughan Williams gave in Brentwood, Essex, when he was introduced to Mr Pottipher, a local shepherd, who sang for him the folksong 'Bushes and Briars'. The composer was inspired by this encounter: he immediately noted down the tune, and over the next decade collected more than eight hundred folksongs.[4]

In addition to this fieldwork, Vaughan Williams also became involved in the Folk-Song Society. Two months after encountering 'Bushes and Briars', he met with Cecil Sharp and Lucy Broadwood, who, in her diary, recorded that they discussed the 'Folk Song Society and made a scheme for reviving its dying embers'.[5] In 1906, Vaughan Williams disseminated his work by publishing a collection of fifty-eight songs in the *Journal of the Folk-Song Society*.[6] This anthology contained songs from seven counties, and demonstrated that the same song could be found in disparate geographical locations.[7] There can be no doubt that the experience of collecting folksongs in person had a profound effect on Vaughan Williams. It would influence his musical language, and, for the rest of his life, he would seek opportunities to share these songs with a wide audience.

A particularly significant opportunity to return folksongs 'to the mouths of the people' emerged at an early stage when, in 1904, Vaughan Williams was appointed musical editor of the first edition of *The English Hymnal*. With no shortage of historical precedents to draw upon, Vaughan Williams continued the tradition of taking secular tunes and employing them in a sacred context. The first edition of the *Hymnal* contained thirty-five tunes based on English folksongs: to give just one well-known example, the hymn 'He Who Would Valiant Be' was derived from the folksong 'Our Captain Calls', which Vaughan Williams had collected from a Mrs Verrall in Horsham, Sussex, on 22 December 1904.[8] By these actions, a tune that was part of a tradition nearing extinction was given new life. Understandably, attention is often paid to the use of such English material, but it should also be noted that Vaughan Williams drew on a wide range of sources for the *Hymnal*, including German, French, Swiss, Italian, Spanish, Flemish, Dutch and American tunes. As he later put it, he aimed to create a book that would 'be a thesaurus of all the finest hymn tunes in the world'.[9]

The musical editor's workload was significant, and continued over a two-year period, but it provided Vaughan Williams with a rare opportunity to address the failings of *Hymns Ancient and Modern* that he had identified in the Bournemouth lectures. This argument was continued in the preface of the new hymnal, with several barbed remarks about current practice: 'No doubt it requires a certain effort to tune oneself to the moral atmosphere implied by a fine melody; and it is far easier to dwell in the miasma of the languishing and sentimental hymn tunes which so often disfigure our services.'[10] With these words Vaughan Williams demonstrated his willingness to confront convention and his ambition to reshape existing practice.[11]

Given that Vaughan Williams undertook a significant amount of original compositional work in the period 1900–14, alongside editing and folksong collecting, it seems remarkable that he had any time for other musical activities; yet his commitment to amateur music-making is also clearly evident. Although his spell as a church organist at St Barnabas, Lambeth, between 1895 and 1899 had been somewhat unhappy, Vaughan Williams thrived on his later work with amateurs. In 1905, the Leith Hill Musical Festival was first held as a small local event, with Vaughan Williams conducting a selection from Handel's *Judas Maccabaeus*; three years later the number of choirs participating from surrounding villages had grown to nine. This was the beginning of an association with the Festival that would last for the rest of the composer's life.[12] Vaughan Williams also participated in local music-making in London as a member of the Bach Choir, and in other smaller groups. To give just one example: he played in the Passmore

Edwards Settlement orchestra under Holst in a performance of Bach's cantata 'Wachet auf, ruft uns die Stimme' (BWV 140).[13]

By 1914, Vaughan Williams had made substantial progress in addressing the problems he identified in the Bournemouth lectures: his new hymnal was providing an alternative to Victorian 'sentimental' hymns, and his folksong arrangements were giving new life to an important musical legacy. Vaughan Williams had gradually emerged to become a significant figure of national importance. He was also a leading figure in his own local community as musical director of the Leith Hill Musical Festival. But all this work was about to be interrupted, as war began.

At the start of World War I Vaughan Williams was, at the age of 41, older than the average military recruit. Enrolment in military duties was voluntary although strongly encouraged (conscription was not introduced until 1916), but, given Vaughan Williams's age, he could have promoted the war effort in a civilian role without reproach. This view was held by Parry, who wrote to Vaughan Williams a few months after his former pupil had enlisted: 'You have already served your country in very notable and exceptional ways and are likely to do so again; and such folks should be shielded from risk rather than exposed to it. We may admit the generosity of the impulse, and feel – I will not say what.'[14] Despite the other choices open to him, Vaughan Williams began his direct and practical contribution to the war effort by joining the London Special Constabulary, and then enlisting with the Royal Army Medical Corps.

While army service prevented new compositional work, Vaughan Williams found opportunities to make music with his fellow troops. During the first part of the war, he formed a choir from among his fellow members of the London 2/4th Field Ambulance Unit. They first rehearsed while training in Britain, and even found some spare moments to get together during a deployment treating soldiers in the trenches at Ecoivres.[15] Christmas music provided a strong link with home: the Hereford and Sussex carols were performed on the slopes of Mount Olympus in 1916; and in December 1918, when members of the Royal Garrison Artillery were not tending to 200 horses on a long and grim march to Germany, opportunities were created for some group singing. Four decades later, Vaughan Williams's death prompted a former officer to record his memories of wartime music-making:

> [Vaughan Williams] spent a lot of such spare time as he had in getting up
> concerts, vocal, by and for the troops, mostly drivers. I can't think he
> enjoyed them much, in view of the talent available. I saw him once or twice,
> drooping despondently over the keyboard of a ghastly wreck of a piano while
> drivers sang sentimental songs – execrably as a rule, to his
> accompaniment.[16]

This recollection illustrates Vaughan Williams's unquestioning commitment to active participation in practical music-making. The value of his work in this area was formally recognized in the final months of his period of service, just after the war itself had ended, when he was appointed to the post of Director of Music of the First Army, British Expeditionary Force, in France. Vaughan Williams travelled widely, encouraging officers and other soldiers with musical interests to lead choral and orchestral groups; his successor as Director of Music, E. R. Winship, recalled that after just a few months 'there were already nine choral societies, three classes, an orchestra and a band'.[17] In this role, and during his previous postings, Vaughan Williams's leadership of music-making raised morale, perhaps offering some temporary relief and consolation in extraordinary and often harrowing environments.

Within the first few months of his return to civilian life, Vaughan Williams's profile began to rise and new opportunities emerged. An honorary doctorate was awarded by Oxford University in the summer of 1919, and in the autumn he began teaching composition at the Royal College of Music.

Many of Vaughan Williams's former pupils have recorded memories of their encounters with a teacher who firmly believed in achieving a secure technique in harmony and counterpoint, but otherwise took a responsive rather than a didactic attitude to teaching composition. Support often extended beyond lessons, as Vaughan Williams made trips to hear rehearsals and concerts, and showed the more successful new works to publishers. In some cases, especially in later years, financial support was provided to enable first performances. Elizabeth Maconchy was one of those to receive lessons at the RCM; when she left, in 1929, Vaughan Williams wrote on her report card, 'Very sorry to lose her – but I can teach her no more – she will work for her own salvation & will go far'.[18] Maconchy echoed these comments when she wrote of Vaughan Williams that 'he had no use for ready made solutions: he had worked out his own salvation as a composer and he encouraged his pupils to do the same'.[19] The biblical allusion emphasizes the ethical dimension to Vaughan Williams's work: composers had a duty to explore and express themselves through their music.[20]

Vaughan Williams took on regular conducting work from 1919, first with the Handel Society, before being appointed Director of the Bach Choir in 1921.[21] This new post provided a significant opportunity to perform the works of a composer whom Vaughan Williams held in the highest regard. The first programme note reveals Vaughan Williams's characteristically unapologetic attitude to using modern forces, including a choir of over three hundred, to perform Bach cantatas in the vernacular.[22] Two years later, Vaughan Williams was able to conduct his first *St Matthew Passion* adopting the same performance principles: a piano was used in place of a harpsichord continuo; lengthy 'da capo' repeats were curtailed; and some numbers were cut. The Bach Choir received several invitations to repeat the work in suburban locations, and a total of six performances were given between 14 February and 22 March 1923.[23] Vaughan Williams incorporated a fair amount of British music into his Bach Choir programmes, including the first London performance of Holst's *Ode to Death*, and the premiere of his own *Sancta Civitas* in 1926, the latter marking the choir's fiftieth anniversary. Younger composers also received an airing; orchestral works by Robin Milford and Gerald Finzi, both in their mid-twenties, were included in a 1928 programme, for example.[24]

In 1929 Adeline Vaughan Williams's increasingly bad health led the couple to make the difficult decision to move away from London, where Ralph participated in so many musical activities, and take up residence in Dorking. This caused Vaughan Williams to give up his association with the Bach Choir. One benefit, however, was that the new home provided an ideal location for participating in the Leith Hill Musical Festival, which was continuing to grow. In the 1920s, the festival had started to include larger choral works, and, once a new hall had been completed, it became possible for the festival forces to give their first performance of the *St Matthew Passion*. Vaughan Williams later described this event: 'It was a "massed" performance with seven hundred singers. Of course they did not all sing all the time, but they did all sing the chorales and when the seven hundred voices whispered "Be near me Lord" they made a magical sound which I shall never forget.'[25] This concert, held in 1931, would be the first of twenty-three performances of the work that Vaughan Williams conducted in Dorking, a statistic that confirms the importance of this work to the composer's outlook.[26]

During the 1930s Vaughan Williams's reputation continued to rise. When Arthur Bliss presented to him the Gold Medal of the Royal Philharmonic Society at the beginning of the new decade, he surely surprised no one by saying that younger composers regarded Vaughan Williams as their leader.[27] After Elgar's death, in 1934, Vaughan Williams's position as the unofficial figurehead of British music was confirmed. He was offered Elgar's position as Master of the King's Music, but refused it.[28] The next award that caused Vaughan Williams some concern was the offer of the Order of Merit, in 1935.[29] This time, however, he decided to accept; and this was to be the highest honour he would hold, as he later declined a knighthood. These dilemmas demonstrate that Vaughan Williams was wary of the obligations that were attached to official recognition. He nevertheless did accept many invitations to play important roles in public musical life; in particular he contributed to state occasions at the request of Sir Walford Davies (who had accepted the post of Master of the King's Music), by writing music marking the death of George V in 1936, and the coronation of George VI the following year.

This unofficial position as a leader of British musical life would cause Vaughan Williams to face a further difficult choice. In 1937, he was invited to become the first recipient of the Shakespeare Prize, offered by Hamburg University to strengthen cultural ties between Germany and Great Britain. Vaughan Williams was immediately unsure whether to accept it, fearing that, if he did so, he would be unable to express freely his own political views about the Nazi regime. A deciding factor appears to have been an understanding that the award would be 'in fact a gesture of recognition to the whole art of music in England through me as one of its representatives', and that 'it implies no political propaganda'.[30] It may seem a curious decision for Vaughan Williams to have accepted an award of this kind when it would surely have been easier for him to have declined it. Indeed the visit to Hamburg caused Vaughan Williams some anxiety and he was relieved to come home; as Ursula Vaughan Williams explained, 'by being very British and very formal, he had avoided giving the Nazi salute or saying Heil Hitler'.[31] The setting aside of his initial concerns may have reflected an optimistic belief that an award could offer some kind of hope in contrast to the bleak political prospects of pre-war Europe. As Alain Frogley has shown, however, Vaughan Williams was deliberately misled by the Hamburg authorities as to the motivations behind the award, and at home the 'miniature drama' of the Shakespeare prize coincided with 'the ill-fated British political policy of appeasement'. In the event both unravelled, as Vaughan Williams's music was banned in Germany not long before the war began.[32]

The consequences of the German regime were already having an impact on life in England by this time. One example of this was the Dorking Committee for Refugees from Nazi Oppression, established in December 1938, of which Vaughan Williams was an active member; he frequently visited the lodgings the Committee had established to house some of the refugees.[33] When the war began Vaughan Williams became involved in other community activities: he made some of his field available for allotments, and dug his own potato patch; he also joined in with collecting salvage, and attended fire-watching training so that he could operate the stirrup pump in case of emergency.[34] Later, in 1940, Vaughan Williams was given a more substantial position, as Chairman of the Home Office Committee for the Release of Interned Alien Musicians. This role allowed the composer to use his knowledge and experience to make a real difference.

The other important aspect to Vaughan Williams's wartime work was his support for practical music-making, even in difficult circumstances.

The war made him more determined that people should have access to music, both as listeners and as amateur performers. For example, he supported the organization of lunchtime concerts at the National Gallery, and ensured that the Leith Hill Musical Festival went ahead, on an appropriately reduced scale. Vaughan Williams promoted music-making of this kind, describing his local plans for Dorking in a Home Service broadcast that was intended to encourage others to follow this example. He was also asked to write a preface for a military music competition songbook. The following remarks, in characteristically blunt style, assert the importance of music-making among the troops:

> I understand that some military authorities consider that music is 'softening' for the soldier. I would remind them that Socrates held that certain kinds of music put courage to the heart of the soldier, that David was an expert harpist but managed to slay Goliath, that Mr Valiant-for-Truth carried his marks and scars with him across the river and that when he passed over all the trumpets sounded for him on the other side. Who shall dare say that music is not an essential part of the soldier's equipment?[35]

However idiosyncratic the means of expression, there can be no doubting the authenticity of this sentiment: it is undoubtedly coloured by Vaughan Williams's own experience on the ground during World War I.

In the years after the war, Vaughan Williams continued with a busy schedule of composing, practical music-making and musical campaigning. For example, commissions were fulfilled for three large-scale community music-making events to be held at the Royal Albert Hall: *Folk Songs of the Four Seasons* was sung by 3,000 members of the Women's Institute in June 1950; a Concerto Grosso for strings was premiered later in the same year by over 400 players under the auspices of the Rural Music Schools Association; and 800 schoolchildren sang in the first performance of *The Sons of Light* in May 1951.[36] Such performances, with their emphasis on mass participation, seem ideally suited to Vaughan Williams's vision of a musical society. It is hard to imagine a greater contrast between these events and the concerts of the Society for the Promotion of New Music, which Vaughan Williams attended as President. In this role he continued to support young composers, even when their idiom was not to his personal taste. Vaughan Williams provided practical help as well, with donations to musicians on an ad hoc basis. In 1956 this work was formalized by the creation of the RVW Trust, which reinvested the composer's Performing Rights income into a range of musical activities including local festivals and premieres of new works.[37]

Vaughan Williams continued to campaign on musical issues in his later years. When the BBC Third Programme was scaled back he played a central role in the protests as a Vice-President of the Sound Broadcasting

Society (originally established as the Third Programme Defence Society). He wrote to newspapers, had an article published in the magazine *Music and Musicians*, and took part in a high-level lobby group that visited the BBC to protest. A press conference after this meeting, held at Vaughan Williams's house, received national coverage.[38]

The Leith Hill Musical Festival played an important role in the last years of Vaughan Williams's life. In 1953 he had signalled, with regret, his intention to stand down as conductor of the main festival, although he continued to conduct concerts of the *St Matthew Passion* which involved many of the same performers, augmented by a number of professionals. The last of these concerts, given on 5 March 1958, was recorded; it is a performance that reflects a lifetime's dedication both to the music of Bach and to community music-making.[39]

The short summary above cannot pay full justice to nearly six decades of musical activism, but it certainly indicates the range of activities that Vaughan Williams either led or promoted. This relentless work must have consumed vast swathes of the composer's time, and poses a more fundamental question: what motivated him to make such a substantial commitment? There can be no simple answer, but a clear indication of the underlying rationale is revealed in the composer's writings. The remaining part of this chapter seeks to uncover the essence of Vaughan Williams's vision of music in an ideal society. In this light, his commitment to practical music-making, by both amateurs and professionals, may be more fully understood.

Vaughan Williams: the writer

The best known of Vaughan Williams's writings is *National Music*, a short book published in 1934, based on a lecture series that he had given in America two years earlier. It would be impossible to account fully for the process by which the composer's beliefs developed prior to this publication. Some insights are afforded, however, by identifying the first appearances of key ideas in the published writings. Before turning to *National Music* itself, the brief survey that follows shows that, by the early 1920s, all the central concerns of the book had received at least one public airing.

The earliest articles establish two principles that Vaughan Williams would often repeat in his published writings. The first of these is that the concept of evolution underpins the history of music. Vaughan Williams expressed this unequivocally in 1897, in his first venture into print, when he wrote that 'no movement which is out of the straight line of musical evolution has ever produced any good results'.[40] The idea of musical evolution had been given full expression four years earlier in Parry's *The Art of Music* (1893), a book which itself is indebted to the broader application of evolutionary principles to society and culture found in the work of Herbert Spencer.[41] The second principle was that of self-expression: 'A musician who wishes to say anything worth saying must first of all express himself – in fact, his music must be the natural utterance of his own natural emotions'.[42] Again this idea reflects the influence of Vaughan Williams's old teacher and mentor: 'Parry's great watchword was "characteristic". He was always trying to discover the character revealed in even the weakest of his students' compositions.'[43] There is a potential tension between this pair of concepts, which suggest that a composer should express his or her own identity through music, but at the same time should build on the achievements of the preceding generation. This potential tension, and attempts to resolve it, would be at the heart of later disputes over the influence of folksong and musical nationalism.

As noted above, folksong is the focal point of the 1902 Bournemouth lectures. Vaughan Williams argues that, in modern times, composers had been 'using folk-songs more frequently as a basis of their compositions. . . . Each composer [has] blended his own individuality with that of his nation.' This 'naturally led' the composer 'to use the folk-songs of his own country as a vehicle for his own personal moods'.[44] According to this view, personal expression and national identity happily are moulded into one. Yet in these particular lectures, Vaughan Williams does not argue that folksong is a viable basis for new English music. Instead he points out that English folksongs are not very well known, although where this leaves the future of English music is not addressed. Indeed, earlier in the year, Vaughan Williams had taken a much stronger line, arguing that in England 'it is surely doubtful if any good result will follow the extremely artificial course of setting before a composer music which is entirely foreign to his temperament, and which even the peasantry have long since ceased to sing'.[45] His concern at this point appeared to be that to use folksong as a basis for national music would be simply to adopt a ready-made external model, a course of action that would lead only to insincerity of expression.

In the following years, however, as his appreciation of English folksong deepened, Vaughan Williams allowed his own musical language to be influenced profoundly by this source of musical inspiration. The composer finally gave a full account of his revised views in an essay entitled 'English Folk-Songs', published in 1912.[46] He acknowledges the importance of his personal experiences: 'I am like a psychical researcher who has actually seen a ghost, for I have been among the more primitive people of

England and have noted down their songs'.[47] The encounter with 'Bushes and Briars' is recounted: 'a shepherd began to sing a song which set all my doubts about folk-song at rest'.[48] And then, after some further examples of folksongs and their variants, Vaughan Williams summarizes the broader issue:

> We do really find . . . among those people whose utterances must of necessity
> be spontaneous and unsophisticated . . . a form of musical art, unwritten,
> handed down by tradition [which] . . . has in it the germ of all those
> principles of beauty, of expression, of form, climax and proportion which we
> are accustomed to look for in the highly developed compositions of great
> masters.[49]

It is worth pausing over this sentence as it addresses two key issues: the nature of folksong, and its relationship with art music. Folksong is understood here as music that is transmitted orally; it is the product of generations of refinement and modification by individual singers, either consciously or by accident. This might be said to illustrate the law of evolution in practice, as weaker songs, or weaker versions of an individual song, are forgotten while stronger ones – those which the singers regard as a form of self-expression – survive the process of oral transmission; thus, once again, evolution and self-expression form a union in the folksong. Of course, as Vaughan Williams acknowledges, these conditions did not always apply: singers were influenced by published songs, sometimes subconsciously, so it was impossible to prove that a folksong had been transmitted only orally. In addition, a collector might unknowingly encounter a song which was recently invented by one person. As the quotation confirms, however, the ideal that Vaughan Williams cherished most was to find folksongs that were the creation and property of a local community. From Vaughan Williams's perspective this intimate bond of music and people made folksong a unique source of the expression of national identity, one which he would celebrate repeatedly in his later writings.

The quotation from 1912 above reveals a further reason why folksong was a particularly suitable basis for art music, as both were understood to exemplify similar aesthetic principles, such as beauty, form and expression. Parry had made this connection in *The Evolution of the Art of Music*, when he concluded that 'the same principles which appear in folk music were instinctively adopted in all the forms of mature art'.[50] In Parry's account folksong therefore represents a vital evolutionary stage, containing in embryo the musical properties that composers would employ on a larger scale in later centuries. This argument also implies a clear basis for the values of art music identified above; a symmetrical formal pattern, for example, is not just an abstract idea, but something whose origins are authenticated in the instinctive expressions of 'unlettered' people. This idea fascinated both Parry and Vaughan Williams as it constructs a role for art music as a refinement and celebration of human instincts expressed through folksong. Therefore it is no surprise to find Vaughan Williams argue that 'The evolution of the English folk-song by itself has ceased, but its spirit can continue to grow and flourish at the hands of our native composers'.[51] He develops the point in another essay published in the same year, 'Who Wants the English Composer?', where he proposes a broader range of musical materials that could inspire original musical works:

> Have not we all about us forms of musical expression which we can take and
> purify and raise to the level of great art? For instance, the lilt of the chorus at
> a music-hall joining in a popular song, the children dancing to a barrel
> organ . . . The composer must not shut himself up and think about art, he
> must live with his fellows and make his art an expression of the whole life of
> the community – if we seek for art we shall not find it.[52]

Taken together these two articles – 'English Folk-Songs' and 'Who Wants the English Composer?' – make clear that Vaughan Williams's idea of national music had already developed significantly by 1912. His vision was in part a response to his personal experiences of collecting folksongs, and of living in central London, and the argument also shows the influences of Parry noted above.

Although many of the ideas subsequently explored in *National Music* had already been broached by the composer before the First World War, one topic that receives surprisingly little attention in the pre-1914 sources is the spiritual nature of music. This is tackled head on, however, in 'The Letter and the Spirit', an essay published just after the war. In a frequently quoted passage Vaughan Williams writes:

> Before going any further may we take it that the object of an art is to obtain a
> partial revelation of that which is beyond human senses and human
> faculties – of that, in fact, which is spiritual? . . . The human, visible, audible
> and intelligible media which artists (of all kinds) use, are symbols not of
> other visible and audible things but of what lies beyond sense and
> knowledge.[53]

From here on the term 'spiritual' features with some regularity in Vaughan Williams's writings. We cannot be certain how or when the composer developed the ideas expressed above; these thoughts could well have been in his mind for many years, and he certainly composed a good number of works before 1914, such as the *Five Mystical Songs* or *A Sea Symphony*, that deal with spiritual themes of one kind or another. Nevertheless, 'The Letter and the Spirit' was his first attempt to tackle this topic in a published article. His acknowledgement that music may afford partial access to 'something' beyond takes us into the difficult and sometimes controversial territory of the composer's mature religious beliefs. Though these are beyond the scope of the present discussion, they were clearly rather more complex than the notion of 'cheerful agnosticism' by which Ursula Vaughan Williams has characterized them, as has been discussed by Byron Adams and others.[54]

The core argument in *National Music* draws upon all the issues raised so far, while focusing particularly on folksong as a source of inspiration. Vaughan Williams's conception of national identity varies in tone during the book. In some places, he introduces an essentialist focus on racial qualities that, while certainly not uncommon in the 1930s, is more redolent of an earlier generation of Spencerian principles; for example, he states that 'in the folk-song we find . . . music which has stood the test of time, music which must be representative of our race as no other music can', and then approvingly quotes Parry's inaugural address to the Folk-Song Society in 1899, in which the older composer claimed that 'all things that mark the folk-music of the race also betoken the quality of the race'.[55] On the other hand, other passages in *National Music*, like some of Vaughan Williams's earlier articles, offer a more broadly conceived model of national identity; for instance, at the conclusion of the book nation is defined, without explicit reference to race, as 'any community of people who are spiritually bound together by language, environment, history and common ideals and, above all, a continuity with the past'.[56] Elsewhere, Vaughan Williams emphasizes the cultural dimension of national identity by comparing the folksong tradition with great literary works such as the King James Bible or Homer. He uses a striking phrase penned by the classicist Gilbert Murray to argue that folksongs, like these literary works, contain 'the spiritual life-blood of a people'.[57]

In a separate passage Vaughan Williams adopts his most extreme position on the influence of folksong, when he writes that 'the composer must love the tunes of his own country and they must become an integral part of himself'.[58] The obvious rejoinder is surely: 'why?' The folksong may be *an* exemplar for a composer, but should it be *the* model to hold above all others? Could not such an approach risk stifling the composer's own self-expression? The explanation lies in the context of the quotation: a passage responding to an article by the critic Robert Hull, who had criticized the composition of 'synthetic folk-music', which required 'practically no skill and very little imagination'.[59] Of course, what Vaughan Williams advocates is a much more dynamic relationship between the composer and folksong, which he summarizes by way of another quotation from Gilbert Murray: 'the genius may be a rebel against tradition, but at the same time he is a child of it'.[60] Even taking this point into account, however, the issue remains that Vaughan Williams had found himself in a defensive position on the supreme importance of folksong. By the early 1930s his polemic had to compete in an arena of diverse views on the future of English music, and his response was to take a harder line.

This determined stance created a problem that Vaughan Williams himself acknowledges:

> Nevertheless I do hold that any school of national music must be fashioned on the basis of the raw material of its own national song; and this, in spite of the fact that one could name many composers whose music certainly reflects their own country, but who had confessedly little or no knowledge of their own folk-music.[61]

Examples given to support the latter point are Elgar and Tchaikovsky. Once again one must ask: why give such primacy to folksong? It would appear quite simply that in these controversial passages an ideal is triumphing over reality. In this sense *National Music* is a creative work rather than an academic study; it is not so much an account of what national music is, as an explanation of what Vaughan Williams would wish national music to be in an ideal world. The words of Walt Whitman appear more than once in this text, and the whole argument – regardless of the composer's relatively advanced age – exhibits a sense of the youthful, even naive, optimism of the American poet.[62] In this book Vaughan Williams is attempting to protect national music as a principle, at a time when, in 1930s Europe, it faced severe peril. The forceful and uncompromising style of writing, however, coupled with a single-minded approach to the subject, remains problematic. It is hard to avoid concluding that Vaughan Williams's genuine belief in, and enthusiasm for, folksong has led him into an unnecessarily dogmatic position on its role in contemporary composition. By contrast, in other areas of his work, Vaughan Williams was energetically contributing to the diversity of the 1930s British music scene. Indeed, during his American stay, at the same time as he was extolling the importance of folksong as a foundation for new music in his lectures, he was also at work on the uncompromisingly modernist sonorities of his Fourth Symphony.[63]

Though many of the composer's later writings celebrate folksong, they do not take any further the polemics found in *National Music*. Those that were written during the Second World War stand out for their particular focus on the importance of practical music-making, including both professional performances and 'amateur homemade music which we make for ourselves to satisfy our innate need of self expression'.[64] As Vaughan Williams explains, 'to listen to fine music beautifully played is a great spiritual experience, so, also, is that of making our own music. Both are necessary for a full musical life.'[65] Another of his writings from the war period is a long and rather curious essay on Beethoven's Ninth Symphony; though not published immediately, it would eventually form the centrepiece of his second book, a miscellany of essays published in 1953.[66] A somewhat flippant tone infiltrates the text, and the many subjective criticisms of individual phrases, within an essentially blow-by-blow commentary, fail to penetrate the expressive heart of the work. Had Vaughan Williams been inclined to engage with the work more deeply, he might have explored the message of hope that Schiller's text and Beethoven's music provided in a time when Europe was at war. In another essay drafted in 1942, however, he did consider this context, arguing that the counterpart to a culture of musical nationalism was political internationalism. Paraphrasing his friend the historian George Trevelyan, Vaughan Williams writes, 'the ideal would be for every nation to be different and all at peace . . . what we are tending towards is to be all alike and all at war'.[67]

Vaughan Williams's third and final book, *The Making of Music*, rehearses in a condensed form some of the ideas from *National Music*, and, like the earlier study, was the product of an American lecture tour.[68] The principal difference between the two books is a change in emphasis; the later text focuses on music-making in general terms, before touching briefly on the subject of folksong. It adopts a quasi-philosophical tone at times, while remaining accessible to a non-specialist audience. Vaughan Williams's indefatigable enthusiasm for music and its history are prominent throughout the characteristic prose. The last chapter, titled 'Epilogue', is drawn from a lecture Vaughan Williams gave in December 1954 at Yale University. On this occasion the composer's achievements were being celebrated by the award of a university prize, the Howland Medal. Unusually, a recording of this lecture has survived, and a transcription has been published.[69] Vaughan Williams used the occasion to give a wide-ranging talk, summarizing the core beliefs he had expressed in earlier writings. Naturally, the composer's unshakeable belief in the beauty of folksongs is reiterated, and their historical importance is confirmed. Once again, composers are urged to learn from them and to ensure that their own music is a sincere self-expression, rooted in their own national culture, and not a mere imitation of an existing foreign model. Vaughan Williams thus encapsulates the vision of national music that he had developed in lectures and writings during a career of some sixty years as a public figure.

Reflecting on Vaughan Williams's work as a writer, one can clearly discern an early period of development, in which he grappled with the significance of English folksong, before his core beliefs matured and reached a settled form. These beliefs were not always expressed in the same way, however; *National Music* constitutes their strongest and most provocative formulation, where the importance of folksong stands at the centre of an idealistic vision of cultural nationalism. Of course this particular construction of nationalism was challenged, both in the 1930s and subsequently by competing ideologies, but it forms an integral, if problematic, aspect of Vaughan Williams's creative identity which should not be overlooked in a rounded assessment of his work. One of the interpretative challenges posed to the musical historian is to understand the contrast between the sometimes dogmatic certainty of the writings and the broader range of expression found in the music.

A particular concern pervading the writings is the importance of practical music-making, and, in his work as a musical activist, discussed in the first part of this chapter, Vaughan Williams took up his own challenge. The local rural communities he had encountered before the First World War, where people made music by singing their own folksongs, acted as an idealized exemplar for the composer, inspiring his work within the context of an industrialized and literate society. In the absence of 'spontaneous' musical utterances from the population at large, the twentieth-century British composer had an important leadership role to fulfil, bringing individuals together to participate in musical events, and providing music that could be performed by the local community, from hymns to repertoire for amateur choral and orchestral concerts. Vaughan Williams turned for inspiration to an idealized construction of society with an ancient tradition of folksongs at its spiritual heart; yet in the many musical activities the composer personally led, he did not provide his local performers with a narrow diet of folksong arrangements and rhapsodies. Beethoven symphonies, Bach cantatas or Schubert masses were just as likely to feature, as Vaughan Williams shared his love of a wide range of music with the local community. Although many examples could be chosen to illustrate this, it is perhaps the annual performances of the *St Matthew Passion* at Dorking which stand out: these occasions seem perfectly to fulfil this vision of community music-making, as amateurs and professionals joined together in large-scale performances of the Passion story. In his writings Vaughan Williams articulated a set of artistic ideals; by working with and for amateur musicians, he sought to bring his vision into being, pursuing the goals of self-expression and spiritual discovery through the act of musical performance.

Notes

1 The lecture series was repeated in Gloucester, and again in Brentwood, Essex, during 1903. Although neither notes nor script survive, the content of these lectures was reported in detail in local newspapers. See *KW*, 30–5; and Michael Holyoake, 'Towards a Folk Song Awakening: Vaughan Williams in Bournemouth, 1902', *Ralph Vaughan Williams Society Journal* 46 (2009), 9–15.

2 See, for instance, Nicholas Temperley, 'The Lost Chord', *Victorian Studies* 30 (1986), 7–23, at 7; and Dave Russell, *Popular Music in England, 1840–1914: A Social History* (Manchester University Press, 1987).

3 Holyoake, 'Towards a Folk Song Awakening', 15.

4 Vaughan Williams, 'Let Us Remember . . . Early Days' (1942), reproduced in *VWOM*, 251–3, at 253.

5 6 February 1904 (Surrey History Centre, 6782/18).

6 Vol. 11, issue No. 8.

7 Two years later, Vaughan Williams had a further collection of fifteen songs published as *Folk Songs from the Eastern Counties* (London: Novello, 1908).

8 *KW*, 72; *KC*, 257.

9 Vaughan Williams, *The First Fifty Years: A Brief Account of the English Hymnal from 1906 to 1956* (1956), reproduced in *VWOM*, 116.

10 *The English Hymnal* (1906), reproduced in *VWOM*, 32.

11 Interestingly, the new hymnal attracted controversy on publication: *The Times* reported that the Archbishop of Canterbury had urged his clergy not to use the new book. See *KW*, 74; *The Times*, 3 November and 14 November 1906.

12 *KW*, 64; *UVWB*, 82–3. For more on Vaughan Williams's relationship with the Leith Hill Festival, see Chapter 6 of this volume.

13 *UVWB*, 75.

14 19 January 1915, reproduced in *LRVW*, 107.

15 *UVWB*, 121.

16 Letter from W. A. Marshall to Ursula Vaughan Williams, 1958, quoted in *UVWB*, 129.

17 Letter from E. R. Winship to Ursula Vaughan Williams, 1958, quoted in *UVWB*, 131–2.

18 Jennifer Doctor, '"Working for Her Own Salvation": Vaughan Williams as Teacher of Elizabeth Maconchy, Grace Williams and Ina Boyle', in *VWIP*, 201.

19 Elizabeth Maconchy, contribution to a special issue commemorating Vaughan Williams's death of *Royal College of Music Magazine* 55/1 (1959), 34.

20 Philippians 2:12. 'Wherefore, my beloved, as ye have always obeyed, not as in my presence only, but now much more in my absence, work out your own salvation with fear and trembling'. This topic is, of course, also central to Bunyan's *Pilgrim's Progress*. For more on Vaughan Williams as a teacher, see Chapter 2 of this volume.

21 *UVWB*, 139.

22 Programme note, Bach Choir concert, Central Hall, Westminster, 14 December 1921, reproduced in *VWOM*, 401–2.

23 Basil Keen, *The Bach Choir: The First Hundred Years* (Aldershot: Ashgate, 2008), 113.

24 *Ibid.*, 115, 126.

25 'Reminiscences of Fifty Years' (1955), reproduced in *NM*, 275.

26 *KW*, 341. Vaughan Williams also conducted twelve performances of the *St John Passion* in Dorking.

27 *Ibid.*, 207.

28 *Ibid.*, 255.

29 *UVWB*, 206–7.

30 *Ibid.*, 217.

31 *Ibid.*, 222.

32 Alain Frogley, 'Vaughan Williams and Nazi Germany: The 1937 Hamburg Shakespeare Prize', in Christa Brüstle and Guido Heldt (eds.), *Music as a Bridge: Musikalische Beziehungen zwischen England und Deutschland 1920–1950* (Hildesheim: Georg Olms Verlag, 2005), 113–32, at 117.

33 *UVWB*, 224.

34 *Ibid.*, 229, 233.

35 Introduction to *News Chronicle Musical Competition Festival for HM Forces* (1942), reproduced in *VWOM*, 88.

36 *KW*, 306, 308.

37 *LRVW*, 599–602.

38 'BBC Hear Plea for "Third"', *The Times*, 19 July 1957, 6a.

39 This recording was released for the first time in 2009 on the Pearl label (GEMS 0079).

40 'The Romantic Movement and Its Results' (1897), reproduced in *VWOM*, 13.

41 A revised version was published in 1896 as *The Evolution of the Art of Music*. See Jeremy Dibble, 'Parry as Historiographer', in Bennett Zon (ed.), *Nineteenth-Century British Music Studies*, vol. 1 (Aldershot: Ashgate, 1999), 37–51.

42 'A School of English Music' (1902), reproduced in *VWOM*, 18.

43 Vaughan Williams, 'A Musical Autobiography' (1950), reproduced in *NM*, 181.

44 Holyoake, 'Towards a Folk Song Awakening', 14.

45 'A School of English Music', reproduced in *VWOM*, 18.

46 Published as a series of short articles in *The Music Student* 4/6–11 (1912), and as a separate booklet for the English Folk Dance Society (London: Joseph Williams, 1912). These publications were developed from a lecture given at the Vacation Conference on Musical Education, 10 January 1912, reproduced in *VWOM*, 185–99. A report of a similar lecture, given to the Oxford Folk Music Society, 19 November 1910, can be found in *MT* 52 (1911), 101–4.

47 'English Folk-Songs' (1912), reproduced in *VWOM*, 186.

48 *Ibid.*, 188.

49 *Ibid.*, 191.

50 *The Evolution of the Art of Music*, 81.

51 'English Folk-Songs', in *VWOM*, 198.

52 'Who Wants the English Composer?' (1912), reproduced in *VWOM*, 41–2.

53 'The Letter and the Spirit' (1920), reproduced in *NM*, 122.

54 *UVWB*, 29. For more on Vaughan Williams's religious beliefs, see, for instance, Byron Adams, 'Scripture, Church and Culture: Biblical Texts in the Works of Ralph Vaughan Williams', *VWS* 99–117.

55 *National Music* (1934), reproduced in *NM*, 40. Parry gave the inaugural address to the Folk-Song Society on 2 February 1899; the full text of his address is given in the *Journal of the Folk-Song Society* 1/1 (1899), 1–3.

56 *NM*, 68.

57 *Ibid.*, 23.

58 *Ibid.*, 27.

59 Robert Hull, 'The Cult of Archaism', *ML* 11 (1930), 367–74, quoted in *NM*, 26. For more on the often ambivalent attitude of British critics to folksong, see Chapter 3 of this volume.

60 *NM*, 42.

61 *Ibid.*, 41.

62 An example of this model of distinct national identities, underpinned by universal values, is implied by the following from Whitman's 'Song for All Seas, All Ships', which Vaughan Williams set in the first movement of *A Sea Symphony*: 'Flaunt out, O sea, your separate flags of nations! . . . But do you reserve especially for yourself and for the soul of man one flag above all the rest / A spiritual woven signal for all nations'.

63 Alain Frogley, 'Constructing Englishness in Music: National Character and the Reception of Ralph Vaughan Williams', in *VWS*, 18.

64 'Making Your Own Music' (1939), reproduced in *VWOM*, 76.

65 Introduction to *News Chronicle Musical Competition Festival for HM Forces* (1942), reproduced in *VWOM*, 87.

66 *Some Thoughts on Beethoven's Choral Symphony with Writings on Other Musical Subjects* (London: Oxford University Press, 1953).

67 'Nationalism and Internationalism' (1942), first published in *Some Thoughts on Beethoven's Choral Symphony* (1953), and reproduced in *NM*, 154.

68 Ithaca: Cornell University Press, 1955.

69 'Howland Medal Lecture' (1954), transcript reproduced in *VWOM*, 99–109.

12 Vaughan Williams, Boult, and the BBC

JENNY DOCTOR

In many ways, Ralph Vaughan Williams's relationship with the BBC can be seen as ambivalent. Many of the BBC Music Department's policies, activities and aims were anathema to him, and nowhere more than in the realm of new composition. The BBC sought to commission new works, a venture that Vaughan Williams found counterproductive; the BBC aimed to explain music to its vast body of listeners, which Vaughan Williams thought unnecessary; the BBC's structure, and consequently its broadcasting practices, divided music into higher- and lower-brow classifications, following a discriminating principle that ran against Vaughan Williams's beliefs in the fundamental nature of music across its entire spectrum; and most important, perhaps, the BBC's purpose as a broadcaster promoted the musical experience as a passive pursuit for its mass recipients, negating Vaughan Williams's encouragement of active music-making as an essential human endeavour.

Nevertheless, the BBC played a vital role in Vaughan Williams's career. Of course, it offered him the obvious benefit of a modern platform for the dissemination of his works, as it did for most living composers, British and otherwise. But, as this essay will explore, Vaughan Williams's relationship with the BBC permeated deeper than that: the Corporation played a fundamental role in establishing his reputation and significance, both nationally and internationally. The BBC not only performed Vaughan Williams's new works as a matter of principle and interest, but it regularly repeated works from his 'back catalogue', reinforcing and amplifying on a national and imperial scale the spectrum of his output, across its many styles, genres and functions. Moreover, though it is hard to quantify precisely, much of this activity and interest would seem to have stemmed from the friendship and mutual admiration that existed between Vaughan Williams and a sensitive interpreter of his works, Adrian Boult (1889–1983). Boult served as the chief decision-maker in the BBC Music Department throughout the 1930s and was conductor of the BBC Symphony Orchestra from 1930 until his retirement in 1950. It was surely his influence that convinced the BBC to offer the virtual space in which Vaughan Williams would become truly known and appreciated, as the composer and his music reached across the British sphere and beyond.

The 1920s

By the time the BBC was formed in 1922, Vaughan Williams was already 50 years old and established as a British composer of renown, celebrated not only for his highbrow symphonic works, but also for community-driven contributions to *The English Hymnal* and to the vocal sphere in general. His larger-scale works were aired in the very first season that the BBC initiated rare broadcast concerts of symphonic repertory. The first Vaughan Williams entry in the published Programmes as Broadcast records lists what was probably the earliest BBC performance of an orchestral work by him: *A Pastoral Symphony* (1916–21) was broadcast on 24 February 1924, in an afternoon 'Programme of Sacred Music' given from Southwark Cathedral, conducted by its noted organist, Dr E. T. Cook.[1] Not long afterwards, on 10 April 1924, a prime-time evening programme titled 'Living British Composers' – the earliest BBC series devoted to national art music – featured Vaughan Williams's vocal and chamber works.[2] The very first performance of his opera *Hugh the Drover* (1910–14) on 14 July 1924 was broadcast from His Majesty's Theatre, London, conducted by the young Malcolm Sargent. At that time, when many organizations and artists refused to broadcast, the British National Opera Company was a notable exception, offering to the BBC frequent performances that were generally transmitted in part.[3] Thus Act ii was aired that evening, preceded by an introductory talk by BBC Music Critic, Percy Scholes.[4] Vaughan Williams's first talk over the airwaves also occurred that year, discussing folk carols before a late programme called 'Carols and Waits' on Christmas Eve.[5]

Thus Vaughan Williams's voice, both musical and literal, was heard across the UK from 1924 via broadcasting. His apparent enthusiasm for the new medium aligns with his belief in music's egalitarian place within society: 'music is able to grow out of our ordinary life in a way that no other art can ... Music is above all others the art of the humble.'[6] Such social doctrines, alongside Vaughan Williams's 'distinctly nationalist agenda',[7] closely paralleled the commonality and democratic reach of the young BBC, set to disseminate music and cultural ideas every day across the nation, to make them audible to all at nominal cost, in ways that had previously been unimaginable.

It is impossible to know what conversations Vaughan Williams may have had when first establishing his relationship with the BBC Music Department and with radio generally. The earliest correspondence preserved at the BBC Written Archives Centre commences in 1928, confirming that the composer would conduct *A Pastoral Symphony* at that season's Promenade Concerts.[8] The following year, he agreed to conduct in the Proms again, on condition that violinist Jelly d'Aranyi would be the soloist in his *Concerto Accademico* (1924–5).[9] Correspondence in the early 1930s often arranged for Vaughan Williams to conduct performances, to attend rehearsals, to approve suggestions for performers or, on occasion, to ask about new works that the BBC might broadcast. Most exchanges were with Music Department staff, but frequent letters were also exchanged with Adrian Boult, after he was appointed to a leading role in BBC music in 1930.

Vaughan Williams had a good and mutually beneficial working relationship with Boult. They were leading British musicians whose careers overlapped for more than forty years, yet the positive disposition of their relationship depended on more than synchronicity. They represented a particular kind of statesman who emerged from the Edwardian era and imparted Edwardian values – Boult even sported an Edwardian moustache. As he wrote of himself in a brief autobiographical description: 'On the rostrum he is an impressive figure, for he is over six feet tall, and has an upright, almost military bearing. He is economical of gestures, for his theory is that a conductor should not distract the attention of the audience.'[10] Moreover, the eulogistic words that Boult wrote of Vaughan Williams shortly after the composer's death paralleled what others might have written about himself: 'He was like many great men, approachable, sympathetic and of a piercing integrity. He was seen at any concert where an important new work was to be played.'[11] Although friends, they were never as close as Vaughan Williams had been with Gustav Holst, for instance;[12] yet the sense of integrity, musicianship and life values that these men shared served as common ground for mutual respect and a fruitful professional association. This bond resulted in a multitude of performances that spanned both their careers, and which we continue to listen to and admire on record today.

Though Vaughan Williams came from an elite, upper middle-class family background compared to Boult's more modest middle-class circumstances,[13] in both cases their families had enough money to support them through the early stages of their careers. Boult was seventeen years younger, yet Vaughan Williams's musical interests took longer to mature;[14] thus they both came of age musically during the Edwardian years, before World War I. Boult first encountered Vaughan Williams's music in 1909 while a student at Oxford, when he sang in a performance of *Toward the Unknown Region* (1907), conducted by his mentor, Hugh Allen.[15] He attended the first performance of *A Sea Symphony* (1903–9) in October 1910, and met the composer the following March, when he performed in its second performance at Oxford. During 1912–13 he studied in Leipzig with Nikisch, and after returning home his conducting career burgeoned, from opportunities that he helped to create both financially and practically. When the First World War broke out, Boult was declared unfit for active service due to a heart condition, and instead served in the War Office, assisting with leather distribution, which gave him the flexibility to conduct concerts both in London and the north of England. Through these concerts he soon became noted for his promotion of English music; in particular, he became close friends with Holst, conducting the premiere of *The Planets* at Queen's Hall in September 1918.[16] Boult also established a warm alliance with Vaughan Williams, when he conducted *A London Symphony* (1911–13) at Queen's Hall in both February and March 1918. Although the February concert was 'rather spoiled by a Zeppelin raid',[17] the composer famously wrote to thank Boult:

> for giving such a fine performance – it really was splendid – you got the score right into you & through you into your orch:
>
>   May I say how much I admired your conducting – it is real *conducting* – you get just what you want and *know* what you want – and your players trust you because they know it also.[18]

Before the March performance, Vaughan Williams 'came to my room in a distant outcrop of the War Office and sat among the samples of boots . . . and made some cuts in the score'.[19]

In 1919, one newspaper remarked that 'inside a year . . . Boult had risen from obscurity to a leading place among British conductors'.[20] He often featured Vaughan Williams's music in his concerts, both in London and in his role as conductor of the City of Birmingham Orchestra (1924–9). The spirit of musical understanding, admiration and trust described in Vaughan Williams's letter formed the basis for a long collaboration between composer and conductor, leading to the BBC partnership that is under particular scrutiny here.[21]

The 1930s

In May 1923, six months after its foundation, the British Broadcasting Company appointed as Music Director the eminent conductor Percy Pitt, known for his promotion both of British opera and of continental contemporary music. Pitt played a highly significant role during the 1920s in shaping the BBC's Music Department and musical output, but in 1929 he was forced to resign due to the BBC's new policy of retirement at age sixty – which may have been implemented with Pitt in mind.[22] After the BBC became a Corporation in January 1927, its musical ventures included taking over the Promenade Concerts in March of that year and the creation of a permanent, contracted BBC Symphony Orchestra.[23] The Corporation was determined to create an ensemble that equalled, in eminence and quality, the best orchestras in Europe and the United States – with a conductor to match. Thomas Beecham was the first choice, but when negotiations with him irrevocably collapsed,[24] the BBC turned to Boult, who had served on the BBC Music Advisory Committee since 1928.[25] Boult was persuaded to return from Birmingham to become BBC Director of Music in May 1930; in October he launched the BBC Symphony Orchestra in its first season, and some months later was appointed as the orchestra's Chief Conductor.

Boult's assumption of these positions was propitious for many reasons. His background had prepared him well for the post, not least because of his close association with British music. But he also had sufficient interest in recent continental trends, music that BBC managers then symbolically valued as a means of 'carry[ing] into the greatest possible number of homes everything that is best in every department of human knowledge, endeavour and achievement'.[26] Boult demanded from his players the discipline, concentration and tenacity needed to pull off worthy performances of unfamiliar, difficult works within limited rehearsal time. Although less charismatic than leading European conductors, it was Boult's all-round, everyday skilfulness and intelligence, as administrator as well as daily broadcasting conductor, that certified him as the musician best suited to lead BBC music in that first decade; this was, after all, a critical period in the Corporation's development from pioneering corporation into top-level broadcaster, on a par with the best in Europe and North America.

The steady availability of a high-quality symphony orchestra emboldened the BBC to showcase orchestral works throughout the 1930s, including those by Vaughan Williams. In 1934, after the deaths of Elgar, Delius and Holst, he became known as the leading living British symphonist.[27] As the decade progressed, nationalist tendencies waxed in parallel with political tensions, and Vaughan Williams's works were regularly broadcast, generally planned and conducted with Boult's and/or his own involvement. The works most commonly broadcast in the early 1930s include *Flos Campi* (1925), *A Pastoral Symphony*, *A London Symphony*, the *Fantasia on a Theme by Thomas Tallis* (1910)[28] and *Job* (1930), his 'masque for dancing',[29] while the mid-1930s added performances of *A Sea Symphony*, *Dona Nobis Pacem* (1936) and the Symphony No. 4 (1931–4). Much correspondence was exchanged arranging for the composer to attend rehearsals or concerts, or when he sent congratulations on successful performances, given not only domestically but also by BBC personnel overseas.[30] The BBC consistently sought opportunities for Vaughan Williams to conduct his own works in broadcasts; for instance, he conducted at least one work in many of the Proms seasons.[31] Moreover, he was occasionally invited to conduct full concert broadcasts.[32]

An important occasion for the BBC was the celebration in 1938 of the jubilee of Henry Wood's conducting career, marked by a concert of combined forces – including three London orchestras and massed choirs – at the Royal Albert Hall on 5 October. At Wood's special request, Rachmaninov was invited to participate, and a commission to Vaughan Williams resulted in the *Serenade to Music* (1938) for sixteen solo singers and orchestra. Although the first half of the concert could not be aired, as Rachmaninov refused to broadcast live, the *Serenade* in the second half was transmitted on the BBC National Programme.[33]

The BBC competed fiercely for opportunities to give first European performances of Vaughan Williams's works, such as the Piano Concerto (1926–31) once it was completed.[34] In his negotiations with the Corporation, Vaughan Williams remained loyal to the performers with whom he associated specific works. The Piano Concerto is a case in point, as he wrote a confidential letter to Boult in 1935:

> I hear a rumour that my Pfte Concerto is to have a studio performance – In case there is any truth in this – I want it reserved for Harriet Cohen for once more partly because I like her playing of it and partly because she has been so adventurous in producing unknown works & deserves recognition for it.[35]

Boult clearly disagreed with Vaughan Williams, believing that

> It is surely common knowledge that Harriet Cohen's performance of [it] caused it to be completely dropped since it was first performed. The work . . . was laid out for a pianist of the Busoni calibre, and though she made a very valiant effort, she could get nowhere near the spirit of it or even the notes in many passages.[36]

Rather than confronting Vaughan Williams, Boult was among those who persuaded him to re-score the extremely difficult solo part for two pianos.[37]

In 1934, when Boult inquired about the work that turned out to be the Symphony No. 4 in F minor (1931–4), the composer responded:

> As regards my symphony – I have been writing it for about 3 years now & I believe it is finished – I have made a 2 pfte arrangement & will get that tried through to see if I can bear it . . . The bits I have shown to people they do not like – Gustav [Holst] heard it all in an early version on 2 pftes – & was puzzled by most of it & disliked the rest.[38]

Undeterred, Boult arranged for the BBC to give the first performance the next season, smoothing over the half-promise of the premiere that

Vaughan Williams had given to Malcolm Sargent.[39] While Boult prepared for the performance, a paragraph appeared in the *Radio Times* asserting that Arnold Bax and Sibelius were the 'greatest living symphonists'.[40] Boult was so annoyed that he wrote to the magazine's editor:

> I do not feel that a statement of that kind should ever be allowed to appear unsigned in the programme pages of The Radio Times. It surely represents in the minds of most people the corporate opinion of the B.B.C., and I think there are plenty of people inside the B.B.C. also who would consider that Vaughan Williams is a far greater symphonist than either Bax or Sibelius.[41]

He also wrote a letter of apology to Vaughan Williams, who took it in his stride.[42]

The following year, Boult wrote to Vaughan Williams to request 'a large and comprehensive lesson from you re the performance of sundry R.V.W. works – if <u>you</u> can be bothered – e.g. Sea Symphony. We are doing it at Queen's Hall in October, and if there was anything in the performance (if you heard it) that irritated you, I should much like to hear about it and put it right'.[43] Vaughan Williams asked to attend a rehearsal,[44] and the result was a performance that prompted an effusive letter from the composer:

> There seem to be two essentials of great conducting.
> (1) Faithfulness to the composer
> (2) The power of the conductor to express *himself* to the full *at the moment* – to feel himself in the music & the music in himself. . .
> Yesterday we had (1) + (2) – a great performance & great conducting for which I thank you from the bottom of my heart.[45]

The spirit of this letter would have been enormously gratifying for Boult.

On occasion, Vaughan Williams asked to attend BBC rehearsals of works by his contemporaries, such as Schoenberg's Five Pieces for Orchestra, broadcast on 18 November 1931,[46] and sometimes Boult served as liaison between Vaughan Williams and internationally acclaimed conductors who had engagements with the BBC. For instance, in May 1935 Boult arranged for the composer to meet both with Serge Koussevitzky and – at Vaughan Williams's request, as 'I should like so much to see how it is done' – Arturo Toscanini. Though 'practically everyone has been refused', Boult offered Vaughan Williams a choice of Toscanini rehearsals to attend.[47]

Given his standing with the BBC, Vaughan Williams sought opportunities also to promote the music of his pupils, such as when he conducted a studio broadcast in December 1934 featuring orchestral works by former students Elizabeth Maconchy, Grace Williams and Robin Milford, by RCM colleague R. O. Morris, and by himself.[48] He also found ways to champion the music of Holst.[49] In the same way, Boult looked out for Vaughan Williams, determined to promote his lesser-known works; for example, in September 1933, he wrote: 'Hearing "The Shepherds of the Delectable Mountains" . . . last week performed in a way which made a lot of it sound almost ugly, I felt I should very much like sometime to give a carefully prepared performance of it . . . Properly done I have known it to make a most profound effect.'[50]

Thus Vaughan Williams was increasingly associated with British radio of the 1920s and 30s, interacting frequently and cooperatively with the new medium as it developed. But alongside this ease of access, the composer began to develop misgivings that distressed him. In 1934, he wrote:

> A musical nation is not a nation which is content to listen. The best form of musical appreciation is to try and do it for yourself; to get really inside the meaning of music. . . The temptation to become a mere listener is nowadays very great. Gramophones and wireless have brought the world's riches to the doors of the humblest, but if we all become listeners there will soon be no one left to listen to.[51]

Interestingly, although Boult agreed that music-making was an essential activity, he distinguished between the music produced by amateur and professional musicians: '[amateurs] are the aristocracy of music, and it is for them that we professionals live and work, and through them that we get our audiences and most of our inspiration'.[52] Boult recognized that radio fostered new connections in the performer–listener relationship, amateur and professional musicians each serving as an incentive and inspiration to the other.

The war years

According to Ursula Vaughan Williams, 'the beginning of the war made Ralph feel desperate for useful work'.[53] The BBC provided an outlet for this, serving as an official body to which the composer could communicate his views, and, given his considerable connections there, he had confidence that they would be heard. On a number of occasions he challenged BBC policies or practices, or championed issues that paralleled the values that civilians or those serving in the armed forces daily risked their lives to protect. In other instances, he agreed to contribute to BBC-led schemes by arranging suites from his popular film scores, or composing occasional works to engage the attention and voices of the British people. As he said in a broadcast talk soon after the war started:

> The composer feels that he would like to be able to serve the community
> directly through his craft if not through his art . . . Are there not ways in
> which the composer without derogating from his art, without being untrue
> to himself, but still without that entire disregard for his fellows which
> characterizes the artist in his supreme moments, [might] use his skill, his
> knowledge, his sense of beauty in the service of his fellow men?[54]

Interactions with the BBC offered Vaughan Williams ways to achieve
exactly that, amplified through radio transmission to reach homes across
the nation and internationally.

In September and October 1939, Vaughan Williams joined with Henry
Wood and other leading musicians in voicing objections to the music that
the BBC chose to broadcast in the initial weeks of the war. As the
Corporation effected its difficult and cumbersome evacuation from
London, cinema-organ music was aired for hours at a time. Vaughan
Williams, apparently with Boult's encouragement,[55] wrote a long and
passionate letter to the Director-General:

> In times like these when so many people are looking for comfort &
> encouragement from music . . . surely we ought to give them something that will
> grip. I believe that really great music, especially if it is familiar[,] will
> grip everybody (in a category of great music I include a Beethoven Symphony, a
> Schubert song and a fine marching tune)[.] I admit that very bad music
> does grip certain minds but this halfway-house stuff grips nobody . . . Are we not
> missing a great opportunity which may never recur?[56]

Vaughan Williams wrote on in support of the many musicians who would
lose their livelihoods through lack of work, as had occurred during the
First World War.[57]

In those early months, Vaughan Williams offered the BBC assistance in
two other ways that reflected his social convictions. Firstly, he gave a talk,
'Making Your Own Music', on 3 December 1939,[58] encouraging active music-
making as a response to national crisis: 'If we neglect the amateur side of
music and become a nation of mere passive listeners all the life will go out of
our art – Art must be creative if it is to be vital.'[59] Secondly, he worked closely
with BBC staff to build two half-hour programmes, recommending 'such
folksongs as he considers would be very suitable for marching purposes';[60] he
prepared scripts to explain these 'tunes with real blood in their veins and real
muscles in their limbs. I don't believe that you could help stepping out to
them even when you are tired after a long day's march.'[61]

As the war developed, Vaughan Williams's own works, such as *Flos
Campi*, the *Wasps* overture (1909), *Job*, the *Five Variants of 'Dives and
Lazarus'* (1939) and the Mass in G minor (1922), were broadcast, often
with Vaughan Williams's and/or Boult's involvement. A year after the

war's commencement, the Ministry of Information suggested that the Corporation develop a 'scheme for commissioning patriotic songs',[62] and Vaughan Williams was invited to compose a 'song or lay hymn, with orchestral accompaniment, the theme patriotic but not necessarily war-like'; the text should avoid 'the word "England" ... as a synonym for Britain'.[63] He set a W. E. Henley poem for baritone solo, double chorus, unison voices and orchestra, sending a draft version to Boult and others for criticism in late October 1940,[64] and soon after, submitting the work to the BBC. Imprudently, Vaughan Williams had set Henley's 'England, my England', but Boult was untroubled by the text: 'it seems to me to hit every nail on the head, except ... the prejudices of Wales and Scotland, and I really do not think we can worry about this'.[65] The BBC lost no time in arranging the work's premiere, planned for broadcast on 4 April 1941.

In March, however, Vaughan Williams wrote an angry letter to the Director-General, protesting against the banning from broadcasts of works by the composer Alan Bush, who was a member of the Communist Party. Though he did not share Bush's political views, Vaughan Williams 'wish[ed] to protest against this victimization of private opinion' by withdrawing the commissioned work.[66] The question of the BBC's policy towards 'artists holding certain religious or political opinions' was raised in the House of Commons,[67] and the Corporation soon reversed its position;[68] Bush's compositions were no longer banned. Once the furore died down, Vaughan Williams's publisher wondered if plans for the premiere might be resumed,[69] but only in the autumn did the BBC again consider a broadcast. By this time 'Vaughan Williams himself ... regretted very much that other circumstances, not connected with the song itself, prevented the original arrangements with the B.B.C., being carried out'.[70] The first domestic broadcast,[71] on 14 December 1941, took place in a programme 'Spirit of the Empire', presenting 'four songs by British composers inspired by this war'.[72] A subsequent performance in February 1942 disappointed the composer. 'I was particularly sorry because the tune is rather a ewe lamb of mine & I feel that if it got a proper send off it might hit the nail on the head – But I felt on Sunday night that it had been strangled at birth.'[73]

In the meantime, wartime conditions made it too difficult logistically for Boult to hold both his BBC positions. From April 1942, Arthur Bliss, a long-time friend and colleague of both Boult and Vaughan Williams, took over the duties of Director of Music,[74] while Boult carried on as Chief Conductor of the BBC Symphony Orchestra. The BBC continued to broadcast Vaughan Williams's works, such as *The Poisoned Kiss* (1936),[75] a suite of film music from *49th Parallel* (1940),[76] and the 'Pavane' from *Job*, the latter ending a programme to celebrate Empire Day 'on a note of slow dignity'.[77] The noteworthy Vaughan Williams event of 1942, however, was his seventieth birthday, which the BBC marked vigorously with 'a week's celebration – one programme each evening, ending on the Saturday with a broadcast of the Celebration Concert by the Royal Philharmonic Society', which presented '"birthday gift" compositions' by friends and colleagues.[78] About all these broadcasts, Vaughan Williams wrote to Gerald Finzi: 'The more I hear my own stuff the more I dislike it – where I shall be at the end of the week I don't know – & I shan't have the courage not to listen'.[79] Boult too was unhappy,[80] as, of the major works, he was scheduled to conduct only *A Pastoral Symphony*.

> May I in all humility remind the great of the Music Department of the B.B.C. that *Job* is dedicated to me; that I conducted the first performance of the F minor symphony; that I was intimately concerned with the first performances of 'The Shepherds of the Delectable Mountains'; that 'Sancta Civitas' is Vaughan Williams's favourite work; and that Tertis has urgently asked me to allow him to take part in a performance of 'Flos Campi'.[81]

To placate him, Boult was invited to conduct the Fourth Symphony in a November broadcast.[82]

In spring 1943, Vaughan Williams worked on incidental music to a radio production of John Bunyan's *The Pilgrim's Progress*.[83] In February, while working on that score, Vaughan Williams wrote to tell Henry Wood that his new symphony 'must now go forward "for better, for worse"', and Wood accepted the Fifth Symphony sight unseen for the 1943 Proms.[84] In that wartime season, the Proms concerts were patriotically filled with works by living allied and Empire composers, and a new Vaughan Williams symphony provided a substantial homeland contribution. Despite overstretched resources, Boult offered: 'We should be most happy to put aside a rehearsal as soon as you like to go through the work and enable you to test the Parts, etc.'[85] The private play-through took place on 25 May 1943 at the BBC's Maida Vale studio. A number of guests were invited to attend, 'a good indication of those who were musically closest to Vaughan Williams at this time'.[86] The first public performance was scheduled for the Proms on 24 June in the Royal Albert Hall, conducted by the composer.[87] Boult was pleased with the performance, particularly given wartime concerns:

> Everything seemed clear and well balanced, & I thought the orchestra played very finely: on the top of their form (which doesn't often happen nowadays) . . . It isn't for me to judge compositions but . . . its serene loveliness is completely satisfying in these times & shows, as only music can, what we must work for when this madness is over.[88]

In the final eighteen months of the war, works by Vaughan Williams were frequently aired, many conducted by Boult, including *Job* and the Fourth and Fifth Symphonies.[89] In February 1944, Vaughan Williams was asked to give a talk about Elgar for the tenth anniversary of his death, but the composer declined: 'I had very little personal acquaintance with Elgar – I used to meet him for a few minutes once a year at the 3 Choir Festivals – he was always very kind & friendly – but we were never intimate.'[90] Interestingly, Vaughan Williams agreed to write and record four short talks for WQXR, the New York station, in December 1944.[91]

Meanwhile, several years before the end of the war, the War Office and BBC wanted to be ready with material with which to greet the peace. The BBC commissioned Vaughan Williams to write a ten-minute Victory Anthem for mass consumption, to be sung at Westminster Abbey,[92] and he composed a work for soprano solo, large chorus, children's chorus, full symphony orchestra, organ and narrator. *Thanksgiving for Victory* was pre-recorded on 4 November 1944, conducted by Boult and in the composer's presence, 'for immediate use when the moment comes ... We would presumably have to [have the right forces ready] when it comes to a grand performance in the Albert Hall in the presence of Their Majesties on some special occasion later on.'[93] Copies of the discs were distributed internationally for overseas use, with strict injunction that they not be aired until after the official first broadcast, once peace was declared.

The first performance took place in a service of thanksgiving on the Sunday after Victory in Europe day (13 May 1945). After all the planning and promises, the work's public emergence was awkwardly subdued. Boult believed that the problem was in part technical: 'the recording ... utterly failed to place the various levels of tone in proper perspective.'[94] By this time, Victor Hely-Hutchinson had succeeded Bliss as the BBC Director of Music, and he attributed the problem to lack of public awareness, 'express [ing his] profound regret at the complete absence of publicity for it in the "Radio Times"'; the music broadcasts for Victory Week were to have been introduced in an article that was omitted due to space restrictions.[95] Others took up the cry for a live broadcast with full forces as part of the victory festivities, but a live performance was not mounted by the BBC until the 1945 Proms.[96] During that Promenade season, three concerts presented major works by Vaughan Williams, and the first public performance of *Thanksgiving for Victory* took place on 14 September.[97]

After the war

In the years after the war the BBC, like Britain generally, was musically behind the times, as a function of conservative attitudes among the staff members in decision-making positions. Music for general audiences continued to be broadcast in the Home Service; in addition, the pioneering Third Programme was launched in September 1946 as an evening radio canvas dedicated to exploring all aspects of the fine arts, old and new. Even with the Third Programme, the Corporation was slow to follow Europe musically on the wave of new developments stemming from serialism, not investing in it wholeheartedly until later in the decade; nevertheless, the BBC's attitude towards Vaughan Williams in those conservative years was surprisingly restrained. He was lauded at major birthdays, he took his stand at the podium during Proms seasons, and his symphonies and other popular works were broadcast on a regular basis. But the unceremonious, creative partnership between Corporation and composer became a thing of the past.

Vaughan Williams's seventy-fifth birthday in October 1947 was celebrated in style. The composer conducted *A London Symphony* in the Royal Albert Hall for the opening of that season's Symphony Concerts, broadcast on the Home Service on 15 October.[98] He conducted a repeat performance from a studio the following evening, when the Music Department held a party in his honour.[99] Each evening of the birthday week, *This Week's Composer* presented a gramophone recording retrospective of his best-known works.[100] At the composer's request, *Sancta Civitas* was featured in a Third Programme studio concert on 13 October.[101] On the birthday itself (the 12th), *Music Magazine* included tributes by Harriet Cohen, Constant Lambert, Vaughan Williams's friend and admirer Alan Kirby, and Boult.[102] Boult gave homage to Vaughan Williams as 'the undisputed leader of English musical life', but, interestingly, also addressed the issue of international recognition:

> Perhaps the insular position and attitude of England makes all our work less apt for export. It is indeed probable that there are a number of his works which no one could expect a foreigner to understand unless he already knew some of Vaughan Williams's preceding output and could have some idea of the development of his, and our, musical language.[103]

Pre-recorded in English, German and Italian, the different versions of this talk were broadcast on the BBC's European Service on Vaughan Williams's birthday.[104]

However, after the 1947 birthday celebrations, the strength of the BBC's commitment to Vaughan Williams's music began to decline. His standing as the leading living British composer prompted those in authority to take notice at important moments, but otherwise musical attention was turned sharply on the younger generation – particularly on Britten, after *Peter Grimes* achieved such outstanding success just as the war ended.[105] Vaughan Williams continued to loom, but it was not long before the ideals he championed – in particular, music for the people, heartily expressed in choral settings or large-scale symphonic land-scapes – came to seem uncomfortably outdated, relics of a war-torn time from which people so painfully wished to disconnect; that is, his causes were increasingly out of step with a post-war musical environment that, as the 1950s unfolded, looked increasingly to Europe's art-for-art's-sake milieu for inspiration.

Yet Vaughan Williams's *oeuvre* still fitted well within post-war BBC programming schemes, in that the Music Department liked to broadcast sets of works. Thus all the Vaughan Williams symphonies to date were given in the 1946 Proms, with the composer conducting *A London Symphony* on 31 July.[106] The Corporation also continued to take interest in first performances. In 1948, the composer offered to the Third Programme the premiere of his Partita for Double String Orchestra, which was broadcast on 20 March[107] and 'diagonalized' on the Home Service the day after;[108] the work was given its first concert performance on 29 July in the 1948 Proms, conducted by the composer. Moreover, the Corporation continued to promote new Vaughan Williams symphonies. The Music Department urgently wished to broadcast the first performance of Symphony No. 6 in spring 1948. Boult had been invited to a piano play-through at the Royal College of Music on 5 June 1947,[109] and an orchestral run-through took place on 16 December,[110] conducted by the composer with Boult assisting; a BBC recording was made for Vaughan Williams's private use.[111] The first performance, conducted by Boult, was given on 21 April 1948 on the Home Service, diagonalized on the 24th on the Third Programme, and repeated on 11 May on the Home Service to promote greater comprehension through repetition – and to arouse further attention and acclaim for the BBC. The symphony was performed again on 4 August, in the 1948 Proms, conducted by Basil Cameron.

The 1949–50 season was marked by the BBC's choosing *Hugh the Drover*, alongside Verdi's *Falstaff*, 'as repertory productions for the whole winter season'; as a result, six broadcasts of Vaughan Williams's opera were given between October and May on the Third Programme.[112] The composer was present for rehearsals leading to the initial broadcasts, and even for subsequent rehearsals, 'simply for the pleasure of the thing'.[113] In August 1950, Vaughan Williams expressed interest in writing incidental music for a series based on Thomas Hardy's *The Mayor of Casterbridge*;[114] he subsequently arranged some of the music into an orchestral Prelude, and made this available to the BBC in September 1952.[115] The following year, he was invited to write incidental music for Hardy's *The Dynasts*, but declined the invitation.[116] Throughout this period, Vaughan Williams continued to work on his *Pilgrim's Progress* opera, and when the BBC Director of Music, Steuart Wilson, asked if it would be ready for performance in the 1951 Festival of Britain, Vaughan Williams immediately sent the score.[117] The opera was given its first performance and broadcast on 26 April 1951 from the Royal Opera House, Covent Garden,[118] and a second broadcast aired on 30 April.

From around this time, Vaughan Williams's interactions with the BBC became fewer and less personal, undoubtedly due to the fact that Boult was no longer on the staff there. Boult had left his position as BBC Director of Music during the war, and ultimately, in April 1950, he left the Corporation altogether. He retired from his position as Chief Conductor ostensibly due to the BBC's mandatory retirement age; as when Percy Pitt had been forced to leave under the same rule twenty years before, however, the matter was handled disagreeably, leaving a bitter aftertaste.[119] After Boult's departure, Vaughan Williams works were still broadcast – four of the symphonies were given at the 1951 Proms, for instance – but he was rarely invited to conduct. The BBC began to treat Vaughan Williams and his music monumentally, broadcasting major works of the past, rather than recognizing an individual whose outlook and musical language continued to develop and change.

Concerning Vaughan Williams's eightieth birthday in October 1952, the BBC Head of Music, Herbert Murrill, asked: 'What are we going to do about Vaughan Williams? . . . Although he is not a controversial figure in the Schönberg manner he seems to me to deserve some considerable gesture.'[120] The full set of six symphonies was presented at that summer's Proms, with the Fifth on 3 September conducted by the composer.[121] A retrospective of choral works and songs was proposed for the Third Programme in the final quarter of the year,[122] but the idea was dropped: 'if the symphonies are given at the Promenade concerts . . . I rather doubt if it is right to do much more than this'.[123] For the birthday itself, Murrill first considered a studio production of *The Pilgrim's Progress*, as it 'represents a crystallization of the composer's thought and style over thirty years or more';[124] but that plan also proved too onerous to realize, and instead a performance of *On Wenlock Edge* was broadcast in a late-night Third Programme recital.[125] The String Quartet in A minor aired on the Third Programme on 13 October, and the Home Service carried 'a symphony concert of the composer's best-loved works', conducted by Malcolm Sargent.[126] Thus the five years that had passed since the war were telling; whereas the BBC celebrated the composer's seventy-fifth birthday heroically, with all stops pulled out, the Corporation approached his eightieth reductively, as a 'best-loved' anachronism.

In this vein, the first performance of *Sinfonia Antartica*, given in Manchester on 14 January 1953 by the Hallé Orchestra, conducted by Sir John Barbirolli, was not at first going to be broadcast; though 'something of an event in British music',[127] a new Vaughan Williams symphony no longer warranted BBC attention. Two regional Home Services, however, bravely decided to broadcast the first performance,[128] and the Third Programme aired the Hallé's second performance the next night; it was diagonalized from London on the basic Home Service on 21 January. The Corporation mounted its own broadcast in a BBC Symphony Concert conducted by Sargent on 11 March, with a studio repeat diagonalized the following night.[129] The Light Programme wondered whether it might approach Vaughan Williams about a broadcast talk, 'to get him to illustrate his new symphony for a popular audience ... with the object of getting him to bridge the gulfs between the great masses who cannot read a score and the musical cognoscenti'.[130] But the Music Programme Organiser reported: 'V.W. summed up "All my life I have refused to talk about my own music and I'm certainly not going to start at 80". He loves us very much – but not that much.'[131]

The major event of 1953 was of course the coronation, and Vaughan Williams's *A Sea Symphony* was included in the Coronation Concert on 27 May 1953, an all-British event that received major coverage on the BBC Home Service.[132] A profound broadcasting effect of the coronation was that it was televised, bringing the phenomenon of television more firmly into the nation's sitting-rooms. It is interesting, then, that around that time the BBC proposed to televise a performance of *The Bridal Day*, a ballet written by Vaughan Williams in 1938–9 to a libretto by Ursula Vaughan Williams, based on Spenser's *Epithalamion*.[133] When the composer rediscovered the score in 1952, he sent it to Stanford Robinson, who wondered whether it could 'be done twice in the Great Hall at Hampton Court, by the London Opera Club, during the Coronation Season'. Kenneth Wright, then head of music for television, believed that 'a new work, with visual possibilities, by our greatest composer, and based on a great Elizabethan poet, might be an attractive idea'.[134] The first performance was televised from a London studio on 5 June 1953, narrated by Cecil Day Lewis and conducted by Robinson. Ursula Vaughan Williams later recalled:

> Neither of us was happy about its performance on the screen, where dances that seemed spacious in a hall became a congested muddle, unrelated to the music. There was only one day of rehearsal in the studio with cameras, lighting, and costume, so it was too late for suggestions. The music was well sung and played, but we were embarrassed by the performance and both felt that television was not for us – and certainly not for this work which needed, we saw, a stage performance.[135]

In 1955, BBC radio featured several first Vaughan Williams broadcasts,[136] but the most significant transmissions of his music that year featured all seven symphonies, given between February and June on the Home Service by the City of Birmingham Symphony Orchestra. 'They represent in a way easily discernable by the average music-lover the process by which a seer-composer of wide sympathies and great mental power assimilates the major experiences of life through music.'[137] The performances aired on Sunday evenings, each introduced by Frank Howes. Vaughan Williams conducted *A Sea Symphony* in the first concert on 6 February; Boult was invited to conduct No. 5 and *Job* in a concert on 1 May, and the final concert with *Sinfonia Antartica* on 19 June; and the rest were conducted by Rudolf Schwarz.

Nevertheless, declining interest in Vaughan Williams resulted in there being no *Radio Times* promotion for the first performance and broadcast of the Symphony No. 8 from Manchester, given by the Hallé Orchestra, conducted by Barbirolli, on 2 May 1956. Similarly, the *Radio Times* issue for the first Proms performance on 29 August, given again by Barbirolli and the Hallé, offered no special coverage of the symphony.[138] Thus it is not surprising that for Vaughan Williams's eighty-fifth birthday in October 1957, the BBC's plans seem rather thin and obligatory, reflecting minimal enthusiasm. The plans included a tribute in *Music Magazine* (6 October) and part of a Royal Philharmonic Society concert (9 October), conducted by Boult;[139] the *Songs of Travel* were aired on the birthday itself, but at the rather subdued hour of 9.25 a.m. When chastised for this half-hearted effort, the BBC explained, 'we do not normally celebrate half-decades – we are saving up for 1962!'[140] The composer's publisher found this all 'rather grim', particularly as the BBC was 'not broadcasting any work later than 1922'.[141] The Corporation did rustle up a further performance on 17 October, presenting the Fifth Symphony.[142]

In spring 1958, Vaughan Williams invited the BBC's Eric Warr to a run-through of Symphony No. 9 at St Pancras Town Hall on 21 March,[143] at which the work was played twice.[144] Despite the 'coolness of the critics' reception of the music',[145] the first performance on 2 April, given by the Royal Philharmonic Orchestra conducted by Sargent, was broadcast on the Home Service with adequate BBC promotion. Sargent and the BBC Symphony Orchestra gave the work again on 5 August at the Proms, with the composer in attendance.[146] Following the composer's death on 26 August 1958 – the day that Boult was scheduled to record the Ninth Symphony – the commemorations started, and the following year all nine symphonies were done at the Proms.[147]

Epilogue

In a world that relied more and more on modern technologies for musical experience, Vaughan Williams's passion for music as 'the art of the common man'[148] was played out through a process that was largely dependent on the BBC's partnership, particularly when directed by Adrian Boult. During his fifteen years in leading roles with the Corporation, the conductor contributed enormously to modern music of his time, especially contemporary British music. But what he did for Vaughan Williams, in particular, can be attributed not only to his fundamental belief in his music, but also to a number of profound convergences in their musical, spiritual and political viewpoints.

Boult frequently wrote, taught and lectured about conducting as a fundamentally pragmatic art;[149] yet, his performing aspiration emerged from a more essential source. In effect, his basic view on musical performance complemented Vaughan Williams's own. Vaughan Williams maintained that

> The composer has a vision and he wants others, out of earshot, to share that vision; so he crystallizes that vision into definite musical sounds. Then he devises a series of black dots, circles, and so on which will explain what sounds must be made in order to realize his vision . . . Those who are going to translate these black dots into sound . . . must learn to realize, when the sounds are made, the connection between the various notes which they produce and the ultimate meaning of it all. Then, and then only, can they realize in sound the vision that has passed through all these stages and back again.[150]

From his point of view as a conductor, Boult heartily agreed about his deferential role within that connective process:

> The Conductor's real job is to convey the message that lies inside the music, to make his listeners catch the thrill that the composer felt when he first wrote it, for music surely grows in a composer's mind, not just as sound, but as the deeply felt impression of something that cannot be conveyed in words . . . With the right keenness from everyone, we conductors can feel deeply privileged as we get ourselves keyed up again and again . . . ready for the great work of helping to summon up and renew the wonderful sounds once heard by a Bach or a Beethoven, and to live again the thrill that they must have felt when these great ideas were first sent to them, to put on paper for us all.[151]

Vaughan Williams and Boult thus held in common this fundamental view of music-making.

Spiritually, Boult retained a religious belief that Vaughan Williams, as an agnostic, denied. In one of his writings, the conductor stated baldly:

'Music is the language of God ... Surely it is not possible for the mystery that is music to have evolved naturally without some commanding author-ity.'[152] Nevertheless, the two musicians shared an understanding of music's spiritual function. For Vaughan Williams, 'music is not only a form of enjoyment, it is also a spiritual exercise in which all have their part'.[153] Boult went further in his view: 'music opens up immense spiritual and psychological resources in the task of lessening some of the misun-derstandings which result in political conflicts and their attendant social disasters'.[154] Throughout his long career, Boult published articles and gave lectures and radio talks about his musical perceptions and experiences, relating his conviction that music performance at its best provided a framework for tapping spiritual resources:

> Beneath [the music's structure] there is a spiritual unity which seems to hold the work up – this tenuous stream of sound which passes so quietly through our consciousness – and, after the experience of performance is over, sustains it before us as a whole, like a great piece of architecture. As we contemplate it, it lifts us off our feet with its ennobling power just as the first sight of a great landscape or of a great building can purify us.[155]

Thus at music's foundation was a unity that spiritually purified and fortified the human condition.

Both Boult and Vaughan Williams lived through two world wars, which had an immense impact on their political perceptions of the world. When the threat of war re-emerged in the 1930s, Vaughan Williams became profoundly attracted to an organization that seemed to offer a solution. The Federal Union advocated 'democratic self-government for the prevention of war, the creation of prosperity and the preservation and promotion of individual liberty'.[156] Vaughan Williams set up a branch of the Federal Union in Dorking, acting 'not [as] an authority on F.U. only [as] a layman who strongly believes in it'.[157] Boult came through World War II also believing in this kind of political unity as the way forward for modern Europe. He was a delegate at the Congress of Europe in May 1948, a 'gathering of Europe's finest citizens and most prominent statesmen', coming together to explore the convic-tions of 'the European Union of Federalists, along with Mr. Churchill's "United Europe" and other movements'.[158] When the Korean War became a further threat, Boult spoke out in support of international political unity as the only viable path.[159] Although Vaughan Williams pursued these views less actively late in his life,[160] on the first anniversary of his death a Royal Festival Hall concert was held in support of the Federal Trust, an educational offshoot of the Federal Union. In Boult's introduction to the concert, he made particular reference to Vaughan

Williams's belief that 'politically the world lacks a fresh vision of its own unity and that it is often for the artist to show the way'.[161]

It is clear, then, that in a variety of important ways, Vaughan Williams and Boult shared world-views that underpinned their long bond of friendship. Forged during the first decade of the twentieth century and lasting until Vaughan Williams's death over forty years later, their alliance was characterized by a number of vital elements: a shared sense of musical principles in the realm of music-making, a shared sense of music in relation to the spiritual, and a shared sense of music in relation to the political – core values that fundamentally framed their artistic identities. In part due to Boult's lifetime of performances and his strong influence at the BBC, Vaughan Williams continues to be remembered today as – in Boult's words – 'one of [the] great men – some of us would say [the] very greatest man'[162] of British music of the mid-twentieth century.

Files of unpublished documents held at the BBC Written Archives Centre

[abbreviations used in footnotes appear to left]

RVW1	RCONT1, Ralph Vaughan Williams, Composer, 1a (1928–33)
RVW2	RCONT1, Ralph Vaughan Williams, Composer 1b (1934–8)
RVW3	RCONT1, Ralph Vaughan Williams, Artists 1 (1930–40)
RVW4	RCONT1, Ralph Vaughan Williams, Composer 2a (1939–41)
RVW5	R41/241, PCS, Ralph Vaughan Williams (1939)
RVW6	RCONT1, Ralph Vaughan Williams, Artists 2 (1941–55)
RVW7	RCONT1, Ralph Vaughan Williams, Composer 2b (1942–3)
RVW8	R19/921, Features, 'Pilgrim's Progress' (1936–54)
RVW9	RCONT1, Ralph Vaughan Williams, Composer 2c (1944–6)
RVW10	RCONT1, Ralph Vaughan Williams, Composer 3 (1947–51)
RVW11	RCONT1, Ralph Vaughan Williams, Composer 4 (1952–62)
ACB1	S32/7, Special Collections, Boult, Autobiographical Material (1928–65)
ACB2	S32/26, Special Collections, Boult, Articles: Ralph Vaughan Williams (1958–62)
ACB3	S32/12, Special Collections, Boult, Conducting (1946–61)
ACB4	S32/10/1–2, Special Collections, Boult, Thoughts on Conducting & Trumpet
ACB5	S32/30, Special Collections, Boult, Lectures (1929–61)
ACB6	S32/31, Special Collections, Boult, Lectures – The Broadcasting of Music (1932)
ACB7	S32/32/1–5, Special Collections, Boult, Scripts
ACB8	S32/32/2, Special Collections, Boult, Scripts (1944–50)
ACB9	S32/24, Special Collections, Boult, Articles (1928–67)

Notes

1 Performed by the LSO; *BBC Programme Records, 1922–1926*, 50.

2 Performed by baritone Gilbert Bailey with pianist Maurice Cole and the Snow String Quartet; *BBC Programme Records, 1922–1926*, 59.

3 See Jennifer Doctor, *The BBC and Ultra-Modern Music, 1922–1936* (Cambridge University Press, 1999), 63.

4 *BBC Programme Records, 1922–1926*, 74.

5 *Ibid.*, 102.

6 Ralph Vaughan Williams, 'National Music: VIII. Some Conclusions' (1934), in *NM*, 63. Vaughan Williams first published such egalitarian ideas in his article, 'Who Wants the English Composer?', *The RCM Magazine* 11/1 (Christmas Term 1912), 12–15.

7 Byron Adams, Introduction to *VWE*, xvii.

8 Queen's Hall, 4 October 1928; letter, Kenneth A. Wright to Vaughan Williams, in RVW1, 14 July 1928.

9 Queen's Hall, 26 September 1929 (later renamed Concerto in D minor for violin and string orchestra). Vaughan Williams also conducted songs from *Hugh the Drover*, sung by Walter Widdup; RVW1, 27 May–5 June 1929.

10 'Sir Adrian Cedric Boult' [autobiography, typescript], in ACB1, 11 October 1962.

11 'Dr Ralph Vaughan Williams, O.M.', [typescript], in ACB2, 1 October 1958.

12 Vaughan Williams wrote to Boult consistently as 'Dear Adrian' rather than 'Dear Boult', as he did to professional associates at the BBC, so their relationship was clearly a friendship.

13 Boult's father, Cedric Randal Boult, was an oil merchant; Michael Kennedy, *Adrian Boult* (London: Papermac, 1987), 3.

14 For a brief description of Vaughan Williams's life up to World War I, see Hugh Cobbe, 'Earliest Letters (*c.* 1895) to the Outbreak of the First World War: 1895–1914', in *LRVW*, 8–12.

15 Kennedy, *Adrian Boult*, 41.

16 *Ibid.*, 62–6.

17 Adrian Boult, *My Own Trumpet* (London: Hamish Hamilton, 1973), 35.

18 Letter, Vaughan Williams to Boult, 20 February 1918, in *LRVW*, 119.

19 Adrian Boult, 'Tributes to Vaughan Williams', *MT* 99 (October 1958), 536.

20 Paraphrased in Kennedy, *Adrian Boult*, 68.

21 Drawing on many of the same BBC files used as sources for this essay, Duncan Hinnells has cogently argued that institutions such as the BBC and Vaughan Williams's publisher, Oxford University Press, helped to construct Vaughan Williams's nationalist image. See Duncan Hinnells, 'The Making of a National Composer: Vaughan Williams, OUP, and the BBC' (DPhil thesis, University of Oxford, 1999).

22 Doctor, *The BBC and Ultra-Modern Music*, 153–4.

23 Nicholas Kenyon, *The BBC Symphony Orchestra* (London: BBC, 1981), 15–48.

24 *Ibid.*, 32–4.

25 Doctor, *The BBC and Ultra-Modern Music*, 392.

26 J. C. W. Reith, *Broadcast Over Britain* (London: Hodder and Stoughton, 1924), 34.

27 Arnold Bax was also recognized as a British symphonic composer of significance.

28 Vaughan Williams campaigned tirelessly for the title of this work to be shown correctly in the *Radio Times* and other BBC publicity; e.g. see letter, Vaughan Williams to Concert Organiser, in RVW2, where he complains that a recent BBC advertisement for a performance of the work has substituted the word 'Variations' for 'Fantasia' [undated, April 1938].

29 Interestingly, a performance of Vaughan Williams's *Job* was televised on 11 November 1936 (performer details unknown); *BBC Programme Records* [television], 283.

30 For example, *A Sea Symphony*, conducted by Boult, broadcast from Stockholm, 19 January 1939 (see *LRVW*, 271); also the first performance of *Five Variants of 'Dives and Lazarus'*, conducted by Boult, in a programme of new British works, New York World's Fair, June 1939; RVW4, 13 January, 6 February and 4 April 1939. See also Kennedy, *Adrian Boult*, 185.

31 Vaughan Williams conducted Proms in 1930 (*A Pastoral Symphony*), 1931 (*Flos Campi*), 1933 (*A Pastoral Symphony*), 1934 (*A London Symphony, Fantasia on 'Greensleeves'* and *Running Set*), 1935 (*A Pastoral Symphony*), 1937 (Symphony No. 4), 1938 (*A Pastoral Symphony*), 1943 (Symphony No. 5), 1945 (Suite: *Story of a Flemish Farm*), 1946 (*A London Symphony*), 1948 (Partita and *A London Symphony*), 1950 (Symphony No. 5), 1952 (Symphony No. 5); Proms Archive database, www.bbc.co.uk/proms/archive (accessed 30 August 2012). Aborted performances include the *Five Variants of 'Dives and Lazarus'* on 15 September 1939 (season cancelled once war was declared) and the first performance of *Six Choral Songs to be Sung in Time of War* on 10 September 1940 (season cancelled after 7 September, due to heavy bombing).

32 Sunday Orchestral Concert, 18 February 1934, London Regional programme; RVW3, 11

January–4 February 1934. BBC Northern Orchestra, 25 February 1939; RVW3, 6–9 January 1939.

33 'Broadcasting: Sir Henry Wood's Jubilee', *The Times*, 5 October 1938, 5E.

34 Letter, Kenneth A. Wright to Vaughan Williams, in RVW1, 20 November 1931. First performance: Harriet Cohen (piano), BBC SO, conducted by Boult, 1 February 1933.

35 Letter, Vaughan Williams to Boult, in RVW2, 27 September 1935.

36 Memo, Boult to Arthur Bliss, in RVW7, 15 September 1942, reprinted in *LRVW*, 346. Thanks to Byron Adams for reminding me of this significant letter.

37 *KW*, 263.

38 Letter, Vaughan Williams to Boult, in RVW2, 19 August 1934.

39 Queen's Hall Symphony Concert, 10 April 1935, in RVW2, 11 September 1934, 4–19 March 1935.

40 *Radio Times*, 1 March 1935.

41 Memo, Boult to Maurice Gorham, *Radio Times* Editor, in RVW2, 4 March 1935 (misfiled among papers from March 1936).

42 Letters, Boult to Vaughan Williams, in RVW2, 7 and 14 March 1935.

43 Letter, Boult to Vaughan Williams, RVW2, 6 August 1936.

44 Letter, Vaughan Williams to Boult, [undated], and response from Mrs Beckett (Boult's secretary), in RVW2, 15 October 1936.

45 Letter, Vaughan Williams to Boult, *c.* 22 October 1936, in *LRVW*, 245–6. The broadcast concert opened that season's Wednesday night BBC Symphony Concerts, Queen's Hall, 21 October 1936, featuring the BBC Symphony Orchestra and BBC Choral Society, with Noel Eadie (soprano) and William Parsons (baritone); *BBC Programme Records, 1936*, 218.

46 Letter, Owen Mase to Vaughan Williams, in RVW1, 31 October 1931.

47 Letter, Mrs Beckett to Vaughan Williams, 20 May 1935, Vaughan Williams's response [undated] and Mrs Beckett's return, in RVW3, 21 May 1935.

48 Programme included: Maconchy's *Comedy Overture*, Williams's Two Psalms for soprano and chamber orchestra, Morris's Concertino, Milford's Two Pieces for orchestra and Vaughan Williams's *Five Mystical Songs* for baritone, chorus and orchestra; BBC 'Programmes as Broadcast' record, National Programme, 28 December 1934; see also RVW3, 31 October–21 December 1934.

49 Letter, Vaughan Williams to Boult, in RVW2, [undated, *c.* 29 July 1934]. *The Planets* was scheduled for that season's Wednesday

Symphony Concerts, while the Scherzo of Holst's unfinished symphony was planned for a later date. Vaughan Williams typically requested that the latter be presented, 'not at a memorial concert . . . but for its own sake at an ordinary concert'.

50 Memo, Boult to Kenneth Wright, in RVW1, 12 September 1933.

51 Vaughan Williams, 'National Music: VIII. Some Conclusions' (1934), in *NM*, 67–8.

52 Lecture II, Birmingham University, in ACB5, 1944, 13.

53 *UVWB*, 229.

54 'The Composer in Wartime, 1940', in Ralph Vaughan Williams and Gustav Holst, *Heirs and Rebels: Letters Written to Each Other and Occasional Writings on Music* (London: Oxford University Press, 1959), 92. This article was first published in *The Listener* 23 (1940), 989, reprinted in *VWOM*, 83–6; the original script has not been traced.

55 Boult sent a telegram stating, 'Grateful if you would write Director-General'; in RVW4, [17?] October 1939.

56 Letter, Vaughan Williams to Ogilvie, 18 October, and the BBC's response, 23 October 1939, in RVW5; both letters reprinted in *LRVW*, 290–1.

57 In fact, to avoid such hardship, the government stepped in from 1940 to fund programmes such as the Council for the Encouragement of Music and the Arts (CEMA) and Entertainments National Service Association (ENSA) which kept artists employed and encouraged the British public and the troops through musical and dramatic entertainment.

58 Sir Walford Davies, then Master of the King's Music, launched the idea; letter, Davies to Vaughan Williams, in RVW3, 9 November 1939.

59 BBC Written Archives Centre scripts, Ralph Vaughan Williams, 3 December 1939 [microfilm of typescript], 2–3. Although less formal and differently structured, this script is related to the lecture of the same name, published as the Epilogue of *The Making of Music* (1954), reprinted in *NM*, 237–42.

60 Letter, P. S. G. O'Donnell, director of the BBC Military Band, to R. S. Thatcher, Deputy Director of Music, in RVW4, 9 October 1939. The programmes aired on 2 January and 27 March 1940. See also correspondence, in RVW3, 6 October 1939–29 March 1940, and in RVW4, 9 October 1939–20 March 1940.

61 From script for the second programme, in RVW3, 27 March 1940, reprinted in *LRVW*, 298–9. The script for the first programme has not been found.

62 Memo, B. E. Nicolls, Controller (Programmes), to Deputy Director of Entertainment, in RVW4, 17 August 1940.

63 For the commissioning letter, see Boult to Vaughan Williams, in RVW4, 2 September 1940, and Vaughan Williams's response, [undated], both letters reprinted in *LRVW*, 304–5.

64 Letter, Vaughan Williams to Boult, in RVW4, 26 October 1940, reprinted in *LRVW*, 309–10. For detailed responses, see Boult to Vaughan Williams, in RVW4, 31 October and 12 November 1940.

65 Letter, Boult to Vaughan Williams, in RVW4, 31 October 1940.

66 Letter, Vaughan Williams to the BBC Director-General, in RVW4, 9 March 1941, reprinted in *LRVW*, 314; see also 'Dr. Vaughan Williams', *The Times*, 15 March 1941, 6F.

67 'Broadcasting of Opinions', *The Times*, 13 March 1941, 2E. For further discussion about this policy debate, see Chapter 1 in this volume, 21.

68 'BBC and People's Convention: Ban on Artists Removed', *The Times*, 21 March 1941, 4E; see also 'Parliament: B.B.C. Ban Lifted', *The Times*, 21 March 1941, 2A.

69 Letter, Hubert Foss of OUP to R. S. Thatcher, and Thatcher's response, in RVW4, 4 and 8 April 1941.

70 Letter, Foss to B. E. Nicolls, in RVW4, 26 September 1941.

71 First broadcast: 16 November 1941, broadcast to Sweden, programme celebrating the opening of the extended Swedish Service; see letter, Leonard Isaacs, European Music Supervisor, to Vaughan Williams, in RVW4, 26 November 1941.

72 Memo, R. S. Thatcher to B. E. Nicolls, in RVW4, 10 October 1941. The other patriotic songs included were George Dyson's 'Motherland', Roger Quilter's 'A Song of Freedom', and John Ireland's 'O Happy Land'.

73 Letter, Vaughan Williams to Boult, in RVW4, [c. 10 February 1942], reprinted in Jerrold Northrop Moore (ed.), *Music & Friends: Seven Decades of Letters to Adrian Boult from Elgar, Vaughan Williams, Holst, Bruno Walter, Yehudi Menuhin and Other Friends* (London: Hamish Hamilton, 1979), 138 (Moore mistakenly places the letter in response to the first performance).

74 Arthur Bliss returned to the UK from California in March 1941, when he began working as BBC Assistant Director of Overseas Music. The Corporation had attempted to recruit him for the Director of Music post since 1933, but he had always turned it down, as he believed it would disrupt his creative work.

During the early 1940s, he agreed to it as a contribution to the war effort.

75 Letter, Stanford Robinson to Vaughan Williams, in RVW4, 14 November 1941. About this broadcast (Home Service, 28 November 1941), Robinson wrote: 'The reports of our Listening Research Department ... were very encouraging as to the number of people who listened to it and so I hope to broadcast it again next year', in RVW4, 24 December 1941, and Vaughan Williams's response, in RVW7, 4 January 1942, reprinted in *LRVW*, 333.

76 Letter, Leonard Isaacs, European Music Supervisor, to Vaughan Williams, and Vaughan Williams's response, in RVW4, 26 and 27 November 1941.

77 Letter, Boult to Vaughan Williams, and Vaughan Williams's response, in RVW7, 30 April and 2 May 1942.

78 Memo, Kenneth Wright, in RVW7, 29 June 1942, reprinted in *LRVW*, 341. Devised in collaboration with Hubert Foss of Oxford University Press, the planning of this week, 11–17 October 1942, spanned eight months; see RVW7, 25 February–17 October 1942. Performances included: the Hallé Orchestra, conducted by Malcolm Sargent (Tallis Fantasia); BBC Orchestra, conducted by Adrian Boult (*The Lark Ascending* and Piano Concerto); BBC Symphony Orchestra, conducted by Henry Wood (Symphony No. 4 in F minor); BBC Northern Orchestra, conducted by Boult (*Magnificat, Four Hymns, Benedicite*); BBC Symphony Orchestra, conducted by Ian Whyte (*Five Variants of 'Dives and Lazarus'*); a vocal concert (*On Wenlock Edge*); and the BBC Military Band and Theatre Orchestra (smaller-scale works). On 12 October, the concert included new works by Gordon Jacob, Elizabeth Maconchy, Edmund Rubbra, Alan Bush, Robin Milford, Constant Lambert and Patrick Hadley. Memo, Assistant Director of Music to Director of Music, in RVW7, 3 September 1942.

79 Letter, Vaughan Williams to Gerald Finzi, in RVW7, 13 October 1942, reprinted in *LRVW*, 350.

80 Memo, Boult to Arthur Bliss, and Bliss's response, in RVW7, 15 and 16 September 1942, both reprinted in *LRVW*, 346–7.

81 Memo, Boult to R. S. Thatcher, in RVW7, 13 October 1942, reprinted in *LRVW*, 347.

82 On 15 November 1942; memo, Herbert Murrill, Director of Music, to Music Library, in RVW7, 21 October 1942.

83 Programme aired: 5 September 1943, with John Gielgud playing Christian. For details, see Eric Saylor's essay in this volume. Vaughan Williams continued to work on *The Pilgrim's*

Progress as a morality stage work, largely completed in 1947–8 and performed at Covent Garden in 1951. Nathaniel G. Lew, '"Words and Music that are Forever England": *The Pilgrim's Progress* and the Pitfalls of Nostalgia', in *VWE*, 184.

84 Letters, Vaughan Williams to Henry Wood, in RVW7, 5 and 9 February 1943, reprinted in *LRVW*, 356.

85 Letter, Boult to Vaughan Williams, and Vaughan Williams's response accepting the offer, in RVW7, 11 February and 1 May 1943, reprinted in *LRVW*, 357.

86 *LRVW*, 358. For the list of invitees, see letters from Vaughan Williams to Mrs Beckett, Boult's secretary, in RVW7, 6 and 21 May 1943; the latter reprinted in *LRVW*, 358; see also letter from Mrs Beckett to Vaughan Williams, in RVW7, 21 May 1943, summarizing guests whom Boult invited, and two additional names from Vaughan Williams, in RVW7, 23 May 1943.

87 Letter, Arthur Bliss to Vaughan Williams, and Vaughan Williams's response, agreeing to conduct, in RVW7, 7 and 10 May 1943. Since May 1941, when Queen's Hall was bombed, the Prom seasons had taken place in the Royal Albert Hall.

88 Letter, Boult to Vaughan Williams, in RVW7, 27 June 1943, reprinted in *LRVW*, 359–60.

89 Memo, Boult to Kenneth Wright, Assistant Director of Music (Programmes) about *Job*, in RVW7, 18 October 1943. Fourth Symphony: Royal Albert Hall, conducted by Boult, 12 May 1944; 'Concerts', *The Times*, 10 May 1944, 6G. Fifth Symphony: broadcasts 22 March and 1 August 1944; letter, Boult to Vaughan Williams, 6 March, and memo, Boult to Wright, in RVW9, 4 August 1944.

90 Letter, Vaughan Williams to George Barnes, Director of Talks, in RVW6, 8 February 1944.

91 Memo, Philip Bate to Arthur Wynn, 27 November 1944, and contract, in RVW6, 4 January 1945.

92 Memo, Kenneth Wright to J. G. Roberts, Administrative and Establishment Officer (Programmes), in RVW7, 13 September 1943.

93 Memo, Wright to Music Booking Manager, in RVW9, 23 August 1944.

94 Memo, Boult to Victor Hely-Hutchinson, in RVW9, 14 May 1945.

95 Letter, Victor Hely-Hutchinson to Vaughan Williams, in RVW9, 14 May 1945, and memo, Hely-Hutchinson to Editor, *Radio Times*, in RVW9, 15 May 1945; see also letter, Hely-Hutchinson to Vaughan Williams, 25 May 1945, for a complete explanation of what happened.

96 For example, see memo, Rev. J. W. Welch, Director of Religious Programming, to Controller (Programmes), in RVW9, 15 May 1945. An earlier performance was given (but not broadcast) by the Luton Choral Society on 26 June 1945; letter from Oxford University Press to Hely-Hutchinson, in RVW9, 21 June 1945.

97 Elsie Suddaby (soprano) and Valentine Dyall (speaker). Letter, Hely-Hutchinson to Vaughan Williams, and letter, Mrs Beckett to Vaughan Williams, in RVW9, 22 May and 24 August 1945. Other Vaughan Williams Proms works: Suite from *Story of a Flemish Farm* on 31 July, conducted by Vaughan Williams, and the *Five Tudor Portraits* on 30 August.

98 Memo, W. W. Thompson, Concert Organiser, to Herbert Murrill, and memo, Kenneth Wright to Boult, in RVW10, 9 and 30 April 1947.

99 Letter, Wright to Vaughan Williams, in RVW10, 7 October 1947.

100 *Radio Times*, 10 October 1947.

101 Letter, John Lowe, Third Programme, to Vaughan Williams, and Vaughan Williams's response, in RVW10, 19 and 21 February 1947, both reprinted in *LRVW*, 410–11. Memo, Lowe to Wright, letter, Wright to Vaughan Williams, and Vaughan Williams's response, in RVW6, 1, 23 and 31 May 1947; see also further correspondence, in RVW10, 5 June–30 September 1947. Other works performed: *Flos Campi*, Suite for viola and small orchestra (1934) and *Four Hymns* for tenor, viola and strings (1914), Lionel Tertis (viola) and Eric Greene (tenor).

102 Letter, Julian Herbage to Vaughan Williams, in RVW10, 6 October 1947.

103 Boult, 'R. Vaughan Williams, O.M., Mus. Doc.', script for *Music Magazine* contribution, in ACB8, 12 October 1947, 1–2.

104 The talk was not given in French, but a letter written by Edward Lockspeiser, the French music expert in the Overseas Music Department, to the British Council sheds light on the BBC's influence. Apparently Irène Joachim was so impressed with *A London Symphony* that she was going to recommend it to the French conductor Roger Désormière, who 'could do more in the interests of Vaughan Williams in France than anyone else.' Letter, Edward Lockspeiser to Miss Seymour Whinyates, in RVW10, 20 October 1947.

105 The opera was first performed at Sadler's Wells in June 1945.

106 Letter, Victor Hely-Hutchinson to Vaughan Williams, in RVW6, 6 May 1946; see also Alison Garnham, 'The BBC in Possession:

1949–59', in Jenny Doctor, David Wright and
Nicholas Kenyon (eds.), *The Proms:
A New History* (London: Thames & Hudson,
2007), 145.

107 Letter, John Lowe to Vaughan Williams,
in RVW10, 18 January 1948.

108 'Diagonalization' was a BBC practice in
which a work would be broadcast on either
the Home Service or the Third Programme,
often from a public concert, and repeated the
next evening in a studio performance
broadcast on the opposite network. This
allowed the public to hear important works
more than once, and was inexpensive to
produce, as the second broadcast required no
rehearsal.

109 Letters, Vaughan Williams to Boult, [both
undated], and Mrs Beckett's responses, in
RVW10, 20 February and 16 May 1947. The
play-through was given by Vaughan
Williams's former pupil, Michael Mullinar.

110 Letter, Vaughan Williams to Boult, in
RVW10, 30 July 1947, reprinted in *LRVW*, 416.

111 Letter, Boult to Vaughan Williams,
memo, Boult to Assistant Director of Music,
and letters, Mrs Beckett to Vaughan Williams,
and Vaughan Williams to Mrs Beckett, in
RVW10, 11, 17, 27 December 1947 and 22
January 1948.

112 'The Third Programme Plans for 2
October–31 December 1949', quoted in
Humphrey Carpenter, *The Envy of the World:
Fifty Years of the BBC Third Programme and
Radio 3* (London: Weidenfeld and Nicolson,
1996), 98.

113 Letter, Vaughan Williams to Stanford
Robinson, in RVW10, 16 November 1949.

114 Memo, Frank Gillard, Head of West
Regional Programmes, to Herbert Murrill,
Director of Music, in RVW10, 8 August 1950.
See Eric Saylor's Chapter 8 in this volume for
details about this production.

115 Memo, Frank Gillard to Acting
Controller, Home Service, in RVW11,
15 September 1952.

116 Letter, Douglas Cleverdon, producer, to
Vaughan Williams, and Vaughan Williams's
response, in RVW10, 9 and 11 March 1951.
Vaughan Williams suggested that the BBC
approach Gerald Finzi, but in the event,
Anthony Smith-Masters composed the
required music; memo, Cleverdon to Music
Booking Manager, WAC R19/290/2,
Entertainment/The Dynasts 2 (1947–54),
13 April 1951.

117 Letter, Steuart Wilson to Vaughan
Williams, in RVW10, 5 August 1948. The work
was given a private run-through by the Arts
Council on 2 December 1948; letters, Eric

W. White, Arts Council, to Wilson, in RVW10,
20 and 24 November 1948.

118 Lew, 'Words and Music', 190. This article
describes the Covent Garden production in
1951 in detail.

119 Kennedy, *Adrian Boult*, 214–18.

120 Memo, Herbert Murrill to Controllers,
Home Service, Third Programme and Light
Programme, in RVW11, 7 January 1952.

121 Letter, Eric Warr, Acting Head of Music,
to Vaughan Williams, and Vaughan Williams's
response, in RVW11, 8 and 16 April; letter,
W. W. Thompson, Concert Organiser, to Alan
Frank, Oxford University Press, 25 April;
letter, Thompson to Vaughan Williams,
25 July 1952.

122 Memo, Leonard Isaacs to Harman
Grisewood, Controller, Third Programme, in
RVW11, 10 January 1952.

123 Memo, Grisewood to Isaacs, in RVW11,
16 January 1952.

124 Memo, Herbert Murrill, in RVW11,
7 January 1952.

125 On Wednesday, 15 October, at 10.25pm,
by René Soames and the Hirsch String Quartet.
Memo note, Lindsay Wellington to Murrill,
and memo, Isaacs to Grisewoood, in RVW11,
9 and 16 January 1952.

126 On Sunday, 12 October, on the Home
Service; programme: the Tallis Fantasia, *A
Pastoral Symphony* and *Sancta Civitas*. Memo,
Eric Warr to Herbert Murrill, 18 January, and
memo, Peter Crossley-Holland to Malcolm
Sargent, in RVW11, 31 March 1952.

127 Memo, Peter Crossley-Holland to
Godfrey Adams, in RVW11, 6 June 1952.

128 The North of England and Northern
Ireland Home Services; memo, Leonard Isaacs
to Maurice Johnstone, and Johnstone's
response, in RVW11, 9 and 13 June 1952.

129 Letter, Eric Warr to Vaughan Williams,
and Vaughan Williams's response, in RVW11,
26 and 23 [i.e. 27?] May 1952.

130 Memo, Kenneth Adam, Controller, Light
Programme, to Warr, in RVW11, 18 August
1952.

131 Memo, F. O. Wade to Kenneth Adam, in
RVW11, 4 September 1952. In the 1950s,
Vaughan Williams occasionally gave broadcast
talks on music by others, for example on Bach
for the composer's bicentenary (pre-recorded
13 July, broadcast 28 July 1950, Third
Programme), a tribute to Sibelius on the
composer's 85th birthday (pre-recorded
23 November, broadcast 10 December 1950 in
Music Magazine, Home Service); on the
Stanford centenary (pre-recorded 13 August,
broadcast 30 September 1952, General
Overseas Service, and subsequently

domestically); on the teaching of Parry and Stanford (recorded 17 November 1955 live at the Composers' Concourse, broadcast 1 January 1956, Third Programme) or on the Elgar centenary (unscripted talk, pre-recorded 21 March 1957, Home Service); correspondence and contracts in RVW6. Scripts, for these and other Vaughan Williams radio talks, survive at the BBC Written Archives Centre.

132 The *Sea Symphony* was followed by the Walton Viola Concerto and Holst's suite from the ballet *The Perfect Fool*.

133 Performance plans were interrupted by the war; memo, Desmond Osland to Leonard Isaacs, in RVW11, 13 October 1952.

134 *Ibid*.

135 *UVWB*, 335.

136 First London performance: Christmas cantata *Hodie* ('This Day'), 19 January 1955, by the BBC SO, Chorus and Choral Society, conducted by Sargent; letter, Alan Frank, OUP, to Johnstone, and Johnstone's response, in RVW11, 25 March and 14 April 1954. First broadcast: The *Prelude on Three Welsh Hymn Tunes*, pre-recorded by the Salvation Army International Staff Band, broadcast 11 March 1955; Vaughan Williams had planned to attend the pre-recording, but had to cancel through illness; memo, Rodney Pelletier, and memos, Harry Mortimer, in RVW11, 8 December 1954, 24 February and 2 March 1955. First broadcast: Tuba Concerto, 25 July 1955, Philip Catelinet (tuba) and the BBC Symphony Orchestra, conducted by John Hollingsworth; letter, Assistant Concerts Manager to Vaughan Williams, in RVW11, 13 July 1955.

137 Memo, John Lowe, in RVW11, 31 August 1954.

138 Letters, Assistant Concerts Manager to Vaughan Williams, in RVW11, 10 July and 4 September 1956. Other Vaughan Williams works at the Proms that season: the Tallis Fantasia, *A London Symphony* and the *Sinfonia Antartica*. The following year the same works were given, except the *Wasps* overture was given in place of the *Fantasia*; letter, Assistant Concerts Manager to Vaughan Williams, in RVW11, 17 June 1957.

139 The programme included *A Pastoral Symphony* and the orchestrated version of *On Wenlock Edge*, performed by the London Philharmonic Orchestra.

140 Letter, Maurice Johnstone to Alan Frank, OUP, in RVW11, 23 August 1957.

141 Letter, Frank to Johnstone, in RVW11, 28 August 1957.

142 Letter, Johnstone to Frank, in RVW11, 2 September 1957.

143 Letter, Ursula for Vaughan Williams to Eric Warr, in RVW11 [undated, February 1958].

144 Alain Frogley, *Vaughan Williams's Ninth Symphony* (Oxford University Press, 2001), 20.

145 *Ibid*.

146 *Ibid*., 21.

147 Memo, Maurice Johnstone to T. M. Whewell, in RVW11, 19 November 1958.

148 *NM*, 63.

149 Adrian Boult, *Thoughts on Conducting*; Boult, 'On Conducting', in *Boult on Music*, 123–50; numerous typescripts of talks and drafts survive at the BBC Written Archives Centre, including in ACB2–ACB7.

150 *NM*, 216.

151 Boult, 'For Cyril Taylor, Royal School of Church Music' [lecture typescript], in ACB5, 27 May 1954, 2.

152 Boult, 'Music, a Definition', [article draft, undated], in BL Add. MS 72660, Boult Papers, Writings (1909–73), f. 51.

153 *NM*, 67–8.

154 Boult, [untitled article draft, October 1949], intended for *European Affairs*, in ACB9.

155 Boult, 'Music and Religion', talk given at Leeds, 2 December 1948, in BL Add. MS 72661, Boult Papers, Writings (1908–1976), f. 45.

156 Clarence K. Streit, *Union Now: A Plea for the Union of the Democratic Nations* (London, 1939), quoted in *LRVW*, 290.

157 *LRVW*, 290, and letter, Vaughan Williams to an unidentified correspondent, 12 June 1940, in *LRVW*, 300.

158 Boult, [untitled draft article], 10 January 1951, in BL Add. MS 72660, Boult Papers, Writings (1909–73), f. 165.

159 Boult, [untitled draft article], 10 January 1951, in BL Add. MS 72660, Boult Papers, Writings (1909–73), f. 164.

160 Cobbe, 'The Second World War: September 1939–May 1945', in *LRVW*, 282.

161 Vaughan Williams, quoted in Boult, [draft introductory talk to concert by Phyllis Sellick and Cyril Smith, 'A Concert in Aid of the Federal Trust', Royal Festival Hall], 12 October 1959, in ACB5.

162 Boult, 'Dr. Ralph Vaughan Williams, O.M.', [typescript], in ACB2, 1 October 1958.

13 Fluctuations in the response to the music of Ralph Vaughan Williams

MICHAEL KENNEDY

Fluctuations in critical and popular reaction to the music of Ralph Vaughan Williams are hardly surprising when one considers the length of his creative career – effectively from 1895 to the day of his death sixty-three years later. Or, if one measures it from his first childhood composition, *The Robin's Nest*, in 1878 the total becomes eighty years, a huge span stretching in musical terms from the lifetime of Brahms and Wagner to the experimentations in electronic music by Pierre Boulez and Karlheinz Stockhausen. Vaughan Williams's music began to be noticed by a small coterie of keen musicians in the 1890s when some songs, part-songs and chamber works were performed at Cambridge University and elsewhere. His teachers at Cambridge and the Royal College of Music between 1892 and 1895 included two of the most influential figures of the day both as academics and composers, Sir Hubert Parry and Sir Charles Villiers Stanford. Both were impressed by Vaughan Williams and put his name forward to enterprising concert-giving bodies. The first of his works of any significance to have been performed in London seems to have been the *Heroic Elegy and Triumphal Epilogue* for orchestra, which Stanford conducted at the Royal College of Music on 5 March 1901. It was generally admired and he revised it in 1902. After more performances in England, the last known in Leeds in January 1905, nothing more was heard of it until the score surfaced in the United States in about 1970.

In 2006 it was performed, published and recorded. While clearly immature, it was recognisably Vaughan Williams in style and showed why three leading critics singled out the work and its composer for special mention in surveys of the British musical scene that they contributed to periodicals in 1903. An anonymous writer in *The Strad* mentioned Vaughan Williams's 'ideas of real beauty'.[1] W. Barclay Squire in *The Pilot* named Cyril Scott, Vaughan Williams and Cecil Forsyth as 'the most interesting' of England's promising composers and found Vaughan Williams the most interesting of all.[2] The *Heroic Elegy* had impressed him, as had the 'strong poetical feeling' of the setting of Rossetti's 'Silent Noon' which he had heard a few days earlier when it had its first performance. He anticipated the 'birth of a really individual school of English composers'.

Edwin Evans in *The Musical Standard* wrote in detail of the *Heroic Elegy* and of how Vaughan Williams had been described to him as 'somewhat in the unhappy state of "not yet having found himself". ...This was true enough', Evans wrote, but Vaughan Williams was 'rather painfully conscious' of it and 'has a disposition to be less satisfied with what he does than would be desirable as an incentive to push on ... [He] has little reason for this extreme diffidence as there are amongst his works many which reveal a subtle personality with individual traits none the less calculated for being presented free of the remotest suggestion of blatancy.'[3] This was an extraordinarily prescient analysis of Vaughan Williams's attitude to his work for most of his life, and partly explains why he withdrew or took no further interest in his chamber works of the first decade of the twentieth century, which have been revived only since 2000. It is hard to understand why he apparently made no attempt to encourage any performance of his setting for soprano, chorus and orchestra of Swinburne's *The Garden of Proserpine* (1897–9), which, as its first performance in 2011 established, contains many traits of the mature composer. Perhaps he took his eye off the ball after 1903 when he began to collect folksongs in earnest and also agreed to edit what became *The English Hymnal*.

The opinions quoted above demonstrate that it was more than the popularity of his song 'Linden Lea', which was published in 1902, that made his name mean something in musical circles. The 1904 *Songs of Travel* soon went into the repertoire of baritones seeking something new but accessible for their recitals. *Toward the Unknown Region*, his setting of words by Whitman for chorus and orchestra, was chosen for the 1907 Leeds Festival where it was clamorously received. The music critic of *The Times* was moved to describe it as the 'perfect maturity of his genius' and to rank Vaughan Williams, who was thirty-five, as 'the foremost of the younger generation'.[4] Vaughan Williams had advanced to this eminence in the space of fewer than ten years, at a time when Bantock, Bridge and several others were writing fine works. But he was still dissatisfied with his music. If he had been writing reports on himself he would often have used the phrase 'Could do better'. His solution was a crash course of lessons in 1907–8 with the French composer Maurice Ravel, after which he never looked back. In the period from 1908 to 1914 he composed, or completed, the String Quartet in G minor, *On Wenlock Edge*, music for *The Wasps*, *A Sea Symphony*, *Fantasia on a Theme by Thomas Tallis*, *Five Mystical Songs*, the Phantasy Quintet, the *Fantasia on Christmas Carols*, folksong arrangements, incidental music for plays at Stratford-upon-Avon and *A London Symphony*. He went to war leaving an opera, *Hugh the Drover*, in vocal score, and the orchestral rhapsody *The Lark Ascending* in an unrevised violin and piano version. In spite of the composer's tinkering between 1918 and 1934 with the score of *A London Symphony*, this ambitious work, a success at its first performance in 1914, kept its place in the repertory. This symphony was the first to reach the United States of America when it was played in Chicago, Boston and New York during 1920–1.[5] It was championed by Frederick Stock in Chicago, who programmed it in six out of ten seasons during the 1920s, and three times in the 1930s; it was similarly popular in New York. It is not clear exactly when Vaughan Williams's music was first introduced to the USA, but it is probable that one of the *Songs of Travel* was included in recitals given by visiting singers such as Harry Plunket Greene, who toured the country in 1905. The impact of the song-cycle *On Wenlock Edge* for tenor and piano quintet (1909) can be documented: it was performed in Boston in 1919, and Eric DeLamarter, Assistant Conductor of the Chicago Symphony Orchestra, arranged the work for performances with the orchestra in the 1919–20 season. The success of *A London Symphony* probably lay behind the invitation Vaughan Williams received to conduct his new symphony, the *Pastoral*, at the Norfolk Music Festival in Connecticut on 7 June 1922, only a few months after its premiere in London on 22 January. This festival had been founded in the 1890s by Carl Stoeckel, a wealthy music-lover (Vaughan Williams called him 'my millionaire') who had persuaded Sibelius to be his guest composer in 1914 and to conduct the first performance of *The Oceanides*. Stoeckel lavished hospitality on Vaughan Williams and Adeline. In a letter to her sister Cordelia Curle, Adeline wrote that 'Ralph feels a little restive from a surfeit of kindness! . . . Meals are too rich and wine flows all the time!'[6] The growth of the composer's American reputation was further stimulated by the release in 1925 of one of the first recordings of his music, on the Aeolian label, which featured the ballet *Old King Cole* (1923) conducted by the composer himself. In 1926 he provided the score of *On Christmas Night*, a masque with dancing, singing and miming, freely adapted by Adolph Bolm and Vaughan Williams from Dickens's *A Christmas Carol*. This was first performed in Chicago by the Bolm Ballet on 26 December 1926 conducted by Eric DeLamarter, who possibly had commissioned it. If so, this was a unique occurrence; Vaughan Williams was asked on several other occasions to accept an American commission, notably by the Library of Congress and Elizabeth Sprague Coolidge in 1926, but he never accepted. Curiously, however, this awakening of American interest in Vaughan Williams's music in the mid-1920s did not include what might have been regarded as his 'American works': neither of his two most ambitious Whitman settings from the first decade of the century, *Toward the Unknown Region* (1907) and the great *Sea Symphony* (1909) were widely performed, despite the fact that no American composer had yet identified themselves strongly with this poet's mystical vision of democracy.

But if *A London Symphony* opened doors for the composer on both sides of the Atlantic, the next symphony, the *Pastoral*, first performed in 1922 in London, gave Vaughan Williams his first taste of an antagonism towards his style. Although Samuel Langford, the *Manchester Guardian's* critic, hailed it at once as 'among the masterpieces of the time',[7] the majority of critics were less perceptive and fastened only on what its title seemed to imply. They looked for folksongs where none existed. Nobody at that date connected it with the war which had ended only three years earlier and in which Vaughan Williams had served. They looked for larks ascending and the tranquillity of the Cotswold landscape. Sir Hugh Allen, director of the Royal College of Music, was reminded of 'VW rolling over and over in a ploughed field on a wet day'. And Philip Heseltine (Peter Warlock) likened the symphony to 'a cow looking over a gate'. Years later Elisabeth Lutyens coined the phrase 'the cowpat school' to denigrate English works of a pastoral nature. Holst and Herbert Howells admired the *Pastoral* and noticed its darker side, but no one noticed that it was a 'war requiem' and not 'lambkins frisking' (Vaughan Williams's phrase). The spectral 'Last Post' in the second movement and the girl's lamenting voice in the finale were not noticed until well after the end of the Second World War.[8]

Although this chapter is mainly concerned with the last phase of Vaughan Williams's life, study of the earlier years shows that his changes of style even disconcerted many of his admirers. His desire to explore, even if it led him into strange byways, resulted in 1925 in one of his most experimental and also sensuous compositions, *Flos Campi*, which for want of a better word he described as a suite for solo viola, small chorus and small orchestra. The chorus is wordless and each of the six movements is headed by a quotation in Latin from the Song of Solomon. The music has an erotic flavour deriving, as it is now known, from Vaughan Williams's passion for a Royal College of Music student. But one could be forgiven for assuming a religious context, as many listeners obviously did. For a performance at a Royal Philharmonic Society concert on 3 November 1927, two years after its premiere, Vaughan Williams supplied a programme note in which he said that he had 'discovered that most people were not well enough acquainted with the Vulgate (or perhaps even its English equivalent) to enable them to complete for themselves the quotations from the "Canticum Cantorum", indications of which are the mottoes at the head of each movement of the Suite'. Even the title and the source of the quotations gave rise to misunderstanding:

> The title 'Flos Campi' was taken by some to connote an atmosphere of 'buttercups and daisies', whereas in reality 'Flos Campi' is the Vulgate equivalent of 'Rose of Sharon' (*Ego Flos Campi, et Lilium Convallium*, I am the Rose of Sharon and the Lily of the valleys). The Biblical source of the quotations also gave rise to the idea that the music had an ecclesiastical basis. This was not the intention of the composer.[9]

This work puzzled H. C. Colles, the music critic of *The Times*. In his review of the first performance he complained that Vaughan Williams had 'wilfully surrounded the flowers of his musical thought with a thorny hedge of riddles . . . One may be a little irritated by the surface eccentricities of a very sane mind, but one cannot listen for long without being assured of the sanity.'[10] In a further article, Colles raised objections to the use of a wordless chorus because the melody, sung simply as 'Ah', lacked the eloquence of the same melody played on Lionel Tertis's viola. Moreover, the references to the Song of Solomon, 'whether given seriously or not, are certainly not explanatory. He has, rather, wilfully raised barriers in the minds of his hearers which the music itself may not be strong enough to sweep away.'[11] He even suggested that the work would benefit from revision and expansion. Another view of this composition was that of the composer and critic Cecil Gray who found *Flos Campi* to be music of a very intimate and subjective order, devoid of any programmatic implications. 'In this work Vaughan Williams seems to have acquired a sureness of touch and a concision which had hitherto been lacking in his art without thereby impairing the apparent spontaneity which has always characterized it.'[12] Gray objected to the use of the word 'sincerity' as the highest praise for Vaughan Williams's music. It was a negative virtue possessed more often by mediocrities. 'Almost alone today, he is entirely without self-consciousness and has the courage to write simply as he feels, without misgivings. He is not afraid to write the kind of music that anybody could have written, with the paradoxical result that he has evolved a more personal style than almost any other composer in this country.' Another composer, Joseph Holbrooke, in a book published in 1925, attributed Vaughan Williams's failings to his having had

> a fairly smooth path. . . There is no overwhelming horror ever felt in the music of this composer. . . There is no splendid uncontrollable passion in him or his music to be discerned or felt. . . The only misgiving one may have with the dreamer like Vaughan Williams is whether he can hold his own with the men who feel savagely, who feel enormously, who feel very very deeply on all things and willy-nilly put it into their music. There is a heavy suspicion to many when any artist meets favour from the academics in power. Vaughan Williams has had this huge misfortune. His art pleases the dull ones of our profession.[13]

Vaughan Williams would have recognized the social envy which lay behind Holbrooke's array of chips on his shoulder, and he would have ignored it.

Of more concern to him was the lack of sympathy shown by his close friend Gustav Holst, whose *Choral Symphony* to words by Keats had its first performances on 7 October 1925 at the Leeds Festival and in London on 29 October. The two composers, friends since 1895, had shown each other their compositions from the earliest stages and had been fearlessly honest in their mutual criticisms. Yet Vaughan Williams could only muster 'cold admiration' for this latest work, while admitting that the Leeds chorus's performance had been poor. He had not wanted

> to get up & embrace everyone & then get drunk like I did after the H. of J. [*Hymn of Jesus*]. . . I couldn't bear to think that I was going to 'drift apart' from you musically speaking . . . so I shall live in faith till I have heard it again several times and then I shall find out what a bloody fool I was not to see it all first time.[14]

Holst's reply was to confess to a similar response to *Flos Campi* which he had not been able to 'get hold of at all' and was therefore 'disappointed with it and me. But I'm not disappointed in *Flos*'s composer because he has not repeated himself. Therefore it is probably either an improvement or something that will lead to one.' Other friends were also puzzled by *Flos Campi* (had they forgotten that Vaughan Williams had studied with Ravel?) and in the following year they were baffled again by his oratorio *Sancta Civitas*. Today, in *Flos Campi* the keen listener can hear anticipations of *Riders to the Sea* (1925–32) and the *Sinfonia Antartica* (1949–52). Nothing in the *Pastoral Symphony* had led listeners to expect the exotic harmonies of these works. The neoclassicism and back-to-Bach style of the *Concerto Accademico*, as the Violin Concerto was at first known in 1925, were other signs that it was never going to be easy to pin down this composer. Had Vaughan Williams's contemporaries looked into his sketchbooks between 1926 and 1930, they would have found ideas for a piano concerto, a Christmas masque, more Housman songs, a musical comedy, a Shakespeare opera, an opera based on Synge and a Blake ballet (or masque), not to mention work on *Songs of Praise* and *The Oxford Book of Carols*.

The 1920s were his most fertile period. During the course of the decade he became recognized by musicians as the obvious successor to Elgar, but when the post of Master of the King's Music became vacant in 1924, Elgar was appointed. The royal household brought forward the name of Vaughan Williams but he was turned down as not being as well known by the general public as Elgar (which was probably true); and he refused the appointment after Elgar died in 1934 but filled the vacancy in the Order of Merit in 1935. Vaughan Williams had his champions among British conductors but his works were not as frequently played as those by Elgar, even though Elgar was out of favour with academics and some critics. Moreover, there were newcomers in the field: Bax, Bliss and Howells represented the generation after Vaughan Williams, while Walton and Britten were the strongest contenders among those born in the twentieth century.

Vaughan Williams made his second visit, lasting two months, to the USA in the autumn of 1932 to give the Mary Flexner lectures at Bryn Mawr College, Pennsylvania.[15] His theme was 'National Music' (the eventual title of the published lectures), and it covered, among other things, the evolution of nationalism and the history of folksong. Vaughan Williams tactfully steered clear of his views on American contemporary music. We do not know how much of it he had heard. He does not mention Henry Cowell or Charles Ives, nor Aaron Copland. But he met and encouraged a young student at the Curtis Institute in Philadelphia, Samuel Barber, who played him his setting of Matthew Arnold's 'Dover Beach', a poem Vaughan Williams had begun to set in 1899 before abandoning the project. He heard the Boston Symphony Orchestra, the Philadelphia Orchestra and the New York Philharmonic. In Boston, Serge Koussevitzky asked him which of his own works he would like the orchestra to play; he chose the Tallis Fantasia because of the orchestra's renowned string section.

The year 1935 was to be a turning point for Vaughan Williams, when the harsh dissonance of his F minor Symphony (No. 4) burst upon a musical public which had not listened carefully enough to the way in which his music was developing in recent works such as *Sancta Civitas* (1923–5), the Piano Concerto (1926–31) and most of all *Job: A Masque for Dancing* (1930). Listeners and commentators are uncertain about the context of the F minor Symphony even after the passage of eighty years. A belief persists that it was a warning of the wrath to come after the rise of Hitler; yet Vaughan Williams began to write it in 1931, two years before the Nazis came to power in Germany, and he finished it early in 1935. The first performance was on 10 April when Adrian Boult conducted the BBC Symphony Orchestra. The enthusiastic ovation was 'almost hysterical', one report stated. The critics generally welcomed the change of style as a divergence from his folksong period – 'no corduroy tunes', said Edwin Evans. H. C. Colles, music critic of *The Times*, mentioned the humour in the Scherzo.[16] Eric Blom, in the *Birmingham Post*, described Vaughan Williams as 'one of the most venturesome composers in Europe. The new symphony was as harshly and grimly compromising in its clashing dissonant polyphony as anything the youngest adventurer would dare to fling down on music paper.'

Although William McNaught thought the symphony was 'masterly', this judgement demanded first that 'we grant the abandonment of the humanities'.[17] Harsher criticism came from Neville Cardus in the *Manchester Guardian*. For all his admiration of its parts, he could not believe that it was likely to be listened to twenty years from today. The music failed to warm the senses, Cardus wrote, or to enter the mind as an utterance of conviction. 'The content of Vaughan Williams's music . . . is respectably middle-class English, and the technique, as I have suggested, is old-fashioned, looked at from standards unashamedly modern.'[18] Cardus was echoing reservations expressed by Copland after he had attended a performance of the *Benedicite* in London in 1931. 'Inherent banality' and 'bourgeois grandeur' were two of Copland's verdicts. Vaughan Williams, he decided, was 'the kind of local composer who stands for something great in the musical development of his own country but whose actual musical contribution cannot bear exportation. Besides, he is essentially not modern at all . . . His is the music of a gentleman farmer, noble in intention but dull.'[19] Nevertheless, Copland was in a minority among American musicians at the time, and it was the Fourth Symphony that accelerated assessment of Vaughan Williams in the USA after 1935. Several American conductors championed the work, notably Dimitri Mitropoulos and Leonard Bernstein, both of whom recorded it with the New York Philharmonic.

It is noteworthy that reviewers on both sides of the Atlantic made little reference to the violence of the music and there is no attempt to draw a parallel with international events. Colles had asked, 'Is its daring and its gaiety really new, or does it hark back to something which Vaughan Williams left on one side with the works of pre-war days, an old impulse newly revived?'[20] Personal reactions from friends were telling. Elizabeth Trevelyan, wife of the writer R. C. Trevelyan, heard 'your poisonous temper in the scherzo'. The folksong scholar Maud Karpeles confessed to having 'missed the clue' to the symphony. 'Someone said it should have been called "Europe 1935" and that is rather what it conveyed to me.' Nearly two years later Vaughan Williams wrote to his friend R. G. Longman, the publisher, who had heard no beauty in the work. Vaughan Williams replied: 'I *do* think it is beautiful – not that I did not *mean* it to be beautiful because it reflects unbeautiful times . . . I wrote it not as a picture of anything external – e.g. the state of Europe – but simply because it occurred to me like this – I can't explain why'. He had written earlier in the letter that 'I am not at all sure that I like it myself *now*. All I know is that it is what I wanted to do *at the time*.'[21] As is often quoted, he said at a rehearsal of the symphony: 'I don't know whether

I like it, but it's what I meant'. Asked what it really did mean, his answer was 'F minor'. On another occasion: 'I wish I didn't dislike my own stuff so much when I hear it – it all sounds so *incompetent*'.[22]

As he told me on one occasion, he did not like the practice of attaching 'meaning' to works. But his Fourth and Sixth Symphonies have attracted many theories. Of the Fourth, the most plausible theory is that he began it after reading a review and description in *The Times* of a performance of a twentieth-century work (possibly Webern's Symphony) at a modern music festival. He certainly used Beethoven's Fifth Symphony as a model. The resemblances are several, notably the brief motifs on which the whole work is founded and the linking passage between the Scherzo and Finale. His widow Ursula favours this genesis in her biography and adds that the symphony was also a self-portrait.[23]

Fourteen years separated the *Pastoral* and Fourth Symphonies. By now, Vaughan Williams was regarded as the leader of English music: Elgar's successor as the musical spokesman for the nation. Although he held no official post, it was true that no state occasions, celebratory or commemorative, could be imagined without a work by Vaughan Williams. His 1936 cantata *Dona Nobis Pacem* was an unconcealed warning of the dangers now obviously brewing in Europe. When war came in 1939, several of his works were found to be in tune with the mood of the times. He found a new outlet as a contribution to the war effort by writing in 1940 his first score for the cinema, *49th Parallel*. It was followed by four more during the war and several afterwards. He enjoyed the disciplines imposed by film-making.

Widespread celebration of his seventieth birthday in 1942 left no doubt of the British musical public's affection for him. The principal work-in-progress on his desk had been started in 1938 when he had decided that his ongoing plan, first materializing in 1906, for an opera based on John Bunyan's *The Pilgrim's Progress* would come to nothing. Themes intended for it were now commandeered for his Fifth Symphony, which was completed and first performed in 1943. The lyricism and serenity of this work were at the opposite extreme from the furies of the Fourth. It is not fanciful to say that the arrival into his life in 1938 of Ursula Wood (later Ursula Vaughan Williams), thirty-nine years his junior, was a catharsis which had a profound effect on him in every respect. She sent him a scenario based on Spenser's *Epithalamion* from which they devised a masque called *The Bridal Day*. Plans to perform it for the English Folk Dance and Song Society were a casualty of the war and it reappeared in 1951 adapted for television. Mrs Wood also assisted him in choosing the Shakespeare text for the *Serenade to Music*, which he composed for Sir Henry Wood's golden jubilee as a conductor. This masterpiece, written for sixteen solo singers associated with Wood, was never merely a *pièce d'occasion*. Its exquisite harmonies and luminous orchestration have endeared it to performers and audiences ever since the first performance in October 1938 and it takes its place among his greatest achievements.

This work, and the *Five Variants of 'Dives and Lazarus'*, written for the New York World's Fair in 1939, must have reassured his admirers that the Fourth Symphony was a development of an existing strand rather than a new path. It looked back, not forward. The Fifth Symphony, coming as it did in the midst of war and just when he had reached three-score-years-and-ten, could have been taken as a benediction, a farewell, 'Now lettest thou thy servant'. It is dedicated (without permission) to Sibelius, whose Fifth Symphony also begins with a horn call, and it explores conflicts of keys and tonal/modal contrasts as thoroughly as the Fourth becomes a dissertation on semitones. The Fifth is 'about' ambiguous tonality fixated on D and G, but it is unlikely that one would listen exclusively to this musical argument and forget *The Pilgrim's Progress* and the strongly programmatic undercurrent. The nostalgic Oboe Concerto (1942–4) and the Second String Quartet (1942–4) are side-shoots of the symphony. The concerto in particular is a bigger work emotionally than it may have seemed at first.

In the last fifteen years of Vaughan Williams's life, the contrasts between the lyricism he had always been able to summon to his aid and the sense of musical citizenship he had described in 1912 became even more apparent.[24] Film music and the music he wrote for the coronations in 1937 and 1953 were a part of this. He was by now the 'grand old man' – a term he hated – of English music, revered not only as composer but as teacher, conductor, writer and lecturer. He encouraged some of his young friends to call him 'Uncle Ralph' and this misled some people into thinking that his approach to music tended sometimes to be avuncular and that the later works could be regarded as *péchés de vieillesse*. Some composers were more wary: William Walton, for instance, who met him in April 1942 while visiting Oxford University Press's London office. Norman Peterkin of OUP described the encounter (when Vaughan Williams left Peterkin's office) in a letter to Sir Humphrey Milford, Publisher to the University of Oxford:

> Walton came into my room remarking 'Well, the old pussy cat has gone at last.' I suppose I must have shown some astonishment for he went on to say that 'of course V.W. was a really big pussy with very sharp claws' and was 'the biggest intriguer of the lot'; that it was astonishing how nobody noticed it (except W.W. apparently) and how he managed to get away with it as a result.[25]

Between 1944 and 1958 Vaughan Williams wrote four symphonies staggeringly different in style and mood. He told a friend that he had so much music in his head that he knew he would not have time to write it all down. While he was completing the Eighth Symphony in 1955, he wrote to me: 'I hope it is going to be all right. But I feel rather nervous... At my age ... I cannot afford to let out anything 2nd rate – which is not really straight from the fountain-head'.[26] Those who comforted themselves with the thought of the Fifth Symphony as a summing-up of the Vaughan Williams they knew and loved were in for a rude awakening when the Sixth Symphony was announced for 1948. He had begun it in 1944. The themes, or motifs, which open the second and fourth movements were based on music written in 1943 for the film *The Flemish Farm* but not used. The first performance was given in the Royal Albert Hall on 21 April 1948 by the BBC Symphony Orchestra conducted by Sir Adrian Boult. It had been played through months earlier on two pianos and (on 16 December 1947) by the orchestra. After this performance, Vaughan Williams's friend, the émigré composer Robert Müller-Hartmann wrote to express 'the overwhelming impression' it had made on him. 'It seems even to transcend your symphonies in F and D [Fourth and Fifth].'[27] The public and critical response to the work was the zenith of his whole career. Only Britten's opera *Peter Grimes* in 1945 had aroused comparable excitement. The symphony's hundredth performance was given by the Hallé Orchestra on 6 July 1950. In the previous two years it had been performed in America, Australia, Holland and elsewhere. It was recorded by HMV on 78 rpm discs in February 1949 and the revised Scherzo was later re-recorded with the same catalogue number.

Most attention was paid to the Finale, which is marked to be played *pianissimo* throughout. 'The music', says the composer's programme note, 'drifts about contrapuntally, with occasional whiffs of theme' – after which it fades into nothingness.[28] Not unexpectedly there was widespread speculation about the programme behind this mysterious movement, which follows a tempestuous opening allegro, a sinister slow movement and a jazzy scherzo. It is 'like nothing else in music', wrote Richard Capell in *The Daily Telegraph*. The symphony, he decided, 'takes a new direction. It will challenge every hearer ... The music says that the soul of man can endure pain and face the thought of a remoteness beyond the outermost of the planets.'[29] Strangely, he did not mention 'Neptune' in Holst's *The Planets* as a possible source of musical inspiration for the finale. Frank Howes in *The Times* drew nearer to an analogy with the atomic bombs dropped on Japan in 1945. An annotator of the symphony fifty years hence, he averred, 'will certainly relate the symphony to the experiences of war, its challenges, its sinister import for ultimate values, its physical bombardment even. But what will he make of the ghostly epilogue? Here the composer seems to be seeking not answers but the right questions to ask of human experience.'[30] Howes returned to his theme in a review of the work in August 1949 in which he described it as a 'War Symphony'.[31] This brought him a personal reply from Vaughan Williams: 'I dislike that implied connotation very much. Of course there is nothing to prevent any writer from expressing his opinion to that effect in a notice. But it is quite a different thing, this reference to a supposed title as if it was official on my part.'[32]

A critic of a younger generation, Desmond Shawe-Taylor, referred to Vaughan Williams's 'serious and courageous glimpse into the future, to have meditated on first and last things with a grasp and profundity worthy of Beethoven'. This was nearer the mark, as can be deduced from the composer's letter to me about the finale dated 22 January 1956: 'I do NOT BELIEVE in meanings and mottoes, as you know, but I think we can get in words nearer to the substance of my last movement in "We are such stuff as dreams are made on, and our little life is rounded with a sleep."'[33] The critic and scholar Deryck Cooke wrote some years later of the effect on him of the first performance as 'nothing short of cataclysmic'. He cited

> the violence of the opening and the turmoil of the whole first movement; the sinister mutterings of the slow movement, with that almost unbearable passage in which the trumpets and drums batter out an ominous rhythm, louder and louder, and will not leave off; the vociferous uproar of the Scherzo and the grotesque triviality of the Trio; and, most of all, the slow finale, *pianissimo* throughout, devoid of all warmth and life, a hopeless wandering through a dead world ending literally in *niente* (Vaughan Williams's favourite word for a final fade-out of any kind) – nothingness . . . I was no more able to applaud than at the end of Tchaikovsky's *Pathétique*.[34]

In the 1940s Vaughan Williams's music for films had undoubtedly spread his reputation further in the United States. Besides the symphonies, smaller works such as *The Lark Ascending* were heard often in broadcasts; more interestingly, the American premiere of Britten's *Peter Grimes* – the musical sensation of 1945 – at Tanglewood in 1946, conducted by Bernstein, was preceded by Vaughan Williams's one-act opera *Riders to the Sea*. But it was the excitement over the Sixth Symphony in 1948 that raised his American reputation to a new height, and it continued to grow over the subsequent decade. A survey in the periodical *Musical America* reported that in the 1956–7 concert season American orchestras had played the music of Vaughan Williams more than that of any other foreign-born twentieth-century composer except Stravinsky and Hindemith; it placed Vaughan Williams ahead of Bartók, Barber and Shostakovich, and equal with Gershwin and Copland. In the same periodical's report on the 1951–2

season, with thirty-one performances he surpassed Copland (sixteen performances) by a margin of nearly two to one.[35] In equivalent surveys throughout
the 1950s, his performance tallies were ahead of those of Bartók, Shostakovich
and, among Americans, Roy Harris, who was then at the height of his
popularity. But after Vaughan Williams's death in 1958, this number of
performances declined sharply. Conductors such as Bernard Herrmann,
André Previn and Leonard Slatkin tended to conduct his music while abroad
rather than in American concert halls. Surprisingly, there is no reference to
his impact on American musical life in any of the primary texts on the history
of American music published from 1958 to the present day. Only after the
mid-1980s was there serious research on Vaughan Williams (and indeed
other British composers) in the United States.

This is to run ahead somewhat, however. In the years after the war
there is little doubt that Vaughan Williams and Britten were the leading
living English composers. The decades of the 1940s and 1950s saw a
marked decline in Elgar's reputation. Of course he had a host of admirers
and his music kept its place in programmes because most of the English
conductors of the day championed his music – Adrian Boult, John
Barbirolli, Malcolm Sargent and others. But among many critics and
scholars, he was considered to be outdated and was tarred with the
adjective 'imperialist'. Of course, Vaughan Williams had shown that he
could write patriotic music and martial tunes, as a list of his wartime
compositions shows – *Six Choral Songs to be Sung in Time of War*;
England, My England; 'A Call to the Free Nations'; 'The Airmen's
Hymn'; *Thanksgiving for Victory*, later retitled *A Song of Thanksgiving*.
And there was the film music. But for the most part he avoided the kinds of
associations that would come to dog Elgar in the 1950s, as the patriotism
of the Edwardian era was increasingly vilified.

Before he began to sketch the Sixth Symphony, Vaughan Williams
returned to the task that had tantalized him since 1906 – making an opera
from Bunyan's *The Pilgrim's Progress*. Convinced it would never reach the
stage, he used some of its themes in the Fifth Symphony. At some point in
1942, the BBC asked him for incidental music for a radio adaptation by
Edward Sackville-West of Bunyan's book. This was the stimulus he
needed. The result was a major score comprising thirty-eight sections.
Some of it was already written for the opera, some of it (with references to
the Tallis Fantasia) linked to the Reigate performance of over thirty-five
years earlier. Much of the radio music was excluded from the final version
of the opera (or 'morality'), on which he resumed work from 1944 to 1949
and which would be produced at Covent Garden in 1951.[36] None of his
previous operas had been staged at the Royal Opera House. But 1951 had
been designated for the Festival of Britain, which the government had

planned as a nationwide celebration of the arts and recovery from the war. Most events were in London, which opened the new Royal Festival Hall for the occasion. English music was a central theme. Covent Garden decided on *The Pilgrim's Progress* as its chief offering, with the premiere fixed for 26 April. The opera was received politely rather than with the fervour the composer's friends anticipated. Capell in *The Daily Telegraph* dismissed the production as 'anti-theatrical'. Musically, he thought, fulfilment had come in the symphonies and in the ballet *Job*. 'The admirable score', as he rather coolly described it, 'will find its niche, but this will not be in the theatre.' In *The Times* Frank Howes took the opposite line: 'The stage can show the inner conflict of principles as well as the outer conflict of action'. He wrote of the 'astonishing ringing of changes on diatonic tunes and simple triads that lifts the heart to something beyond the power of language'.[37]

No one could pretend that it had been anything but a failure. It was dropped as soon as the second set of performances in the 1951–2 season was over. It received only one performance, at Leeds on 12 July 1951, in the provincial tour which Covent Garden undertook every year. Vaughan Williams was deeply hurt. He said to Ursula Wood: 'They don't like it and they won't like it and perhaps they never will like it because it hasn't got a love story or any big duets, and it's not like the operas they are used to, but it's the sort of opera I wanted to write, and there it is'.[38] Happily, a production at Cambridge in 1954 enabled him to see something much closer to his vision. Opinions of the work were, except in a few cases, either ambivalent or lukewarm.

For the coronation in June 1953 of Queen Elizabeth II, he contributed an unaccompanied part-song, 'Silence and Music', with words by Ursula Vaughan Williams (as she had become since February 1953), to *A Garland for the Queen*, in which British composers and ten poets paid tribute to the new monarch. It was dedicated to the memory of Stanford and his 'Bluebird', beside which it is not unworthy to stand. Feeling that the congregation were overlooked in the coronation service, he made a grand ceremonial arrangement ('a mess-up' he called it) of the *Old Hundredth Psalm Tune* ('All People that on Earth Do Dwell') for mixed choir, congregation, orchestra and organ. The large brass section was to include 'all available trumpets' which made an unforgettable sound in the Abbey on 2 June. But his most treasurable contribution to the service was the exquisite unaccompanied motet 'O Taste and See', the quintessence of his hymnal style, music with the innocence and timeless freshness of 'The Woodcutter's Song' he had added to *The Pilgrim's Progress*.

From the *Pilgrim* premiere we can date the beginning of a falling-off in esteem for Vaughan Williams as a composer, though not as the acknowledged head of the profession, as the tributes to him on reaching his eightieth birthday in 1952 testify. Cardus found the right note for the occasion. He wrote:

> His music is an atmosphere. It does not woo the impressionable senses, it does not satisfy all the moods of pleasure-loving and sinful man. The greatest of it comes from a certain order of our national way of living, independent and natural as a growth out of the earth, refreshed by all the weathers and humours and dispositions of the reserved but romantic English.[39]

Yet as he began his ninth decade, Vaughan Williams became more adventurous than ever before. One is tempted to think that his obvious employment of a richer and more exotic instrumentation stemmed from two causes: the film companies' willingness to employ larger numbers of orchestral players, and, for all that he missed Holst's advice, perhaps a feeling of slight relief that his friend's candid criticisms were no longer on tap. He became interested in the solo capacities of such instruments as the harmonica, writing a Romance in D♭ in 1952 for the American virtuoso of the instrument, Larry Adler, whom he consulted about its capabilities. Shortly after giving one of the smallest instruments a place in the sun, he did the same (although in a less original manner) for one of the largest, the bass tuba, in a three-movement Concerto in F minor, first performed in London in 1954. This piece quickly established itself; and its slow movement, bearing the title 'Romanza', always a signal that the music was of special significance to him, was arranged as a separate piece for euphonium, bassoon, cello and piano. He also wrote several of those short and exquisite works, like the *Serenade to Music*, which seem always to have existed and rank him with the best of Purcell, Tallis and Byrd. These include the *Three Shakespeare Songs* of 1951 for unaccompanied mixed chorus, the second of which contains the lines which inspired the Sixth Symphony finale: 'we are such stuff as dreams are made on'. Other works of this period which showed that there was no risk of his drying up include the cantata *Folksongs of the Four Seasons* (1949), written for the Women's Institutes, the ill-advised revision of the Piano Concerto for two pianos (1946), the *Fantasia (quasi variazione) on the 'Old 104th' Psalm Tune* (premiered at the Three Choirs Festival in 1950), and the Concerto Grosso for strings (1950) which catered for various standards of playing among schoolchildren. These were the kind of works he was happy to supply as part of his credo that music was not only for the technical wizards, but for everyone. One haunting work, which slipped out almost unnoticed in 1949, was *An Oxford Elegy*, a setting for speaker, small chorus and orchestra of extracts from Matthew Arnold's *The Scholar Gipsy* and *Thyrsis*. This is music to rank with the *Serenade to Music* and has gradually become recognized as such. Ernest Newman, never a whole-hearted – or even half-hearted – admirer, complained in the *Sunday Times* that Vaughan Williams had deliberately distorted Arnold's poems for his own purposes in order to give extra emphasis to the poet's emotion for Oxford.[40] That will not bother most listeners to this deeply moving work.

The first substantial book devoted to Vaughan Williams and his music was published in 1950.[41] It was written by his former publisher Hubert Foss and gave a non-technical summary of his works, relating them to the English literary tradition. It contained also the composer's contribution in the shape of his 'chapter of musical autobiography' which since has been printed elsewhere and, for musicians, is as quotable as *Hamlet*. Vaughan Williams thanked him for sending him a copy of the first edition and added: 'I am quite overpowered by the affection and thought in your book. I feel hopelessly unable to live up to it.'[42] Seven months later he sent Foss a list of over thirty amendments and corrections. These included wrong datings of the Tallis Fantasia, which were repeated by other writers and in *Grove's Dictionary* for some years (and sometimes still are).

Since the end of the war the climate of British music had changed as the old gave place to the new. For the younger generation, Vaughan Williams now represented an entrenched traditionalism which also claimed Britten although few of his followers noticed it. For instance, Britten's views on the composer's place in society are not very different from those expressed by Vaughan Williams in 1912 in 'Who Wants the English Composer?'[43] The 1950s were a time for the reappraisal of reputations and the exploration of avant-garde composers native and foreign. There was a strong reaction against late Romanticism. Serialism was all the rage. The music of Strauss, Rachmaninov, Elgar, Sibelius, Walton and many others of their ilk was disparaged by academics; and the music of Schoenberg, Webern and Berg was exalted despite its continuing unpopularity with the general concert-going public. It was no longer *de rigueur* that the conductor of the BBC Symphony Orchestra should be British. At the BBC itself the appointment in 1959 of William Glock as Director of Music was bad news for middle-of-the-road composers (although not quite as bad as has sometimes been made out). Britten was regarded as a special case, and Vaughan Williams's death in 1958 removed his personality from the scene but affected performance of his music much less than might have been expected.

From the vantage-point of sixty years later, one can pinpoint 1954 as the *annus horribilis* in which Vaughan Williams's reputation took its first serious knocks. *The Pilgrim's Progress*, *Sinfonia Antartica* and the Christmas cantata *Hodie* were the works which began the critical slide. The opera, fruit of a life's work, was regarded as weak dramatically and static musically, while the symphony was . . . well, what was it? Re-hashed film music or an old man playing games with unusual instruments? At the Three Choirs Festival in Worcester in September 1954, he conducted the first performance of *Hodie*, a large-scale work for soprano, tenor and baritone, mixed chorus, boys' voices and orchestra. The text was compiled by the composer from the Bible, prayer books, Coverdale, Milton, Hardy, Drummond, Ursula Wood and others. The music belongs in style to various periods of Vaughan Williams's career, and those who loved it from the start will have agreed with the critic and author J. H. Elliot who wrote in the *Hallé Magazine* in December 1954 that there was as much vigour of spirit and execution as there was in his music of twenty years earlier.

> But it has something else which I can only call the fullness of wisdom – spiritual tranquillity that is not mere resignation and a simplicity that is grander than any intimacy of performance or bold and exultant splendour of expression. . . . It is the music of old age in the truest sense, the final maturity of a great mind. It breathes a deep peace of soul.[44]

No other critic came as near as that to assessing the true nature of this still-undervalued masterpiece, but the general reaction was favourable. However, the periodical *Musical Opinion* in its April and May issues of 1955 asked the critic Donald Mitchell for a survey of Vaughan Williams's work.[45] He took aim at *Hodie*, which he regarded as 'grossly over-praised and grossly under-composed'. He continued:

> If this is the kind of music that rouses cries of exaltation, then our musical culture is in a worse condition than I thought possible. Of course, a good deal of the whooping is positively Pavlovian . . . There is a level below which 'directness' and 'forthrightness' of utterance – qualities for which Vaughan Williams is praised – deteriorate into a downright and damaging primitivity . . . It is doubly damaging when his contemporaries are so blind (or deaf perhaps) that they mistake patent coarseness as evidence of genius.[46]

Mitchell then turned his guns on the collection of writings by Vaughan Williams published by OUP in 1954 with the title *Some Thoughts on Beethoven's Choral Symphony*. He described them as 'often reminiscent in their creaking humour of that arch-comical bore, though brilliant analyst, Sir Donald Tovey'. They led him to Vaughan Williams's references to his own 'amateurish technique' which had

> more than a grain of uncomfortable truth . . . When listening to a work of the character of *Hodie*, where, I suspect, Vaughan Williams's compositional conscience was at a low ebb, it suddenly becomes very noticeable how clumsy his technique can be, and how much he relies on his inimitable

idiosyncrasies to pull him through. At the same time one is reminded, rather disturbingly, of many a more masterful composition of his where his technique has not seemed fully adequate to his needs . . . The composer who pioneers in the national field loses that very freedom of artistic expression which his pioneering activities confer upon his successors. In a sense he becomes the first – perhaps only – victim of his revolution . . . I believe Vaughan Williams will be regarded as a major minor composer . . . His very real and personal genius will keep his music alive, though I fear the limitations which circumscribe it will become increasingly apparent.[47]

Mitchell was shrewd in citing Vaughan Williams as a victim of his own pioneering. The next generation of English composers – Britten in particular – had embraced Austro-German developments just as Vaughan Williams had immersed himself in folksong and French influences. But the new English generation was fixated on Schoenberg and his followers dedicated to atonality, many of whom had settled in Britain after the war and had penetrated British musical life at many points, notably the BBC. Vaughan Williams had no time for atonality – 'the worst kind of German music' – and did not endear himself to its followers by his contribution to the symposium in *Music & Letters* on the death of Schoenberg in 1951: 'Schoenberg meant nothing to me – but as he apparently meant a lot to a lot of other people I daresay it is all my fault'.[48]

The principal composition of this period was the *Sinfonia Antartica*, first performed in January 1953. This was the outcome of the music he had written in 1947–8 for the film *Scott of the Antarctic* which was first shown in November 1948. The story of Captain Robert Scott's expedition to the South Pole in 1912, which ended with the death of Scott and his four companions, seized Vaughan Williams's imagination. Man against nature was a theme he had explored in other works. He was full of admiration for their heroism but was shocked by the inefficiency with which the expedition was planned. He decided in 1947 to expand the film music into a symphony in which he could also indulge his taste for illustrative orchestral colouring. This had always been a trait – the imitation of mouth-organs in *A London Symphony*, for example, and the gathering of birds in *Five Tudor Portraits*. The women's voices in the howling Antarctic winds were foreshadowed by the sea-machine and the keening in *Riders to the Sea* and by Apollyon's followers in *The Pilgrim's Progress*. The icy bleakness of the Antarctic landscape was akin to the finale of the Sixth Symphony and to some of the 1946 music for the film *The Loves of Joanna Godden*.

The choice of this subject for a symphony aroused keen public interest. And it aroused critical scrutiny. Film music, even when written by Prokofiev, Shostakovich, Bliss, Walton, Britten, Malcolm Arnold or

Vaughan Williams, bothered the critics. I remember the scorn and derision which were poured on William Alwyn's First Symphony at Cheltenham in 1950. He had composed much film music and so a straightforward symphony was highly suspect. Was *Antartica* a symphony or a tone poem? No one was quite sure. However, perhaps attitudes were changing and minds getting broader. One of the younger critics, Colin Mason in the *Manchester Guardian*, had no doubts. He singled out the work's 'masterly and completely unified symphonic form', its originality of design and the symphonic logic of the treatment of the material. He ended: 'Nothing could better demonstrate the rightness of his attitude to his art than the new symphony'.[49] Frank Howes was also firmly for the work, asserting that Vaughan Williams had broken new ground 'not in the fact that he uses a larger orchestra but that he has found in sheer sonority devoid of thematic significance a means of conveying his vision and placing it within a symphonic scheme'.[50]

It was Cardus in the *Manchester Guardian* who came nearest to the heart of the matter: 'The *Sinfonia Antartica* seems to me the most powerfully imaginative of all the composer's works ... For sheer brilliance, vividness and spontaneity in the moulding and releasing of tone, in a swift imaginative blending of instrumental colours, everything serving the composer's inner vision, Vaughan Williams has never equalled this latest of his scores.'[51] Yet despite appreciation of this nature, and although Vaughan Williams was riding high in public esteem and was revered by most of his colleagues, mutterings were to be heard from some critical outposts where a cooler wind was blowing. In continental Europe he was scarcely mentioned in academic circles and any opinion (when there was one) would most likely have been similar to Aaron Copland's quoted earlier. What could the *Five Tudor Portraits* mean in Paris? *Sinfonia Antartica* raised a few eyebrows: was the old boy beginning to be seduced by his own image? The answer in 1956 was the Eighth Symphony, his shortest and lightest, dedicated to John Barbirolli, dubbed 'Glorious John' by the composer after the first performance of *Antartica*. Its first sketches date from 1953. The four movements comprise a set of variations 'in search of a theme', a Scherzo for wind, a Cavatina for strings with a cello solo in tribute to the dedicatee (a cellist) and an exuberant Finale which required a large percussion section 'including all the "phones" and "spiels" known to the composer' (in fact, side drum, bass drum, triangle, cymbals, vibraphone, xylophone, glockenspiel, tubular bells, three tuned gongs and celesta). The symphony was enthusiastically received when Barbirolli conducted the first performance in Manchester on 2 May 1956, only a minority wondering if it was a concerto for orchestra. The critic Frank Howes suggested it might be better called a sinfonietta, but got short shrift from Vaughan Williams: 'I am not taking your advice', wrote the composer. 'I feel the thing is a symphony and it is going to remain one.'[52]

Colin Mason, in a long *Guardian* review, was the most perceptive of the critics. He thought the symphony did not quite satisfy

> as a complete musical form, as the *Antartica* satisfied those who listened for its form as well as for its antarcticness. Nor are all the sound-effects justified by any real musical significance ... The first movement is most beautiful and original both in shape and content ... What is also refreshing in this first movement is the modal variety and flexibility of the melodic line which are more elegant, easy and graceful in motion, less tied to his usual distinctive but rather lumpish modal formulae than any he has ever written and show him at 83 still extending his musical range. As this is the most sophisticated, civilized and universal music he has ever written, so the second movement is the wittiest ... This movement made the audience laugh, and in the old days, when audiences knew their own mind and did not hesitate to express it, an immediate encore would have been demanded.[53]

No one has discovered a detailed subtext to the Eighth, though it has been suggested that the flute solo in the first variation of the opening movement relates to the 'human' music in the Intermezzo of *Antartica* and also to Holst's tune for the Remembrance Day hymn, 'O Valiant Hearts'.[54] Variations 2 to 5 were written first, which explains the 'searching for a theme'. An American critic, Paul Henry Lang, noted the resemblance of the principal theme of the *Cavatina* slow movement to the Passion chorale 'O Sacred Head'. Vaughan Williams replied: 'I was thinking about the slow movement and how I wanted a cello tune and it suddenly occurred to me how lovely that chorale would sound on the cellos so as far as I can remember, without deliberately adopting it, the two themes got mixed up in my mind with the result you know. I am quite unrepentant!'[55] Critical response to the symphony was on the whole favourable and friendly but with an overlay of patronizing surprise that a man of his age could write such youthful music and still be aware of contemporary trends, notably in his treatment of percussion. The public liked it and it was programmed in eight cities in Europe, including Vienna, within six months of its premiere. Stokowski conducted it in New York, and it also won the New York Critics' Circle award for the best new symphonic work performed there in 1956.

Vaughan Williams's reputation in America was at its zenith in the 1950s and his third (and last) visit was awaited like a musical state occasion. His friend the English baritone Keith Falkner, who was teaching at Cornell University, arranged a period of residence in Ithaca. Accompanied by his wife Ursula, Vaughan Williams sailed from Liverpool to New York early in October 1954. At Cornell he gave a series of lectures on *The Making of Music* (its published title) and some composition tutorials. After ten days he flew to Toronto to give a lecture. He had intended that this visit should be a holiday and he had to fight hard to keep it that way. He refused more invitations than he accepted, and at a party in his honour annoyed his publishers, Oxford University Press, by spending more time talking to ordinary people than to dignitaries.[56] He refused to appear on NBC television in a coast-to-coast interview, one of a series in which Einstein, Bertrand Russell and Carl Sandburg had previously appeared; he also declined an opportunity to conduct the New York Philharmonic in one of his works. But he had a long private talk with the *New York Times* critic Olin Downes, who had always admired his music. Explaining his attitude to these invitations, he wrote to the organizers: 'I fear I am being difficult, but we do want to enjoy ourselves in America, and that we definitely shall not do, our natures being what they are, if we are besieged by invitations to dinners and theatres and concerts. And I want my time which is not occupied by my duties at Cornell to be peaceful and quiet in order to see whether America will not stimulate me with new ideas.'[57] Before returning to London, he went to Yale University to receive the Howland Prize, which, thirty years earlier, had been awarded to Holst. At a dinner in New York before sailing, he met the composer William Schuman, and renewed his acquaintance with Samuel Barber.

No one could fail to admire the fertility of a composer on the eve of his eighty-fifth birthday who could produce a symphony as compelling as the Eighth, and it was soon known that a Ninth was on the way. This had its first performance in London on 2 April 1958 and was not well received except by a small minority. The gist of more than one critical notice was 'composing for the sake of composing'. Words like 'silly' and 'asinine' (the second movement) had never before been applied to his music. His own comment to a friend the next morning was 'I don't think they can quite forgive me for still being able to do it at my age'.[58]

Once more it was Cardus who fully appreciated what he had heard. Writing in the *Manchester Guardian* he called the symphony 'an astonishing production'. He continued:

> Much of the technical formula is familiar; his music is much an art of cadence, with blocks of harmony the supporting pillars. But this Ninth Symphony is not repetitive of the content of the immediately preceding ones. The changes go deeper than the externals of instrumentation – saxophones and flugelhorn, and so on. The texture of musical brainwork is different and more direct, subtle yet simple . . . Vaughan Williams's great achievement has been to dispense with the current musical coin of the period of his basic culture and maturity and to modulate to the contemporary tone and language without obvious iconoclasms. He is of our period and yet he is full of harvest – which means to say that he is a master.[59]

In what were to prove to be the last weeks of his life he went on holiday, revisited favourite places in the West Country, attended performances of his opera *Sir John in Love* and went to the Proms (where the Ninth was performed). He also began to compose an opera with Ursula as his librettist. Most of the obituary tributes acknowledged that he was a great composer and a remarkable man. Respect and affection were everywhere expressed. But as so often happens after a composer's death, a dip in his reputation and in the frequency of performances set in, although not drastically. There was never a time when it was difficult to find a Vaughan Williams performance; he still had conductors who championed him and the record companies issued new discs of the symphonies, operas and other works. Nothing like the neglect of Bax and Bliss came his way. It was in the universities that he was virtually *persona non grata*. His death coincided with the arrival of a new wave of avant-garde composers with a passionate interest in the Second Viennese School and its successors. And it looked as though Parry's remark that the British only like one English composer at a time might be true once again. Now it was Britten. It would be wrong to call Vaughan Williams a neglected composer at any period of his career, but the question was bound to be asked whether Donald Mitchell was right when he said that Vaughan Williams would be regarded by posterity as a 'major minor composer', the equivalent, though not so flattering, of Richard Strauss's classification of himself as 'a first-rate second-rate' composer. For a while in the 1970s, Mitchell seemed to have persuaded a vocal group to come near to his own judgement. But taking a broad view of the fifty years after Vaughan Williams's death, one can say that he always occupied a high place in the English pantheon. Who in the 1950s and 1960s would have dared to forecast the present popularity and high rating of Elgar? Even the most devoted supporter of Vaughan Williams must have been taken aback by the immense surge of interest in his music in 2008. Suddenly it was everywhere – and this enthusiasm and interest did not fade when the anniversary year was over but continues, intensified, at the time of writing.

Not only did the major orchestras extend their acquaintance to more than two or three of the symphonies in concert halls, but the BBC devoted hours of air-time to his works. The Proms revived the Piano Concerto. Two long and detailed television films were made (and shown several times). Radio programmes held polls to discover the best liked English works: *The Lark Ascending* and the Tallis Fantasia dominated the voters' choices. But even more pleasing was the belated recognition that the Ninth Symphony, far from being the 'the mixture as before', as so many of its first listeners casually and thoughtlessly described it, could even be considered as a culminatory summit, opening up a new phase. Alain Frogley's intensively researched and well-balanced monograph on the work ushered in a deeper and more comprehensive appreciation of its mastery and originality.[60]

Several other excellent books on his music have been published in recent years. Performances in the United States and in Europe have steadily increased. Although there had been a marked diminution of interest in America after his death in 1958, there had never been a total eclipse. In the *Musical America* review of orchestral performances in the 1961–2 season, Vaughan Williams was the twelfth most performed foreign contemporary composer, ahead of Britten, Kodály, Webern and Sibelius. While the surge of interest after the fiftieth anniversary in 2008 was not as great as in Britain, it was still remarkable. In Britain, what would have pleased him most of all is the revival of interest in his operas. *The Pilgrim's Progress* has convinced many critics that it is the masterpiece its admirers believe and opera companies in several countries have staged it or have plans to do so. There were seven performances in London by English National Opera in November 2012 at the Coliseum. These were the opera's first professional staging in the capital since its premiere at Covent Garden in 1951–2.

Encouragingly, many of the less often played works have found advocates. *The Poisoned Kiss*, for example, has had more performances after 2008 than it had had in the previous seventy-five years. And this is true not only of his operas. We now can have a different perspective on his development into one of the greatest of composers, with the publication and performance since 1996 of early works that were withdrawn. These include chamber music, the Mass (*A Cambridge Mass*) he wrote in 1899 for his doctorate, his first choral masterpiece, *The Garden of Proserpine*, the *Bucolic Suite*, the Serenade of 1898, and other orchestral works. Now we can hear the complete Vaughan Williams.

Notes

1 *The Strad*, 13/9 (March 1903), 37.

2 'Some English Music', *The Pilot*, 4/1 (21 March 1903), 280.

3 'Modern British Composers. vi.', *MSt* 65/2034 (25 July 1903), 52.

4 12 October 1907, 6.

5 I am deeply indebted to Alain Frogley, who made freely available to me his research material on Vaughan Williams and America.

6 Letter of 8 June 1922, quoted in *UVWB*, 144.

7 *The Manchester Guardian*, 27 June 1922, 16.

8 The quotations are as follows: Heseltine: Robert Nichols, 'At Oxford', in Cecil Gray (ed.) *Peter Warlock: A Memoir of Philip Heseltine* (London: Jonathan Cape, 1934), 78–9; Allen, *KW*, 156; Lutyens, generally credited to

lectures at Dartington Summer School some time in the 1950s; 'Lambkins frisking' letter, Ralph Vaughan Williams, Dorking, to Ursula Wood, London, 4 October 1938, quoted in *UVWB*, 121.

9 Programme note for *Flos Campi*, 1927; reprinted in *VWOM*, 347.

10 *The Times*, 12 October 1925, 9.

11 *The Times*, 17 October 1925, 10.

12 *The Nation and the Athenaeum* 38/8 (21 November 1925), 290.

13 Joseph Holbrooke, *Contemporary British Composers* (London: Cecil Palmer, 1925), 96–8.

14 *LRVW*, 150.

15 *UVWB*, 192–3.

16 *The Times*, 11 April 1935, 12.

17 *MT* 76 (May 1935), 452.

18 *The Manchester Guardian*, 11 April 1935, 6.

19 Aaron Copland, *Copland on Music* (London: André Deutsch, 1961), 197.

20 *The Times*, 11 April 1935, 12.

21 Trevelyan and Karpeles quoted in *KW*, 245 and 246 respectively. The Longman letter is in *LRVW*, 254–5.

22 *KW*, 246.

23 *UVWB*, 190.

24 See 'Who Wants the English Composer?', *RCM Magazine* 9/1 (1912), 11–15, reprinted in *VWOM*, 39–42.

25 24 April 1942; *LRVW*, 338.

26 15 October 1955; *LRVW*, 568.

27 *KW*, 300–1.

28 *VWOM*, 367.

29 *Daily Telegraph*, 22 April 1948.

30 *The Times*, 22 April 1948, 7.

31 *The Times*, 9 August 1949, 8.

32 10 August 1949; *LRVW*, 453.

33 *KW*, 302; *LRVW*, 573.

34 Deryck Cooke, *The Language of Music* (Oxford University Press, 1959), 252–3.

35 The 1956–7 survey appeared in *Musical America*, 79/7 (August 1957), 15 and 28, the 1951–2 survey in 74/6 (July 1952), 6 and 24.

36 For a more detailed discussion of the composer's different musical responses to *The Pilgrim's Progress* see Chapter 8.

37 *The Daily Telegraph*, 28 April 1951, 6; *The Times*, 27 April 1951, 8, quoted in *KW*, 310–11.

38 *KW*, 315.

39 *KW*, 320–1.

40 *The Sunday Times*, 12 April 1953, 9.

41 Hubert Foss, *Ralph Vaughan Williams: A Study* (London: George G. Harrap & Co., 1950).

42 *LRVW*, 466.

43 *Royal College of Music Magazine*, 9/1 (1912), 11–15; reprinted in *VWOM*, 39–42.

44 Quoted in *KW*, 330.

45 Donald Mitchell, 'Contemporary Chronicle: Revaluations: Vaughan Williams', *MO* 78 (1955), 409–11, 471, quoted in *KW*, 330–31.

46 Mitchell, 'Contemporary Chronicle', 471.

47 *Ibid.*

48 'Arnold Schoenberg (1874–1951)', *ML* 32/4 (1951), 322.

49 *The Manchester Guardian*, 15 January 1953, 3.

50 'A New Symphony: Vaughan Williams's "Antartica"', *The Times*, 15 January 1953, 3.

51 *The Manchester Guardian*, 23 January 1953, 5.

52 *UVWB*, 358.

53 *The Manchester Guardian*, 3 May 1956, 5.

54 See Oliver Neighbour, 'The Place of the Eighth among Vaughan Williams's Symphonies', in *VWS*, 213–33 at 230–1.

55 Letter to Paul Henry Lang, 18 October 1956, quoted in *LRVW*, 597.

56 This was at a large tea-party that Lyle Dowling at the New York office of OUP had finally managed to put together, about which Dowling reported back to the publisher's London office. Speaking of the many missed opportunities such as the television interview, he adds ruefully: 'But to compensate for all this, there remains the fact of his extraordinary character – and the pleasure, not unmixed, of dealing for a change with a celebrity who is 100 percent un-commercial; a rare event in my life, I can assure you.' Internal OUP memo of 4 January 1955 from Dowling to Alan Frank, OUP, London.

57 Letter to Lyle Dowling, 6 June 1954.

58 *KW*, 343.

59 Neville Cardus in *The Manchester Guardian*, 7 August 1958, quoted in *KW*, 345.

60 Alain Frogley, *Vaughan Williams's Ninth Symphony*, Studies in Musical Genesis and Structure (Oxford University Press, 2001).

14 Vaughan Williams and his successors: composers' forum

PETER MAXWELL DAVIES, PIERS HELLAWELL,
NICOLA LEFANU AND ANTHONY PAYNE IN
CONVERSATION WITH AIDAN J. THOMSON

As Michael Kennedy has shown in the previous chapter, Vaughan Williams's posthumous reception has followed a pattern familiar to music historians: respectful mourning at his passing, comparative neglect as a younger generation of composers takes centre stage, and then gradual rehabilitation, in Vaughan Williams's case one that was complete by the fiftieth anniversary of his death. It is, one might say, the transition of a composer of the present – the apogee of a living tradition, known personally to those who performed and wrote about his music – to a composer of the past, known to performers and critics alike through that music and the scholarly discourse on it. Vaughan Williams's reception today has thus been coloured by the historical distance of which this transition is both a cause and a symptom. Most obviously, it has been affected by twenty-first-century audiences' experiences of – and changing trends in – post-war music: the Vaughan Williams that we hear today is inevitably going to sound different from the composer heard by the audiences who attended his premieres because of our knowledge of composers like Boulez, Stockhausen, Cage, Ligeti, Xenakis, Glass, and Murail. On the other hand, Vaughan Williams's centrality to the renaissance in British music in the first half of the twentieth century – both as a composer and, as David Manning has observed in Chapter 11, as a public figure who encouraged music-making in all levels of society – means that, at least in Britain, his successors are part of his legacy.

The relationship between Vaughan Williams and his British successors is sometimes rather tense. As both Kennedy and Jenny Doctor have shown in their chapters, the reception of Vaughan Williams's later music was affected by the emergence of Benjamin Britten as Britain's unofficial composer laureate; in turn, Britten's own reception was affected by the emergence of the British avant-garde in the 1960s, perhaps most spectacularly in the form of the New Music Manchester group, headed by Harrison Birtwistle, Alexander Goehr and Peter Maxwell Davies. The neglect of Vaughan Williams in the 1950s and 1960s was evidence that, in the era of the Angry Young Men, there was no longer a place for a Grand Old Man: Vaughan Williams was a symbol of everything that a younger generation wanted to sweep away. But as the tide of high modernism has ebbed, to be replaced by a more pluralist musical culture that is equally accepting of minimalism and acousmatics, Vaughan Williams has re-emerged, and his central position within the canon of British composers is now taken for granted. And so this raises the question: how is Vaughan Williams regarded today by those British composers who came to the fore in the 1960s, 1970s and 1980s, and whose work may be seen as part of the reaction against him?

Given that a feature of this volume has been the idea of 'Vaughan Williams the Progressive', the editors made the decision to include a composers' forum, in which four contemporary British composers (Sir Peter Maxwell Davies, Piers Hellawell, Nicola LeFanu and Anthony Payne) were interviewed about Vaughan Williams. In certain respects, all four composers share traits with Vaughan Williams, whether it be that their works investigate the relationship between music and nature, or that they have written music for amateurs to perform, or that they have been actively involved in teaching composition. Each interview lasted just under an hour, during which the composers were asked nine questions, listed below. The transcripts that follow are thus edited highlights of longer conversations; for the sake of brevity, this has sometimes meant combining two questions in one.

- When and how did you first encounter Vaughan Williams's music, and which work was performed?
- How would you describe the impact his music had on you in that first encounter?
- How has your view of his music changed, if at all, since you first heard it?
- What do you consider to be the most distinctive aspects of his music?
- Which of Vaughan Williams's works do you consider the most important?
- How would you evaluate Vaughan Williams's influence on British music and musical life, particularly in terms of its positive or negative effects on subsequent generations of composers?
- How would you evaluate Vaughan Williams's place in the broader international perspective of twentieth-century music?
- Are there any aspects of his music beyond specific choices of national literary texts etc. that can be reliably identified as British, or English, or that are linked to broader notions of British or English national identity?
- Do you feel he has in any way influenced your own music, or your attitudes to music in general, or your view of the role of the composer in society?

An analysis of these interviews is revealing. It is perhaps unsurprising that among the first works by Vaughan Williams encountered by all four composers is the *Fantasia on a Theme by Thomas Tallis*; that this work and the middle-period symphonies (*A Pastoral Symphony* and the Fourth, Fifth and Sixth) were among the works that they ranked most highly; and that Vaughan Williams's use of folksong, modality and early music were among his most distinctive stylistic features. More striking is the extent to which they draw attention to Vaughan Williams's skill as an orchestrator and his ear for unusual sonorities, and, above all, the extent to which Vaughan Williams should be considered in a pan-European context, not within a purely English or British one. One feature that united all four composers was their sense of gratitude to Vaughan Williams for having played such a huge part in the creation of a contemporary British art-music compositional tradition; as Piers Hellawell puts it, Vaughan Williams gave 'a tradition for people like me to exist within'. Perhaps that is the best legacy of all.

∗∗∗

Interview with Sir Peter Maxwell Davies (Dublin, 3 May 2011)

Sir Peter Maxwell Davies is one of the outstanding British composers of his generation. One of the leaders of the New Music Manchester group in the 1960s, he was influential in introducing the sounds of the post-war avant-garde to British art music. His later music has been strongly inspired by the landscape and culture of Orkney, where he has lived since 1971, and where, in 1977, he established the St Magnus Festival. An acknowledged master in all the main compositional genres, his vast output includes nine symphonies, seven operas, many other works for orchestra, stage, voices, chamber ensemble and solo instrumentalists, and a significant number of shorter, lighter works, of which perhaps the best known is *An Orkney Wedding, with Sunrise* (1985). Since 2004 he has been Master of the Queen's Music, a position from which he retires in 2014.

> AT: When and how did you first encounter Vaughan Williams's music, which work was performed, and what impact did it have on you?
>
> PMD: I can't remember, because I must have been very young. I know that when I was eleven or twelve I was thrilled to bits with things like *The Wasps* Overture and the Tallis Fantasia, but the one that really knocked me out was the first performance of the Sixth Symphony in 1948. The cataclysmic opening which resolves into that very lyrical second subject, and the utter desolation of that last movement – I had never heard anything like it, and I don't think I have since, either. I made it my business to hear the other symphonies as soon as I could. I got a recording of the Fifth and heard it a few times, and fell in love with it, too. I've conducted the Fifth and the Sixth quite a lot, and having got to know them from the inside, I think that, as a boy, I was absolutely right in thinking that they, and also 4, were very great works. And more recently I've got to know the later symphonies. They're more introverted, but great symphonies, too.

AT: Was it the fact that the Sixth Symphony was written when it was, and that you experienced it when you did, that perhaps made its effect so drastic and dramatic?

PMD: I don't know. Obviously I had been through the war and he wrote this very much as a reaction after it, and I suppose one does connect it with that. But I think when I heard it, it was just its moods and its changes. That work is so personal to my being that I can't really say.

AT: How far has your view of his music changed, if at all, since you first heard it?

PMD: My interest in his work has deepened over the years quite extraordinarily. When I was still at school, I heard the first performance of the Antarctic Symphony with John Barbirolli and the Hallé.[1] I bought a 7/6 ticket for that concert, hoping I would get a glimpse of Vaughan Williams and Ursula, his very pretty young wife, and I sat quite close to them. I never met him, of course, but to get that close and just be able to watch his reactions to his own work was a wonderful experience; I think he realized that Barbirolli and the orchestra loved him and his work, and he just seemed to enjoy the whole thing. I got to know Ursula quite well later, and we talked about that particular event when she came to the first performance of my own *Antarctic Symphony*, which was commissioned by the Philharmonia and the British Antarctic Survey to mark the fiftieth anniversary, more or less, of the Vaughan Williams.[2] Of course, unlike Vaughan Williams, I experienced Antarctica first, which was wonderful.

AT: And were the penguins anything like Vaughan Williams's depiction of them?

PMD: When you're there, you realize that they're schizophrenic creatures on land; they aren't like he depicts them. But I remember when three penguins came out of the water, just in front of me, while I was walking along the shore near Rothera, the main British base. They were doing a kind of Vaughan Williams dance, and were looking at me; I'm sure they were saying to each other, 'What a funny-looking penguin'.

AT: In an interview about your student days, you mention your interest in 'dangerous' composers, among whom were Stravinsky, Bartók, Vaughan Williams and Britten.[3] What did you feel was dangerous about Vaughan Williams?

PMD: His extraordinary way of going places that nobody else was going to. He's not given enough credit for that. The extraordinary polyrhythms at the beginning of the Sixth Symphony: they're as 'advanced' as anything in *The Rite of Spring*. They get into your physical system like very little music that I've conducted. And the last movement of that symphony is one of the most desolate things that's ever been written. You hear similar desolation in Dowland, and in some of the motets of Byrd; I don't know whether it's a particularly British or English thing, but the metaphysical melancholy in some of his work has resonances that I haven't had from anything else.

AT: What do you consider to be the most distinctive aspects of Vaughan Williams's music?

PMD: In his early work, the sheer sense of space, which connects him in my mind to landscape. One distinction I make is that some composers write music that exists inside the concert hall, and other composers write music that really exists outside it, in nature. Even something like the Tallis Fantasia, which is to do with the spaces inside Gloucester Cathedral, to me sounds like an 'outside' piece, because of its extraordinary majesty of spaciousness. Vaughan Williams's symphonies sound as if he's been walking outside and just listening; they have that outdoor feel.

AT: One 'outdoor' work that springs to mind is *A Pastoral Symphony*, particularly the end of it.

PMD: I took some time to get used to it. I listened to it a lot and thought, well, it's not got that direct line, it's meandering about a bit. But then you realize that it's very tightly controlled, and that his use of vocal line is very dramatic. The gentleness of some of it is unusual in twentieth-century music. You think of gentle music by Debussy and Ravel, but the Third Symphony is like a spiritual oasis in his line of symphonies.

AT: Which of his works do you consider the most important?

PMD: I think I shall have to pass on that. Obviously there's the Sixth, and I love the Fifth, but then *Riders to the Sea* is overwhelming. And the Tallis Fantasia, which I heard as a boy and thought was just the most beautiful thing ever, which it probably is in its way. I'm still coming to terms with some of his work, such as the Ninth Symphony. When I first heard it, I thought 'that's an old man's music'; maybe it is, but it's a very constructive view on old age. As you get older, you begin to take these things more seriously than you did when you were in your forties, say.

AT: How would you evaluate Vaughan Williams's influence on British music and musical life, particularly in term of its positive or negative effects on subsequent generations of composers?

PMD: There was a generation shortly after me who didn't really take much interest. But you listen to your students. In the '70s, particularly, they didn't talk much about Vaughan Williams; they were more interested in more 'radical', but possibly more quickly forgotten, composers. But these days, students are more interested, and they take his symphonies very seriously. Also, there is a growing realization that he is technically very competent. His manuscripts aren't pretty and tidy, but that doesn't mean that his thought is untidy; it's *very* precise. He obviously could work out things in his mind very clearly before he put the pencil to paper.

AT: Vaughan Williams envisaged a role for the composer as a public figure. Do you think this is still relevant today?

PMD: I think it's even more relevant. He helped make his and other people's music available to the public. He wrote choral pieces which anyone could sing, and I think that was an expression of his love for the people who actually performed his work, and a counterbalance to the infantile approach of composers who, in the '60s and early '70s, were saying, 'You don't take any notice of the performers or your audience; you just do what you want, and to hell with the public'. The composer has a role in society, and Vaughan Williams fulfilled that. I can understand perfectly well why he edited *The English Hymnal*; he had a social duty to do so.

AT: How would you evaluate Vaughan Williams's place in the broader international perspective of twentieth-century music?

PMD: I would put him highly. Having conducted his work in Scandinavia and in Germany, I wonder why he's not done there more. I think if people knew his work they would appreciate it. And as for saying, 'Oh, it's too English, and it won't be understood here', well, that's rubbish. My experience in Germany is exactly the opposite; they're very interested *because* it's English, and something quite specific. They had no preconceptions of Vaughan Williams's music; they didn't know it.

AT: Given this absence of preconceptions, how far might someone listening to Vaughan Williams for the first time think, 'that sounds Ravelian, that sounds Sibelian' etc., and perhaps hear threads that listeners more familiar with him might miss?

PMD: Good question. I suspect that Vaughan Williams's personality is strong enough to come through, and people who take that tack are probably looking for excuses not to like it, or not to come to terms with it.

AT: In your view, are there any aspects to Vaughan Williams's music beyond the specific choices of national literary texts, etc., that can be reliably identified as British, or that reflect broader notions of British national identity?

PMD: It's hard to say, because you're very close to it. For instance, I have claimed that Birtwistle's music sounds quintessentially English and people think I'm mad. But I don't think so; it's got something of that extraordinary eccentricity of Tippett, and of Vaughan Williams in his more experimental works like the Fourth and the Sixth symphonies. I think I hear that kind of Britishness in Vaughan Williams's work. But I wonder if it's something that should concern us, because what one is really concerned with is the quality of the music. If a composer writes interesting music, and Vaughan Williams certainly does, you take on that flavour, and you enjoy it. I take it for granted that if a composer is genuine, something of his own country will come through. With Vaughan Williams it's inevitable, as he was interested in folk music, and that flavours it very much – very beautifully, too.

AT: It's interesting that you mention eccentricity, because alongside the violent eccentricity of the Fourth and Sixth there's also a comic eccentricity: works like *Sir John in Love*, which is just very funny a lot of the time, or *The Poisoned Kiss*. When placed alongside more serious pieces that were being written at the same time – *A Pastoral Symphony*, or later on *Riders to the Sea* or *Job* – the eccentric comic works stick out that bit more, and yet they form a very distinct strand of his music.

PMD: I think we try to put composers into pigeonholes, and they've got to behave themselves and stay in their pigeonhole. I get a lot of flak for writing different kinds of music, and I can understand that people don't like it because it doesn't fit into a pigeonhole. It's much the same with Vaughan Williams; it's resented that he could be terribly funny, or that he wrote light pieces. But you have many personalities as a composer, and music expresses all kinds of things. Think of Mozart writing those very superficial German dances shortly before he died: well, he was interested in dancing, so why not? He enjoyed it.

AT: Do you feel that Vaughan Williams has in any way influenced your own music, your attitudes to music in general, or your view of the role of the composer in society?

PMD: Yes, he has: the fact that he's publicly engaged, that he writes different kinds of music, and that he can be wonderfully eccentric. I think he was a wonderful example, quite apart from his technical competence.

AT: Was Vaughan Williams's sense of space, and depiction of landscapes and seascapes, an influence on your own work?

PMD: It certainly has been an influence, together with Debussy and Britten. But yes, Vaughan Williams was a big influence in that respect.

AT: Religious music, and the influence of religious music, has also played a big part in your own output, despite your being an atheist; could one say that there is a parallel with Vaughan Williams, who also wrote a lot of religious music despite his being a self-professed agnostic?

PMD: There is a parallel, and this was brought home to me when Westminster Cathedral wanted me to write a Mass for them. I said, 'Well, I've heard a lot about Christianity, but I'm not a Christian, and certainly not a Catholic'. They said, 'It's all right, we commissioned Ben Britten and he was an Anglican; they [the Church of England] commissioned Vaughan Williams and he was an atheist. What we want is a decent piece of music.' I'm quite happy to write a decent piece of music, if I can do such a thing, for the serious religious purpose which is going to help people develop spiritually and musically. There are many things in Christianity that I can't agree with, but it hasn't prevented me from setting a poem by the Archbishop of Canterbury, with permission; he's a marvellous poet and a wonderful human being.[4] My dear friend George Mackay Brown, the Orcadian poet, was a very staunch Catholic convert. And I love and respect Jimmy MacMillan who is a wonderful composer; I think his Catholicism helps him tremendously with his work.

AT: We touched on the public role of the composer. Do you feel that things have changed since Vaughan Williams's day because of the nature of modern media, and the amount of time that's given to art music?

PMD: I think that with serious music there is a big problem. There's a couple of generations now who have had no introduction to 'serious' music, classical music, whatever. And I think this is everyone's loss. There is music that doesn't have words; there is music that goes through development and variation, transformation, transition – the equivalent, if you like, of a long poem, a novella, or even a novel – and people have no idea that it's there. I think that that's a terrible denial of their inheritance.

AT: A hundred years ago, Vaughan Williams belonged to a movement that saw folksong as a way of teaching young people how music worked, particularly British or English music. What similar ways, if any, might we adopt today to get people to understand music as music?

PMD: As far as I'm concerned, a place doesn't exist unless there's music that is composed about it, and sung and played about it. And that's what folk music does. It makes a place come to life musically. If you do that through any kind of music, you will bring people in. When people create music, they become interested in music. If they improvise or compose music, whether in groups or individually, even at a very rudimentary level, they are interested in how it works. And I think that's the way.

***

Interview with Piers Hellawell (Belfast, 27 April 2012)

Piers Hellawell is Professor of Composition at the Queen's University of Belfast, and was Gresham Professor of Music in London between 2000 and 2003. One of the UK's leading composers, his works include *Inside Story* for violin, viola and orchestra (1999), which was premiered at the BBC Proms, and a substantial amount of music for smaller ensembles. He is also an award-winning teacher of composition and a public commentator on the teaching of composition, and of music in the education system more generally.

AT: When and how did you first encounter Vaughan Williams's music, which work was performed, and what impact did his music have upon you in that first encounter?

PH: I think that it must have been the Tallis Fantasia, and that I heard it in Winchester Cathedral when I was at school, probably in the early 1970s. I have a memory of the sonority in the building, which of course was astonishing.[5] It's hard to think of another modern work that delivers a simpler, more thunderous, uncomplicated message in sound. The impact was to do with pastoralism more generally, and I think Vaughan Williams was at the centre of that. My teens were very strongly coloured by an idea of a lost English pastoral and the sense of wanting to regain it. I suppose this was because I was at school in what one could call Wessex, and when I was about fifteen I read all the Thomas Hardy novels. The sense of forgotten, unspoiled places was a kind of Romantic ideal that was huge for me, and I was particularly taken with the idea of a Wessex kind of idyll. I think that Vaughan Williams – and other music, such as Delius – and Hardy, informed a sense of where I was: I wanted to believe that there was still a 'hidden England'. And I think that pieces like *The Lark Ascending* and the Tallis Fantasia embodied that. I'm less comfortable with that whole pastoral thing now, but at the time it articulated where I wanted to believe the country still was.

AT: That suggests that your sense of a pastoralist ideal is still recoverable, whereas one might say that some of Vaughan Williams's work *doesn't* recover that ideal, or it does so only very fleetingly, before turning away again.

PH: Even as you say that a line of Housman comes to mind: 'Land of lost content, where once I was and cannot come again'. In a sense I think the point of pastoralism *is* its unrecoverability; the idea of loss is essential to it. Something else that I remember from my schooldays was that the music master at Winchester, Angus Watson, organized some really incredible concerts, and sometimes conducted the Bournemouth Sinfonietta when they visited. Angus said that he didn't think that Vaughan Williams was as effective in darker pieces, like the Fourth or Sixth symphonies, as he was in the pastoral works; he was less good at being angry and coloured by war than his European contemporaries, such as Bartók, Stravinsky or Schoenberg. And I think that I have inherited that view. To me Vaughan Williams is less authentically an angry composer than he is a pastoral one, and so I don't tend to know those pieces so well, whereas *The Lark Ascending* side, or the *Tallis* side, or the *Wenlock Edge* side, is to me a more contented sort of place, and that tends to be the music that I've associated with him.

AT: How has your view of his music changed, if at all, since you first heard it?

PH: As a teenager, I probably had a sort of 'snapshot' view of Vaughan Williams's music, which had evoked something very particular for me; and the extent to which I became frustrated by that probably explains why I stopped listening to him when I was a young adult. But then, of course, you find that any really substantial composer is far more complex and diverse than you thought. My view has changed to the extent that I've taken on board the very important aspect of the European dimension for great British composers. The thought that we are hopelessly defined by some kind of parochial insularity that matches our geography is very depressing; any composer aspires to some kind of breadth of universal expression, however short of it we may fall. It always seems important to me to see Elgar as a European late Romantic composer; increasingly I think the same of Vaughan Williams, and the pieces that now interest me are in no way parochial or restrictive. For example, the Vaughan Williams work that has come to mean most to me in recent years is his early Piano Quintet: a piece that most people don't know, and perhaps not even recognisably Vaughan Williams. But it continually amazes me; it's a late Romantic piece that you might listen to in the same way that you would early Fauré. Nationhood or national identity is totally unimportant when I'm listening to that piece. So that has definitely changed. And it's a good example of how a composer who lived as long as Vaughan Williams is always more than we give them credit for as young listeners, or more than I did, anyway.

AT: What do you consider to be the most distinctive aspects of Vaughan Williams's music, and which of his works do you consider the most important?

PH: In terms of works, I greatly enjoy parts of the more pastoral-type symphonies, like 3 and 5. And the opening of *A Sea Symphony* is a never-to-be-repeated moment. But I can't imagine that anything comes close to the Tallis Fantasia as an individual achievement; I think of it as a kind of landmark like the *Rite of Spring*. Interestingly, another work that I regard as among the greatest of the period is Tippett's *Corelli Fantasia*, which is, I suppose, its natural heir. I think both of them stand beside anything of their time.

As for your first question, I would say Vaughan Williams's most distinctive feature is his harmony; his achievement was to do something utterly original with his historical situation. At a time when there were so many different exits from European late Romanticism, he avoids total chromaticism and instead adopted a Debussian approach of recontextualizing tonal materials as non-functional sound objects. But he does it differently from Debussy. I think that is huge in terms of individuality; those sonic experiments with overlapping triads in the Tallis Fantasia are extraordinary, and wonderfully controlled. I think the use of historical modes to create a post-tonal language is extraordinarily individual, and that's probably the most important thing for me.

AT: Of course, there was a lot of suspicion of Debussian harmony in Britain around that time; for Vaughan Williams to study with Ravel, and then to come up with something so distinctive was really very radical.

PH: The whole reception issue is interesting in itself. Composers who live a very long time do one of three things: they develop and are always part of their time, like Stravinsky; or they largely stay the same, like Vaughan Williams; or they stop writing, like Sibelius. Vaughan Williams continued to compose into the '40s and '50s, but he wasn't part of any of the new things that were going on then, such as Darmstadt; so in a sense his reception is affected by the fact that he 'stayed himself'.

AT: And yet even though his new work wasn't radical by Darmstadt standards, he still experimented with new sonorities and new media. One thinks of the film scores and the unusual sounds in both the *Sinfonia Antartica* and the Eighth Symphony.

PH: But he's still cast in the role of the canonic symphonist, something that's under great challenge everywhere else in the '50s. I wonder how far the reason we're timid about Vaughan Williams, as a musical nation, might be because we're aware that he continued to be one thing when newer, if perhaps more trivial, things were opening up elsewhere.

AT: How would you evaluate Vaughan Williams's influence on British music and musical life, particularly in terms of its positive or negative effects on subsequent generations of composers?

PH: I think it's reasonable to say that Vaughan Williams is at the close of a phase of English music, although, of course, there are lots of exceptions to that. To me, the big inheritor of that tradition of doing something international with English symphonism is Tippett, who is enormously great to me, and perhaps slightly eclipsed at the moment; I feel a really palpable affinity from Vaughan Williams to Tippett, although I have no idea if Tippett did. But otherwise, in the '70s, '80s and '90s, I don't think he has been that influential, except on those composers who have continued to evoke a conscious sort of lyricism.

AT: There have been perhaps three generations of British composers between Vaughan Williams and you: the generation born in the 1900s and '10s, such as Tippett and Britten; the generation that emerged after Vaughan Williams's death, such as Maxwell Davies and Birtwistle; and then your own generation, which came to the fore after the death of Britten. Might one say that each generation's reinterpretation of Vaughan Williams reflects their own position in British musical history?

PH: There's a line from Gaelic poetry: 'It's not history, but memory.' Something like the loss of the *Titanic* is just on the cusp of becoming history, because there are still people who were told about it by those who remembered it first-hand, and I think it's the same with art. I remember Tippett being alive; I remember when Stravinsky died; I met Lutosławski here. For me, those are 'living' composers, whether or not they're actually still alive; Vaughan Williams is ever so slightly historical to me, in a way that he might not be to some older composers.

AT: How would you evaluate Vaughan Williams's place in the broader international perspective of twentieth-century music?

PH: I think it's too early to say. For me, what makes a composer solidify in the canon is ultimately individuality. If we can get something from a composer that we don't get anywhere else then people will go on listening. And I'm absolutely certain of that with Vaughan Williams; I think he's a composer of immense expressive range, not all of which I've encompassed as a listener. I don't get the impression that there's a huge amount of his work being played at the moment, but I think that there is real range, expressive depth and individuality.

AT: It's interesting that you raise the issue of how much Vaughan Williams is played. Obviously, crowd-pullers like the Tallis Fantasia and *The Lark Ascending* are performed frequently, whereas quirkier works like the Piano Concerto tend to get less of an audience.

PH: I was thinking of the Piano Concerto, too. But then one thinks of the Ireland Piano Concerto, which is from the same period, and encapsulates the English pastoral in that genre. In a sense I think it's quite a crowded market; some works will struggle to get heard.

AT: In your view are there any aspects of Vaughan Williams's music beyond specific choices of national literary texts etc. that can be readily identified as British, or that are linked to broader notions of British national identity?

PH: I suppose those are the ones with which I began. There are folksong-informed melodies, and rhythmic, quite scherzando material that I think places him in early twentieth-century England. But we've already linked the pastoral harmonies to Debussy and Ravel, and so they're not as English as often thought. I suspect that if there are aspects of Vaughan Williams that can be tied down, they might be derived from the English cathedral tradition – I'm thinking here of *Five Mystical Songs* – or from the discovery of early English polyphony, such as in the Tallis Fantasia. I'm more doubtful that his symphonic style is typically English – sometimes you hear symphonies by lesser-known composers from other parts of the world whose work is similar to Vaughan Williams – but I think his acknowledgement of the English polyphonic tradition is perhaps a distinctive national trait.

AT: Do you feel that Vaughan Williams has in any way influenced your own music, your attitudes to music in general, or your view of the role of the composer in society?

PH: In a specific sense, I would have to say no. Going back to the question of generations, I think I might be the wrong age for that to be the case; when I was younger I conceptualized Tippett as a contemporary composer in whom something English and authentically of its time came together. But I think that the fact that Vaughan Williams did so much to establish the idea of Englishness through folksong and the rehabilitation of earlier English musical traditions gives a tradition for people like me to exist within. It makes it possible for us to function in the profession, as it were.

AT: You have written that composers influenced by earlier composers' works are 'mentally in the zone of [their] own'.[6] In other words, what may influence or inspire them is unlikely to be a work's surface detail, but rather something that can point them to new ways of thinking.

PH: Absolutely, yes. If an influence is worth enumerating it's not going to be of a 'that sounds like that' type, but something from beneath the surface, because any artistic work of value absorbs whatever it is on its own terms. The idea of a sonority, and an exploration of sonority and harmony in a way that is possible within English terms, is very important to me, and perhaps more so as I get older. Vaughan Williams did this in apparently traditional frameworks, which actually turned out to renew themselves expressively for each generation.

AT: Vaughan Williams's approach to composition was always practical: as something to be performed, not least by amateurs, rather than something that existed in the abstract. Would you subscribe to that legacy? I think of your keenness to get student work performed at the earliest opportunity, for instance.

PH: For me, the ideal not only of non-professionals, but at least professional non-*specialist* new music performers being able to perform things is hugely exciting. And I think that belongs to that tradition, although it's not a conscious Vaughan Williams thing. I've been a major contributor to the Schubert Ensemble scheme, Chamber Music 2000, writing short chamber pieces for young people; and a couple of times I've had students in university recitals sing work that's not easy for professional ensembles. Those things are incredibly important to me. We now think of this amateur participation as exceptional, but of course those were the players for whom music was written two hundred years ago. And I think we need to hang on to this tradition.

***

Interview with Nicola LeFanu (York, 21 June 2010)

Nicola LeFanu taught composition at King's College London before becoming Professor of Music at the University of York in 1994, a post she held until her retirement in 2008. An experienced and widely performed composer in all media, she is perhaps best known for her operatic works, notably her monodrama for soprano and thirteen instruments, *The Old Woman of Beare* (1981), and an extensive corpus of vocal and choral music, much of it with a chamber-ensemble accompaniment. Uniquely among the interviewees in this chapter, she met Vaughan Williams in person.

AT: When and how did you first encounter Vaughan Williams's music, and which work was performed?

NL: That's very hard to remember because I was eleven when he died, and for those eleven years he was a very important person in our family life. I met him on a number of occasions: my mother, Elizabeth Maconchy, was a very close friend of Ralph and of Adeline, and later of Ursula Vaughan Williams, and my parents often visited them. My first real memory of a particular Vaughan Williams piece is actually a negative one. It was the Ninth Symphony premiere; I was deemed too young to go to it, and he sent me a programme which said, 'For Nicky, Love from RVW'.[7] I first became aware of the music in my teens, but I can't pick out an individual work because I would have heard a lot. The first works that I think I could identify came later, probably when I was sixteen, because the Fifth Symphony was a set work at school, so I really knew the score very well. I probably knew *Job* quite early on; I saw a wonderful performance of it, but I am pretty certain that was in my later teens, not in my early childhood.

AT: How would you describe the impact his music had on you in that first encounter? Given that your early encounters with Vaughan Williams's music were almost incremental I suppose that that would be very hard to say.

NL: My memory of *Job* was that it was an exciting work. The Fifth Symphony was the first piece that I analysed, and naturally got me interested in the Fourth and Sixth symphonies as well. The Fifth made a deep impression on me; I found it a beautiful piece, particularly the way that he moved between modal and tonal harmony. But when I was sixteen and seventeen what was really exciting were the early works of Goehr and Maxwell Davies; so I never had the experience of hearing Vaughan Williams as new. One of the real contradictions for me was that while Vaughan Williams held radical views – he believed in change and socialism – I knew his music as a music of the past.

AT: How has your view of his music changed, if at all, since you first heard it?

NL: I think there are three stages. When I studied the Fifth Symphony in my mid-teens, I knew a great deal about his music: more, probably, than I ever have since, in that I got to know not only the symphonies, but also his choral music, and I also saw *Sir John in Love*. I loved some of it, was much more critical of some of it, and so on. Then in my twenties, his music was less important to me, because I was immersed in discovering my own language as a composer, and in the new music of this country. What remained important was Vaughan Williams the man, because it angered me that he was described as if he were an elderly, genial, jingoistic Englishman. That was absolute rubbish, and I never missed an opportunity to correct people if they spoke about Vaughan Williams in that way. And then, finally, there's been a third stage, in which I now enjoy listening to his pieces without being critical in the sense that I might have been in my twenties.

AT: The point about jingoism is interesting. Would you say that in the '60s some people constructed Vaughan Williams as an Elgar-like figure as a way of asserting their own radicalism?

NL: It's partly that. But it's also probably a question of taste; the reasons I like Vaughan Williams are perhaps swayed by the fact that it [his music] ran through my childhood. And in any case he had qualities that Elgar doesn't have. It's funny that people never think of Vaughan Williams as having a lightness of touch, and yet to me there is sometimes a very beautiful, luminous, radiant quality to his music.

AT: As in, for example, *A London Symphony*?

NL: Certainly. But I think there is another important thing, which is that sometimes Vaughan Williams's music is described as nostalgic. Now, I think this is misleading. As a composer, I think nostalgia is absolute death; a composer must live in the present. Of course, Vaughan Williams lived to be so old that it's perhaps not surprising if the works of the last two decades have a valedictory quality, and therefore that some people interpret it as nostalgic. But the trouble is that there's a huge industry in England for promoting nostalgia, even among scholars and critics. So I think that that may explain why, in my middle years, I was less involved with his music, and why, when I listen to his music today, I try to counter ascriptions of nostalgia when they arise in people's conversations.

AT: What do you consider to be the most distinctive aspects of his music?

NL: The way he used his understanding of English folksong melody to create extended works is remarkable. And his use of tonality and modality is very interesting; his understanding of functional tonal harmony and his own distance from it really came from the work he did as a young man on *The*

English Hymnal and in recording folksong. What fascinates me about *The English Hymnal* is the meeting in Vaughan Williams's ears of English folksong and Bach. He knows Bach inside out, and at the same time hears these other melodies; his aural imagination is fascinating. That first decade was really the crucial period, not so much in the music that he produced, but in terms of what was happening in his mind, and the fruits of it are works like *Flos Campi*. The other important thing is the influence of Holst, which I think was considerable, particularly in the music of the early 1920s.

AT: Which of Vaughan Williams's works do you consider the most important?

NL: I find that hard to answer, because I tend not to rank works in terms of importance, and it's not a category I tend to encourage. But I think you mean which works represent his musical language at its best? Perhaps the three central symphonies are one aspect of his work that is clearly very important. The Tallis Fantasia may be the most important for me, but that doesn't necessarily mean it's the most important work. It's a key work, but that's different.

AT: How would you evaluate Vaughan Williams's influence on British music and musical life, particularly in terms of its positive or negative effects on subsequent generations of composers?

NL: I think it happened in two ways. Compared with other European countries Britain has a tradition of amateur music-making, and Vaughan Williams devoted a huge amount of time to that: writing for amateurs, conducting amateurs, performing the *St Matthew Passion* every year, and so on. He wasn't the first person to do it, but among well-known composers he was perhaps the one who spent the most time doing it. Then, in terms of his musical language, there was obviously an immediate influence on many of his students, particularly those who composed for the Anglican Church. Of course, some of his students, such as my mother, wrote music less directly influenced by him; I suspect that that's why she was said to be his favourite student, because he preferred the independent student to the one who was so similar.

AT: As Ravel said of Vaughan Williams himself, 'Of all my pupils, he's the only one who doesn't sound like Ravel'.

NL: Yes, that's right. People often assume that the generation who emerged in the '60s had turned over a new leaf, and that the influence of European music was so strong that we could hear no influence of either Britten or Vaughan Williams in their work. But actually that's not true; some Birtwistle, such as *The Triumph of Time*, is in a direct line from Holst's *Egdon Heath*. I think we'll hear a stronger Vaughan Williams influence over time; by, say, 2058 the distances between generations may seem quite small.

AT: How would you evaluate Vaughan Williams's place in the broader international perspective of twentieth-century music?

NL: I think that he's a major figure; he is played a huge amount in the United States and across the world. Interestingly, a lot of the orchestras who play minimalist music and apparently enjoy it also play Vaughan Williams symphonies. This suggests that there is a substantial audience for music that isn't overtly modernist, and that historians fifty years from now may see Vaughan Williams as important because he became one of the most performed composers.

AT: Are there any aspects of his music beyond specific choices of national literary texts etc. that can be reliably identified as British, or English, or that are linked to broader notions of British or English national identity?

NL: I'm very dubious about the notion of Englishness in a musical context; I think it's meaningless, because when composers are working they think in music's terms. I think a great deal of what is ascribed to Vaughan Williams's Englishness is actually what other people have overlaid. Yes, he had a feeling for English texts – but then he had a feeling for Bach. I think for every example one can find of quintessentially English Vaughan Williams, one can find an example of something non-English that was just as important in his writing.

AT: One example of that is *Riders to the Sea*. As an Anglo-Irish composer, if I may call you that, how successfully do you think Vaughan Williams set Synge's play?

NL: I think he found something in *Riders* that spoke very deeply to him. I think he had a kind of fellow-feeling with Synge, because Synge was not himself an Irish peasant, and yet he went to live on the Aran Islands, and knew what it was like to subsist on a turf fire, and so on. In the same way Vaughan Williams came from a very privileged background, but when he recorded an elderly man singing a folksong, he could intuit what it was like to be that person, and he wanted to share the privilege. That kinship with Synge enabled him to realize something quite special in his setting of *Riders to the Sea*. The final aria of that work is extraordinarily moving.

AT: Do you feel he has in any way influenced your own music, or your attitudes to music in general, or your view of the role of the composer in society?

NL: I'll take the last one first, because it's the easiest. I'd say very definitely, because I've always believed that the composer has to have a role in society, and needs a social conscience. It's meant a huge amount to me to work with many different kinds of musicians: children, amateurs, the highest professionals, whatever. And aspects of Vaughan Williams's personality were definitely influential on me, such as when he spoke up for Tippett when he was imprisoned for being a conscientious objector. I don't know whether my early knowledge of his work influenced my own music. If so it's probably something that would have appeared much later, and is not so much an influence of language as an idea of what you might do: that a voice and an oboe on their own have a wonderful sound, or that you can write a large orchestral work with dense textures without having to have a Germanic kind of formal shape.

In 2008, Anthony Payne, Jeremy Dale Roberts and I were invited to set a poem by Ursula Vaughan Williams for her memorial concert at the Royal College of Music. I chose a poem called 'Finding', and in my setting I quote some of his music deliberately.[8] They're mostly Fifth

Symphony moments, because the poem dates from the early 1940s, which was when the Fifth Symphony was composed; and the period when I was studying the Fifth Symphony, in the early 1960s, was when I knew Ursula best myself. It was both a beautiful and also quite a difficult thing to write, so that it retained a LeFanu voice and yet incorporated the Vaughan Williams without its standing out as somehow in the wrong place.

AT: A thread that runs through your own career is the evocation of place or landscape. Are you conscious of such evocations in Vaughan Williams's work, and, if so, how far does he do it in specific ways that you might do similarly or differently?

NL: Interestingly, I think my ideas about music and landscape came from getting to know Birtwistle's work. So there's something of that line of British composers that we were talking about earlier. I often have the first ideas for a piece when I am walking outside, so the piece would be intimately connected with where I was. Beyond that, I think of landscape as an important metaphor: you can take in large geological shapes and the implications of huge areas of time, and also, at the same time, tiny details and things that are very fleeting. This is something we all learnt from Messiaen. As far as I know, Vaughan Williams never used landscape as a metaphor in that way. But I imagine it was quite important to him at an unconscious level, because that's what's happening in his work.

***

Interview with Anthony Payne (London, 16 June 2010)

One of Britain's most experienced composers, Anthony Payne has worked extensively in most of the main compositional genres, particularly chamber music and orchestral music, among which *Spirit's Harvest* (1985), *Time's Arrow* (1990) and *Visions and Journeys* (2002) were premiered at the Proms. In addition to this, he is a noted critic and writer, who has published monographs on both Schoenberg and Bridge, and in 1997 completed a performing version of Elgar's Third Symphony based on his elaboration of the composer's sketches.

AT: When and how did you first encounter Vaughan Williams's music, and which work was performed?

AP: In my teens, I had already fallen in love desperately with serious music, but I hadn't heard any by English composers. When I first heard a Vaughan Williams piece – it was almost certainly the Tallis Fantasia – it had an extraordinary effect on me; it just immediately spoke to me. I began to pursue other works: the Fifth Symphony also had a profound impact on me, and I remember listening to the composer's own recording of the Fourth Symphony, which I found very difficult but fascinating. I heard an early performance of the Sixth Symphony at the Albert Hall, maybe in 1949 or

1950. I didn't really understand it, especially the Scherzo, which I still think is a very difficult movement; but I thought the Finale was extraordinary. And also the first movement: when it eventually breaks down into that great restatement of the lyrical theme, I thought that somehow it didn't belong; it seemed to come from another world. It took me quite a long time to realize its significance. It was a brave statement of something that never comes back, and every time I hear it now I think how incredibly poignant, especially the way the music closes down after it, and goes back into the dark world.

AT: How would you describe the impact his music had upon you in those early encounters?

AP: It made a really deep impression on me. I wasn't composing at this stage – I started composing reasonably late on – but when I started to compose, Vaughan Williams's harmony hit me for six. Unlike my contemporaries, I didn't know anything about the Second Viennese School; the most modern music I knew was Bartók's string quartets and Vaughan Williams in his modernistic mode. I was very influenced by Vaughan Williams's polymodal techniques, and wrote several pieces in an English 1930s idiom. It was only later that I realized it was terribly out of date, and I would have to do something else.

AT: How has your view of his music changed, if at all, since you first heard it?

AP: I admire him more as the years go by; he is a sort of spiritual godfather for me along with some other composers. When I began to take off as a composer, I was very disappointed at how indifferent my contemporaries were to that music, and how they felt this was a great shadow hanging over them. In those days, to belong to the composer community, I often felt you had to be able to talk about Ligeti, Varèse, Messiaen, Boulez, and so on; you couldn't talk about Elgar, Delius, Vaughan Williams and Holst. I loved what was coming out of a lot of modern continental composers, but I also adored all the early twentieth-century English composers, and I think Vaughan Williams was the greatest of them.

I now wholeheartedly think that he is one of the great composers of the century, and sometimes ask why we are listening to someone like Shostakovich, for instance, when we have a composer greater than Shostakovich who covers some of the same ground. The Sixth Symphony is quite a Shostakovich-like piece. There's also something slightly Mahlerian – I think of the Scherzo in Mahler's Ninth – about the way Vaughan Williams flings together his ideas in the Scherzo of the Sixth, though I don't think that Vaughan Williams would admit to the influence of Mahler; he came to it by a different route.

AT: What do you consider to be the most distinctive aspects of Vaughan Williams's music?

AP: The breadth of style. People ask me what they should listen to, to get to know Vaughan Williams, and I say 'listen to Symphonies 3, 4, 5 and 6; you'll be absolutely astonished at the totally different world in each of those symphonies, and yet they all sound as if they're by the same man'. He's got an amazingly wide style. Some critics said that he had that in common with Beethoven, and of course everyone poured scorn on that later, but I don't see why you shouldn't compare them in that respect: no composer since Beethoven has had the sheer breadth that Vaughan Williams has got. And it's amazing how he was willing to go into new territories. He changed course on two or three occasions, and then you get *Scott of the Antarctic*, which introduced a whole new strange world. It's absolutely amazing.

AT: He began in the Parry tradition, and ended with works that perhaps anticipated the modernism of the generation that came to the fore in the late '50s: that's a huge transformation within a single lifetime.

AP: And the fact that all who came after him wanted to go down a different pathway: you could say that Vaughan Williams was a *big* enough figure for that to happen; he compelled you to think for yourself and do something different, perhaps.

AT: Which of his works do you consider the most important? You have already mentioned the Third, Fourth, Fifth and Sixth symphonies.

AP: Yes, and the other symphonies are important as well. When I was reading about the famous conversation between Sibelius and Mahler about what the symphony should be like, it struck me that Vaughan Williams encompasses both those definitions,[9] because *A London Symphony* is really a Mahlerian symphony – it's the whole of the world of London, welded together – whereas *A Pastoral Symphony* is absolutely pure; it's a Sibelian work. And the Sixth is Mahlerian, but the Fifth is Sibelian.

I think his operatic works have been neglected unjustifiably. *The Pilgrim's Progress* is a fine piece, as is *Sir John In Love*. And we've got our own *Bartered Bride* in *Hugh the Drover*. Why don't we perform that more often? It's wonderfully tuneful and invigorating, and has some of the sexiest love music imaginable. A kind of English Puccini, someone said, quite rightly.

Among the choral works, I think very highly of *Sancta Civitas*; it's a wonderful visionary statement. I have a great affection for the *Five Tudor Portraits*. And a work that I've heard only once or twice, but it did impress me, is the *Magnificat*. Actually, there are very few pieces of Vaughan Williams I don't respond to on their own level. *The Lark Ascending* is a wonderful piece; it's really haunting.

AT: It's astonishing that whereas *The Lark* quickly got an established following, slightly earlier works like the Tallis Fantasia did not receive as much critical acclaim until after the First World War.

AP: I think that shows you the sheer newness of the Tallis Fantasia. It was a new world of sound, and so different from anything else at that time – utterly unlike Elgar, for instance. It seems to encompass sixteenth-century counterpoint in a funny kind of way, with all of those parallelisms that you get from Debussy. To think of Vaughan Williams as being a little Englander is really strange because he had a lot of French in his early music; the Finale of *A Pastoral Symphony* is very like the 'Magic Garden' in Ravel's *Mother Goose Suite*, for instance.

AT: How would you evaluate Vaughan Williams's influence on British music and musical life, particularly in terms of its positive or negative effects on subsequent generations of composers?

AP: I think that the sheer creative generosity of Vaughan Williams might have affected some people; I think of him going along in the late '40s to early concerts of the Society for the Promotion of New Music and saying why he didn't really care for the stuff but he was keen to know what was going on. He was generous in supporting people with opposing views to him, like Britten, and participatory, particularly in writing music for amateurs; I think that probably had an effect on some of the composers who came after him.

I'm not sure whether composers of my generation feel that he affected them in matters of style. There were real hang-ups about him, especially from people who would regurgitate Peter Warlock's famous comment about *A Pastoral Symphony*: 'like a cow looking over a gate'. But they don't say what he said next: 'but after all, it's a very great work'. Warlock was being bitchy, but he could see that this was a visionary work.

And as Vaughan Williams himself said, *A Pastoral Symphony* isn't 'lambkins frisking at all'. A few years back I saw an exhibition of paintings by the Australian artist Arthur Streeton, who went to the First World War as an official war artist. One of his war paintings, *The Somme Valley Near Corbie*, was extraordinary. I looked at this great, flat, level plain, with clouds and slightly brown/green, rather majestic landscape, and more clouds on the distant horizon – and when I looked carefully at it, I suddenly realized that it was gun smoke. I thought, my God, this is Vaughan Williams's *Pastoral Symphony*. War happening against a peaceful background, deep ambivalence and irony: that's the strength. I find that in all Vaughan Williams's so-called 'pastoral' works; there's a deep undertone of something else.

AT: How would you evaluate Vaughan Williams's place in the broader international perspective of twentieth-century music?

AP: Very highly. I think he's England's greatest twentieth-century composer. I know Elgar and Britten and Tippett and my contemporaries, and I think he's at the top, for his visionary genius and his great emotional variety. All this stuff about his style being a bit untidy and amateurish, and his orchestration being clumsy, is nonsense. In something like *A Pastoral Symphony* it's luminous.

AT: Vaughan Williams perhaps hasn't travelled as well as he should have done. Is one problem the type of modernism that he represents, and the extent to which pre-avant-garde modernism has become so synonymous with Stravinsky and Schoenberg that it hasn't made enough room for others who have gone down different paths?

AP: Yes, I think it hasn't quite done so. I often think that the really great music at that time was being written in between the cracks of those various categories. But you'd be astonished how much Vaughan Williams's music has been done abroad. I don't know why people are unaware of this. He's been done in the States. He's not particularly done in France, but there is a coterie of people in France who think quite highly of him.

AT: Are there any aspects of his music beyond specific choices of national literary texts etc. that can be reliably identified as 'British', or that are linked to broader notions of British national identity?

AP: There is folksong, which became so much a part of his style especially when he developed modal writing into producing synthetic modes of his own devising. People constantly look into Bartók for that sort of thing, but they don't with Vaughan Williams. I suppose that slight 'folkiness', where he seems to be composing his own folky material that is not based on any specific folksong, is a rather English thing about him. And there is something in his connection with Bunyan – that tie-up with English poetry and words and philosophy, which is not easy to pin down – that to me makes him specifically English-sounding, much more so than, say, Elgar.

AT: And similarly, perhaps, in his connection with Blake and the 'radical pastoral' tradition as well.

AP: Yes, that comes through in Vaughan Williams. He ties up a lot of threads.

AT: Do you feel that Vaughan Williams has in any way influenced your own music and your attitudes to music in general, or your view of the role of the composer in society?

AP: As I said earlier, he was a composer whose music spoke to me: the first really modern composer that I heard who had that quality. And that's influenced me enormously; I really want to speak to my listeners. But there are so many magical moments in Vaughan Williams that I've longed to reproduce in my own music, in my way. I thought it was delightful when he said that any other person's music is up for grabs; that you can crib from other people, as long as you make it your own, or some such phrase. And he proceeded to say how he cribbed Beethoven's F major quartet in 'Satan's Dance of Triumph' in *Job*.[10] You find such things all over: the beginning of the Fourth Symphony is obviously cribbed from the Finale of Beethoven's Choral Symphony. But he's made it his own; it's palpably Vaughan Williams. If you can do that, it's fine, and I do hope that I've done it sometimes.

AT: In your *Time's Arrow*, I was struck that something in the trio-like section – the violin melody, and the throbbing brass in the background – had faint echoes of the second subject of the first movement of Vaughan Williams's Fourth Symphony.

AP: Oh my goodness, you're absolutely right. Often with Vaughan Williams, I'm fascinated by the processes, and the constant jamming chord, with this great expansive prose melody on top, is an effect that I've always wanted to produce. In all honesty I'd forgotten that particular reference.

AT: Some of your language is based on third-based chords, and four- or five-note motifs, some of which might be pentatonic. Might these contain traces and likenesses that recall Vaughan Williams?

AP: I find a way of creating order in my harmonic texture is by having bitonal or polytonal chords with thirds belonging to one tonal region, often underpinned by a major second. That comes, probably, from Vaughan

Williams's Fifth Symphony, where you get the C and the D at the beginning and end of the first movement. The line traced by the top notes is often quite simple: tonal, or as you say, pentatonic, which somehow steadies up each string of chromaticism that is going on in the middle.

In Vaughan Williams, you can probably hear those absolutely searing false relations that he got from the early Renaissance, and which you also get in Purcell. I think some of my harmony has that, and I love the idea of a major/minor effect. But it's usually more complicated, and built out of the thirds you were talking about.

AT: How far has Vaughan Williams played a role in shaping your view of the composer in society, if at all?

AP: I rather wish he'd played more of a part, because I'm not the kind of person who very easily writes pieces for amateur performance. I've always had a feeling that I have a poetic world, and I just don't think I'm quite skilled enough also to take on board the problems of writing for amateurs and young people, which is a shame.

Notes

1 This took place on 14 January 1953, at the Free Trade Hall, Manchester.

2 This took place on 6 May 2001, at the Royal Festival Hall, London, and was performed by the Philharmonia Orchestra, with Davies himself conducting.

3 Highlights from 'Max Speaks: A Recorded Interview', in *Peter Maxwell Davies: A Portrait. His Works, His Life, His Words*, Naxos CD 8.558192, track 6.

4 'Advent Calendar' for SATB chorus and organ (2011), to a text by the Most Revd Rowan Williams, Archbishop of Canterbury, 2002–12.

5 For a recent examination of the relationship between Vaughan Williams's *Fantasia* and cathedral architecture, see Allan W. Atlas, 'On the Structure and Proportions of Vaughan Williams's *Fantasia on a Theme by Thomas Tallis*', *Journal of the Royal Musical Association* 135/1 (2010), 115–44.

6 Piers Hellawell, '"Who Are You Like" – A Blog about Influence', www.piershellawell. com/writings.asp?ARTICLE=8 (accessed 7 January 2013).

7 This took place on 2 April 1958 at the Royal Festival Hall in London; Sir Malcolm Sargent conducted the Royal Philharmonic Orchestra.

8 See *The Collected Poems of Ursula Vaughan Williams*, with an introduction by Stephen Connock (Albion Music, 1996), 23. The poem appears in Ursula Vaughan Williams's

collection *Fall of Leaf* (Oxford: Basil Blackwell, 1943). The poems set by LeFanu, Roberts, and Payne can be found in the collection *Finding Ursula Vaughan Williams* (University of York Press); see www.uymp.co.uk/works.php? work_id=879 (accessed 30 January 2013).

9 Sibelius and Mahler discussed the genre of the symphony when they met in Helsinki in 1907. Sibelius professed admiration for the 'profound logic that creates an inner connection between all the motifs' of a symphony; Mahler replied that 'the symphony must be like the world. It must contain everything.' See Andrew Barnett, *Sibelius* (New Haven: Yale University Press, 2007), 185. While Mahler's conception of the symphony does not necessarily exclude Sibelian logic, its emphasis on gigantism and drama is often viewed as the polar opposite of Sibelius's more transformational approach.

10 'Musical Autobiography', *NM*, 177–94 at 189–90: 'The duty of the composer is to find the *mot juste*. It does not matter if this word has been said a thousand times before as long as it is the right thing to say at that moment. If it is *not* the right thing to say, however unheard of it may be, it is of no artistic value. Music which is unoriginal is so, not simply because it has been said before, but because the composer has not taken the trouble to make sure that this was the right thing to say at the right moment.'

Select bibliography

Adams, Byron, '"No Armpits, Please, We're British": Whitman and English Music', in Lawrence Kramer (ed.), *Walt Whitman and Modern Music: War, Desire, and the Trials of Nationhood* (New York and London: Garland, 2000), 25–42.

Adams, Byron, and Robin Wells (eds.), *Vaughan Williams Essays* (Aldershot: Ashgate Publishing, 2003).

Atlas, Allan W., 'On the Structure and Proportions of Vaughan Williams's *Fantasia on a Theme by Thomas Tallis*', *Journal of the Royal Musical Association* 135/9 (2010), 115–44.

Baker, H. W., and Walter Howard Frere, *Hymns Ancient and Modern for Use in the Services of the Church, with Accompanying Tunes* (London: W. Clowes, 1909).

Banfield, Stephen, *Sensibility and English Song* (Cambridge University Press, 1985).

Bawden, John, 'The Music of *The English Hymnal*', in Alan Luff (ed.), *Strengthen for Service: 100 Years of The English Hymnal 1906–2006* (Norwich: Canterbury Press, 2005), 133–54.

Beckerman, Michael, 'The Composer as Pole Seeker: Reading Vaughan Williams's *Sinfonia Antartica*', *Current Musicology* 69 (2000), 42–67.

Benjamin, Arthur, 'A Student in Kensington', *ML* 31/3 (1950), 202–3.

Boden, Anthony, *Three Choirs: A History of the Festival: Gloucester, Hereford, Worcester* (Stroud: Sutton, 1992).

Boult, Adrian, *Boult on Music: Words from a Lifetime's Communication* (London: Toccata Press, 1983).

  My Own Trumpet (London: Hamish Hamilton, 1973).

  Thoughts on Conducting (London: Phoenix House, 1963).

  'Tributes to Vaughan Williams', *MT* 99 (1958), 535–9.

Bradley, Ian Campbell, 'Vaughan Williams' "Chamber of Horrors" – Changing Attitudes towards Victorian Hymns', in Alan Luff (ed.), *Strengthen for Service: One Hundred Years of the English Hymnal 1906–2006* (Norwich: Canterbury Press, 2005), 231–43.

C[apell], R[ichard], 'Three Choirs Festival – Gloucester, September 5–10'. *MT* 78 (1937), 909–10.

Carpenter, Humphrey, *The Envy of the World: Fifty Years of the BBC Third Programme and Radio 3* (London: Weidenfeld and Nicolson, 1996).

Cobbe, Hugh (ed.), *Letters of Ralph Vaughan Williams 1895–1958* (Oxford University Press, 2008).

Connock, Stephen, '"It Will Be Alright in the End": The Complex Evolution of the Libretto', *Journal of the RVW Society* 26 (2003), 6.

Cooke, Deryck, *The Language of Music* (Oxford University Press, 1959).

Copland, Aaron, *Copland on Music* (London: André Deutsch, 1961).

Day, James, *The Master Musicians: Vaughan Williams*, 3rd edn (Oxford and New York: Oxford University Press, 1998).

Dickinson, Alan E., *Vaughan Williams* (London: Faber and Faber, 1963).

Doctor, Jennifer, *The BBC and Ultra-Modern Music, 1922–1936: Shaping a Nation's Tastes* (Cambridge University Press, 1999).

Erlebach, Rupert, 'Dr. Ralph Vaughan Williams, O.M.', *The RCM Magazine* 55/1 (1959), 30.

Etter, Paul James, 'Ralph Vaughan Williams's *Hodie*: An Analysis and Performance Guide for the Choral Conductor' (DMA dissertation, Texas Tech University, 2002).

Evans, Edwin, 'English Song and "On Wenlock Edge"', *MT* 59 (1918), 247–8.

'Modern British Composers. IX. Ralph Vaughan Williams', *MT* 61 (1920), 232–4.

'Modern British Composers. X. Ralph Vaughan Williams (Contd.)', *MT* 61 (1920), 302–5.

'Modern British Composers. X. Ralph Vaughan Williams (Concluded)', *MT* 61 (1920), 371–4.

Foreman, Lewis (ed.), *Ralph Vaughan Williams in Perspective: Studies of an English Composer* (London: Albion Music, 1998).

Foss, Hubert, *Ralph Vaughan Williams: A Study* (London: Harrap, 1950).

Frogley, Alain, '"O Farther Sail": Vaughan Williams and Whitman', in Julian Rushton (ed.), *Let Beauty Awake: Elgar, Vaughan Williams and Literature* (London: Elgar Editions, 2010), 77–95.

'Vaughan Williams and Nazi Germany: The 1937 Hamburg Shakespeare Prize', in Christa Brüstle and Guido Heldt (eds.), *Music as a Bridge: Musikalische Beziehungen zwischen England und Deutschland 1920–1950* (Hildesheim: Georg Olms Verlag, 2005).

Vaughan Williams's Ninth Symphony (Oxford University Press, 2001).

(ed.), *Vaughan Williams Studies* (Cambridge University Press, 1996).

Garnham, Alison, 'The BBC in Possession: 1949–59', in Jennifer Doctor, David Wright and Nicholas Kenyon (eds.), *The Proms: A New History* (London: Thames & Hudson, 2007), 130–67.

Goddard, Scott, 'The Three Choirs Festival', *MT* 95 (1954), 615–16.

Gray, Cecil, *A Survey of Contemporary Music* (Oxford University Press, 1924).

Grimley, Daniel M., 'Music, Ice, and the Geometry of Fear: Vaughan Williams's *Sinfonia Antartica*', *MQ* 91 (2008), 116–50.

Hinnells, Duncan, 'The Making of a National Composer: Vaughan Williams, OUP, and the BBC' (DPhil thesis, University of Oxford, 1999).

'Vaughan Williams's Piano Concerto: The First Seventy Years', in Lewis Foreman (ed.), *Ralph Vaughan Williams in Perspective: Studies of an English Composer* (London: Albion Music, 1998), 118–63.

Holbrooke, Joseph, *Contemporary British Composers* (London: Cecil Palmer, 1925).

Holyoake, Michael, 'Towards a Folk Song Awakening: Vaughan Williams in Bournemouth, 1902', *Ralph Vaughan Williams Society Journal* 46 (2009), 9–15.

Howes, Frank, *The Music of Ralph Vaughan Williams* (Oxford University Press, 1954).

Hull, Robert, 'The Cult of Archaism', *ML* 11 (1930), 367–74.

Jacob, Gordon, 'Dr. Ralph Vaughan Williams, O.M.', *The RCM Magazine* 55/1 (1959), 31.

Keen, Basil, *The Bach Choir: The First Hundred Years* (Aldershot: Ashgate, 2008).

Kennedy, Michael, *Adrian Boult* (London: Papermac, 1987).

   A Catalogue of the Works of Ralph Vaughan Williams, 2nd edn (Oxford University Press, 1996).

   The Works of Ralph Vaughan Williams, 2nd edn (London: Oxford University Press, 1980).

Kimberling, Clark, 'Hymn Tune Descants, Part i: 1915–1934', *The Hymn* 54/3 (2003), 20–7.

Leith Hill Musical Festival, *Music Won the Cause: 100 Years of the Leith Hill Musical Festival, 1905–2005* (Dorking: Leith Hill Musical Festival, 2005).

Maconchy, Elizabeth, 'Dr. Ralph Vaughan Williams, O.M.', *The RCM Magazine* 55/1 (Easter 1959), 33–4.

Manning, David, 'Harmony, Tonality and Structure in Vaughan Williams's Music' (PhD dissertation, Cardiff University, 2003).

   (ed.), *Vaughan Williams on Music* (Oxford University Press, 2008).

McGuire, Charles Edward, *Elgar's Oratorios: The Creation of an Epic Narrative* (Aldershot: Ashgate Press, 2002).

   'From *The Apostles* to *Sancta Civitas*: The Oratorios of Elgar and Vaughan Williams', in Norris, Neill and Kennedy (eds.), *A Special Flame*, 99–115.

   Music and Victorian Philanthropy: The Tonic Sol-fa Movement (Cambridge University Press, 2009).

Mellers, Wilfrid, *Vaughan Williams and the Vision of Albion* (London: Barrie and Jenkins, 1989).

Mitchell, Donald, 'Contemporary Chronicle: Revaluations: Vaughan Williams', *Musical Opinion* 78 (1955), 409–11 and 471.

Moore, Jerrold Northrop (ed.), *Music & Friends: Seven Decades of Letters to Adrian Boult from Elgar, Vaughan Williams, Holst, Bruno Walter, Yehudi Menuhin and Other Friends* (London: Hamish Hamilton, 1979).

Neighbour, Oliver, 'Ralph, Adeline, and Ursula Vaughan Williams: Some Facts and Speculation (With a Note About Tippett)', *ML* 89/3 (2008), 337–45

Newbery, Celia (ed.), *Vaughan Williams in Dorking: A Collection of Personal Reminiscences of the Composer Dr. Ralph Vaughan Williams O. M.* (Dorking, Surrey: The Local History Group of the Dorking and Leith Hill District Preservation Society, 1979).

Newman, Ernest, 'Concerning "A Shropshire Lad" and Other Matters', *MT* 59 (1918), 394.

Norris, John, Andrew Neill, and Michael Kennedy, *A Special Flame: The Music of Elgar and Vaughan Williams Based on the Proceedings of an International Symposium Jointly Organised by the Elgar and RVW Societies Held at the British Library, Saturday 29 & Sunday 30 March 2003* (Rickmansworth: Elgar Editions, 2004).

Onderdonk, Julian, 'Vaughan Williams and the Modes', *Folk Music Journal* 7/5 (1999), 609–26.

Ottaway, Hugh, *Vaughan Williams Symphonies* (London: British Broadcasting Corporation, 1972).

'Riders to the Sea', *MT* 93/1314 (1952), 358–60.

Ottaway, Hugh, and Alain Frogley, 'Vaughan Williams, Ralph', in *Grove Music Online, Oxford Music Online*, www.oxfordmusiconline.com/subscriber/article/grove/music/42507 (accessed 30 May 2013).

Raverat, Gwen, *Period Piece: A Cambridge Childhood* (London: Faber and Faber, 1960).

Routley, Erik, *The Music of Christian Hymnody* (London: Independent Press, 1957). *Twentieth Century Church Music* (Oxford University Press, 1964).

Rushton, Julian (ed.), *Let Beauty Awake: Elgar, Vaughan Williams and Literature* (London: Elgar Editions, 2010).

Russell, Dave, *Popular Music in England, 1840–1914: A Social History*, 2nd edn (Manchester University Press, 1997).

Savage, Roger, 'Vaughan Williams Brings in the May: Sydenham, 1911', *Journal of the RVW Society* 28 (2003), 12–14.

Saylor, Eric 'Dramatic Applications of Folksong in Vaughan Williams's Operas *Hugh the Drover* and *Sir John in Love*', *Journal of the Royal Musical Association* 134/1 (2009), 47–58.

'The Significance of Nation in the Music of Ralph Vaughan Williams' (PhD dissertation, University of Michigan, 2003).

Scholes, Percy A., *The Mirror of Music, 1844–1944: A Century of Musical Life in Britain as Reflected in the Pages of The Musical Times*, 2 vols. (London: Novello & Company, Limited; Oxford University Press, 1947).

Schwartz, Elliott S., *The Symphonies of Ralph Vaughan Williams* (Amherst: University of Massachusetts Press, 1964).

Seddon, Eric, 'Beyond Wishful Thinking: A Re-Evaluation of Vaughan Williams and Religion', *Ralph Vaughan Williams Society Journal* 36 (2006), 14–23.

Shaw, Watkins, 'Church Music in England from the Reformation to the Present Day', in Friedrich Blume (ed.), *Protestant Church Music: A History* (New York: W. W. Norton, 1974), 691–732.

Talbot, Michael, *The Finale in Western Instrumental Music* (Oxford and New York: Oxford University Press, 2001).

Temperley, Nicholas 'The Lost Chord', *Victorian Studies* 30 (1986), 7. *The Music of the English Parish Church*, 2 vols. (Cambridge University Press, 1979).

Vaughan Williams, Ralph, 'The Composer in Wartime, 1940', *The Listener* 23 (1940), 989.

Folk Songs from the Eastern Counties (London: Novello, 1908).

Letters of Ralph Vaughan Williams 1895–1958, ed. Hugh Cobbe (Oxford University Press, 2008).

The Making of Music (Ithaca: Cornell University Press, 1955).

National Music and Other Essays, 2nd edn (Oxford: Clarendon Press, 1987).

'Review of *Six Suffolk Folk-Songs*, collected and arranged by E. J. Moeran', *Journal of the English Folk Dance and Song Society* 1/3 (1934), 173.

Some Thoughts on Beethoven's Choral Symphony with Writings on Other Musical Subjects (London: Oxford University Press, 1953).

Vaughan Williams on Music, ed. David Manning (Oxford University Press, 2008).

'Who Wants the English Composer?', *The RCM Magazine* 11/1 (1912), 12–15.

Vaughan Williams, Ralph, and Gustav Holst, *Heirs and Rebels: Letters Written to Each Other and Occasional Writings on Music*, ed. Ursula Vaughan Williams and Imogen Holst (London: Oxford University Press, 1959).

Vaughan Williams, Ursula, *R. V. W.: A Biography of Ralph Vaughan Williams* (Oxford: Clarendon Press, 1964).

Weltzien, O. Alan, 'Notes and Lineaments: Vaughan Williams's "Job: A Masque for Dancing" and Blake's "Illustrations"', *MQ* 76/3 (1992), 301–36.

Index of Vaughan Williams's works

General index

Cambridge Companions to Music

Instruments